D0340766

IN THE
BEGINNING

IN THE
BEGINNING

———◆◆◆———

The Advent of the Modern Age
Europe in the 1840s

JEROME BLUM

CHARLES SCRIBNER'S SONS
NEW YORK

MAXWELL MACMILLAN CANADA
TORONTO

MAXWELL MACMILLAN INTERNATIONAL
NEW YORK   OXFORD   SINGAPORE   SYDNEY

Charles Scribner's Sons   Maxwell Macmillan Canada, Inc.
Macmillan Publishing Company   1200 Eglinton Avenue East
866 Third Avenue   Suite 200
New York, NY 10022   Don Mills, Ontario M3C 3N1

Macmillan Publishing Company is part of the Maxwell Communication
Group of Companies.

Library of Congress Cataloging-in-Publication Data
Blum, Jerome, 1913–1993.
    In the beginning: the advent of the modern age—Europe in the 1840s / Jerome Blum.
        p.   cm.
    Includes bibliographical references.
    ISBN 0-684-19567-4
    1. Europe—History—1815–1848.
I. Title.
D385.B58   1994
940.2'83—dc20
1572

Macmillan books are available at special discounts for bulk purchases for sales promotions,
premiums, fund-raising, or educational use. For details, contact:

Special Sales Director
Macmillan Publishing Company
866 Third Avenue
New York, NY 10022

10 9 8 7 6 5 4 3 2 1

Printed in the United States of America

95-5

To
Constance Carter,
who aided and abetted

CONTENTS

INTRODUCTION

In a letter of 21 July 1850, Prince Clemens von Metternich, long-time Austrian chancellor now in exile, compared the Europe of that day to the first day of creation. "On that first day," he wrote, "the Creator said 'Let there be light,' and the light illuminated the chaos." Others shared Metternich's perception that they lived in the dawn of a new age whose configurations lay hidden to them. Baron Stockmar, trusted counselor of Prince Albert, Queen Victoria's consort, wrote the prince in 1845 that "A new epoch seems to me to have run into the mould, but still being there, hardly anyone can tell of what metal it is composed, or what shape it has taken." A few years later the German historian J. G. Droysen wrote that "This is the present: everything is tottering immeasurably confused, tumultuous, unmanageable. Everything old is exhausted, debased, worm-eaten, past hope. And the new is formless, aimless, chaotic, only disruptive. We live at a time of great crisis, that leads from one world epoch to another." In 1851 Wilhelm Riehl, editor of Germany's leading newspaper, the *Augsburger Allgemeine Zeitung,* and later a professor at the University of Munich, in his book *Die bürgerliche Gesellschaft (The Civil Society),* explained that the materials that for so long had served as the pillars of civilization were disintegrating, but out of the decay a new and exotic life was germinating.[1]

In other times, including our own, men have voiced the same sense of confusion and alienation, the same uneasiness because things were not the way they had been. But the 1840s saw the onset of the most amazing epoch

Introduction

that the world had yet seen. That epoch was our own modern world with its astonishing achievements, along with its problems, tensions, and internal conflicts. It was a time of endings and beginnings, of changes of great magnitude in science, social structure, communications, politics, political and economic thought, and literature. These changes led to revolutionary transformations in the way that men for long centuries had lived and thought.

Changes in the preceding decades had prepared the way for the innovations and the dislocations of the 1840s. An explosion in population, the growth of cities, shifts in property and income among sectors of the social order, the technical and social impact of early industrialization, the emergence of new social and economic elites and an enormous increase in the uprooted and the propertyless, a chronic social crisis rising from mass pauperism, a slow revolution in agricultural production, and a long-lasting monetary deflation had produced new and disturbing tensions. By the 1830s a sense of impending crisis accompanied by convulsive changes evidenced itself among thoughtful people, and in the succeeding years spread widely. In France supposedly ancient prophecies foretold calamities in 1840 and frightened credulous people. Many are said to have fled from France, and especially from Paris, which was to be the epicenter of the cataclysm. Wiser heads, with better evidence at their command, were certain that convulsive change would soon engulf society. Alexis de Tocqueville, visiting England in 1833, wrote that "a spirit of discontent with the present and hatred of the past shows itself everywhere" and warned that the British were on a dangerous course. The middle class, he said, was becoming more numerous and more restless, and the poverty of the common people "gives birth to ideas and excites passions which would have perhaps long continued to sleep if the country had been more prosperous." The level-headed and perceptive Freiherr C. F. Kübeck von Kubau, born a tailor's son who rose to high rank in the Austrian government, confided to his diary in January 1836 that the calm that prevailed in Europe was not a harmonious adjustment to the revolutions of 1830 but was rather a temporary paralysis that would be followed by still stronger paroxysms. In the early and mid 1840s, K. A. Varnhagen von Ense, indefatigable diarist, gossip, and political commentator, reported on the intellectual discontent and unrest that he encountered everywhere. Europeans, he wrote, were anxiously seeking new configurations for living to which they could adjust. Everything was in flux. Philosopher Victor Cousin and statesman François Guizot each warned that overeducated young men, feeling themselves unappreciated and unrewarded by their societies, were creating widespread unrest and joining and often leading every outbreak of disorder. In eastern Europe, too, young men, most of them sons of the nobility, had become alienated from the values and practices of the existing order and sought new solutions to old and aggravating problems.[2]

What was happening was that by the 1840s a new generation who shared a common historical experience had reached maturity. Born after the French Revolution, they grew up in an age of wars, devastations, disruptions, and renewals. They were confronted with the challenge of establishing a new ordering of society. The twenty-six-year-old Alfred de Musset, himself of the generation, in 1836 wrote, "Three elements entered into the life of these young men; behind them a past forever destroyed, still quivering in its ruins with all the fossils of centuries of absolutism; before them an aurora of an immense horizon, the first gleams of the future; and between these two worlds—like the ocean which separates the Old World from the New—something vague and floating, a troubled sea filled with wreckage, traversed from time to time by some distant sail or some ship trailing thick clouds of smoke; the present, in a word, which is neither one nor the other, which resembles both, and where one cannot know whether at each step, one treads on living matter or dead refuse."[3]

It was a generation born into an era in which the explosion of population that had begun in the mid-eighteenth century continued at an even more accelerated rate. In 1800 Europe had an estimated population of 186.8 million. By 1850 that figure had increased by 43 percent to 267 million. The spectacular increase meant a population of young people full of the hopes and ambitions that mark youth. Cities grew at an even more rapid rate. Between 1800 and 1850 London's population rose from 1.1 million to 2.685 million, Paris's from 547,000 to 1,053,000, Vienna's from 247,000 to 444,000, St. Petersburg's from 220,000 to 485,000, Berlin's from 172,000 to 419,000, Edinburgh's from 83,000 to 202,000, and so on.[4] The cities grew not by natural increase but by an influx of people from rural areas, all characteristically young, all drawn to the cities by the opportunities they hoped to find there for employment and for careers in the arts and sciences, in journalism and commerce. The great influx created severe shortages in housing, and the newcomers crowded into inadequate lodgings, cellars, and garrets. Many were reduced to dependency upon public and private charity. And they still came.

It was a generation that shared a restlessness of mind and spirit that made them dissatisfied with the way things were. They distrusted and scorned the thinking, habits, and beliefs of the older generation. Full of self-confidence, they eagerly sought for change in every sphere of life. They were so very young: in 1840 Hermann Helmholtz was nineteen, Karl Marx twenty-two, Friedrich Engels twenty, Courbet twenty-one, Dickens twenty-eight, Thackeray twenty-nine, Bismarck twenty-five, Turgenev twenty-two, Dostoyevsky nineteen,

Cavour thirty, Darwin thirty-one, to list a scant few names who were the creators of the new age. They were the men of the new generation who reached maturity and influence in the 1840s. It was sheer chance that this new generation counted so many men of supreme talent. "The distribution of men with the highest creative power," wrote W. A. Lewis, "seems to be a rare statistical accident, in place as well as in time. The circumstances of place and time help to determine whether these qualities will be recognized and used, but they cannot create what is not already there."[5]

Those of the older generation found themselves bewildered and sometimes horrified by what they saw as the excesses of their successors, and warned of chaos and disruption. They had the bad luck of straddling two historical epochs. Lytton Strachey once wrote that the "fortunate generations are the homogeneous ones which begin and end, comfortably, within the boundaries of a single age. It is the straddlers who are unlucky." Varnhagen von Ense, born in 1785, put it well when in a diary entry of February 12, 1842, he wrote, "That world to which I belong recedes and a new world ascends to which my spirit comes close to belonging, but my life does not. In its battles and victories I will take part only in spirit." Nobles, born when the aristocracy carried all before it, saw their power and exclusivity divided and diminished by a new aristocracy of wealth and commerce. Nor were they the only ones confronted and confused by a strange new world. Men of the working class, proud of their skills and their workmanship, found themselves disoriented and displaced by the transition of manufacturing from the old ways of handicraft production to the new industrial age. Most striking of all, the old world was transforming itself from a society of orders into a class society. In the Old Regime society had divided itself into orders or estates (as they were called). Each order, whether of nobles, burghers, or peasants, was determined by birth. The orders remained, but increasingly the strata became classes determined by economic interests and economic roles, rather than determined by being born into a certain order. "We are entering on a new political dispensation," wrote Lord Ashley in 1848, "and many of us probably will outlive the integrity of our aristocratical institutions." Wilhelm Riehl, more certain, wrote in 1852 that the society of orders no longer belonged to the realm of the possible.[6]

Notwithstanding the confusions and perplexities that accompanied the emergence of a new kind of world, much of the old order remained and, indeed, survived for many decades. Above all, the people of the forties, and for long years thereafter, save for a small and sometimes fractious minority, accepted without question the rule of hereditary monarchs. That seemed to them the way it had always been, and they saw no reason to abandon their loyalty to an ages-old institution. No trait seemed more prevalent among the great mass of the people of Europe than their traditional veneration of and allegiance to the throne. The monarch could goad, irritate, even persecute his subjects; he could be profligate, corrupt, and practice the darkest vices. Yet so long as he had a legitimate claim to the throne, his subjects remained steadfast in their loyalty to their ruler. In their rare rebellions against legitimate rulers, and their brief romances with other forms of government, the people returned to hereditary monarchy and to their old loyalty to the throne. Those who became sovereigns through their own effort always aroused the envy and resentment of rivals, and their motives were questioned with all the distrust of rivalry. Those born to the royal prerogative were above jealousy, for even though policies could be questioned, their legitimacy and their superiority were beyond cavil.[7]

The popular loyalty to the throne persisted, but changes began to overtake the objects of that loyalty. The political authority and power of the monarch suffered a gradual slippage, to the benefit of the upper strata of their subjects. It started very tentatively. When monarchs in western and central Europe yielded to popular pressures and granted constitutions, they pretended that this was a voluntary exercise of the absolute power of the ruler. The new prominence of the middle classes, who were less appreciative of tradition, the growth of a popular press that often questioned authority, advances in transportation that allowed people to break away from old roots, the emergence of new ideologies, and increased bureaucratization all served to lessen the role and the authority of monarchs.

Other changes accompanied the diminution in the power of princes. The royal court had once been the center of social life. People had gauged their own importance and the importance of their peers by their proximity to the throne. The ceremonies, the lavish displays, and the etiquette remained, along with the privileges and honors in the gift of the monarch. But these things held far less importance and interest than once they had. New centers had formed, and the life of the court seemed increasingly unimportant to the social, intellectual, and business elites of the era. People still felt honored by invitations to the court and still danced attendance upon the rulers and their families. But their diaries and letters showed that they were bored by the ceremonies and by the insipid conversations of the royal hosts and their fellow guests.[8]

Although their functions and their powers were showing signs of erosion, rulers still retained great significance in the affairs of their kingdoms. This, of course, was especially true of the absolute monarchies of Prussia, Russia, and Austria, where the will of the monarch (or of his surrogates) dictated national policy, though their claims to absolute power were being challenged. In constitutional monarchies the monarchs played a lesser but a still significant role. The ruler was still considered the ultimate source of power and was invested with a majesty that gave strength and permanence to the institutions of government.

Royalty served as instruments of national policy. In one famous instance in the early 1840s, men of similar views in France and England thought that an understanding between their two lands would serve to dispel the threat of war. So in 1843 they arranged a rapprochement at the personal level by having Queen Victoria and Prince Albert visit the French royal family at their Chateau d'Eu, on the French coast. It was the first visit to France of a reigning British sovereign since Henry VIII's visit in 1520 to the Field of the Cloth of Gold near Calais. In a letter to Prince Albert, his mentor Baron Stockmar pointed out that the visit of the royal couple "flattered not a little the national vanity of the French . . . and allayed the irritation of their feelings." Guizot, the French minister who had engineered the visit, was so elated with its results that he wrote to a friend that, in contrast to Jeanne d'Arc, who drove the English out of France, he brought the two nations together. "This day is for me," he continued, "what the coronation of the king at Rheims was for Jeanne d'Arc." In 1845 King Louis Philippe of France and his queen came for a stay at Windsor Castle, the first visit ever made to Britain by a ruling French monarch. Unfortunately, that brief era of good feelings lasted only a short time, shattered by the brouhaha engendered by the affair of the "Spanish Marriages."⁹

Marriages in reigning families remained, as they had long been, matters of political importance. The pride and prestige of the family demanded that every marriage serve to enhance the fame of the dynasty, to raise its stature among its fellow royal families, and to cement alliances with other states. Typically the planning and the diplomatic negotiations that preceded the making of a royal match paid little attention to the wishes of the prospective wedded couple. Grand Duke Friedrich of Baden recalled a dinner in Strasbourg in 1846 with the duc de Montpensier, a younger son of King Louis Philippe, when a special dispatch arrived for the duke from his father. Montpensier paled as he read the message, then passed it to Friedrich. It read, "The King to the duc de Montpensier. I have today concluded an agreement with the queen of Spain that your Royal Highness will consider yourself betrothed to the Infanta Maria Luise, sister of Queen Isabella. I congratulate your Royal Highness and will soon send you a picture of your bride." Montpensier wept, but he obeyed his father—and thereby became a pawn in the infamous affair of the Spanish Marriages.¹⁰

Introduction

The Spanish Marriages was the penultimate time that a dynastic marriage brought on the threat of war between powers. (The last time was the Hohenzollern candidacy for the throne of Spain that served to precipitate the Franco-Prussian War of 1870.) The story of the Spanish Marriages was a twisted tale, complicated by the instability of the Spanish government, by the meddling of the powers, and by intrigue, deceit, and fraud. A wise old historian observed that "looking at the dispute over the Spanish Marriages is somewhat like seeing Rome: one must do it very superficially if it is not to take an unconscionable amount of time." With that counsel in mind, suffice it to say that Spain was in turmoil with a young, new, unmarried queen, Isabella, whose uncle, Don Carlos, contested her right to the throne. France and Britain each had its own candidate for the hand of the youthful queen. The presumption was that the successful candidate would establish French or British domination of Spanish policy. The jockeying for position became so heated that there was talk of war. The French outflanked the British, and in the end, the hopes and fears engendered by the Spanish Marriages turned to sand. The ouster of Louis Philippe in the revolution of 1848 ended French hopes of a dynastic alliance that would make Spain a French dependency. Spain continued to be racked by internal disorder and near anarchy.

The significance of the 1840s as a seminal decade has been overshadowed by the single year 1848, the year of revolutions. Countless historians have written and still write copiously about these uprisings, though as revolutions they were notable failures. The revolutions were not unexpected. From the late 1830s on, politicians, diplomats, journalists, and other observers of the contemporary scene, aware that a new kind of society was germinating, had warned of the specter of revolution. By the second half of the 1840s, popular unrest and the longing for change had increased markedly at nearly every level of society.

Civil war in Switzerland in November 1847 served as a prelude to the revolutions of 1848. That brief conflict—it lasted less than a month—settled a long-standing quarrel about the need for revision of the Swiss constitution. The so-called liberal cantons wanted to establish a stronger central government and a secular state free of religious influence. Seven Catholic cantons, opposed to more centralization and in order to protect their religious interests, leagued together in the *Sonderbund*. In the war that broke out, the *Sonderbund* was quickly defeated, though it had the support of France and other powers.

The revolutionary year began with a rising in Sicily, but happenings there were too peripheral to affect the rest of Europe. The event that set much of Europe afire came when revolution erupted in Paris in the last days of

February. In a few weeks, the fire had spread to Austria, Hungary, Prussia, and other German states, to Lombardy, Venetia, and other Italian states, and to Romania. The near simultaneity of these revolutions stimulated contemporaries and later writers to advance explanations that would be common to all of the risings. Some placed primary responsibility upon economic conditions. Poor harvests throughout much of Europe brought on unrest in the countryside and bread riots in the cities. Artisans were being displaced by factory industry workers. A severe financial crisis brought on widespread unemployment and much suffering, above all to the urban poor. Others stressed political demands. The revolutionaries, and especially those of the growing middle class, wanted written constitutions and representative government, an independent judiciary, the abolition of censorship, and the establishment of independent national states in Italy, Germany, Austria, and Romania.

Economic and social considerations were of much importance, especially among the peasantry and sectors of the urban proletariat. But the revolutions of 1848 were essentially political revolutions, inspired by the ideologies of liberalism and nationalism. More specifically, they were inspired by the political ideologies of journalists, professors, philosophers, lawyers, and students. L. B. Namier called 1848 the Revolution of the Intellectuals. Nearly all of them were men of the rising generation, activists who drew up petitions, wrote articles, organized meetings and demonstrations, and formed secret societies. They were motivated far more by hope than by despair—hope, as one of them put it, "for a better order in government and in society."

No one has ever determined the exact number of revolts that shook state after state and city after city, but one educated estimate counted over fifty of them.[12] The Netherlands, Belgium, Scandinavia, Britain, and Russia escaped the fury of the storm, but the winds of change reached all of them. In the Netherlands and in Denmark, popular pressure resulted in new constitutions, in 1848 and 1849 respectively, that established constitutional monarchies. In Belgium, when disturbances broke out, the government made timely concessions that siphoned off revolutionary inclinations and thwarted efforts by radicals at insurrection. In contrast, British and Russian governments adopted an opposite course. In Britain, a renewal of the working-class movement called Chartism and the threat of revolt in Ireland threw a fright into the ruling elite. The government responded by a series of repressive acts that included making it a felony to advocate the establishment of a republic, and suspending the writ of habeas corpus in Ireland. In Russia, Tsar Nicholas responded to the news of revolution by intensifying the repression that marked his rule, and directing it especially against intellectual activity. Only Spain and Portugal, torn by decades of political strife and revolts, were all but untouched by the currents of revolution.

Although many people expected revolutions, no one, strangely enough, was prepared for them when they came, neither governments nor the revolutionaries. Everyone was taken by surprise. Indeed, a consideration of the seemingly fortuitous events that touched off the revolutions raises questions about their inevitability (though as someone once remarked, nothing is inevitable until it happens). Governments had neither the wisdom nor the will to ward off revolutions, and the revolutionaries themselves had little or no organization nor plan. Had monarchs been wiser, and willing to yield the modest reforms called for by the discontented, the revolutions might never have happened. But as luck would have it, the monarchs were inept and ill-advised and unprepared or unwilling to meet the challenges of the reformers. When they refused to make changes, crowds formed in the streets of their capitals. When they called out the troops to control the crowds, shots were fired in Paris, in Berlin, and in Vienna, either by accident or by panicked soldiers, and people were killed and wounded. Outraged mobs, incited by agitators, turned to violence; demonstrations turned into revolutions and spread to other centers.

The revolutions were almost exclusively urban phenomena. Disturbances and violence occurred in the countryside, but they were of secondary importance. The revolutions were fought out in the cities. The narrow winding streets, blocked with ripped-up paving stones, trees and lumber, inhibited the movement of regular troops and so fed the fires of insurrection. The fighting was done almost exclusively by people of the working class, the laboring poor. Only a scattering of men of the middle class and students joined in actual combat. Working-class successes on the barricades forced monarchical governments to grant concessions. But the concessions they made were those demanded by the liberal bourgeoisie who wanted constitutions that gave them a voice in the government—but excluded the workers—and that protected individual rights, such as freedom of the press and of assembly, trial by jury, and the creation of national states.

For a brief moment, the revolutionaries tasted the fruits of victory. Everything seemed to be going their way. France had become a republic. An all-German parliament met to establish a united Germany. A national assembly had convened in Vienna. Nationalist risings threatened the very existence of the Austrian empire. A united Italy with Rome as its capital seemed within the realm of the possible. It was a time of excitement and exaltation. People thought that a new era had arrived. The Germans called these first few weeks of revolution the Springtime of the Peoples, a time of brotherhood and good-will that held the promise of a bright new future.

The euphoria lasted for only a few weeks. In late spring, the tide of revolution began to ebb as discord appeared among the revolutionaries. Radicals began to push for social and economic reforms and gained the support of the workers who had fought the battles of the revolutions. That frightened the liberal bourgeoisie, who feared for their property and even for their lives. They withdrew from the revolution that they had invoked, longed for the restoration of peace and social order, and welcomed the return to power of their old rulers. The revolutions in Central Europe had freed the peasants there from the remaining servile bonds that had held them to their seigniors. Their goal achieved, they, too, withdrew from the revolutions. Before the summer had ended, the defeat of the revolutions was all but assured. By winter, only Hungary and parts of Italy remained in revolt and the risings there were crushed by the middle of 1849. All of the old regimes had been restored with the exception of France, where a republic had been established. It lasted only until 1851, when it yielded to the autocratic rule of Napoleon III.

The revolutions, failures though they were, served as catalysts for momentous developments. The reaction that followed in every land that experienced revolution held back reforms for decades to come. Liberalism stood discredited. The revolutions brought down the curtain on the idealistic view of peace and freedom that liberals had cherished. A new view of the world and its workings called "realism" seized men's minds. It stressed power and material progress and glorified struggle and conflict. The nationalistic strivings of Germans, Italians, Poles, Czechs, southern Slavs and Hungarians, frustrated during the revolutions, gained new strength and soon won great victories in Italy and Germany, and put new and threatening strains on the Austrian empire. The revolutions also hastened the growth of modern socialism. The so-called utopian socialists of pre-1848 believed that men could transform society by appeals to reason and by a moral reformation of mankind. The failure of the revolution dispelled these dreams. A new kind of socialism materialized that stressed class warfare between workers and bourgeoisie, and preached revolution to shatter the existing order.

In contrast to the failure of the revolutions of 1848, successful revolutions of great consequence in the creation of the modern world marked the decade of the 1840s. These revolutions are the subjects of the first part of this book. A revolution in communications took place that included a great expansion in the building of steam railroads, the ocean-going steamship, the electric telegraph, photography, and a postal revolution. Rapid and inexpensive travel to places far and near, the speedy transmission of news and messages by telegraph, photographs, and cheap mail opened up new horizons to the people of Europe, and ultimately, to the rest of the world.

Another kind of revolution that was destined to have equally enormous consequences took place in the sphere of social relations. The first steps in the creation of the modern welfare state were taken in Britain, when the government, in the name of the public interest, accepted some degree of responsibility for the welfare of its subjects. The forties, too, saw the development of a social conscience among the upper classes, again first in Britain. Simultaneously, the plight of the poor, and of the working class in general, encouraged the proliferation of radical social movements. Their proponents talked of a new order of justice and equality, characterized usually by the abolition of private property and the collectivization of wealth.

The revolutionary movement of nationalism that has shaped so much of world history had its roots in Romanticism. Beginning as a movement of fraternal love and peace among nations, nationalism soon took on menacing tones. By the 1840s, nationalism had become chauvinistic, with nation pitted against nation. The 1840s, too, saw the demise of Romanticism that had its origins in the last quarter of the eighteenth century. Now a new outlook, a new cast of mind, became dominant that came to be known as realism. The transition from Romanticism to realism was mirrored in the works of Europe's authors and artists. They rejected the idealism and sentimentality of their Romantic predecessors and sought to portray life as it really was.

The decade of the forties was distinguished, too, by the inception of a revolution in the world of learning, above all in the natural sciences. That revolution began the modern era in the history of science, which has given mankind a new understanding of the physical world, and indeed, of the universe. The social sciences, too, experienced revolution, though not so compellingly as the revolution in the natural sciences. Inspired by the success of the new breed of natural scientists, scholars tried to apply the methodology and the objectivity of the natural sciences to social phenomena.

Part Two deals with the changes that transpired in the 1840s in the five great powers that dominated Europe: Great Britain, France, Prussia, Austria, and Russia. In Britain, the world's first industrial society, the forties saw the end of the personal rule of the crown, the beginnings of the modern party system, the world's first organized political pressure group, a militant working-class movement with its own agenda, and the onset of the Victorian Age. In both France and Germany, the forties marked the beginning of their respective "take-offs" into self-sustained economic growth. In France, for the first time in European history, the bourgeoisie became rulers of a great power.

In France, too, upward social mobility became more possible than it had ever before been, with careers open to talent. For the first time, too, France had a ministry responsible to the elected representatives of the people.

In Germany the forties witnessed the end of the passive acceptance of the wave of reaction that had followed the defeat of Napoleon in 1815. A new kind of Germany began to evidence itself, one that reflected the interests and values of the growing middle class and that incorporated a vibrant nationalism and a demand for national unification. In contrast, the Austrian Monarchy was the classic land of routine, where the government not only avoided change but abhorred it. Confusion, delay, and stagnation became the normal state of affairs. There were muted sounds of discontent, especially from the middle class, and the first steps were taken in industrialization and transportation. In the last seven years of the decade, the empire was shaken by revolutionary nationalism, but in the end, the absolutism reestablished itself.

Russia, the most underdeveloped of the great powers, was also ruled by an autocrat who opposed change. Yet in the forties, despite himself, the tsar readied his nation for the ending of the serfdom that bound so many of his subjects. And despite the suppression and censorship that characterized his rule, the forties saw a spectacular intellectual outburst that earned its name as the Golden Age of Russian Culture.

PART ONE

CHAPTER ONE

Revolution in Communications

Shortly before his death in 1835, Emperor Francis I of Austria refused to grant permission for the building of a steam railroad lest revolution come into his country. Francis's fellow autocrat, Tsar Nicholas I of Russia, did consent to the building of railroads, but with much reluctance. In 1845 he told a French visitor that "the improvements in the means of communication will change everything and the dregs that rested in the depths will rise to the top." He thought railroads absorbed enormous amounts of capital unproductively and considered their speed a luxury that promoted "the spirit of inconstancy which characterizes our century." Nicholas's finance minister, Count Kankrin, not only opposed railways because they would increase vagabondage, but also prophesied that in twenty years railways would no longer exist when governments realized that they served more to unify scattered revolutionary elements than they did to promote trade.

Nobles joined monarchs in their opposition to the railway. They saw it as destructive of the patriarchal way of life that they cherished. The mobility that railroads would provide would give common people advanced ideas unsuitable to their station in life and would arouse new and dangerous ideas. Nobles were much vexed, too, by the fact that on the train they ceased to be privileged individuals and instead became indistinguishable from the other passengers. They could have added to their condemnation of the railway the other great innovations in communications of the 1840s—the transatlantic steamer, the postal revolution, the electric telegraph, and photography. These advances contributed mightily to changing forever the quality of European—and ultimately the world's—life and the structure of society.[1]

There were other objections and condemnations of the railway that ranged from the serious to the trivial to the ludicrous. People feared with some reason that the sparks from the wood-burning locomotives would set fire to forests and crops and to the thatched roofs of houses near the tracks. Peasants in Baden, observing that the railroad and the disease that killed their potato crops appeared simultaneously in their land, reasoned that soot from the locomotives' stacks caused the disease. Many years passed before they abandoned that belief. Peasants were not alone in blaming calamities on the railroad. Grave doctors and learned scientists made even more frightening claims. The Bavarian board of health warned that the speed of the trains would cause severe brain damage not only to their passengers but also to those who saw the trains go by. They insisted that to protect the nonpassengers a high fence should enclose the tracks. On a more serious albeit equally fallacious note, leading economists of the era, like J. R. McCulloch in Britain and Adolphe Blanqui in France, doubted the utility of the railroads and questioned their future. The highly respected *Quarterly Review* in 1825 deemed that those who thought of making railways general throughout the United Kingdom were "unworthy of notice."[2]

The doubts vanished as soon as the railroad became a reality. Then people everywhere greeted it with enthusiasm and fervor and with hopes for what the railroad could do for mankind, their expressions prefiguring Neil Armstrong's "one small step for a man, one giant leap for mankind" a century and a half later. The railway, with its seemingly endless rails, with smoke rising from the locomotive's stack, and with its then-unbelievable speed, made the new industrial age visible for all to see, and brought home the realization that the world had indeed changed. No one expressed these emotions more affectingly than did Heinrich Heine in May 1843, when two new rail lines opened in Paris. "The thinking man," he wrote, "experiences an eerie feeling that we always experience when an unheard of and tremendous thing happens whose results cannot be foreseen nor calculated. We know only that our entire existence is forced into new paths and disrupted, that new circumstances, new joys, and new sorrows await us, and that the unknown has its uncanny attractions, alluring and at the same time anguishing. So much our forefathers felt when America was discovered, when the first shot announced the invention of gunpowder, when the printing press sent the first proof sheet of the word of God into the world. Like these, the railroads are a providential happening bringing mankind a new revolution that changes the color and form of life. A new chapter begins in world history and our generation can boast that we were there at the beginning. What changes must now happen in our outlook and our perceptions? Even the elementary ideas of time and space totter. The railroad annihilates space and only time remains."

Judge Henry Cockburn of Edinburgh dreaded that the railroads would mar the beauty of the hills and glens of his beloved Highlands. Yet in 1845 he confided to his diary that "the ultimate miracles of railways are obvious. . . . The globe is in the course of being inhabited as one city or shire, everything known to and everything touching everybody. The consequences cannot yet be foreseen fully, but there is no reason to doubt that on the whole, the result must be good. It will give force to public reason, and thus give great advantages to civilizations over barbarism, and to truth over error." The revolutionary journalist Karl Ludwig Borne, in exile in Paris from his native Germany, thought that the railroads would have "immense political consequences, including making both despotisms and war impossible." Unfortunately, wars and despotisms did not cease, and truth did not triumph over error, nor civilization over barbarism. But thirty years later, the *Times* of London would say that, "No change in the history of the world is greater than the change which was effected by the introduction of the railway."[3]

The anticipations, the enthusiasms, and the hopes inspired by the coming of the railroad become understandable in the light of the all but incredible state of European communications. Roads almost everywhere were unpaved, deeply rutted, quagmires after rains, covered with ice and snow in winter, and the despair of travelers in all seasons and everywhere. In 1820 a French writer called the high roads that led out of London disasters. Thomas Macaulay, traveling on the Continent in 1838, dreaded the return home through France "in the depth of winter, on the vilest highways that are to be found in a civilized country." In Germany, roads were aptly called calamities.[4] Nowhere were the roads as bad as they were in Russia, that is, those parts of Russia that had roads. In most of that land, there were only footpaths in summer; in winter, people drove cross-country in sleds. In Spain the additional menace of highway banditry confronted the traveler. Robbers infested the roads, apparently without fear of punishment. In neighboring Portugal roads were so few and so poor that a visitor in 1845 found that he could travel only by foot or on the back of a mule.[5]

General ignorance of how to build a good road prevailed until the last years of the eighteenth century. The principles laid down by a Frenchman, P. M. J. Tresaguet, and two Scotsmen, Thomas Telford and J. L. MacAdam, provided the guides to satisfactory road building. All three proposed the use of broken stones for the roadbed. MacAdam's unique contribution was to insist upon the draining of the subsoil. If kept dry, deep foundations would not be needed, and the roadbed, rarely more than eight inches deep, would be easier to build and less expensive to maintain. The broken stones, each no larger than could fit in a man's mouth, and sharp edged, were tightly packed so that rain could not penetrate the road's surface.[6]

Armed with the knowledge of the way to build good roads—but not always employing it—government and private individuals set out to answer the rising demand for improved means of transportation. Increases in trade and industry, the growth of urban populations who had to be fed, and military considerations created that demand. England, the world's most advanced economy, led the way, or more precisely, English private enterprise led the way. Britain had no national roads built by the central government. Instead, it had turnpike trusts, owned by private companies, and parish roads, built and maintained out of local tax revenues. England had privately owned turnpikes from early in the eighteenth century covering only a few hundred miles. The number grew after 1750 but the heyday of the turnpike came after 1815. By the beginning of the 1840s, there were over 1,100 turnpike trusts, each created by a private act of Parliament. Each controlled its own ten or twenty miles of road, save for a few consolidated trusts that owned sizable stretches of highway. Together the turnpikes covered up to 22,000 miles of major trunk and crossroads, and in 1837 had a combined revenue of 1.5 million pounds in tolls. Nearly all of the turnpikes were macadamized and well maintained in contrast to the mud and ruts of the 120,000 or so miles of parish roads in town and country.

The turnpikes' heyday proved short-lived. With the expansion of the railway network in the 1840s, the turnpikes went into a tailspin. By 1877 only fifteen still survived, and the last one disappeared in 1895.[7]

In France between 1814 and 1841, the central government, and especially after 1830 under the July Monarchy, built 7,000 kilometers of main roads, and the departments built 22,000 kilometers of secondary roads. The era of road building in Germany began only in the late 1830s. Until then most roads were in deplorable condition. New improved roads built by governments, by turnpike companies, by private individuals, and by communities quickly proved their economic value. Tolls were a nuisance, especially in the petty states. In a two-hour trip in 1846 from Frankfurt to the spa at Homburg, the diarist Varnhagen von Ense paid tolls six or seven times because the road passed through strips of land belonging to separate rulers. In Austria, the central government had initiated a road-building program in 1815. By the 1840s a network of improved highways reached out spokelike from Vienna, and lesser complexes centered on other major cities. Between

1831 and 1847, the state built 1,413 miles of primary roads. Nearly everywhere these roads, like the ones built earlier, were poorly maintained. The financially strapped central government made no attempt to build or repair secondary roads. Local governments and the owners of estates and factories in the western half of the empire assumed that task, and between 1831 and 1847 built 29,000 miles of road. Despite the poor quality of these roads and the rest of the network, the increase in the number of passengers carried in mail coaches provides a measure of the importance of the new roads. In 1831 the coaches carried 53,615 passengers, in 1847, 278,350 passengers, plus large increases in mail, parcels, and money shipments. Russia, as in just about everything else, lagged behind the other powers. The state did build a hard-surfaced road of over 450 miles from St. Petersburg to Moscow, completed in 1834 and reportedly well maintained.[8]

Passengers (save for the wealthy who had their own coaches) traveled by horse-drawn stagecoaches. Nostalgia has transformed these vehicles into cheerful reminders of bygone days, with stout, red-cheeked, smiling coachmen and happy passengers. In actuality no end of discomfort attended coach travel. The coaches were excessively uncomfortable, crowded, ill-smelling, and unheated vehicles. Passengers pitched and rolled as the coaches, at best inadequately equipped with springs, rode over the poorly maintained roads. Frequent and often fatal mishaps occurred when axles or wheels gave way to the beatings they took from the appalling roadbeds. The coaches carried four to six passengers inside, and as many as eleven atop the coach. Those inside were packed in like herring in a barrel, especially in winter when the passengers were wrapped in cloaks and rugs and wore fur boots. The discomfort of those inside paled when compared to what those riding atop the coach had to endure. With a hard plank for a seat, and if lucky, an iron rod for a back rest, they had no protection from the weather, and were always in danger of being thrown from their high perch by an accident or by falling asleep. France had its own variety of stagecoach, called the *diligence*, that offered more comfort than the ordinary coach. Much larger than the ordinary, it was divided into three separate compartments and was drawn by six or more horses. Three passengers sat in the first and most expensive compartment, six in the second compartment, and six in the third. There were also seats on the roof.[9]

The building of new and better roads did allow improvements in the speed, comfort, and reliability of coach services. Still, the time consumed by a journey compounded the disabilities of travel. Coach speed in the 1840s averaged around five miles an hour. In France, at the end of the eighteenth century, the average had been 2.1 miles per hour. At five miles an hour, even short trips ate up time, and long journeys must have seemed "beyond all comfort, not to say beyond all endurance," as one weary traveler remarked. Henry Vizetelly recalled that it took eight hours from London to Dover, "several hours of misery crossing the Channel, and twenty-two hours of additional torment to get to Paris." The coaches stopped at regular intervals at inns or posting stations to change horses. That took only a few minutes if the fresh horses were ready for the arrival of the coach. Inns varied in quality, with some described as having all of the comforts of home. Mail coaches, introduced early in the century, were the express lines of the era. They stopped only to change horses—every ten miles in Britain—and to pick up mail. They averaged twice the speed of regular coaches. They were even less comfortable than ordinary coaches. In Britain, they carried four passengers inside on narrow seats and three outside, plus the coachman and an armed guard to protect the mails.[10]

In much of Europe, there were no public stagecoaches. Travelers had to hire vehicles and drivers, or if they could afford it, travel in their own coach. Relay stations provided changes of horses and the rudest of accommodations. In Russia public coach services, introduced only in the 1820s, ran between Moscow and St. Petersburg and a few other major cities. Elsewhere in that vast empire, the traveler had to depend upon what he could hire. That usually turned out to be a remarkably uncomfortable peasant cart, called a *telega*. It was little more than a topless box mounted on four wheels, without seats or cushions, much less springs. The posting stations provided no facilities beyond renting the *telega* and horses, so that the passenger had to carry his own food and bedding and sleep in the *telega*. A special category state of peasants, called *iamshchiki*, had the obligation of manning the relay stations, providing horses and drivers, and carrying mail and parcels to the next relay station. In return, they received a fee from private travelers (travelers on government business paid no fee), and they were exempted from most of the obligations other peasants had to pay the state.

In Russia the carriage of most goods, and especially of heavy wages, had to wait upon the coming of winter when the snow cover allowed transport by sledge. Then the landscape became alive with literally millions of peasants, required by their masters to carry all manner of merchandise and foodstuffs. Winter travel had its perils, and each year many succumbed to cold and storms, or lost their way in the unmarked and endless fields of snow and perished. If by some unlucky chance the winter brought only light snowfall, transport by sled became difficult, and gluts piled up on the land while townspeople suffered shortages and high prices.[11]

Everywhere freight shipped in wagons over land moved at a snail's pace. It took thirty-six to forty days to send a loaded freight wagon from Paris to Lyon. The costs of feeding and maintaining the carters and horses made overland shipping extremely costly, so that freight wagons carried wares relatively light in weight and high in value. Heavy commodities, such as coal, stone, or timber were carried over land for only short distances. Typically, they were carried along canals, navigable rivers, or by coastal shipping.[12]

In Great Britain canal building on a large scale began in the mid-eighteenth century, and by 1845, the island kingdom had about 2,500 miles of these waterways. Save for two in Scotland, private enterprise had built all the canals. Parliament fixed the tolls and left the operation of the canals to their proprietors. In addition, Britain had around 1,300 miles of navigable rivers, and, of course, the island had extensive coastal shipping. In France successive regimes since the seventeenth century, but especially after 1815, had built canals, and by 1858 the country had over 2,300 miles. In contrast, Germany and Austria lagged far behind. The particularism that divided Germany into thirty-seven states had retarded the building of canals, and by 1850 Germany had only about 450 miles. In Austria the mountainous terrain of much of the empire made canal building prohibitively expensive so that few were constructed. In Russia canals built by the state in the eighteenth and nineteenth centuries had connected major rivers and eliminated costly portages.

Freight on canals moved slowly, rarely more than 2.5 miles an hour under the best conditions. The canals were frequently poorly maintained and often were closed by ice, fog, flooding, or shortage of water. Nor did they always prove profitable, at least in Britain where a considerable number paid no dividends to those who had invested in them. Horses usually provided the motive power for barges on canals and riverboats sailing up stream. In Russia men supplanted the horses. In 1815 an estimated four hundred thousand of these human draft animals worked on the Volga, Russia's busiest river. The hardships and brutality of their occupation took a heavy toll. Reportedly, seven thousand perished on the job each year, and thousands more returned to their villages broken in body and spirit.[13]

Nothing indicated better the inconveniences and expense of coach travel and overland freight shipments than the swiftness with which they disappeared with the coming of the steam railroad. In the late 1830s thousands of coaches had taken off from London for all over Britain. Within six months of the opening of the London and Birmingham Railway, the coaches had ceased running, and in 1846 the last coach left the capital. The same thing happened everywhere in Britain. The last coach line in all of the kingdom shut down in 1874 in the north of Scotland when the Highland Railway began operation.

The spectacular difference in the speed of the railway—in England an average of 29 to 36 miles an hour in 1843—over coaches, and in comfort, at least for first- and second-class passengers, made coaches obsolete. Canals managed to survive the competition of the railroad, but their importance declined with the increase in rail mileage. The greater speed and carrying capacity of the railways enabled them to transport goods at reasonable rates and far more expeditiously.[14]

The "Age of the Railway" began in England with the opening of the twenty-seven-mile-long Stockton and Darlington steam railway in 1825. Actually, Europe had long known railways: horse drawn railways typically not over ten miles in length and often less. They carried heavy commodities, frequently serving as feeders for nearby canals. The quick success of the Stockton and Darlington awakened governments and entrepreneurs alike to the advantages and the potentialities of the steam railroad. After considerable planning, discussion, and legislation, serious construction of railroads began in the 1840s. The United Kingdom had 1,454 miles of operating rail lines in 1840 and 6,088 miles in 1850. Germany had 291 miles in 1840 and 3,639 miles in 1850. France and Austria lagged well behind. In France the comparable figures were 255 miles in 1840 and 1,811 miles in 1850; in Austria, 80 miles in 1840 and 843 miles in 1850. Russia, as usual, brought up the rear, with 17 miles in 1840 and 311 miles a decade later.[15]

Governments, entrepreneurs, and combinations of state and private enterprise built the new railroads. Belgium, which in 1830 had won its independence from the Netherlands, set the pattern for state planning and construction. In 1835 the Belgian Parliament authorized the construction of a state-owned system, radiating out from Brussels, the capital, to the frontiers. After building the trunk lines, the government, beginning in 1842, granted concessions to private companies to build the rest of the rail network. In other lands, too, the state built railroads, or joining with private enterprise, participated directly or indirectly in their financing and construction.

The United Kingdom proved the exception. Unaided private enterprise built the British railway network. There was no overall plan as there was in continental lands. Needing only permission by act of Parliament, companies built railroads helter-skelter. They paid no heed to military and strategic considerations that influenced the location of the railways in continental lands with their exposed frontiers. The people of the island kingdom did not have to worry about overland invasions. But sometimes the railway entrepreneurs neglected economic considerations, building lines in locations where demand did not justify the investment, or where they competed with existing railways. The role of the government pretty much ended with the act of Parliament that authorized the proposed railroad to raise capital and acquire land, specified how much the promoters could raise by sale of shares and how much by borrowing, and prescribed maximum freight rates. In 1840 Parliament did establish a Railway Department at the Board of Trade to inspect new lines and to issue safety regulations.

Britain's first railroad, built to connect the coal field of Darlington in northeast England to the port of Stockton-on-Tees, used its locomotives to haul coal. Then in 1830 the thirty-one-mile-long Liverpool and Manchester Railway, the first line designed from the outset to carry both passengers and freight, began operation.[16]

The quick success of these first two steam railroads led as quickly to the founding of new railway companies. Like the two pioneers, the new lines were rarely more than thirty miles in length and began as local enterprises, nearly always financed locally by men of the commercial classes. Capitalists in London, wary of the profitability of the railroad, did not invest on a large scale until the mid-forties.

It cost surprisingly large amounts of money to get railways organized and built. Contemporary estimates put average costs at £35,000 to £40,000 per mile, and costs could skyrocket to hundreds of thousands of pounds for railways in and around major cities where land and construction costs were highest. Legal and so-called Parliamentary expenses were remarkably high. They could run as much as £100 per mile, and in some cases much more, and that was before a foot of land had been purchased.[17]

Total lack of any plan for a national rail network, extravagant claims of promoters and wishful thinking of investors, lack of concern for social costs, wild-eyed speculation, and sometimes purposeful deception characterized the first years of British railway history. The planlessness continued until the mid-1840s. Then, in a whirlwind of speculation and fraud, amalgamations of scores of independent small railway companies became the order of the day. Once begun, the mergers continued after the frenzy subsided. By 1860 twelve large companies accounted for seven eighths of England's railway mileage and capital; in Scotland three companies controlled three quarters of the mileage and capital of that land. By that time Britain had over nine thousand miles of track in operation.

In 1859 a financial journalist named David Morier Evans wrote that "it would seem to the casual observer that the construction of these lines was the mere realization of sagacious and wise views on the part of those who promoted them, when in fact, a great majority owe their creation to the most extravagant deceptions and the wildest illusions—to financial speculation rather than to any intelligible appreciation of the practical bearings of railway undertakings." Evans was writing about a man named George Hudson, the central figure in the beginnings of the amalgamation frenzy.[18]

Three principal prototypes appeared at the dawn of the Railway Age who characterized not only the Age of the Railway but the entire modern industrial order. They were the promoter, the visionary, and the financier. George Hudson was the archetypical promoter. He began life in 1800 as the son of a moderately prosperous Yorkshire farmer. At sixteen he left his village home for the city of York, reportedly because he faced a charge of bastardy. In York he apprenticed to a cloth merchant, six years later married into his employer's family, and became a partner in the family business. In 1827 his great uncle died, leaving Hudson a reputed fortune of £30,000. The legacy made Hudson, at twenty-seven, one of the wealthiest men in York. He became a civic leader and in 1833 took over as head of the local Tory political machine. The purchase of votes had long been a staple of English politics, and Hudson became a master of that art and of political corruption in general. He quickly led his party to electoral victories, though York had been a Whig stronghold. In 1835 he became a town councillor, in 1836 an alderman, and in 1837 became Lord Mayor of York.[19]

In 1833 he helped found the York Union Bank, which later became a principal instrument in the financing of his enterprises. In that same year, he attended a meeting called by promoters to consider the building of a twenty-mile railway from York to Leeds. Named to the committee to study the project, Hudson became so intrigued that he subscribed in advance to five hundred shares. In 1837 the York and North Midland Railway Company was established, with Hudson as its unanimous choice for chairman of the board of directors. That began what can only be called a meteoric career.

Hudson took complete charge, and the new railroad opened on May 29, 1839. His success—and his raising the stock dividend to 10 percent—quickly established his reputation as a wizard in railway management. He was put in charge of the foundering North Midland Railway Company and quickly restored it to solvency by ruthless cutting of costs. Then he embarked on a program of amalgamations, annexations, and reduction of competition among railways, the boldness of which dazzled the public. He won—and gloried in—the popular title of the "Railway King," or, as some put it, the "Railway Napoleon." He became chairman of the board of four major railway companies and ruled over them with an iron hand. His directors, awed by his spectacular success and his enormous self-confidence, contented themselves with endorsing his decisions. Acting as if these companies were his private property, he treated lesser companies like pawns in a game of chess, leasing them or absorbing them into one of his own companies if he so pleased. By 1848 his companies were worth thirty million pounds and controlled 1,450 miles out of the 5,000 miles of railways then in operation.[20]

Hudson's appearance and manner seemed perfectly fitted to the kind of man that he was—a supremely self-confident promoter who commanded attention and who sought money and power. Of slightly less than medium height, he had a burly, broad-chested and bull-necked frame that was thick around the middle. His strong and hard face had full lips, a strong jaw, broad brows, and small, quick, and piercing eyes—a face that looked out on the world with almost a sneer and a dare. He had an abrasive manner, was arrogant and dictatorial, and apparently did not mind giving personal offense. He had great stores of energy that allowed him to work long hours without cease. He cowed his associates and others by his complete mastery of the details and even the minutiae of the many enterprises in which he involved himself. He awed them, too, by his skill in doing complicated calculations in his head.[21]

He knew little and cared less about the technology and engineering of railroading. He hired people to take care of such matters. His genius lay in his financial skills and, above all else, his ability to bend the wills of others to his own purposes. He was a born promoter, the first of the world's great railroad entrepreneurs, a wheeler and dealer whose busy mind churned out scheme after scheme in his pursuit of wealth and of power over men and things. The *modus operandi* that he used in his ascent was strikingly simple. He played on man's greed and he was totally dishonest. When he took over a line, he increased dividends. Naturally that won the gratitude, support, and admiration of the stockholders. They did not know, or did not want to know, that he paid all or part of the increases in dividends out of capital rather than out of operating income. He gained the support of his boards of directors by awarding them large blocks of new shares at no cost to them. He, of course, took the largest block for himself. No records were kept of these transactions. He gained allies and converted foes by providing them with inside information about coming mergers and acquisitions. He pocketed large sums of company money supposed to be spent for land and construction and used the money for his own purposes. He used his seat in the House of Commons, to which he was elected in 1845 and where he quickly became a front bencher, to harass railway proposals which would compete with his own lines.

A web of circumstances allowed Hudson to get away with these practices. Standard railway accounting had not yet been developed. Hudson added his own special touch to the confusion by cooking the accounts of his companies.

Hudson had a free hand in these malfeasances because of his complete control of his boards of directors. The directors of the Eastern Counties Railway explained that they had invited Hudson to become their chairman at the insistence of their stockholders, who envied the dividends paid by Hudson's companies. As almost his first action as chairman he raised the dividend on company shares from 2 to 6 percent. Of £545,714 paid out in dividends between 1845 and July 1848, only £225,141 came from income. The remainder was provided by alterations of the accounts and charges to capital. When asked by investigators why they allowed this, the directors claimed that whenever they protested Hudson threatened to resign. Knowing the enthusiastic support of the shareholders for Hudson, the directors felt they had to go along. On one occasion the directors of the Midland Railway, another line of Hudson's empire, screwed up their courage in advance of Hudson's appearance at their meeting to demand that Hudson tell them of some deal he was making that concerned the company. When Hudson entered the board room, he asked whether anything had happened. A spokesman for the directors declared that since they bore equal responsibility for the company's actions they were, as the spokesman expressed it, "desirous of knowing the nature of your future plans." "You are, are you?" Hudson replied, "Then you will not!" Whereupon the meeting of the board proceeded to other matters as if nothing had happened.[22]

The shortcomings of railway accounting, Hudson's arrogance, his dishonesty, and the compliance and cowardice of his directors help explain Hudson's success in his manipulation of money and men. Above all else, he succeeded because the times were with him. Economic depression in the early 1840s had placed a check on new railway construction. Recovery by early 1844, a low interest rate that made it inexpensive to borrow, the low prices of materials, and the high dividends paid by some lines then in operation encouraged the promotion of new railway companies. By mid-1844 the reawakened interest in railway building ignited a speculative fever that swept across Britain. Earlier outbursts of speculation in railroad securities had occurred, especially in 1836–1837. These outbursts could not compare with what came to be known as the Railway Mania of 1845–1847. The widely known and envied success of George Hudson inspired others to try to make their fortunes in the railroad business. Contractors and engineers and lawyers, seeking new business, stirred up public interest. And always there were promoters who promised certain success for their enterprises.

Whatever the stimulus, people began to hallucinate about fortunes to be won by buying railway shares cheap and selling them dear. In November 1845 that level-headed Scotsman, Judge Cockburn, observed that "Britain is at present an island of lunatics, all railway mad. The patients are raving, even in the wildest recesses of the Highlands." People surrendered to a euphoria that convinced them that Britain could absorb all the new railway schemes and that their profitability was unlimited. A few voices, including the Governor of the Bank of England, the *Times*, and the *Economist* warned of the inevitability of a crash, but they were damned as alarmists and doomsayers. People of small means and large could not resist the temptation to buy the new issues of stock. Charles Greville, who belonged to the topmost level of British society, wrote in his diary of his peers that "half of the fine ladies have been dabbling, and the men most unlikely have not been able to refrain from gambling on shares, even I myself (though in a very small amount), for the warning voice of the Governor of the Bank has never been out of my ears." The middle ranks of society provided the heaviest investors.[23]

To attract investors the new companies heavily discounted the price of their shares, thereby adding fuel to the speculative fever. They offered their shares at 5 to 10 percent of their face value (usually £25 per share), with the balance payable upon calls made when the company needed more cash to continue construction. The companies did not ask for deposits from applicants for their shares, and they rarely made inquiries about the financial position of the prospective buyers. Not surprisingly, applications for allotments far exceeded the number of shares being offered, sometimes as much as ten or eleven times over. Those who received allotments of the new issues found eager buyers for their certificates. Before 1845 England had only three stock exchanges, in London, Liverpool, and Manchester. During 1845 thirteen new exchanges opened in cities scattered across the nation, scores of new brokerage houses opened, and temporary exchanges and brokerage houses sprang up in small towns. People traded in stock in coffee houses, inns, and other places of public accommodation, and so-called "alley men" sold small amounts in the streets.[24]

The delirium of the public provided a golden opportunity for unscrupulous promoters to announce the creation of a new railway company. The promoter needed only a map of Great Britain on which he drew a line connecting towns of some size. He had the map lithographed, printed a prospectus abounding in specious statistics, and ran glowing advertisements in the newspapers. To impress prospective buyers of shares, the promoter lured well-known local figures, impecunious younger sons of peers, and seedy baronets to serve on their provisional committees. If the committee included a peer, the promoter, exploiting the deference Britons paid to a title, usually made the nobleman chairman of the committee. The opportunities for skullduggery and fraud proved irresistible to sharp operators and confidence men.

Shares were priced without reference to the property on which they were based. Promoters paid bribes to buy off opponents of their proposals, and reportedly, though it was never proved, bribed members of Parliament to buy their support for the act of Parliament that authorized the establishment of a railway. The law required so-called independent audits of company books, but these were farces. The companies had no external checks or inspections of their operations until a law in 1849 ordered that a government auditor had to go over the books with the company's own auditor.[25]

The promoters were not alone in benefiting from the public's obsession with railways. Lawyers and engineers lined their pockets with the exorbitant fees they charged for their services, contractors grew rich, and the promoters' advertising campaigns proved a bonanza to the press. The demands for materials for railroad construction benefited more legitimate enterprises. The business-oriented wife of a Welsh iron master noted in her diary for October 7, 1845, "We have sold the Great Western 10,000 tons of rails at £12 which is *now* a great price. But people are wild at this moment about Railways and speculation, and they say that iron will still further advance, which, if the bubble do not too soon burst, may probably be the case."

On January 1, 1844, Britain had 1,950 miles of railway in operation. Between that date and the end of 1847, 628 individual acts of Parliament had authorized the construction of 9,572 miles of railway with a total capitalization of £254,900,000. That amounted to over half of Britain's annual gross national income during these years. Before Parliament would consider a bill for a new railroad, the company had to deposit 10 percent of the capital it wanted Parliament to authorize, to establish the bona fides of the new enterprise. The companies used cash raised from the sale of scrip, the preliminary certificates issued to subscribers to their stock, and money borrowed from a bank to meet the 10 percent requirement. In 1846 Parliament approved at least one railway bill each day that it was in session. In addition, there were hundreds of other petitions for acts of incorporation that failed to receive Parliament's approval. In 1845 alone over six hundred new proposals did not even reach first reading in Parliament, presumably because they could not meet the requirement for a deposit of 10 percent of their projected capital.[26]

Seated in the eye of this hurricane of speculation and deceit was none other than George Hudson, the greatest promoter of them all. He was also the greatest subscriber to new promotions. A parliamentary report of 1845 showed that he had subscribed a total of £319,835 to railway proposals seeking authorization from Parliament. His very name had talismanic effect. A mere rumor of his interest in a company sent the price of its stock to new highs. Companies vied with one another to persuade him to join their boards.

The Railway King stood at the zenith of his power and splendor. In addition to his control over more than a third of Britain's railroads, he was chairman of the company that built new docks at Sunderland in Durham, was a director and shareholder in glass works and coal mines, was chairman of the York Union Bank, owned large tracts of land in Yorkshire, and was part owner of a newspaper.

His success made him a public figure. In his obituary in 1871, the *Times* wrote, "There was a time when not to know him was to argue one's self unknown." John Campbell, the later Lord Chancellor, who met Hudson in 1847—and took a strong dislike to him—wrote that Hudson was then "of more note and consequence than any duke in England, except the duke of Wellington." The press reported details of his everyday life as matters of public interest. When he ran for Parliament from Sunderland, the *Times* chartered a special train to carry the news of the outcome of the election to London. Hudson won the election, which reportedly cost him £10,000. He was appointed a deputy Lieutenant of the county of Durham and a magistrate for Durham and for the East and North Ridings of Yorkshire. He moved to London, bought the largest house in the city, and set out to break into high society. At his behest ladies of the elite invited guests of their social station to the Hudsons' for parties and dinners, and there introduced them to Mr. and Mrs. Hudson. He quickly became a social lion, courted by the high and mighty, all of them hoping for tips and inside information. He and his wife were invited to the town houses and country estates of the social and political elite. *Punch*, for whom Hudson was a favorite target, ran a famous cartoon called "King Hudson's Levee," which showed a host of royals and nobles on hands and knees before the enthroned Hudson. He bought estates for his three sons and set them up as country gentlemen. In 1845 he bought for himself two of the finest and most expensive country seats in Yorkshire, one of them of twelve thousand acres.[27]

To many of the middle class, who like most Britons stood in awe of titles, Hudson's fraternization with peers may have seemed his supreme achievement. The reality, of course, was that the elite tolerated and used him but never accepted him as an equal. The snobbery that marked and marred the ruling elite would never have allowed that. They simultaneously courted him and sneered at him. Hudson, for his part, seemed as contemptuous of those who derided him as they were of him. In a casual conversation with John Campbell, he remarked that "the old nobility, sir, are all paupers. What a sad state my neighbors at Castle Howard are in. I am going tomorrow to Clumber [the estate of the duke of Newcastle] where a large party of nobles is invited to meet me, but I could buy them all."[28]

Reasonable folk should have known that the speculative mania with its paper profits could not last. In 1847 signs of contraction evidenced themselves. Continued spending on the construction of new lines strained companies' finances and prompted reductions in dividends. Meanwhile shareholders in increasing numbers failed to meet calls on the shares they had purchased at 10 percent of their nominal value. Traffic on newly opened lines had not yet grown enough to contribute to net earnings. Companies had to turn to the banks for loans, and interest rates began to rise. By August several major lines announced cutbacks in construction. The bubble was nearing the bursting point. Since railroads were Britain's most important area of investment, the entire economy was affected. By October economic life entered on a downward spiral known to history as "the commercial crisis of 1847." The Railway Mania had run its course and had contributed largely to the creation of the financial crisis, but it was not the only culprit. Short harvests and crop failures had persuaded grain importers that Britain faced a shortage, and they had imported large quantities. The shortage failed to materialize, prices fell, and many grain merchants and some of their banks were forced into bankruptcy. The Bank of England, too, bore responsibility by raising its rates. The crisis set off the panic selling of shares and also of merchandise, as bankers, merchants, and investors sought to convert assets into cash. The price of railway shares plummeted, and the downward slide brought financial ruin to many who had invested heavily. Some wound up in debtor's prison. Others, like Sir William Massey Stanley, who owed £280,000, fled abroad to escape their creditors.[29]

The tide of events that had raised Hudson to the heights now betrayed him. He managed to hold onto power for a while after the bottom dropped out by boldly facing down unhappy directors and shareholders. But by early 1849, stormy meetings and formal investigations forced him to resign his chairmanships. Investigations revealed that his illicit gains from his four principal companies amounted to almost £600,000. He admitted his guilt and immediately set about making arrangements to pay back the money he had taken. He sold his London house (it became the residence of the French ambassador) and his estates and liquidated his other assets. Being Hudson, he did not allow his reverses to daunt him. He continued to present a bold face to the world as if nothing had happened. But it was to no avail. Those who had once courted him now reviled him and rejoiced in his downfall. The burghers of his hometown of York, only recently so proud of him, renamed the street they had named after him, scuttled plans for a monument to him, and defeated by only two votes a motion to remove his portrait from the residence of the Lord Mayor. In London he received the final indignity when Madame Tussaud removed his effigy from her museum.

Twilight surrounded the rest of Hudson's days. He dabbled in various enterprises but always unsuccessfully. He kept his seat in Parliament until 1859. That gave him immunity from arrest when Parliament was in session. When the session ended, he fled abroad to escape the creditors who hounded him. In the elections of 1859, he lost his seat and lived in cheap hotels in France, all but penniless. In 1865, when he returned to England with plans to run again for Parliament, a creditor had him arrested. He was sentenced to a debtor's prison in York but was released in three months because he had nothing left to satisfy his creditors. In 1868 some friends raised £4,800 and bought him an annuity. He died in 1871, sanguine and self-confident to the end.

Hudson was a crook and an inept one at that. A renowned modern economist wrote of him that "the misdeeds that eventually swept him from his leading position were rather primitive. He was obviously not adept at the higher arts of swindling." A ruthless man whose unscrupulous use of power brought financial loss and even ruin to thousands, he had the leading role in lowering the standard of commercial morality in Britain. Yet the early development of the British railway system owed more to this swindler than to any other single man. His leadership in the amalgamation of competing railway lines laid the foundation for the creation of a national rail network that within a few years provided Britain with a rational and efficient system of transport. In place of the many small railroads scattered through Britain, fifteen large companies had emerged. In 1850 they controlled 75 percent of the United Kingdom's gross traffic revenues and accounted for 61 percent of its paid-up capital; and by 1860, as mentioned earlier, twelve companies accounted for seven eighths of railway mileage and capital. The *Times*, in its obituary of Hudson, described him as a man "who united largeness of view with wonderful speculative courage. He went in for bigger things than anyone else. He took away people's breath at first, but he soon succeeded in persuading them that the larger the project and the bolder the scheme, the more likely it was to pay. . . . This is the kind of man who leads the world."[30]

If George Hudson was the archetypical promoter, whose genius lay in his ability to bend the wills of others to his purposes, Georg Friedrich List was the archetypical visionary. He dreamed of a united and industrialized Germany bound together by an integrated rail network. Unlike Hudson, he did not seek control over men, or power and riches for himself. Instead, he wanted to bring the blessings of wealth and power to all the people of his beloved homeland. Unlike Hudson, too, he lacked the ability to persuade his countrymen to share his dream. Indeed, he seemed constitutionally unable to get along with people. His life was a tragic tale of endless rebuffs and disappointments, punctuated only by short-lived triumphs, of never finding a place to settle, a life daunted by bad luck and failure that ended in suicide. Yet his name will always be remembered and honored as the prophet of German railroads and German industry.

The driving force that inspired List to devote his life to the advancement of the German economy rose out of his passionate patriotism. A vision of Germany destined for greatness obsessed him. He wrote and argued for a unified code of industrial legislation, for a powerful German navy and merchant marine, and a German colonial empire. He urged German control of the coasts of the Baltic and North Seas, with Austria, the Netherlands, and Denmark incorporated into the German Confederation, and German commercial supremacy in the Danubian lands and in the Near East.

Above all else, List devoted himself to propagandizing for the building of a German railway system and the expansion of the *Zollverein*, the German customs union. The two were inextricably linked in his mind, as, indeed, they were in fact. He once wrote that railroads and the *Zollverein* were Siamese twins that were born at the same time, had grown simultaneously, and were inspired by the same goal: the unification of divided Germany into a wealthy, powerful, and invincible nation. Without the *Zollverein*, a German national railway network was impossible, and without the railways the German economy and the German people could not achieve greatness. Many shared his enthusiasm for the *Zollverein*, but he stood far in advance of his countrymen in his agitation for the building of a national railway network. He was shunted aside and disregarded during his lifetime, but his arguments and doctrines were destined to influence German statesmen, businessmen, and economists for many decades to come.[31]

List was born in 1789 into a well-to-do middle-class family in the imperial city of Reutlingen, later annexed by the kingdom of Württemberg. He left school at fourteen and entered government service at sixteen. As he rose in the bureaucracy of Württemberg, he submitted proposals for reforms, including the establishment of a program at the University of Tübingen to train students for public service. The Minister of Education liked the idea and appointed the twenty-eight-year-old List as the university's Professor of Public Administration. Entirely unqualified for the post, List met with the resentment and opposition of both faculty and students. In 1819 he resigned his chair of his own accord. That same year, he took the lead in organizing a Union of German Merchants and became its secretary. He quickly came into conflict with the executive committee of the Union and quit his post. In 1820 he was elected to the Württemberg diet as a delegate from his hometown. In short order he antagonized the ruling elite of the kingdom by publishing a pamphlet demanding a host of reforms and criticizing the bureaucratic and judicial establishments. The government accused him of writing a criminal document and sentenced him to ten months in jail. Now married to a widow with children, he had a family to support and so he fled, winding up in Switzerland. Unable to earn a living there, he returned to Württemberg and to prison. The political leaders and bureaucrats who had endured his criticism now saw the opportunity to rid themselves forever of this scourge. They released him from jail after five months on the condition that he renounce his citizenship in Württemberg and leave Germany for good.

In 1825 List and his family sailed for the United States. His American experience turned out to be the great turning point in List's thinking. He was mightily impressed by the boldness of American entrepreneurs and politicians, by the freshness and amplitude of their vision for America, and their concern for its economic development. Until now a supporter of the free trade and laissez-faire doctrines of Adam Smith, he became a convert to the "American System." That system combined tariffs to protect infant industries and a national program of internal improvements to expand the domestic market and lessen American dependence upon imported wares. He settled in Pennsylvania, and after several ventures, organized a coal and railroad company that proved successful. He had always intended to return to Germany and now he could afford to do it. He wanted to go back and convince his fellow Germans of the need for unification and economic development, and of the central role that railroads would have in reaching these goals. He knew that opposition and, worse still, apathy awaited his arguments in the narrow parochialism of divided Germany. He had become an American citizen and returned to Germany with his family in 1832. After an aborted appointment as American consul in Hamburg in 1834 he became American consul in Leipzig in Saxony.[32]

During his American sojourn, List had written letters, articles, and brochures developing his economic views and urging the need for railways in Germany. These writings prepared him for the publication of a trailblazing study that appeared in Leipzig in 1833. It bore the long-winded title, "On the Saxon Railway System as the Foundation of an All-German Railway System, and especially the Construction of a Railway from Leipzig to Dresden." The brochure estimated costs of construction and the operating income of the Leipzig-Dresden line and prophesied that it would pay large dividends and would lead to a great boom in the trade of Leipzig. The most striking feature of the publication was an outline map of Germany in which List had drawn a proposed rail network that he titled, "The German Railway System." It sketched out nearly all the major railway lines that were built in the succeeding decades.

Soon local Saxon businessmen told List that they wanted to work with him in building the Leipzig-Dresden line. They formed a committee with List as a member, speedily raised money to get started and began construction. Almost as quickly, List came into conflict with his fellow committee members over critical decisions. In addition, he antagonized them by his intemperate outbursts and his grandiose plans for future railroads. He made himself so objectionable that he was pushed aside and allotted no shares in the enterprise that he had inspired. The committee finally sent him packing with a gratuity of talers and a gilded silver goblet as a gift from the merchants of Leipzig. The first section of the railroad opened in April 1837. That August List left Leipzig. He had hoped to become manager of the railroad. Justly, he complained bitterly that he had received shabby treatment after four years of hard work and out-of-pocket expenditures of fifteen thousand talers.[33]

List had once again the role of outsider thrust upon him. He had the misfortune of being ahead of his time, a prophet without honor. No statesman recognized his merits, a hidebound bureaucracy thwarted him, and no legislative body would heed him. Much of the blame for his rejection by others lay with the man himself. He had a vehemence in speech and manner that put off people and offended them. A friend of many years described him as "the most impassioned man I've ever met. Whoever has seen him never forgets him. His eyes flash, a storm always hovers around his broad brow, and his mouth always flames like the crater of a volcano." He insisted upon having his own way and would not take "no" for an answer. He was blunt and undiplomatic, spurning the role of courtier or supplicant. He spoke in a loud voice, interrupted by sudden peals of laughter, so loud and unexpected as to be disconcerting. He had a large and expressive face, a fresh complexion, graying hair and beard, and slightly bulging eyes with bushy brows. He seemed a cheerful and lively man, full of life and energy, but he suffered spells of darkest depression that overwhelmed him.

After he left Leipzig, List worked as a free-lance journalist, writing an endless stream of articles for magazines, newspapers, and an encyclopedia. He dealt with a host of subjects, but the great majority concerned railroads and their potential. He barely made a living from his writings. He traveled constantly from city to city and to other European lands in pursuit of a livelihood and to preach his gospel of railroads and economic development. Wherever he went, he sought employment in the railroad industry and never succeeded. His articles and above all his important book, *The National System of Political Economy* (discussed in a later chapter), which appeared in 1840, made him well known and influential. Railway projects that he had outlined became realities. Yet he received no thanks for his contributions, much less monetary rewards. He was not appointed to any office in a bureaucracy, he never received a pension from a grateful government, and in a society that placed high value on decorations and awarded them liberally, he was not even given an order with a ribbon that he could wear on his coat.

List's spells of depression deepened. Robert Mohl, who in 1846 saw much of List in Munich, where he then lived, thought that List had become deranged. According to Mohl, he had developed a persecution complex, saw enemies everywhere, and feared attacks on his life. He fortified his house, equipped the doors with concealed locking devices, and admitted only those who knew the password. Yet, said Mohl, each day he sat at the same table in a favorite tavern and filled the room with his loud voice. In the summer of 1846, he went to England, persuaded no one of his ideas, and returned home deeply depressed and physically exhausted. In November he took a trip to Tyrol to recover, but life seemed ever darker. In despair on November 30, 1846, he committed suicide in a lonely hotel room by a pistol shot to his head.[34]

List, of course, was not alone in Germany in his advocacy of the steam railway. Forward looking and increasingly self confident bourgeois entrepreneurs had early on urged the building of railroads. Less far-seeing and less imaginative than List, they thought in terms of railways for their own towns and states rather than for a national network for a united Germany. The desire to make a profit for themselves and a concern for the development of their city and state motivated them. Like List, they faced formidable opposition. Rulers and their advisors remained unconvinced, fearing the impact of the railroad and of industrialization on the political and social structure and even the independence of their states. Important bureaucrats like P. C. W. von Beuth, long-time director of Prussia's Department of Industry, believed that Prussia had no need for railways. In the Grand Duchy of Baden, the government's technical experts were so dubious of the advantages of the railroad that they refused to have anything to do with the building of Baden's first rail line in 1840. The grand duke had to entrust the direction of the enterprise to the chief of his army's general staff.[35]

Germany's first railroad began operations in Bavaria on December 7, 1835. Named the Ludwig Railroad after Bavaria's king, it opened to the thunder of cannon and with the erection of a monument and the striking of a medal to commemorate the great occasion. It ran for all of five miles between

Nuremberg and Fürth and carried only passengers. The first railroad that hauled both passengers and freight was the Leipzig and Dresden line which List had inspired. That railway, completed in 1839, marked the onset of a boom in railway construction throughout Germany. In 1840 Germany had 291 miles of railroad in operation. By 1850 that figure had risen to 3,639 miles. The boom set off a fever of speculation, though it never reached the proportions of Britain's Railroad Mania. Actually, the government built and operated most of the railroads in the German states except for Prussia. In Prussia private enterprise built and ran the railroads but with the state participating substantially in the financing of the different companies and guaranteeing the interest on their bonds. Early in the 1840s it became obvious that some kind of order had to be imposed on the many small lines scattered through the independent German states. In 1847 forty railroads organized the Union of German Railway Administrations and reached agreement on fares, freight charges, and other common operating matters.[36]

George Hudson was the archetypical promoter, Friedrich List the archetypical visionary. Finally there was the archetypical financier, the money man whose motive was profit. He provided the money needed to build the railroads, whether by the state or by private enterprise, because he saw the opportunity to get a good return on his investment.

Above all others, the Rothschild brothers, the greatest money men of their day, were the archetypical financiers of the Railway Age. These five remarkable men, sons of the equally remarkable Mayer Amschel Rothschild, banker of Frankfurt, headed the branches of their banking house in Frankfurt, Paris, Vienna, Naples, and London. They became the preeminent financiers and builders of railroads in much of Western and Central Europe. Their involvement in the financing of railroads marked a great turning point not only in the history of the House of Rothschild, but in the history of banking. The Rothschilds, like other bankers of that era, made their money by lending to governments, by acting as the fiscal agents of governments, by making short-term loans—usually of three to six months—to merchants and other businessmen, and by discounting commercial notes and bills of exchange. They were reluctant to immobilize their capital in long-term loans to industrial enterprises. The decision of the Rothschilds to put money into the building of railroads not only began their own involvement in the financing of industrial enterprises. Their preeminence as the leaders in the world of banking persuaded other banking houses to follow their lead.[37]

The Rothschilds' involvement with railways began with Nathan, head of the London branch, Mayer Amschel's third and most gifted son. A short, stocky man of considerable girth, he spoke heavily accented English laced often with Yiddish. He had been an interested observer of the debut of the steam railroad in England. The success of the new enterprises convinced him of the potential for profit offered by the railroad. He realized that many Englishmen had recognized that potential, too. So he wrote his brothers on the continent advising them to get in on the ground floor in this new business in their respective lands.

His advice fell on fertile soil in Vienna and Paris. Solomon Rothschild, in Vienna, already had his interests in railroads awakened in 1829 by Francis X. Riepl, a professor at the Polytechnic Institute in Vienna. Solomon sent Riepl and Leopold Wertheimstein, his trusted aide, to England and later to Belgium and Germany to study the building and operation of the new lines in those lands. Solomon was eager to get started but, as mentioned at the outset of this chapter, Emperor Francis, with his dread of all innovation and change, refused to allow the building of steam railroads. In 1835 Francis died and he had hardly been buried when Solomon received permission to build his railroad. He easily raised the money needed for the enterprise, issuing 12,000 shares at 1,000 florins each, selling 4,000 shares to the public—who applied to buy 27,490 shares—and keeping 8,000 shares for the Rothschild bank. The first section of the railroad, from Vienna to Brunn in Moravia, opened in 1839. The line quickly made profits, and by 1845 its stock had more than doubled in price. Rothschild tried to get the concession for a railroad south from Vienna to the Adriatic, but it went to Baron Georg von Sina, another Viennese banker. Construction of other railways got underway in Lombardy, an Austrian possession since 1815, and Hungary in the 1840s. Meanwhile the government had awakened to the political and military importance of the railroad. In December 1841 an imperial decree ordered the construction by the state of four trunk lines, each to run in a different direction from Vienna to the frontiers of the empire. Work began and large sums were expended, but excruciatingly slow progress and financial difficulties persuaded the state to sell its railroad properties. Privately owned railroads continued their growth but at a rate much slower than in other lands. By 1850 the empire had only 843 miles in operation.[38]

In France a young man named Émile Péreire after several years of effort had gained the concession in 1835 from a reluctant government to build an 18-kilometer railroad from Paris to the resort village of Saint-Germain. Émile and his brother Isaac were disciples of the teachings of Count Saint-Simon (1760–1825), and like their fellow Saint-Simonians, they realized the enormous possibilities of industrial technology and praised and promoted material advance as a boon to human welfare. In time the Péreires became great bankers, industrialists, and railroad builders. Now, at the outset of his career,

Émile Péreire wanted to build the Paris–Saint-Germain line as a common carrier of freight and passengers to prove the value of the railroad to a skeptical government and public. Péreire had drawn the attention of James Rothschild, head of the Paris branch of the family firm, to the possibilities of his little railroad. In May 1835, after some hesitation, James, predisposed by what he had learned from his brothers in London and Vienna, took a block of shares in the new venture. Far more important, he lent the enterprise the prestige of his family's name.[39]

Adolphe Thiers, then Minister of Public Works, prophesied that Péreire's line "would never carry a passenger nor a parcel." Confounding Thiers and its other critics the new railway, opening in August 1837, proved an immediate financial and public success. That encouraged Rothschild and other bankers to plan new railroads. Meanwhile, the government passed the Railway Law of 1842 after nine years of debate about railroads as private enterprise versus governmental monopolies, about proposals presented for new lines, about costs and financing, and a multitude of related matters. The law prescribed the routes of the trunk lines for a national rail network and provided for a partnership between the state and private enterprise. The law's favorable conditions encouraged not only French financiers, but also bankers from Britain, Germany, and Switzerland, to invest in French railway construction. Inevitably, the issuance of shares and the promise of quick profits touched off a frenzy of speculation in 1845 and 1846. In mid-1846 the crash came. Share prices fell, foreigners withdrew their money, and money needed to continue construction fell short of demand. Recession in 1847 and revolution in 1848 provided further damaging blows. Financial difficulties led to bankruptcies and cessation of construction in some cases and reduction in the scope of other enterprises. As a result, France in 1850, with only 1,800 miles of operating railroads, lagged far behind Germany and England. Then in 1852, under the aegis of the newly proclaimed Emperor Napoleon III, governmental policy introduced new vigor into France's railway industry. By 1860 France had 5,700 miles of railway in operation, and by 1870 it had nearly as many miles (10,750) as neighboring Germany (11,150).[40]

The involvement in railroads of Solomon Rothschild in Vienna and James in Paris was quickly joined by their brothers. In the forties and fifties, they financed or built lines in Prussia and other German states, in the Kingdom of the Two Sicilies, and in other parts of Italy. They and the other bankers who followed their leads invested in railroads to make a profit, the *métier* of the financier. The initiative of the financiers and their willingness to risk their money in railroad ventures made them pioneers in ushering in the Railway Age.

Economic gains from the introduction of the railways first began to evidence themselves in the 1840s. They increased rapidly in the following years as the new lines joined to form national networks and then an international one. The building of railroads contributed mightily to the growth of other industries, creating a huge new demand for iron and coal and all the other materials needed to manufacture locomotives, rails, and rolling stock and to build stations. Old industries grew and new ones started, and enterprising and talented men introduced innovations that increased productivity and in time gave employment to many thousands.

The railroads themselves provided work for hundreds of thousands. In those days before the advent of earth-moving machinery, railroad building was pick-and-shovel work. In Britain, at the zenith of the railway boom in 1847, a Parliamentary report showed that 256,509 men were employed in building lines then under construction. In the years after the boom, new construction declined so that in the early 1850s, less than 36,000 were employed. Meanwhile, as the railroads grew, so did the number of their permanent employees, who by the mid-fifties exceeded 100,000 workers.[41]

The railroads had other and not so immediately evident effects upon economic life. They became the pioneers in the development of the management of large enterprises. At a time when nearly all businesses were family firms or partnerships, the railroads were corporate enterprises, owned by thousands of shareholders but managed by a corporal's guard of executives and their associates. The railroads formed by far the largest enterprises of their times, with initial costs, assets, operating expenses, payrolls, and the need for a variety of technical skills that far exceeded other industries. Their terminals, warehouses, shops, rolling stock, and employees lay scattered over many miles. They were an entirely new kind of business, and the men entrusted with their management had to find their own way. Every day, they had to direct the activities of hundreds and even thousands of people who were far distant from them and whom they may never even have seen. Through trial and error, they learned how to manage their huge enterprises successfully, and in that process, they led in the development of business management that in succeeding years became standard practice in other industries. They led, too, in the creation of a new kind of bureaucratic elite—the salaried professional manager who could move easily from one industry to another. In Britain these top executives came predominantly from the upper and upper-middle classes. In Germany, many of them were former government bureaucrats who organized their companies in ways that closely resembled the structure of governmental bureaucracies.[42]

The railroads were also responsible in largest part for what has been called the democratization of the money market. Till then wealthy nobles and rich merchants had invested primarily in government securities. The sale of shares to raise the millions needed for railway construction attracted a new investing public, the middle classes. When the opportunities for profitable investment in railroads tapered off, the new investors did not go back to their old habits. Instead, they sought out other opportunities for investment that offered them the yields to which they had become accustomed.[43]

Railroads were once accorded the rank of leading sector in the economic growth of the second half of the nineteenth century. In recent decades some economic historians, skillfully employing sophisticated analytical techniques, have questioned this assumption. They have argued that the railways were not of overwhelming importance in the growth of the economy and that no single innovation was vital for that growth. They maintain that in Britain and the United States, economic expansion would have been only slightly affected if railroads had not existed, with other modes of transportation taking their place. In contrast, students of the German economy maintain that the railroad was unquestionably the leading sector in that land. These and similar studies have much heuristic value, stimulating further careful investigations. The fact remains that the railroads did exist and that despite their possible downgrading, there is general agreement that they had a greater impact upon the economy than any other innovation of the era.[44]

The railroad had an especially dramatic effect upon the lives of ordinary people. It not only greatly reduced the time they spent in travel, but far more important, the railroad could carry far more people and at far lower cost than could coaches. Trains had as many as twelve carriages with 1,200 to 1,500 passengers. The people who crowded into the new lines included many—probably the great majority—who till then could not afford to travel. The railroad with its cheap fares made it possible for them to go beyond the borders of their towns and villages and to gain new experiences, new impressions, and new knowledge. It was as if people from different worlds were meeting for the first time, with the railroad serving as a great leveler. The arrogance of caste continued, but its importance began to lessen when the common man, riding in the same train and often in the same coach, waiting in the same station, eating in the same railroad restaurants, and using the same sanitary facilities, began to see through the veil that separated him from his "betters." At the same time, people began to develop a sense of belonging to a larger society. Local and regional differences and prejudices became less pronounced as people met and learned more about their fellow countrymen.[45]

The railroad builders had severely underestimated the mass appeal of their enterprises. They had concentrated on serving the more prosperous sectors of society with comfortable cushioned first-class coaches and, at least on the Continent, tolerable second-class ones. In Britain second-class coaches had bare wooden benches with straight backs and often with their sides open to the weather. Poorer folk went third class (or fourth in Continental lines). That meant riding in boxes on wheels, without springs, with no roof, with three-foot-high railings, and with no seats. Snow, rain, sparks from the locomotive, and blistering rays from the sun all were the lot of the third-class passenger.[46]

All passengers, regardless of class, shared some discomforts. The trains jolted and jumped as they traveled on uneven roadbeds. The Duchess de Dino complained that there was nothing to see as the train hurtled through the countryside, and the cold, dark tunnels were filled with thick and choking smoke from the locomotive. An Austrian diplomat, ill-tempered after sitting for three hours on a German train because of a breakdown, wrote that "nothing is so badly organized as the lines of railway communication in Germany, in addition to the dirtiness of the carriage and the stations and the vulgarity of the passengers."

So went the plaints of members of the elite. Ordinary people welcomed the railroad, for all its discomforts, for providing them with hitherto nonexistent opportunities for recreation. British railroads introduced excursions at reduced fares at the end of the 1830s, and they became increasingly popular in the succeeding years. Now, for the first time, working-class families could go off for a day in the country or at the seashore. The Great London Exhibition of 1851 owed its spectacular success to the excursions and their low fares. Many of the more than six million visitors who poured into London from every corner of Britain came by rail.[47]

Not everyone traveled on the train or went on excursions. But everyone felt the influence of the railway in the important matter of keeping time. In 1820 a committee of French scientists established the standard for intervals of time. They recommended that the length of the solar day be averaged and that a second be defined as 1/86,400th of the average day. That definition became accepted internationally. However, the periods of time were not standardized. That is, each locality had its own time. Each town or city set its clocks at sundial noon, corrected to allow for variations of the solar day. That occasioned no serious inconveniences until the introduction of the railroads, which operated on a schedule, announcing times of departure and arrivals in railway guides and time tables. Obviously, if time differed from town to town the published schedules would be worthless. A passenger on a train, say from London to Liverpool, who got on at some midpoint would not know whether the announced time of the train's arrival was that of London, where the train originated, the time of the town where he got on, or Liverpool time. So it quickly became necessary to have a uniform system of time. Called at first "railway time," it was set at London time, determined at London's Greenwich Observatory. The Great Western Railroad adopted Greenwich time in 1840, and in the succeeding years, it became the standard time for all of Britain. Other lands, confronted with the same problem as their rail networks grew, at first followed Britain's example by making the time of its chief city as the national standard, but ultimately adopted Greenwich mean time as the basis for standard time throughout the world.[48]

The new railroads had an impact, too, upon the environment in both town and country. Their impact became most marked in the cities. To keep down the costs of land for their rights of way the railways usually went through working-class districts, where land was the cheapest. They did not have to pay for the resettlement of the hosts of the poor whose housing they demolished. These people, compelled to seek shelter wherever they could, compounded the already desperate housing shortage that haunted so many urban centers. Lovers of rural beauty were outraged by the intrusions of the railroads into the countryside. It seemed to them as if the railway builders deliberately sought out places of natural beauty for their lines.[49]

The railways did not everywhere destroy and devastate. By the 1840s passenger fares formed a large and even largest share of their gross receipts. To attract and hold passengers, rail companies built magnificent terminals in major cities, designed by leading architects, luxuriously furnished and illuminated, with excellent food in their restaurants.[50]

The coming of the railroad was hailed as the inauguration of a new age in communications. Actually, the revolution in transportation had begun decades earlier with the steamboat. The steamboat had been the first radical innovation in transport since the second half of the fifteenth century. That was when European boat builders made galleys and single-mast ships obsolete by introducing the full-rigged ships with three or four masts and five to eight sails. Inventors and engineers of the last part of the eighteenth century had experimented with steam engines as motive power for vessels, but the famed voyage on the Hudson in 1807 of Robert Fulton's *Clermont* marked the beginning of commercially successful steamboat operations. Within a few years steamboats became common on the rivers and lakes of the United States. Europeans lagged behind, but by the 1830s and 1840s steamers had pretty much replaced sailing vessels and barges on the rivers and lakes of central and western Europe.

It took longer for steam to conquer the high seas. The risk of mechanical breakdowns, all too frequent in the early days of steam, and the space required for fuel for the inefficient engines, made steam in ocean-going vessels a hazardous enterprise. In fact, steam engines remained so unreliable that almost to the end of the nineteenth century, even the great ocean liners carried masts and sailing rigs as auxiliary power for use in emergencies. Despite the risks, ships equipped with steam engines—and sails—crossed the Atlantic: the first, the *Savannah* in 1819, and several more in the 1820s and 1830s. In 1838 the *Sirius* out of Cork and the *Great Western* out of Bristol raced across the Atlantic. These two voyages of nineteen and fifteen days respectively settled all doubts about the feasibility of travel by transatlantic steamer. In 1838 the British government invited bids for carrying mail from Liverpool to Halifax, Quebec, and Boston. Samuel Cunard, a Canadian, won the contract. With others, he formed a company called the British and North American Royal Mail Steam Packet Company, and on July 4, 1840, began the first regular steamship service between Britain and America.

These first steamers were wooden side wheelers. In 1838 Swedish-born John Ericsson and an English collaborator demonstrated the screw propeller. Superior to paddle wheels in rough weather and delivering more power, screw propellers were quickly adopted by builders and used on new steamships. Meanwhile, already in 1838 shipbuilders had begun to use iron for ships' hulls. Iron hulls were lighter, stronger, and less susceptible to decay than those of wooden vessels, which were, moreover, susceptible to buckling.[51]

The transatlantic steamer easily surpassed the sail ship in the time required to cross the North Atlantic. Trips under sail took around four weeks unless heavy weather intervened. Young John Motley took fifty days to go from Boston to Hamburg in 1831. Dr. Augustus Gordon, bound for France in 1845, spent thirty-three days in a storm-racked voyage from New York to Le Havre. In contrast, the steamer on which Professor Benjamin Silliman of Yale was a passenger made the trip from New York to Liverpool in nearly twelve days. A Cunard packet crossing at the same time took only ten days.

The ocean-going steamship had established itself in the 1840s as a new and valuable means of transportation. Yet despite its superior speed and capacity, the sailing ship remained paramount on the high seas. In 1850 in Great Britain, the world's chief maritime power, out of a total of 3,565,000 tons of shipping, only 168,000 tons were driven by steam. Indeed, the sailing ship reached its peak in size, capacity, and speed in the 1850s when the graceful and beautiful clipper ships ruled the waves. The first clipper was launched in New York, and others soon followed. The fastest of these vessels could make eighteen knots with favoring winds while steamships puffed away at an average of about nine knots. The disparity between sail and steam slowly declined as steamships became more efficient, and in 1883 the tonnage of steamships in Britain finally exceeded that of sailing vessels.[52]

The introduction of railroads and steamships was paralleled by innovations in other means of communication. The first practical innovation came in 1794 when the French revolutionary government adopted the invention of Claude Chappe and his brother that they called the telegraph, from the Greek for "distant writing." A line of towers was built, the towers being six to ten miles apart, each with a wooden beam pivoted at its center so that it could be rotated in a vertical plane, and with movable arms at each end of the beam, making possible a large number of configurations. An operator in each tower, equipped with a telescope and using an agreed upon code, relayed the message he received from one tower to the next one. Messages could be transmitted rapidly, unless rain, snow, fog, and of course, night, obscured the operator's vision and made the system useless. Despite this limitation, the optical telegraph, as it was called, spread across Europe and was still in use in some places in the mid-nineteenth century. France had 556 stations that covered more than 3,000 miles in 1852, when the electric telegraph finally supplanted the Chappe system.

The optical telegraph was reserved everywhere exclusively for the use of governments, and especially for military messages. The only rapid means of communication available to private persons were mounted couriers who raced along the roads of Europe, and the far less expensive homing pigeon with a message in a small container tucked under a wing. Pigeons seemed particularly favored by financiers and speculators. In 1840 T. B. Macaulay reported that pigeons brought news from Paris in twenty-three hours.[53]

Unsuccessful efforts to develop an electric telegraph, using static electricity, reached back into the eighteenth century. The breakthrough came with the discovery by Christian Oersted, at the University of Copenhagen in 1819, of electromagnetism, that is, the production of magnetic effects by the use of electricity. That discovery inspired dozens of efforts to produce an electric telegraph. The first to develop a practical instrument were two young Englishmen, William F. Cooke, recently returned for reasons of health from Britain's East India Company, and Charles Wheatstone, professor of science at King's College, London. In 1837, they formed a partnership to produce an apparatus that would serve as an adjunct to visual railway signals. That same year they patented a device with six wires and five needles. The signaling system was easy to learn, but the need for multiple wires made the apparatus difficult to install. Despite this, in 1838 the Great Western Railway Company tried the device on a thirteen-mile stretch, and it quickly proved successful. The inventors introduced improvements, but a quarrel between them almost from the outset of their partnership retarded the machine's development. Wheatstone frequently claimed that he invented the telegraph, to Cooke's considerable irritation, especially since Cooke had done more to make it a practical device.

In America Samuel F. B. Morse, a portrait painter of distinction and professor of art at New York University, in 1832 began to work on an electric telegraph. His interest in electricity went back to his college days at Yale. It received new stimulus from lectures and colleagues at New York University. In 1835 he produced a telegraph, but the instrument, reflecting Morse's technical inexperience, was crude and impractical. His efforts might have ended had he not received assistance from Leonard D. Gale, a university colleague, Joseph Henry of the Smithsonian Institution, and most important, Alfred Vail. Morse formed a partnership with Vail, and the latter in 1838 completely redesigned the instrument. Morse had first asked Congress in 1837 for a subsidy but his petition went unanswered until 1843. Congress then appropriated $30,000 to run a thirty-seven mile line from Washington to Baltimore. The line was completed in 1844, and Morse demonstrated the practicality of his instrument and inaugurated public use of the telegraph with that famous first message, "What hath God wrought."[54]

After a few years of hesitation, the electric telegraph spread with astounding speed in country after country. By the end of the 1840s, it had firmly established itself as an important medium of communication. The thirteen miles of line in Britain in 1838 had grown to four thousand miles in 1852. The telegraph's first and most widespread use was for railroad signaling and control of rail traffic. Gradually governments became aware of the usefulness of the telegraph, an awareness that was heightened on the Continent by the revolutions of 1848 and 1849. The success of a new line between Berlin and Frankfurt in keeping Berlin immediately apprised of the actions of the National Assembly, which was meeting at Frankfurt, persuaded the Prussian government in 1849 to expand the system. It commissioned Werner Siemens to build lines from Berlin to Hamburg and Breslau, and from Berlin to Cologne, and thence to the Prussian border. There it met the Belgian telegraph system and so became the first international telegraph line. The telegraph became available to the general public in Britain in 1846 when the first privately owned telegraph company was formed. Privately owned companies provided service until 1868, when the post office bought them and took over public telegraph lines. In France a law of November 29, 1850, ordered that telegraph lines, hitherto reserved for government use, be made available to the public.[55]

Railroads, steamships, and the telegraph, triumphs of man's inventiveness and technological skill, brought about revolutionary changes in the pattern and quality of life. Yet none of these great innovations affected the lives of so many people so directly as did a far simpler and nontechnological innovation that was introduced in the United Kingdom and spread quickly from there to the rest of the world. That innovation drastically reduced the cost of mail and so put the writing of letters within the reach of the poorest in society. Called the Penny Post, it was the brainchild of an obscure Englishman named Rowland Hill. Years later, when Rowland Hill, full of honors, was laid to rest, Prime Minister William Ewart Gladstone in his eulogy paid gracious tribute to Hill. "In some respects," said Gladstone, "his lot was a peculiarly happy one even as among public benefactors, for his great plan ran like wildfire through the civilized world, and never perhaps was a local invention (for such it was) and improvement applied in the lifetime of its author to the advantage of such vast multitudes of his fellow creatures."[56]

Until the introduction and spread of Hill's Penny Post, mail had everywhere been available only to governments and to the upper classes who could afford to pay the costs of sending a letter or package. In some lands the state, and in others private companies, provided the mail service. Delivery time improved with the introduction of mail coaches in the late eighteenth and early nineteenth centuries, but it still took much time for letters to travel even relatively short distances.

A letter's postage varied according to its destination, its weight, and even its size and shape. The sender could prepay the postage, but typically the recipient paid the fee on delivery. Britain had over forty separate rates for domestic mail. It cost four pence to send a letter fifteen miles, seven pence for up to fifty miles and so on, so that, for example, it cost one shilling, four-and-a-half pence, to mail a letter from London to Edinburgh, a distance of four hundred miles. Daniel O'Connell, the famed Irish tribune, complained that the many thousands of Irishmen living in England, who filled the ranks of unskilled labor, would have to spend one fifth of their weekly wage to mail a letter to Ireland and get back a reply. In France the government had divided the nation into six postal zones, each with special rates that ranged from six to thirty-two sous.[57]

Not surprisingly, people resorted to all manner of dodges to avoid the postal fees. In Britain stage coaches and freight wagons carried mail in packages and trunks at less than post office rates. Evasion was especially rife on oceanic mail. Coffee houses and ship brokers served as collecting points for letters that went out on ships to all parts of the globe. The franking privilege of members of Parliament provided a legal, albeit grossly abused, method of evasion of postage. During sessions and for forty days before and after sessions, each M.P. could send ten letters and receive fifteen letters free of postage. High government officials also enjoyed the franking privilege. Members of Parliament and officials alike not only franked their own mail but franked letters wholesale for friends and important constituents.[58]

Rowland Hill, whose reform introduced order into the chaotic postal system of Britain, was born in 1795 into a middle-class family that had come down in the world. His father was an impractical idealist, a man without guile, whose friends said of him that he had every sense but common sense. Fortunately, his wife, though lacking in learning, was full of shrewd common sense and strength of purpose. Anticipating the Shavian maxim that those who can, do, and those who can't, teach, she urged her husband, then forty, to open a school. That would provide the family a living and give her sons a better education than the family's resources could have provided.

Rowland Hill, third of the four sons, after trying his hand at a number of things, became secretary in England of a new commission for the colonization of then unoccupied southern Australia. The project met with difficulties, so that Hill had time for other interests. He settled on postal reform. Complaints about the post office reached far back into the past, but the campaign destined to bring about change began in 1833 with a Scottish M.P. named Robert Wallace. He became the spearhead of the attack on the postal system, supported by other reform-minded members. In 1836 Hill's brother Frederic, then Inspector of Prisons in Scotland, introduced Rowland to Robert Wallace. They hit it off immediately, and Wallace provided Hill with a great pile of government reports dealing with the post office. He immersed himself in an exhaustive study of these data and arrived at some startling conclusions. He discovered that the principal costs of the system had very little to do with the costs of the actual delivery of the mail. Instead, the chief expenses of the post office arose from the costs of maintaining the complicated system of rates and the costs of collecting the postage on delivery. He arrived at the obvious conclusion that the post office could save great sums of money by simply making prepayment of letters general practice. His next finding not only startled the supporters of the existing system, but startled him. After long and involved calculations, he found that the cost of carrying a letter in Britain, regardless of distance, was substantially the same. For example, the cost of carrying a letter from London to Edinburgh, for which the post office charged one shilling, four-and-a-half pence, amounted actually to one thirty-sixth of a penny. Obviously, it made sense to charge a single low rate for all domestic mail, thereby making postal service available to the great mass of the public and yet increasing postal revenues.

In January 1837 Hill presented his findings and recommendations in a small pamphlet that he circulated among friends and some high public officials. Dissatisfied with the lack of attention paid to the pamphlet, he put out a second edition, intended for general distribution. In the pamphlet he recommended a uniform rate for all of the United Kingdom of one penny for each half ounce and urged prepayment, but allowed the option of payment on receipt of two pennies per half ounce. Hill proposed the sale at the post office of paper or envelopes prestamped by a hand stamp. It then occurred to him that through ignorance or carelessness people might write a letter on unstamped paper. They would then have to go to the nearest post office to buy prestamped paper or envelopes and readdress the letter. However, in those days of plentiful domestic help, letters were brought for mailing by illiterate servants or messengers who could not readdress the letter. That led Hill, almost as an afterthought, to propose the sale of an adhesive postage stamp. A concern for the convenience of illiterates, who would otherwise have to return to their employers with the letters unmailed, and not public convenience, inspired the use of adhesive stamps that soon became a fundamental feature of postal reform.[59]

The second edition of Hill's pamphlet quickly won wide public attention. Petitions demanding reform, signed by many thousands, poured into Parliament. Meanwhile, in November 1837 a Parliamentary committee headed by Robert Wallace began to hold hearings. The following July, it recommended a uniform postage rate. The government, headed by Lord Melbourne, refused to yield. Popular pressure continued to mount; finally, after 150 members of Parliament urged Melbourne to support the reform, he reluctantly agreed. The bill carried in Commons by a large majority. Queen Victoria gave her assent and the "Penny Post," as it was popularly called, came into effect on January 10, 1840. The sale of stamps and stamped envelopes began in May 1840. The stamps quickly had great popular success. Over 68 million of the famous "Penny Blacks" were sold in the first year of their issuance. The stamps bore a profile of Victoria, taken from a portrait medal struck in 1837, when she was eighteen. The queen liked it so much that for the rest of her long reign, she refused to allow the use of any later portrait.[60]

Hill had triumphed. The great reform that he had proposed had become the law of the land. But he had not achieved the goal he now set for himself.

He wanted to run the Post Office, and with his Penny Post a reality, he set out to win that appointment. When the Whigs returned to office in 1846, he received the appointment of Secretary to the Postmaster General. At last, he was on the inside of the Post Office, but the long-time Permanent Secretary, Colonel Maberly, was in full command. Maberly had originally opposed the reforms, but under his direction, the post office had made remarkable progress. That did not deter Hill from efforts to take over Maberly's position. Finally, in 1854, Hill won his campaign. Maberly was transferred to another department and Hill became Permanent Secretary of the Post Office.[61]

His will to succeed, instilled in him long ago by his mother, carried him to the heights. In 1860 the queen knighted him for his services. When he died in 1879, he was buried in Westminster Abbey amidst the great of his nation. He was a man driven by ambition, and not surprisingly, he made enemies on his way to the top. His own nephew, in a lavishly admiring biography, described him as a cold and reserved man. The novelist Anthony Trollope, who spent many years as an official of the Post Office, was much harsher. He wrote of Hill that "I never came across anyone who so little understood the ways of men—unless it was his brother Frederic [in 1851 he became Assistant Secretary of the Post Office]. To the two brothers, the servants of the post office . . . were so many machines who could be counted on for their exact work without deviation."[62]

By 1850 most of the nations of Europe and some lands overseas had adopted the principle of a uniform rate for postage and the use of adhesive stamps. By the end of that decade, the use of stamps had become all but universal.[63]

The decade of the 1840s saw the introduction of another great new medium of communication. This one brought about a revolution in visual imagery. In 1839 the world learned of the invention of photography. In France, Louis-Jacques-Mandé Daguerre (1780–1851) announced his discovery of the method by which he fixed an image on a silvered sheet of copper, called the daguerreotype after its inventor. Two weeks later in England, William Henry Foxwood-Talbot (1800–1877) reported his discovery that produced a negative image on a sheet of sensitized paper.

Both Daguerre and Foxwood-Talbot, or Fox-Talbot as he was called, had spent years on the development of their processes. A Frenchman named Joseph-Nicéphore Niepce had taken the first real photograph in 1826. Daguerre, a professional scenery painter and producer of dioramas, had been experimenting with the long-known camera obscura. Daguerre learned of Niepce's work and in 1829 formed a partnership with him. After Niepce's death in 1833, Daguerre continued the research and by 1837 succeeded in producing remarkably clear and detailed photographs. In 1839 Daguerre and Niepce's son sold full rights to the discovery to the French government in return for life annuities, and the government placed the discovery in the public domain. Soon thereafter Daguerre wrote a pamphlet describing the process, and the pamphlet immediately became a best-seller. More than thirty editions appeared between 1839 and 1846, and it was translated into eight languages. Daguerreotypes became enormously popular, especially when rapid improvements in lenses and sensitizing techniques reduced the time of exposure from twenty minutes or more to as little as twenty to forty seconds. Till now only the wealthy and the powerful could afford to have their portraits, painted by artists, preserved for posterity. Now ordinary men and women, people of modest means, could have their portraits made and permanently preserved.

The daguerreotype had serious disadvantages, not the least the bulky equipment needed to take the picture, and the fact that it could not be reproduced. The process discovered by Fox-Talbot had the great advantage of producing negatives that could be reproduced in multiple copies and on paper. Fox-Talbot, grandson of an earl, graduate of Harrow and Cambridge, and Fellow of the Royal Society, was very much a member of the elite that ruled Britain. He might well have kept his invention to himself had it not been for the widely publicized announcement of Daguerre's process. He patented his discovery in 1841. The patent impeded the adoption and spread of his process because he imposed restrictions and conditions on licensees that discouraged them, and he brought frequent lawsuits against infringements of his patent. Then in 1851 the English sculptor Frederick Scott Archer introduced the wet-plate process, which quickly came into universal use. The new method, in which the negative was of collodion-coated glass, equaled the daguerreotype in clarity of detail, provided a negative from which paper prints could be made, and was free of patent restrictions. Till then the photograph had been restricted to portraiture. Now mass production of photographs became possible, and photography reached out beyond portraiture to all areas of human life to provide mankind with a unique and invaluable record of the human experience.[64]

Heine had not exaggerated when, in 1843, he compared the coming of the railway to the discovery of America 350 years earlier. Had he shared our wisdom of hindsight, he could have added the ocean-going steamship, the electric telegraph, the advent of inexpensive mail, and the discovery of photography. Just as the discovery of America had opened a new world to

Europeans, these revolutionary innovations of the decade of the 1840s opened a new world of another kind, a world of communications that gave people the opportunity to do and see things and have experiences that till then had been impossible. Now they could travel to places far and near at hitherto unimaginable speeds and at costs that the common man could afford. People who had never ventured beyond the borders of their native villages or towns could discover a world till now unknown to them. They gained a knowledge of the way that other people lived and a degree of sophistication that fitted them for the new kind of society that was emerging. The electric telegraph provided them speedily with news of happenings in near and distant places that only yesterday had taken days and even weeks and months to reach them. The development of photography added a great new dimension to the human experience by providing a means of communication that was destined to become as powerful and as important as the printed word. Finally, the revolutionary innovation of the 1840s that affected the lives of the greatest number of people was the simplest and least technological innovation of them all. A uniform postage rate and adhesive stamps reduced the cost of mail, so that the writing and the receiving of letters came within the reach of everyone. For the first time in history, the poor and people of modest means could communicate with those for whom they cared and from whom they were separated. In Great Britain alone in 1839, a year before the introduction of the Penny Post, 82.5 million letters were delivered by the post office, including 6.5 million franked letters. In 1853 that number had risen almost five-fold to over 400 million, and by 1870 the number was over one billion. Gladstone had not exaggerated when in his eulogy he said that Rowland Hill's simple idea "ran like wildfire through the civilized world." That was true, too, of the other great revolutions in communications that distinguished the decade of the 1840s.

CHAPTER TWO

Reformers and Radicals

In one of the most famed opening lines in all literature, Karl Marx and Friedrich Engels began their *Communist Manifesto* with the words, "A specter is haunting Europe—the specter of communism. All the powers of old Europe have entered into a holy alliance to exorcise this specter." A specter did, indeed, haunt Europe, but not the minuscule Communist League that in 1847 had commissioned Marx and Engels to draft a manifesto. Rather, it was the dread aroused by the emergence of a host of radical movements in the late 1830s and especially in the 1840s, of which the Communist League was one of the least important. Some of these movements sought the introduction of political reforms, such as universal manhood suffrage or the drafting of a constitution that guaranteed equality of all before the law. Others, far more radical, had as their professed aim the transformation of the entire social order. The upper orders did not distinguish among these movements, but tarred moderates and extremists with the same brush. "Where is the party in opposition that has not been decried as communistic by its opponents in power?" asked Marx and Engels in their *Manifesto*.

Actually, most people overestimated by far the importance of these radical movements. They had relatively few adherents, lacked leadership and coherent programs, and were riven with dissension and jealousies.[1] Still, the memories of the violence and the excesses of the French Revolution and of the revolt in Russia in 1773 led by Emelyan Pugachev remained fresh in the minds of the upper orders of Europe. More immediately, the unrest and risings of workers and peasants and the organization of secret societies awakened dark fears among the elite. They often identified these troubles with something they called socialism or communism, though they were unclear what these words meant. As John Stuart Mill explained in 1849, "it is not obvious what there is in this system of thought [socialism] to account for the frantic terror with which everything that bears that ominous name is usually received on both sides of the English Channel." In 1838 Charles Greville warned that few people "are aware of the poison that is circulating through the veins and corrupting the blood of the social mass." The Baden diplomat, Freiherr von Andlaw, wrote that whatever they wanted to call themselves—Republicans, Socialists, Radicals, and so on—they all wanted to undermine state, church, property, family, and every other institution of human society. Karl Biedermann, Prussian academic, publicist, and moderate bourgeois liberal, warned in 1847 of a "red rising of uneducated and coarse elements, a mighty overturn of all institutions from which one could not possibly envision how a peaceful order could be rebuilt out of the abyss."[2]

Dire prophecies heard in every European land in the 1840s of the inevitability of revolution came true in the spring of 1848. These risings inflamed the rhetoric of those who warned of the Red Menace. Queen Victoria's husband, Prince Albert, in a letter of March 6, 1848, to King Frederick William IV of Prussia wrote that the February revolution in Paris loosed "the evil spirit of communism, the hereditary foe of all society, and threatens the fall of other states." Sir Robert Peel in an address on April 6, 1848, told Parliament that socialism could have no other ultimate result than the misery and ruin of the working class. The Austrian high bureaucrat, Baron Kübeck von Kubau, equated socialism with theft, robbery, murder, sedition, and high treason. That indefatigable diarist Varnhagen von Ense foretold a dark future under the red banner of revolution, with blood flowing in the streets in class warfare, vengeful tribunes, and the impoverishment and flight of both the high and the low.[3]

The concept of democracy was held in equal contempt with socialism and communism by conservatives and liberals alike. To the Duke of Wellington, the Reform Bill of 1832, which extended the suffrage, represented a victory of democracy. No matter that the numbers entitled to vote rose by only a mere 300,000 and that 85 percent of Britain's adult males did not have the franchise. To the duke, the mischief was done: "Whereas democracy prevailed heretofore in some places," he said, "it now prevails everywhere." A decade later a petition presented to Parliament asked for passage of the People's

Charter, one of whose six points advocated universal male suffrage. Thomas Macaulay, the famed historian, then a member of Parliament, attacked the petition in a perfervid and lengthy address to the House of Commons on May 3, 1842. That speech could serve as a classic statement of the conviction held by bourgeois liberals in Britain and the Continent that participation of the working classes in government would lead to anarchy. Macaulay told Parliament that "universal suffrage is incompatible . . . with all forms of government, and with everything for the sake of which forms of government exist: that it is incompatible with property, and that consequently it is incompatible with civilization."

Those who supported basic principles of liberalism, such as constitutions that limited the power of the monarch, governments responsible to the electorate, equal justice before the law, and administrative and fiscal reforms, saw grave dangers in popular democratic government. In fairness to these men, their world had little experience in the workings of popular democracy. The brief years of democracy in France during the revolution were marred by terror and arbitrary justice. The contemporary American experience seemed to them to possess many unattractive characteristics. Hugh Tremenheere, a leader in industrial reform, said that Tocqueville's recently published *De la Démocratie en Amérique* (1835) showed clearly that American democracy "is tending rapidly there to degradation of human nature." Charles Lyell, the geologist, who traveled in America in 1841 and 1842, thought that universal education was "the only good result" that tended to counterbalance the evils of universal suffrage. The scientist Alexander von Humboldt wrote that the United States presented to his mind "the sad spectacle of liberty reduced to a mere mechanism in the element of utility, exercising little or no elevating influence upon mind and soul, which, after all, should be the aim of political liberty." Finally, the existence of slavery, state bankruptcies, the repudiation of debts, and brawls in Congress brought the reputation of the United States and of democracy to a low ebb.[4]

The fear of radicalism and revolution was but one side of the coin, on the other side of which, simultaneously, appeared a new awareness of the plight of the poor. The misery and the deprivation of the poor, made increasingly visible with the growth of cities and of factory industry, and urban unrest, aggravated by periods of economic depression and unemployment, explained the rise of radical movements and explained the fears they inspired. They also explained the new concern for the fate of the underclasses. Henry Cockburn put it succinctly when, in 1843, he wrote, "The great masses of poverty by which every spot blasted by manufacturers is now borne down has roused terror as well as sympathy. . . . Of all the new features of modern society in

Britain, none is so peculiar or frightful as the hordes of strong poor, always liable to be thrown out of employment by the stagnation of trade."

Till now, when Europeans had thought at all about poverty, they tended to accept it as part of the divine plan for mankind or to blame it on the poor themselves. In 1798 Thomas Malthus, in his *Essay on the Principle of Population,* had provided the seemingly irrefutable proof of the latter attitude. Population outruns available resources, wrote Malthus, making poverty unavoidable. The poor could escape their destiny only if they practiced "moral restraint," postponing marriage and practicing sexual continence. But now, for the first time, people of the upper classes began to write and talk about what they called the "social question." By that they meant the responsibility of society for its poorest members. An always increasing number of the upper orders agreed with radicals that poverty was not a natural condition but resulted from flaws in the organization of society. They felt that something was awry in a system that allowed starvation wages, slums, unemployment, child labor, and the myriad of other ills that plagued the poor. In 1839 Thomas Carlyle began his pamphlet on Chartism with a warning that something had to be done to ameliorate the condition of the working class. Many of their contemporaries in Great Britain and abroad echoed Carlyle's admonition. An article in *Blackwood's Magazine* in 1841 opened with the words, "The present age is, in a peculiar manner, distinguished by the interest which the social and moral condition of the working classes generally awaken. It is felt that there are other things of moment in human affairs than the nature and causes of the *wealth* of nations; that the most splendid growth of national opulence may be co-existent with the greatest debasement in national character; that wealth may indeed accumulate and men decay."[5]

The fact was that in the 1840s people of the upper classes and to some extent their government, especially in Britain, had developed a social conscience. That development inaugurated a great turning point in the relationship between government and the governed. It marked the first steps in the evolution of the modern welfare state. In the name of the public interest, the state began to intervene through legislative acts or royal decrees in matters till now left to individual responsibility. For the first time governments accepted some degree of responsibility for the protection of their subjects from the excessive exploitation and the diseases of an industrial and urban society. They began with the least and the most vulnerable of their societies. The new legislation regulated such matters as hours of labor in factories and mines, the employment of women and children, public health measures to protect against the spread of disease, and the establishment of supervisory agencies to oversee compliance. A piecemeal approach carried out with a cautious reserve, such measures were designed to accomplish not more than some slight amelioration or modification. But it was the opening act of a movement destined to take on increasing momentum and concern for the public welfare as each successive decade went by. Britain, Europe's most industrialized and urbanized state, took the lead in the movement, despite its traditions of laissez-faire and local government.

Until now, poverty had been largely a rural problem for the simple reason that the overwhelming majority of Europeans were peasants who lived out on the land. The primitive, low-yield agricultural techniques that these people still used, and the demands made of them by lord, state, and church, meant that most of them lived on the bare margin of existence. Peasant life was an unceasing struggle. In the first half of the nineteenth century, that struggle became more difficult for most peasants than it had ever been before because the growth of population steadily decreased the amount of arable land available to each household. The result was a prodigious increase in the numbers of those who had only a hut and a scrap of land, and of entirely landless peasants who lived as boarders in the huts and lean-tos of their more fortunate fellows and who earned their pitiful livelihood as laborers. The dwellings of the peasants reflected their abysmal poverty. Many lived in one- or two-room hovels, and they often shared their huts with their animals. Small wonder that visitors were overwhelmed by the squalor, filth, stench, vermin, and general wretchedness that they encountered. Peasant diets were typically a dreary repetition of a few foodstuffs, with every meal centering on a porridge prepared from grain meal. In the first half of the nineteenth century, potatoes became an increasingly important staple of rural diets from Ireland across to the Polish-Russian border. For most peasants, weeks and even months intervened between meals in which they had meat, and then only in small amounts. When food was available in sufficient amounts, peasant diets, for all of their limited variety, had a satisfactory nutritional value. But all too often, crops failed, and hunger, malnutrition, disease, and death swept through the land.

Nothing spoke more of the miseries of peasant existence than the large numbers of vagabonds and runaways. Some of these people roamed the countryside or lived in the forests. Without roots and beyond the reach of the law, they became beggars, poachers, thieves, smugglers, and the like, and resorted often to violence and crime. But most of them came to the cities in the hope of finding a better life. Although they quickly discovered that city life was harsh and cruel, they stayed nonetheless since anything was preferable to life in their home villages.[6]

The realities of peasant life were there for all to see, if only they had looked. Instead, tradition had long portrayed the peasant as a bumpkin, deserving only of contempt and ridicule, and ignored as less than human. Then late in the eighteenth century and increasingly in the nineteenth, writers "discovered" the peasant and constructed the myth of happy and well-fed villagers, guardians of the antique virtues, who lived contented and peaceful lives. In 1845, in his *Condition of the Working Class in England*, Friedrich Engels contrasted the miseries of the English factory workers with English peasants who were weavers. The latter, wrote Engels, enjoyed a comfortable existence, were strong and well-built, lived "decent, God-fearing lives," enjoyed themselves in rustic games, only occasionally patronized orderly taverns, and reared children who "grew up in idyllic simplicity and in happy intimacy with their playmates." George Sand explained that she wrote her enormously popular romances to show the beauty and simplicity and goodness of French rural life. Russian writers portrayed the peasants as the protectors of something called "the Russian soul."

Not everyone succumbed to this sentimentalism. The hardheaded John Quincy Adams could not conceal his revulsion with what he saw of rural life in a journey in Silesia early in the century. After describing the poverty, filth, and mean-spiritedness of the peasants there, he wrote, "Such is the condition of these venerable and blissful beings, whom we have heard extolled as the genuine children of nature—the true sample of mankind in the golden age." The author of an article in the *Edinburgh Review* in 1844 wrote that a large proportion of Britain's farm laborers lived in "a state of bondage scarcely less degrading and intolerable than that of Russian serfs."[7]

The peasants, living in their isolated villages or lonely farmsteads, were out of the sight of most people of the upper classes and hence out of their concern. A few wrote of the miseries of the rural poor but their writings excited scant interest. When the phenomenon of mass pauperism descended upon the cities in a relatively few decades, urban dwellers could not avoid becoming aware of it. If they averted their eyes from urban mass poverty, a host of books and pamphlets brought home to them the sordid realities. In Britain reports by government commissions documented in starkest prose the brutalities of life in factories and mines and the glaring inadequacies in housing and sanitation. In France L. R. Villermé, at the bidding of the Academy of Moral and Political Sciences, in 1840 published a two-volume work that he called *Tableau de l'État physique et moral des Ouvriers*. A year earlier a young journalist named Eugène Buret wrote a two-volume study titled *De la Misère des Classes laborieuses en Angleterre et en France*. Both authors documented in detail the deplorable living standards of the working classes, their insecurity, and the horrors of their work places and their dwellings.

French socialists of the forties used data drawn from the books of Villermé and Buret to publicize the plight of the proletariat and to win support for their socialist programs. In his *Condition of the Working Class in England* (1845), Engels borrowed heavily from other books, especially from Buret's work, and he was often careless in his use of data. Unlike Buret, he intended his book not so much as a description of the English working class but rather as an indictment of the English bourgeoisie as exploiters of the poor.

In addition to these and similar studies, the forties saw a flood of radical journals and newspapers, most of them short-lived, that devoted themselves in largest part to the "social question." A far greater audience was reached by a new genre of fiction that was unsparing in its portrayal of the miseries and depravity of urban lower-class life. Written by British, French, Russian, and German authors like Charles Dickens, Elizabeth Gaskell, Nikolai Gogol, Eugène Sue, and a host of lesser talents, and usually serialized in newspapers and magazines, these novels received wide readership. They became one of the most effective influences in making the upper and middle classes aware of both the existence and the threat to the social order of an oppressed and cruelly exploited under class.

These studies and journals and novels all told a story of cities deluged by destitute people who fled from their villages in hopes of finding work or charity in the city. Cities grew not by natural increase but by migration from rural areas; overpopulation in the countryside translated into swelling population in the cities. Between 1800 and 1850 London grew from 959,000 inhabitants to 2,681,000; Paris from 547,800 to 1,227,000; Berlin from 172,000 to 500,000. So many sought work that employers could pay starvation wages and get all the labor they needed. Factory hands made up a minority of the labor force. By far the largest numbers of workers still earned their living in domestic service or handicraft trades. But growing numbers of handicraftsmen found themselves unable to meet the competition of an always growing factory industry. Unemployed, or at best underemployed, they were reduced to pauperism. All told, an estimated third or more of Europe's population in the 1840s lived on the margins of subsistence.[8]

Not all of the migrants fled to the cities. In the 1840s emigration to the New World became an increasingly popular way to escape the poverty and deprivation of the Old for those fortunate enough to have the passage money. In 1831 only 1,153 immigrants came to the United States from England, Wales, and Scotland; 2,721 from Ireland; and 1,976 from Germany. In 1851 these numbers had increased to 51,847 from Great Britain, 221,253 from Ireland, and 72,482 from Germany. For Europe as a whole, migration to the United States rose from 7,217 in 1830 to 369,510 in 1851.[9]

In their hopelessness and desperation, both city slum dwellers and impoverished peasants, men, women, and sometimes even children, drank heavily and even passionately to seek escape from the wretchedness of their lives. Everywhere drunkenness was the common vice of rural and urban proletariat alike. A knowledgeable contemporary estimated that in mid-nineteenth-century Poland annual per capita consumption of distilled liquor amounted to at least 3.25 gallons. That was about six times the annual per capita consumption in mid-twentieth-century Poland. In the German and Slav provinces of the Austrian Monarchy, official tax data for 1841 showed an annual per capita consumption of 2.4 gallons of distilled liquor. London alone had 8,659 bars in 1836. In 1840 in Glasgow, one house in ten was said to be a bar.[10]

Youths of both sexes, many of them homeless, roamed the streets to beg, rob, and steal. Thousands of women, including young girls, became prostitutes to supplement their family's income. Obscenities and profanities suffused the language of young and old. Neither religion nor education found any place in their existence. They dressed in tatters that gave them scant protection from the weather. Children often went all year round without shoes or stockings. Fuel was expensive so they lived in barely heated or unheated rooms. The fact was that uncounted millions had reached the outermost limits of human depravity. Their wretchedness was reflected in their stunted bodies and their wan, colorless, and often brutish faces.[11]

For those who found employment in factories, the work day ran from twelve to as much as fifteen hours, with short breaks for meals. These long hours, six days a week, in dirty, noisy, poorly ventilated factories, broiling in summer and glacial in winter, drained the workers physically and mentally. Most inhuman of all was the employment of children, as young as five and six, as full-time workers in mills and mines. The unbelievable demands made of these children and the harsh discipline under which they lived form one of the saddest and most shameful chapters in all of Western history.

The deprivations of the urban poor reached their nadir in the periods of depression and unemployment that punctuated the emerging industrial order. In Manchester from half to three quarters of all workers were unemployed in the depression of 1841–1842. Other industrial centers knew similar mass unemployment in times of economic crisis. Penniless and without resources, the unemployed had to depend upon the meager allowances provided by public relief and private charity, and upon begging and stealing. Accounts of the sufferings during these "heartless visitations" (as one diarist called them) of stagnation in economic life seem almost beyond belief.

As mentioned earlier, most workers earned their living as handicraftsmen in the host of trades needed to meet the demands of the market. The artisans and their helpers toiled long hours in small rooms, often in the backs of crowded houses, and surrounded by filth. A large number—an estimated 14.5 percent of the entire British labor force in 1841—worked as domestic servants, always at the beck and call of their employers, and housed in tiny attics or cellar rooms. Most of these people were no better off than the workers in factories, and some were worse off. Yet it was the plight of factory workers, and more specifically of children employed in factories, that motivated the governmental intervention that marked the beginnings of the modern welfare state.[12]

The movement had its inception in Britain, the land that first knew the Industrial Revolution. Concern about the conditions of child factory labor had already appeared late in the eighteenth century, and in 1802 and again in 1819, Parliament adopted bills that limited the work day for children working in cotton mills, the largest industrial establishments, to twelve hours. The legislation did not apply to children employed in other industries. In any event, the laws lacked machinery for their enforcement and so were universally evaded. Meanwhile, the idea of a ten-hour day for children spread among textile workers in the north of England. Organized agitation began in 1830 with a fiery letter titled "Yorkshire Slavery" that appeared in the Leeds *Mercury* denouncing the evils of child labor. The writer was Richard Oastler, a deeply religious Anglican who worked as a steward for a wealthy landowner. He had shown a burning interest in the abolition of Negro slavery in the British Empire, and friends had taunted him for his indifference to what took place in the mills of his native Yorkshire. He hurried to a nearby mill town, and what he saw there infuriated him. He decided to devote himself to the battle for the ten-hour workday for children and youths. He addressed mass meetings, led demonstrations, and helped form local committees that mobilized support for the ten-hour legislation.[13] Largely through his efforts, an organized movement came into being that pressed for factory reform. Michael Sadler, Yorkshire businessman and Tory member of Parliament, led the fight in Commons, and in 1832 introduced a Ten Hour bill. The opposition claimed that Sadler exaggerated the sufferings of the children and insisted upon the appointment of a committee to investigate the effects of factory work on children.

The committee's findings, reported in the press, made a deep impression upon many of the upper classes who till then had been unaware of the evils of child factory labor. Among those who first learned of these evils was Lord Ashley, heir of the 6th earl of Shaftesbury, who had been a Tory member of Parliament since 1826. When Sadler lost his seat in the election of 1832, Ashley took over leadership of the fight for the Ten Hour bill. The opposition succeeded in blocking Ashley. Yet he won a partial victory in that Parliament adopted the Factory Act of 1833. This law, which came fully into force in 1836, barred the employment of children under nine in plants that used machinery. No child under thirteen could work more than nine hours a day (ten in silk mills) or more than forty-eight hours a week. Those between thirteen and eighteen could not work more than twelve hours a day nor more than sixty-nine hours per week, nor could they work at night. Children under thirteen had to have two hours of school a day in addition to their factory work. Most important, the law ordered the appointment of four traveling inspectors who were to put the law into effect, make sure that it was obeyed, and make regular reports to the appropriate cabinet ministers. That was the critical innovation. The government had decided not only to intervene in the employer-employee relation on behalf of children and youths, but had also decided to use its authority to compel obedience to the law by delegating some of that authority to the factory inspectors. Although the number of inspectors was woefully inadequate, a weakness continued in later factory legislation, the government had taken a significant step in the interests of the welfare of some of its citizens.

The 1833 law applied only to children and youths employed in cotton and silk mills. By 1840 Ashley had successfully insisted upon the appointment of a royal commission to report on the employment of children in general. The commission's first report revealed conditions in the mining industry that aroused horror and disgust. Children of four and five worked in dark, damp, and muddy pits opening and closing the trap door that regulated ventilation and through which the coal trucks passed. Half-naked girls and women crawled on all fours, pulling trucks along passages too low for ponies. Ashley proposed a bill to end these abuses, and after amendments that made the act less stringent, the Miners Act of 1842, the second major industrial reform, became the law of the land. Now for the first time, Parliament had turned its attention to the employment of women. The new act banned the employment of girls and women underground in the mines. It also forbade the employment of boys under ten (Ashley had wanted to set the limit at thirteen).

Once again, the law appointed inspectors to oversee the observance of the legislation. Hugh Seymour Tremenheere, the first inspector appointed, and his handful of fellow inspectors faced a formidable task. To begin with, there were some 2,500 coal mines, employing about 120,000 people, scattered through England, Wales, and Scotland, and often in isolated villages. The inspectors had to put up with the hostility of the mine owners and of some mine workers who resented the loss of family income that resulted from the banning of employment of woman and children. Tremenheere sent copies of the act of 1842 to the leading law firms in mining districts, in which he asked them to gather evidence of violations of the act and send it on to him. If he thought the evidence warranted prosecution he submitted it to the Home Office in London for its opinion. If the Home Office agreed—and it did in every case—Tremenheere ordered the local lawyers to prosecute. Word quickly spread of the conviction of mine owners for violations of the act. Within a year or so the violations had all but ceased.[14]

In his tours of inspection, Tremenheere was appalled by the lack of precautions against accidents in the mines. He submitted a report to Parliament in 1849 on measures to protect both lives and property in the mines. Parliament acted quickly with a Mines Inspection Act. Its provisions reduced accidents and loss of life in the collieries, and stressed the need for better systems of ventilation to protect the health of the miners.[15]

Meanwhile Lord Ashley and his supporters continued their agitation for a bill that would limit the workday of those under eighteen to ten hours a day. He almost succeeded in incorporating the Ten Hour law into a new factory act in 1844, but his efforts foundered on the opposition of the administration. Encouraged by the near success and by widened public support, Ashley and his friends renewed their pressure, and in 1847 Parliament finally adopted the bill, to take full effect in 1850. The new act banned the employment of women and children for more than ten hours a day in the industries specifically listed in the legislation, and it implied but did not order that men should not work more than ten hours.[16]

The government's acceptance of responsibility for its less fortunate citizens extended to prisons and to the insane. The inmates of prisons, all of them under local control, suffered cruelly from the conditions of their places of confinement and the often inhuman treatment by their guards. The Prison Act of 1835 left the administration of the prisons in local hands but subject to inspection by civil servants of the Home Office of the government. The criminal law, too, was reformed. Until 1838 over two hundred offenses had been punishable by death. After the reform of that year, only murderers could be sentenced to execution. The insane were treated even more cruelly than prisoners. Violent and dangerous lunatics were kept chained in solitude in outhouses or cellars or in jails where guards often flogged and tortured them. The harmless insane of the lower classes often roamed the streets or found shelter in parish work houses. Those of higher social status were kept out of sight by their families, locked in an attic or room, or sent to a private asylum. Lord Ashley once again distinguished himself by coming to the defense of these helpless people. In 1845 he introduced legislation that Parliament passed by large majorities. The bill called for the establishment of a Lunacy Commission of three doctors and three lawyers, all salaried, and five unpaid commissioners with Ashley as chairman. The law authorized the Commission to inspect and license all asylums, private and public, at least twice a year and individuals confined in private homes once a year. The act also required each county that did not have an asylum to build one.[17]

Continental lands lagged far behind Britain in the introduction of factory legislation. In Prussia, the government had long known of the abuses that attended the employment of children in the Rhineland, Prussia's most industrialized region. In 1828 the Army declared that the industrial districts could not meet the quotas for Army recruits because their labor as children had impaired the physical fitness of young men for military service. A few years later, a series of articles by a humanitarian employer in the Rhineland awakened public interest, and in 1839 the Prussian government proclaimed a factory act which forbade the employment of children under nine, limited the work day for those under sixteen to ten hours, and so on. But the government did not provide machinery for enforcement of the act, so that most employers disregarded its provisions. Not until 1853 did the government appoint inspectors and then only for the three most industrialized districts.

In France the government as early as 1813 forbade the employment of children in mines, but the question of child factory labor only became an issue in the 1830s. Villermé's book of 1840 on the condition of workers brought the matter to a head. He had long been an opponent of state intervention in private enterprise, but what he saw in his visits to factories moved him to plead for legislative action to protect child labor. The book's impact was such that in 1841 the government passed France's first factory act. It banned the employment of children under eight, set the work day at eight hours for children under twelve, and a twelve-hour day for those under sixteen. But as in Prussia, the government failed to provide an effective system of enforcement, and factory owners evaded the law. Early in 1848 new legislation extended protection to women factory workers and provided for a paid inspectorate. Unfortunately, the outbreak of revolution in late February prevented the law from coming into effect. The legislature of the short-lived Second Republic, established after the revolution, passed a number of laws designed to protect workers from undue exploitation. None of this legislation survived, except an act of September 1848 that set the maximum work day for all labor at twelve hours. Thereby France became the first state to attempt to regulate the employment of adult males. The law was never strictly enforced, but it remained on the books until the introduction of the eight-hour day after World War I.[18]

Meanwhile, the continuing flood of humanity from the countryside over-whelmed the cities. New construction lagged far behind the demand for housing. Hastily built tenements were so badly constructed that sometimes entire buildings collapsed as if struck by an earthquake. The housing shortage compelled the poor to crowd into whatever they could find, including cellars and garrets. Two to three families sometimes huddled into a single room with ragged curtains for partitions. The poor had to do with a few sticks of furniture or empty boxes for tables and chairs. Straw or shavings in a corner served as bedding, with a worn piece of carpeting as a blanket.

Sanitary facilities and sewers, never adequate before the rural invasion, became hopelessly overburdened. An official survey in 1843–1844 reported that one neighborhood in Manchester had only thirty-seven privies to meet the needs of over seven thousand inhabitants. Garbage and human excrement deposited in the narrow winding streets stood in stagnant piles in city after city. In Paris most of the streets, to quote an observer in 1848, were "nothing but filthy alleys forever damp from a reeking flood." In 1851 Paris had eighty-two miles of underground sewers to serve more than 250 miles of streets. Much of the city's sewage wound up in the Seine, from which Parisians drew most of their water. Conditions were no better in smaller cities. Drainage ditches in cities large and small emptied into nearby streams or rivers from which city dwellers drew their water. A miasmic haze that rose from the filthy streets and alleys hung over cities and could be seen from far away. Noxious stenches filled the air, and the smells of cities assaulted travelers from a distance of several miles. In London and in Paris overcrowded graveyards in the midst of the city had bodies buried on top of one another in shallow graves. In Paris coffins of the poor were stacked seven deep. A pestilential odor rose from these cemeteries, their soil saturated with human putrescence. The organic matter from thousands of decomposing bodies polluted the subsurface water that fed wells and ran into the rivers.[19]

Inevitably, sickness, disease, and early death that resulted from the lack of sanitation ravaged the people of the cities. The better off were not spared, but the poor suffered the most. Ill-fed and ill-housed, their life expectancy was much shorter than that of the more fortunate classes. Typhus, transmitted by body lice, was a poor man's disease. So, too, was tuberculosis, an almost exclusively urban disease which thrived among the undernourished, debilitated, and poorly housed. Asiatic cholera, which appeared in Europe for the first time in 1832, killed hundreds of thousands in its periodic recurrences. Carried by contaminated water, it knew no distinction between rich and poor. As urban population swelled, the death rate climbed alarmingly. In the course of the 1830s, the annual death rate for five major English cities rose from 21 to 31 per thousand; in Birmingham, it nearly doubled from 14.6 to 27.2, and in Liverpool, it rose from 21 to 34.8 per thousand. Infant mortality reached enormous proportions. Half of the children born in the cities of Great Britain died before they were six. Half of the babies born to workers in the spinning mills of Mulhouse in Alsace died within fifteen months of their birth. In many cities one third to one half of all infants were illegitimate. Their mothers, unable or unwilling to care for them, often smothered them or let them perish by neglect, or abandoned them in streets or doorways or in foundling hospitals whose facilities were so inadequate that many babies died in them.[20]

Despite the smells, the filth, and the disease that marred life in the cities, the general public remained curiously uninterested in sanitary reform. It was as if people accepted the nastiness of urban life as inescapable, and disease as the will of God. The authors of the novels of social realism spoke out for the urgent need of reforms in factories and in prisons and in education. But they rarely mentioned the even more urgent need for sanitary reform. Fortunately, a handful of men, most of them doctors of medicine, recognized that need. They saw it as their duty to make the public aware that public hygiene affected all facets of social existence. Because of their efforts and the efforts of laymen who campaigned with them, governments in the 1840s began to show concern for the health of their countrymen and especially those who lived in the working class districts of their cities. French physicians took the lead in this crusade. Their interest intensified after 1815 with an outpouring of books and articles. Chairs of hygiene were established in the universities, and a journal, *Annales de Hygiène*, began publication in 1829.

In Britain, too, doctors held places of honor in the movement for sanitary reform. But from 1838 until 1854, a barrister named Edwin Chadwick (1800–1890) held undisputed leadership in the movement. He was a born "take-charge" person whose intensity, drive, and determination carried him to the forefront of the reform movements in which he involved himself. This despite the fact that he was a remarkably unpleasant man who fought constantly with his superiors and with just about everyone who disagreed with him. He was tireless and open-minded in assembling and analyzing data. But once he arrived at his conclusions, he was convinced that he was right and would make no concessions. He never admitted to an error or to bad judgment. A colossal egoist, he lacked a sense of humor and a sense of proportion. Without tact and graciousness, he was intolerant, precipitate, and surly. When he was forced to retire from public service in 1854, the *Times* commented, "We prefer to take our chance of cholera and the rest, than be bullied into health." But he was inspired by a hatred of disease, unnecessary suffering, and economic waste because they reduced the nation's wealth, efficiency, and well-being; and he believed that most social ills were preventable and that the state had the duty to prevent them. As one of his biographers pointed out, he was passionately devoted to the public good, and in the service of the public "he was daring, original, ardent, and indomitable. . . . He *cared*. Whatever his errors of judgment—and they were many—this is his supreme justification."[21]

Chadwick began his career in public service in 1832 as an assistant commissioner on the Poor Law Commission. In 1834 he became the chief executive officer of the New Poor Law Commission established by Parliament. The year before he had joined the staff of the royal commission appointed to investigate and report on the condition of child factory labor. He was the principal author of that report. He also took a leading part in proposals for reform of the police; instigated the establishment of a national bureau to register births, marriages, causes and number of deaths; and made recommendations for the training of the children of paupers, and on burials within city limits.

Until 1838 he showed only minimal interest in sanitation and public health. The initial impetus for his concern about these matters may have been fiscal. The Poor Law commissioners realized that ill health of the poor was a drain on the resources available for relief payments. They reasoned that they could save a considerable amount of money by improving the unsanitary conditions in which the poor lived. A letter drafted by Chadwick to Lord John Russell, the Home Secretary, resulted in the appointment of three doctors experienced in public health to conduct an investigation into the living conditions and the prevalence of disease among the working class of London. Their reports were the first inquiries initiated by the government into the possibility of improvements in the living conditions of the poor. In 1839 the Anglican Bishop of London, probably at Chadwick's instigation, successfully suggested in the House of Lords that surveys like the one made in London be carried out for all of England and Wales. Not surprisingly, the task was assigned to Chadwick. After three years of intensive work, Chadwick submitted his report to the House of Lords. It consisted of two volumes of local reports from all over the country, and a third volume of 279 pages that he wrote himself. Titled *Report on the Sanitary Condition of the Labouring Population of Britain*, that third volume was the first full account of the conditions in which Britain's poor had to live, and without a doubt, its data revealed the connection between these living conditions and the ill health, diseases, and early deaths of the poor. Chadwick's recognition of the linkage between slum life and degraded morality overturned for many the long-held opinion (which Chadwick himself believed only a few years earlier) that the degraded behavior of the poor rose from defects of their character.[22]

Though it had commissioned the report, the House of Lords refused to publish it because of its merciless strictures on governmental agencies and powerful private interests. After negotiations, the authorities consented to the publication of the report under Chadwick's name as his personal opinion. Once the report appeared, Chadwick set out with his usual drive to win supporters and to convert its recommendations into legislation. In 1843 the government created a Health of Towns Commission to substantiate Chadwick's findings and to frame any necessary legislation. Chadwick, although not a member, managed to influence the members of the commission, and, indeed, the first of its two reports, issued in 1844, was largely the work of Chadwick. Meanwhile, a voluntary organization called the Health of Towns Association, established in 1844, initiated a vigorous campaign for sanitary reform. Modeled after the highly successful Anti-Corn Law League (see Chapter Five), it held public meetings and published books and pamphlets promoting its platform. In its first two years, the Association had to compete with the thunder of the Anti-Corn Law League and so ran a poor second to that powerful movement. With the abolition of the Corn Laws in 1846, the public health agitation, its hand mightily strengthened by the ever nearer approach of a new cholera epidemic that was sweeping westward across the Continent, persuaded Parliament to pass the Public Health Act of 1848.[23]

The provisions of the Act fell far short of what Chadwick and his fellow reformers had wanted. Still, it was a landmark in the history of the welfare state: for the first time the British government had accepted a degree of responsibility for the protection of the health of its citizens. The Act created a General Board of Health with three Commissioners as its central authority, to serve for a term of five years. The Act empowered the commissioners to establish local health boards in any town upon receiving a petition from one tenth of its taxpayers, or when the death rate in the town exceeded twenty-three deaths per thousand. The local boards had the power to initiate a broad spectrum of sanitary reforms, but the Act did not require them to do this, and the General Board had limited supervisory powers over the local boards. Obviously, it was a curious piece of legislation that allowed one town to adopt provisions of the Act and its neighbors not, and it gave too much latitude to the local boards. The act's unusual nature reflected the traditional British aversion to the centralization of power in the national government. Nonetheless, the passionate devotion of the members of the General Board to sanitary reform and to public health enabled it to lay the foundations of the national concern for public health, to establish a network of local health authorities, and to initiate a continuing program of research and investigation. In fact, the Board pushed so hard that it aroused the antagonism of important politicians and of local authorities who together shared the opposition to centralization. In 1854 legislation disbanded the General Board of Health, and a newly created committee of the Privy Council took over the problems of public health.[24]

Continental lands followed Britain's lead in sanitary reform after the middle of the century. In Germany the first major improvements came in the mid-fifties in Hamburg, in 1861 for Berlin, and in other cities in succeeding years. In France the clean-up of Paris came during the rebuilding of the French capital that began under Napoleon III in 1853. An often told story relates that when Napoleon III asked the visiting Edwin Chadwick what he thought of his improvements, Chadwick replied, "Sir, it was said of Augustus that he found Rome brick and left it marble. May it be said of you that you found Paris stinking and left it sweet."[25]

In Britain the reforms that marked the beginnings of the modern welfare state could not have come about without the support of men and women of the middle and upper classes. Convinced of the need for reform these people fought an uphill battle against ministerial inertia, against those who regarded any intervention by the government as an unjustified invasion of private rights, and against the many who believed that the poor brought their poverty upon themselves because they were lazy, shiftless, and dissolute. The reformers were neither democrats nor revolutionaries. They wanted to better the lives of the under classes but they did not want to make them their equals. They opposed universal suffrage, were against unions, and feared radicalism. Neither compassion nor a feeling of identity with those they wanted to help motivated them. Instead, they acted out of a sense of moral duty, the conviction that they did God's work and proved themselves worthy of His grace by looking out for the less fortunate. Of course, they also acted in the fervent hope that reform would fend off social unrest. Lady Charlotte Guest, daughter of an earl and wife of a wealthy middle-class ironmaster, expressed the view of the reformers when, in mid-April of 1848, she wrote of "the unsound state of society and the necessity of education, or humanizing the lower grade. But I know one cannot make people good and religious by act of Parliament. The first step is to make them comfortable and happy, and for this purpose all the sanitary and social reforms are most important."[26]

To help make the "lower grade" comfortable and happy, people of the British upper classes formed literally hundreds of philanthropic societies. In

1844 the London metropolitan region alone had over 450 of these organizations. Generally, each society devoted itself to a specific cause, such as soup
kitchens, providing the poor with bread and coal, helping needy domestic
servants, coming to the aid of distressed milliners and modistes, advocating
temperance, spreading religious knowledge, and the like, with "fallen
women" an especially popular cause.[27]

The members of these societies prided themselves on their activism in
doing good works. Evangelical Christians, believing they followed God's will,
showed special devotion to philanthropic endeavors. To many membership in
these societies made them feel good about themselves and also became the
fashionable thing to do. More skeptical Britons looked with jaundiced eye
upon the flood tide of benevolence. The flinty Charles Greville confided to
his diary, "We are just now over run with philanthropy, and God knows
where it will stop, and whither it will lead us." Carlyle denounced the movement as "this universal syllabus of philanthropic twaddle." The skeptics and
the mockers had their point. Victorian benevolence fell far short of making
the under class "comfortable and happy," and the multiplicity and the redun-
dancy of its agencies produced inefficiency and waste. Nonetheless, though it
is easy to criticize and even to ridicule its motives and efforts, these philanthropic societies represented an awareness of social evils and a desire to contribute to their amelioration.[28]

In contrast to the English voluntarism, in continental lands private philanthropy was notable only for its infrequent appearance. In France it had developed somewhat after 1814 during the years of the Bourbon Restoration, partly because of a religious revival among the social elite, and partly as a measure
to ward off revolution. Philanthropy waned drastically after the revolution in
1830 that established the July Monarchy. In Germany, and especially in
Prussia, concerned people formed a number of voluntary organizations to
help the poor. As in Britain, skeptics quickly pointed out the ineffectiveness
of these philanthropic efforts.[29]

Among the many men and women active in British philanthropy, the
name of Lord Ashley towered over all the rest. With justice, he has been
called the personification of the philanthropic spirit of the nineteenth century. Indeed, some might say he carried that spirit to excess. In 1845 the *Times*
wrote of Ashley dashing about "to meeting rooms and taverns, making
speeches and eating dinners on behalf of every scheme that is nominally
devoted to charitable purposes." He maintained his interest and involvement
in these eleemosynary causes up to his death in 1885. At the memorial service for him in Westminster Abbey, 201 philanthropic and religious organizations were represented by deputations. With many of these organizations, he

had close connections, serving as chairman or board member; with others he was less directly involved, but he was interested in all of them.

During his years in the House of Commons from 1826 to 1851, he sponsored or supported important reforms. In some instances his efforts met with success, albeit sometimes limited. He failed with other of his causes, such as the employment of children as chimney sweeps and full civil rights for Jews. He not only sponsored reform legislation but took an active part in its enforcement. He became chairman of the Lunacy Commission and remained in that post until his death, attending weekly board meetings and visiting asylums. As a member of the Board of Health, he remained in London during the cholera epidemic of 1849, working day and night, while those who could, fled the city. He made personal inspections of the worst slums of London to acquaint himself with the living conditions of the poor. When his father died in 1851, Ashley became the 7th earl of Shaftesbury and left Commons for the House of Lords. There he continued unabated his interest and activity in reforms and philanthropy.[30]

Born in 1801, he bore the name of Anthony Ashley Cooper like all the eldest sons of his distinguished lineage. With the confusing British custom of multiple nomenclature, he was known by the courtesy title of Lord Ashley until his father's death, whereupon he became known as the earl of Shaftesbury. One would assume a privileged and happy childhood for someone fortunate enough to have been born into the high aristocracy. Instead, he had a desperately unhappy childhood, deprived of parental love and cruelly neglected. His father and his mother, the daughter of the 4th Duke of Marlborough, were selfish and coldhearted, his father a bully and his mother totally preoccupied with social life. In later years Ashley habitually referred to his mother as "a fiend," and his father fared no better. In a diary entry in 1828, he wrote at length of the cruelty of his parents to their children and concluded with the words, "The history of our father and mother would be incredible to most men, and perhaps it would do no good if such facts were recorded."[31]

Fortunately, a faithful old servant, Maria Millis, formed a strong attachment to the lonely little boy and in return won his love and devotion. A devout Evangelical Christian, she told him stories from the Bible, taught him his first prayers, and instilled in him the deep and simple Evangelical faith that he never abandoned and that inspired him throughout his long life. Maria Millis died shortly after his eighth birthday, but he never forgot her. In her will she left him a gold watch, which he always carried and was fond of showing, saying, "That was given to me by the best friend I ever had in the world."

At eight he was sent to Manor House, a school in London favored by sons of the nobility, where he remained for four years. It was a devastating experience. Many years later he recalled it as a place of bullying, neglect, filth, and harsh treatment—very similar, he said, to Nicholas Nickleby's Dotheboys Hall. He thought that it gave him a horror of oppression and cruelty that he bore for the rest of his life. After the trauma of Manor House, he spent two happy years at Harrow, and after a hiatus of two years, he matriculated at Oxford. There he discovered the joys of scholarship and of reading, and distinguished himself by taking a First in Classics.

After Oxford he lived the aimless life of a young aristocrat about town. Not welcome in his parents' home, deprived of their affection, grave in manner, uncertain of what he wanted to do, he seemed to lack self-confidence, and to be in search of understanding and love. He was a fine-looking man, with an unmistakable aristocratic air. Tall, slender, and graceful in his movements, of him a contemporary wrote that "it would be difficult to imagine a more complete *beau-idéal* of aristocracy." His appearance and manner contributed importantly to his success. "He had those manly good looks and that striking presence," said one of his greatest friends, "which I believe . . . help a man more than we sometimes think, and they helped him when he endeavored to inspire his humble fellow countrymen with his noble and elevated nature."[32]

He finally found the love and understanding that he sought when he married the nineteen-year-old Lady Emily Cowper. The match seemed improbable. Ashley, a strait-laced, puritanical Evangelical and convinced Tory had married into a family of free-thinking, loose-living Whigs. Emily's mother was a Lamb, a niece of Lord Melbourne. No one, not even the bride's mother, could say for sure who had been Emily's father, except that he certainly was not her mother's husband. The finger pointed to Lord Palmerston. Two years after Lord Cowper's death in 1837, the fifty-two-year-old Lady Cowper married Palmerston. In any event, Palmerston showed Emily much love and through her became close to Ashley, an otherwise unlikely circumstance given the difference in the characters of the two men.

Despite the improbabilities surrounding the match, the marriage was enormously successful. Ashley and his wife were deeply in love and profoundly devoted to each other. Remembering his own unhappy childhood, he was a loving and caring father, concerned with their ten children, and delighting in the joys of family life. She always retained her lively nature but apparently had no difficulty in adjusting to his stern view of life.

At twenty-five Ashley did what was expected of a young man who was the eldest son of a peer of the realm and who had taken a good degree at the university. He stood for Parliament in the pocket borough of the duke of

Marlborough. Himself the grandson of the 4th duke, he ran against the son of the 5th duke. After what was reportedly a spirited campaign, he was elected and entered Parliament in 1826. At the outset of his parliamentary career, he remained uncertain about what calling he should pursue. After careful consideration, he decided in 1828 to make politics his life's work: "I have taken political life," he wrote in his diary, "because I have, by God's blessing, many advantages of birth and situation, which, although of trifling value if unsupported, are yet very powerful aids if joined to zeal and honesty. It is here, therefore, that I have the chief way of being useful to my generation." He decided that the first principle of his chosen career would be "God's honor, the second, man's happiness, the means, prayer and unremitting diligence."[33]

He started as an orthodox Tory, but it soon became evident that party loyalty was not of first importance to him. At various times he received invitations to join the cabinet, but he always refused. He spoke often and well in Parliament, in perfectly formed sentences, although an admirer allowed that his voice "was not sufficiently exerted to be generally audible."

As a young man Ashley began to keep a diary that he continued almost to the end of his life, filling twelve quarto volumes, each of several hundred pages. He wrote on unruled paper, yet every line was straight and with scarcely a blot or erasure. The diary is amazingly revealing. Its author committed to its pages his innermost thoughts and emotions, his self-doubts, and his spiritual anxieties. He engaged constantly and at length in often morbid self-analysis, as if he were talking to himself and recording everything that he said. The diary mirrored this strange man's mind, a mind filled with self-pity and imagined slights and enmities, with deep pessimism and bouts of depression, with endless appeals to God's grace, and with the certainty of divine retribution on a sinful world. In a typical outburst of self-pity, in 1842 he wrote, "I confess I feel sadly alone; I am like a pelican in the wilderness, or a sparrow on the house tops. I have no one with whom I can take counsel, no one to aid me, no one to cheer me."[34]

His moralizing in his speeches in Parliament and in his public addresses, his lack of a sense of humor, his conviction that he did God's work and so could do no wrong, made him the kind of man who could set people's teeth on edge. Still, many admired him for his adherence to his principles and his dedication, though as Charles Greville reported in 1839, most people disliked him. In public he was always polite and even friendly with his enemies and had them as guests at his table. In his diary he saw the world peopled by men who hated him and who wanted to thwart his every move. "At times," he wrote, "I almost quail when I think of the concentrated hatred against me. . . . The [Anti-Corn Law] League hate me as an aristocrat, the landowners as a Radical, the wealthy of all opinion as a mover of inconvenient principles. . . . the floating men of all sides, opinions, ranks, and professions, who dislike what they call a 'saint' join in the hatred against me. . . . The working people, catching the infection, will go next and then . . . farewell any hopes of further usefulness."[35]

The gloom and pessimism that so often darkened his mind increased as he grew older. In a diary entry in 1846, he described himself as one of those who saw only what was dark on the far horizon and never what was bright. "Evil is more powerful and lasting than good," he continued, "evil is natural, good is unnatural, evil requires nothing but man as he is, good must find the soil prepared by the grace of God." Another time he wrote, "We should pray for the end of the world. If it come soon, how much wretchedness would be spared." Even on holiday, he could not escape his pessimism. Paris charmed him, but at the moments of his enjoyment, dark thoughts filled his mind. "As I walked through the gardens and the streets," he wrote, "contemplating the numbers of young, pretty, and playful children, I felt as Elisha, and wept to think of the sorrows in store for them, the widowhood, the orphanage, the desolation, the suffering." If gloom and a sense of impending doom did not overtake him on a holiday, a sense of guilt did. In 1829 he spent a few days at the Royal Lodge as the guest of King William III. He admitted to his diary that he enjoyed himself, and now, he continued, "I say with Job 'it may be that I have sinned and cursed God in my heart'." All because he had a good time![36]

Over and over again, he explained and justified his actions and decisions by seeing them as the expression of the will of God. He had an unshakable faith in the literal truth of the Scriptures as the word of the Lord. He believed devoutly in the efficacy of prayer. He once quoted the Psalmist: "Commit thy ways unto the Lord, and he will direct thy paths." That verse (actually he misquoted it) could serve as the motto of his life. Everything he did—in politics, in reforms, in philanthropy—had its roots in his deep religious faith. Religion sustained him, protected him from those whom he, often mistakenly, deemed his enemies, and provided him with the determination and the strength to spend his life in the service of his fellow man. "I desire to be useful in my generation," he wrote when he was only twenty-six, "and die in the knowledge of having advanced happiness by having advanced true religion."

To Ashley true religion meant Evangelical Christianity and its conviction that Christ would return to earth and rule over a Kingdom of Glory for a fixed period before the final Day of Judgment. He believed that the Second Coming of Christ was imminent. He had his envelope stamped with the words in Greek, "So come, Lord Jesus." These same words ended many of his diary entries, which were replete with references to Christ's return. He believed that the Second Coming would not occur until the ingathering of the Jewish people in their ancient homeland, the Land of Israel, and their conversion to Christianity (a belief still common among many Evangelical Christians). To speed matters along he became chairman of a society that sought to convert the Jews and ardently supported Jewish settlement in Palestine. He did not propose the creation of an independent Jewish state, but rather a colony under British protection but still subject to the Ottoman empire.[37]

Ashley shared to the full the prejudices of his fellow Evangelicals, including a fear and hatred of Catholicism. In a fiery address in 1850, he termed the pope "a foreign priest and potentate, who misunderstands and misgoverns his own people, who is kept in his miserable throne, to the oppression of his own subjects and all religious liberty, only by outlandish bayonets." He gave his support to any measure that preserved the strict observance of Sunday as the Lord's Day, a day in which everything closed down. He became almost apoplectic when he learned that Prime Minister Robert Peel had attended a dinner party on a Sunday. When, in 1849, the government decided to keep post offices open on Sunday, he wrote in his diary, "We pray and trust that God will bring to confusion the vile attempt." In May 1850, in Parliament, he moved the cessation of Sunday mail services throughout the kingdom. His fellow members, hoping to please their ultrareligious constituents, voted for the measure in the belief that it would not pass. To their surprise, the measure did pass. On Sunday, June 23, 1850, the collection and delivery of mail in Great Britain ceased. An immediate public roar of protest followed, and in three weeks Sunday mail service resumed. A few years later he had more success when he defeated the effort to open the British Museum and the Crystal Palace on Sundays, and he persuaded the government to cancel its permission for military band concerts on Sundays in London's parks.[38]

Great as was his concern for the less fortunate of this world, the 7th earl of Shaftesbury never forgot that he was a nobleman and they were commoners. He wanted the lower classes to have more of the comforts of life, but he did not want to share status and power with them. He opposed programs and policies that sought to raise the social and political position of the laboring classes. "I protest against universal suffrage on many grounds," he wrote in 1851, "on none more than this, that it has never been found consistent with general freedom. Wherever it has prevailed it has established the freedom, nay, license of the majority, and the restraint, nay, the thralldom of the minority." He put his faith in Christianity, and not democracy or any other political or social program, to bring about a better and more just world.[39]

It was easy to poke fun at Shaftesbury, who took both himself and life with such great earnestness. His younger brother John remarked that, next to a religious ceremony, the most solemn thing he knew was shaking hands with Ashley. Lord Melbourne said of him, "He is the greatest fool, for a clever man, that I have ever met with." An important and scholarly civil servant once remarked of Shaftesbury that "as the record of his charitable enterprises and public function extends, one feels that he is turning into marble before one's eyes." Remarks such as these were neither groundless nor gratuitous. But they are as nothing compared with the achievements of the 7th earl of Shaftesbury. Despite his many faults and flaws, he was a great and good man. He contributed more than any one person of his time toward the well-being of his fellow Britons, and whether knowingly or not, he contributed enormously to the raising of the social conscience of his contemporaries and to the beginnings of the modern welfare state. His life made a difference in the history of his country.[40]

Actually, the condition of the laboring poor, the people about whom Shaftesbury and his fellow reformers were concerned, had begun to improve. Those who long debated the effects of industrialization in Britain, the first land to industrialize, disagreed whether or not improvement in worker income began and proceeded, albeit irregularly, after 1815. But both "optimists" and "pessimists," as the two sides have been labeled, agreed that the real income of labor increased starting in the 1840s. Averages and aggregates reveal nothing about the distribution of income among workers. The available evidence, however, indicates that all but the least fortunate workers, those in declining handicraft industries such as hand loom weaving, did have a slow growth in their incomes. The increase was small, and poverty, often desperate poverty, remained the fate of the working class.[41]

In France evidence indicates an improvement in the workers' standard of living, a conclusion Villermé reached in his study of industrial workers in 1840. He found that many workers no longer lived in hovels without windows and furniture. They dressed better, wore shoes rather than sabots even in rural districts, and had meat and white bread as more common parts of their diet than they had once been. Data on wages indicate a slow increase in real wages in the 1840s that continued on into the second half of the century.[42]

For long centuries workers had accepted their inferior status and powerlessness, which the upper strata of their societies had imposed upon them. They had no sense of solidarity with other workers. Guilds had united artisans into corporate bodies with their own privileges, but they excluded ordinary workmen and, in any event, were declining with the advances of factory industry. In France the *compagnonnages*, organizations of journeymen and apprentices formed in earlier centuries, were, like guilds, in a state of decay by the 1840s. Through the years, riots and revolts of workers had often erupted, but nearly always they had been local and short-lived happenings, set off often by rising prices or shortages of food rather than by discontent with their lowly status or their exclusion from political life. Their risings had no political content and were not intended to overthrow the existing order and replace it with a new kind of society.

In 1840 H. S. Tremenheere, on a tour of inspection of coal mines in South Wales, visited the homes of miners. He reported their astonishment at learning that their government wanted to know about their living conditions, and that sympathy for their plight existed anywhere. He found their ignorance pitiable, though typical. Four years earlier a declaration by the newly formed London Working Men's Association explained that, "Ignorance has caused us to believe that *we* were 'born to toil,' and *others* to enjoy—that we were naturally *inferior*, or should silently bow to the government of those who were pleased to call themselves *superior;* and consequently, those who have governed us have done so for their own advantage, and not ours."[43]

That was an early expression of working-class solidarity and of the conflict between "we" and "they." In the late thirties and especially in the forties, workers in increasing numbers gradually developed a class consciousness, that is, a sense both of corporate awareness and of a corporate role in their societies. They began to realize that by identifying with one another, they had the potential to exert power and to influence the course of events. They had great obstacles to overcome, not least their own ignorance and lack of interest, and the rising antagonism of the propertied classes.

In Britain a collective class consciousness had slowly evolved among skilled craftsmen despite harassment and persecution by the government and the courts. The craftsmen formed many short-lived organizations, among them the aforementioned London Working Men's Association. That organization had as its declared purpose the unity of "the intelligent and influential portion of the working classes in town and country," freedom of the press, a national system of education, and the collection and publication of information on social and political matters. Its founder, a cabinetmaker named William Lovett, wanted to make all workers aware of their common interests and to align them against those who ruled over and exploited them. In 1838 the Association published the People's Charter, which became the founding document of the movement called Chartism, whose history is recounted at length in a later chapter.[44]

In Germany artisans threatened by the factory system formed associations to protect their interests. Their opposition to industrialization alienated factory workers so that a common class consciousness seemed absent. When, during the revolution of 1848, workers fought in the streets of Vienna against the forces of the government, they had no program of their own. Instead, they fought for the interests of the lower middle class. The workers of Vienna, wrote Friedrich Engels, were "hardly awaking not to a knowledge, but to a mere instinct of their social position and proper political line of action."[45]

In France the laws were heavily weighted against the workers. During the Revolutionary and Napoleonic eras, legislation had banned all associations of employees, made strikes and picketing criminal offenses, effectively outlawed collective bargaining, and ordered all workmen to carry a *livret*, a book which listed the names of the worker's various employers. The worker could be hired only if his previous employer had recorded in the worker's *livret* that he had been a satisfactory employee. Despite these restrictions, and possibly in no small part because of them, French workers, especially in Paris, had become ever more restive. They had taken a major part in the July Revolution that had ended Bourbon rule in 1830. They felt cheated because they had received no recognition or reward from the new regime and were instead subjected to new restrictions. Some of them organized secret societies, conducted illegal strikes, and in 1831 and again in 1834, the silk weavers of Lyons rose in revolt. The societies attracted only small numbers, the strikes failed, and the silk weavers of Lyons gained nothing from their revolts.

Meanwhile, a new ideology that came from men outside the working class began to gain the attention of workers. France and specifically Paris became the center of radical thought. The ideas, and especially the slogans, of the radicals seeped down into the ranks of the workers and encouraged many of them to believe that revolution was imminent and that the working class would emerge victorious and take over France.[46]

In these and other European lands, self-appointed would-be leaders of the working class held forth visions of revolutionary solutions to the ills that beset the proletariat. With few exceptions, they were not themselves workers and, for the most part, knew little about working-class life. Save for Russia, where noblemen, alienated from their class, formed the core of the radical movement, most of these revolutionaries were middle-class intellectuals. The radical Russian nobleman, Mikhail Bakunin, writing of the group around Karl Marx in Brussels in 1847, said "the word *bourgeois* had become a catchword repeated *ad nauseam*, but one and all, from head to foot are themselves provincial petty bourgeoisie." The radicals were constantly at odds with one another, each coterie insisting that it had the right key to unlock the door to the future. Alexander Herzen, another radical Russian nobleman, called them "perpetual suitors of the revolutionary Penelope" and said they were "the permanent tribunes of the clubs and cafés, perpetually dissatisfied with everything and perpetually fussing about everything." These radicals were members of what Wilhelm Riehl in 1851 dubbed the "intellectual proletariat."[47]

Most of them were exiles, either forced or voluntary, from their homelands, and most were young men in their twenties and thirties. Homeless, without roots, they fled to cities in Switzerland, in Britain, in Belgium and France, where relative freedom of expression and publication were allowed. Above all, they came to Paris, drawn by that city's reputation as the home of the great Revolution of 1789 and still the center of revolutionary thought. Alexander Herzen, who left Russia for Paris in 1847, explained that "the name of Paris was closely bound up with all the noblest enthusiasms of contemporary humanity. I entered it with reverence as men used to enter Jerusalem or Rome."

The willingness of the host countries to offer asylum to these exiles puzzled and offended conservatives in the homelands of the radicals. On rare occasions the host nation did take actions when pressed by another government. In January 1845, for example, the French, at the insistence of the Prussian government, gave a dozen German radicals, among them Karl Marx, twenty-four hours to get out of France. The host countries sometimes had reservations about the wisdom of accepting radical émigrés. The Belgian government, apparently fearing the influence of radical presence in Brussels, distributed the exiles among villages and small towns.[48] The radicals talked much about international cooperation and a universal uprising that would usher in the new order. Typically, however, each national group formed its own societies and associations. Sometimes they chose such colorful names as the Union of the Righteous, the Union of the Despised, the Legion of the Just, and the Blindfolded.

The stream of refugees rose to flood stage after the collapse of the revolutions of 1848. They came from all over Europe, seeking sanctuary from the vengeful victors in their homelands. Most of them had no money and lived a hand-to-mouth existence. They spent their evenings in taverns where, with much gallows humor, they talked endlessly about themselves, about spies in their ranks, and about their concerns for the future. They lived in a realm of fantasy. Herzen, who knew well his fellow exiles, wrote that "cut off from the living environment to which they belonged, they shut their eyes to avoid seeing bitter truths, and grow more and more acclimatized to a closed fantastic circle consisting of inert memories and hopes that can never be realized." To this was added elements of exasperation, suspicion, exclusiveness, and jealousies that complicated their existence and made it all the more unpleasant.[49]

The doctrines that the radicals espoused and the panaceas they proposed differed from one another, but they all came under the common rubric of socialism. Because of its many varieties, each with its own shadings, it was difficult to define socialism. Whatever their differences, all socialists believed that the abolition of private property would establish economic and political equality, and thereby bring about a just and harmonious society. Almost to a man they were militant atheists. Yet they believed with a faith equal to that of the most committed Christian that revolution, whether violent or peaceful, would overthrow traditional society and replace it with a perfect society where equality and justice prevailed. Theirs was a religious vision of man's redemption through a second coming that would bring eternal salvation in an earthly paradise where man no longer exploited and oppressed his fellow man. Already in 1843 Heinrich Heine had recognized the messianic vision of the socialists and their resemblance to the early Christians. In a dispatch to a German newspaper, he wrote that, like the Galileans, they were a small band, they were despised and oppressed, they held strongly to their faith, were equally determined to destroy existing society, and, like the early Christians, were the wave of the future.[50]

Though the idea of the collectivization of wealth and the abolition of private property had a long pedigree, modern socialist thought began during the French Revolution with the teachings of François-Noël Babeuf. In 1797 he paid with his life for his doctrines, but they lived on in one form or other. Though people continued to talk and dream about the ideas of socialism, they did not at first give it a collective name. Until the mid-1820s, the word *socialism* did not exist in any European language. By the 1840s it had come into common use everywhere. Variations in the word *community*, which figured large in socialist thinking, appeared in 1827. In 1840 relatively obscure leaders of French secret societies introduced the word *communist*. That term was picked up in England that same year, and in Germany two years later. The antonym of socialism, individualism, made its appearance in France in 1827 and came into common use in England in 1840 when it was introduced from France. To some, communism had a meaning distinct from socialism, but most people, including Karl Marx, used the words interchangeably. They remained vague, general terms that referred to any doctrine that proposed a radical solution to the "social question."[51]

Paris continued to be the wellspring of revolutionary thought and action. French theorists like Henri de Saint-Simon (1760–1825) and Charles Fourier (1772–1837) constructed elaborate blueprints of ideal societies that would free mankind's productive energies and create a just and prosperous world. These visionaries believed that their ideas would triumph through education and persuasion. Others advocated violent revolution as the only way to achieve the socialist Nirvana. Whatever their programs, they had little impact upon the working class until the 1840s. The repressive legislation of the July Monarchy, the growing unrest, the strikes, and the unceasing agitation and propaganda of the radicals persuaded increasing numbers of workers to give their allegiance to socialism. And soon it become fashionable among French intellectuals to give at least lip service to the new socialist ideologies.

Knowledge of the doctrines of French socialism reached other lands through the writings of the exiles who gathered in Paris. Their letters and articles influenced intellectuals back in their homelands to read and study the writings of the French socialists. In Germany a two-volume scholarly work called *Socialism and Communism in Today's France* appeared in 1842. Written by Lorenz von Stein, the book had an enormous influence among European intellectuals, and for most of its readers, it was the first introduction to the doctrines of socialism. In far-off Saint Petersburg, the "circles" of the youthful intellectuals began to read and discuss the writings of the French socialists.[52]

In Britain the doctrines of French socialists gained the attention of some intellectuals, but most were not interested in abstract theories of social revolution. In any event, Britain had its homegrown variety of socialism in the teachings of Robert Owen (1771–1858), who wanted mankind to settle in "villages of unity and mutual cooperation." His vision for a new way of life never came to fruition, but the cooperation he advocated became the progenitor of Britain's cooperative movement. In December 1844 twenty-eight Lancashire weavers, led by Owenite socialists, opened a small shop on Toad Street in the town of Rochdale. They called themselves the Rochdale Society of Equitable Pioneers. They had dreams of cooperative manufacturing and farming enterprises, but their little store dealt only in foodstuffs and operated on sales for cash. The profits were divided among the members in proportion to their purchases. Soon workers in neighboring towns adopted the "Rochdale system," as it came to be called. By 1851 the one store on Toad Street had grown to 130 small cooperative enterprises with a total membership of around fifteen thousand. That was the beginning of the consumer cooperative movement that in the succeeding years spread throughout most of the world.[53]

Being intellectuals, the radicals belonged to what the duke of Wellington called "the scribbling set." The written word was their principal weapon. They wrote endlessly, turning out books, pamphlets, newspaper articles, proclamations, manifestos, handbills, and above all else, journals. Government censorship and repression guaranteed the journals short lives, sometimes not more than a couple of numbers. That did not dissuade the editors, who simply started a new journal with a new name or moved to a different place. German radicals, unable to get their writings published in Germany, had them published in Switzerland. Julius Fröbel, himself a political exile who ran a publishing house in Zurich from 1844 to 1847, told how he evaded German customs officials on guard against shipments of publications from Switzerland. He had the writings printed in Alsace, Holland, Denmark, and even the United States, and had them shipped into Germany from these lands.

The usual journals had editorial boards of radical friends and associates of the editors. The board members were disputatious, opinionated, and highly articulate young men, and their meetings sometimes became bedlam. The twelve to fourteen members of the board of the magazine *Vorwärts*, founded in Paris in 1844 by Heinrich Bornstein and Karl Ludwig Bernays, met in the largest room in Bornstein's house, which happened to be the bedroom of the Russian radical Mikhail Bakunin. Everyone argued passionately and at the top of his lungs in order to be heard. They also smoked furiously, so that the room became shrouded in thick clouds of smoke. Bornstein was afraid to open the windows to clear the smoke. With windows open, the commotion would be certain to attract a crowd that might include police agents who would want to know what the shouting was about. In any event, like other radical periodicals, *Vorwärts* had a short life. Its vituperative attacks on the various governments of Germany and their rulers brought protests from German diplomats in Paris, and the French government ordered the suppression of the journal.[54]

Despite its many varieties, socialism divided itself into two principal categories, which were identified by the catchwords *utopian* and *scientific*. The utopians held the stage to the end of the 1840s. They believed that it was possible to transform society peacefully by appeals to human reason, by a moral reformation of mankind, and by the adoption of a new organization of economic and social life that would provide the solution to all of the evils of existing society. In the late 1830s their opponents derisively began to call them utopians, and the term was popularized by the writings of Marx and Engels. The utopians stressed the need for cooperation between the classes. They addressed their appeal to all of society but expressed special concern for the workers because they were the people who suffered the most in existing society. The panaceas they offered differed widely from one another.

Outlandish and, indeed, utopian as their proposals seemed, the utopians won devoted disciples. Utopian communities proved especially attractive in the United States, some of them established by migrating Europeans, others by native Americans. Some of them lasted longer than others, but all of them ultimately collapsed. Despite the failure of these communities, utopian socialism left a lasting heritage. Its idealism and its faith in reason awakened many to the powerful influence of ideas and of ethics and gave them hope for a better and brighter world. Its message of cooperation among classes, of moral suasion, and of peaceful legislation to achieve socialistic goals became part of European socialism.

Among the utopians the most remembered names are those of Saint-Simon, Fourier, Blanc, and Owen. Étienne Cabet, when he is remembered at all, is dismissed as a man who lacked intellectual depth and originality. Yet in the 1840s his utopian teachings inspired a larger following than those of any other socialist movement of the time. By 1848 contemporary estimates of the number of his disciples ran from fifty thousand to as high as two hundred thousand. Already by 1845 he was known as "the chief of the communists." A report written in 1850 for Austria's Minister of the Interior, Alexander Bach, on socialism in France, Germany, and Austria identified him as "the first and most important head of the new revolutionary socialism."[55]

Born in Dijon in 1788, Cabet was the son of a master cooper. He would have followed his father's trade had not his poor eyesight persuaded his father that the youth was better suited for an academic education. In 1812 he took a law degree from the University of Dijon and became a practicing attorney and an active politician. During the Bourbon Restoration, he became a partisan of republicanism and continued his agitation for a republic after the establishment of the July Monarchy in 1830. In 1834 he was sentenced to five years of exile.

He spent his exile in England, where he read widely in works of history and social theory. Borrowing ideas liberally from More's *Utopia*, Rousseau's *La Nouvelle Héloïse*, and the writings of Saint-Simon and Fourier, he formulated his own version of the ideal society. In 1839 he published *Voyage en Icarie*, the book that described that society and that marked the beginning of the remarkable success of his ideas. Published first in French in London and in Paris in 1840, the book went through eight reprintings between 1840 and 1848 and was quickly translated into English, German, and Spanish. Written in the form of a novel, it told of the adventures of an Englishman named Lord William Carisdale. Carisdale, hearing of a classless community called Icaria, somewhere east of Africa, decided to visit there. He found it a land of plenty where everyone lived in luxury and where happiness and contentment reigned. The state, governed by elected representatives, owned everything and provided the people with whatever they needed. In the last section of the book, he abandoned the novel form, and in proper lawyer fashion cited at length authorities from Socrates down to his own time who, he averred, supported the principles of communism.[56]

To the modern reader Cabet's novel is poorly written, with its six hundred pages filled with tedious details. To the French working man of the 1840s, it presented an exciting account of how to achieve a veritable heaven on earth by a few simple concepts. Cabet, a skillful propagandist, decided to capitalize on the success of his book. He published a weekly newspaper that he called *Le Populaire*. Unlike other radical publications, it contained no theoretical or philosophical articles. Instead, it told sensational stories of fallen women, murders, oppression of workers, the sins and moral decay of the upper classes, and always pressed home the need for a communistic society to abolish the ills of the present. The paper had only four pages, printed in larger type than other papers of the time, written in simple language, and sprinkled liberally with exclamation points. Soon *Le Populaire* had the widest circulation of all newspapers.

Encouraged by the popular success of his movement, Cabet decided to put his ideas into practice in an experimental settlement in the United States. He bought a large tract of land in Texas, and in January 1848 an advance party of sixty-nine "Icarians" sailed for New Orleans to ready the way for those who were to follow. After their arrival in New Orleans, they discovered that they had been swindled in the Texas land deal. After further adventures, a community established itself at Nauvoo, Illinois, only recently abandoned by the Mormons who were driven further west. Meanwhile, word had come back to France of the unexpected difficulties and the onset of dissensions and disenchantment. Cabet, in December 1848, decided to go to America to restore morale. Instead of bringing peace and order, he created new dissensions by assuming the role of dictator of the community. Finally, in 1856, the settlers drove him out, and he died shortly thereafter in St. Louis.[57]

Frenchmen took the lead in formulating the doctrines of utopian socialism, whereas "scientific socialism" was a German product that owed its origins to the teachings of G. W. F. Hegel (1770–1831), professor at Heidelberg and then Berlin. Hegel's philosophy dominated German intellectual life for decades. He proposed an all-encompassing philosophical system that aimed at a complete reconstruction of thought. Yet his followers often arrived at conclusions that were contrary to one another. Conservatives, liberals, and radicals all found support for their ideas in his writings. In no small part that happened because of the difficulties, abstractions, and lack of clarity in his voluminous writings, which filled eighteen volumes.[58]

The Hegelians split into two camps, the Old or Right Hegelians, the first generation of his disciples, and the Young or Left Hegelians, the second and radical generation. The Old Hegelians used their master's teachings to provide a new and more rational justification of traditional religion and the authority of the state. They interpreted Hegel's famous dictum that "What is real is rational and what is rational is real" as the justification of the status quo. The Young Hegelians seized upon Hegel's elevation of reason and his use of the dialectical method to prove that everything real is always in flux. The dialectic maintained that the thesis, whatever it may be, gives rise to its opposite, or antithesis, and out of the conflict between thesis and antithesis comes the synthesis. The synthesis is not a compromise of thesis and antithesis, but is new and superior to both. The synthesis then becomes the new thesis, gives rise to its antithesis, and results in a new and still higher synthesis, and so on. The status quo, therefore, cannot be rational, and so Hegelianism becomes a revolutionary doctrine. The Young Hegelians believed that through the operation of the dialectic history was moving toward the final goal of freedom for all, but that human effort and action were needed to remove the obstacles that impeded the historical process. The radical views of the Young Hegelians kept them from appointments to the faculties of German universities. Some of them went into exile and devoted themselves to pamphleteering, agitation, and endless and often bitter quarrels with one another. They were few in number and their contemporaries paid them and their theories scant attention. Yet Young Hegelianism was destined to have an enormous influence, for it provided the intellectual climate out of which Marxian socialism emerged.

"Scientific socialism," as the Marxists called it, developed under the aegis of Karl Marx and Friedrich Engels. They derided utopian socialism as idealistic, ineffective, and out of touch with the currents of history. In contrast, they described "scientific socialism," or communism, as they chose to call it, as realistic. The violence eschewed by the utopians was necessary because bourgeois capitalistic society was itself employing violence to maintain its supremacy. Yet beneath Marx and Engels's claim that they presented a scientific analysis of the triumph of communism lay the same messianic urge that inspired the utopians: the redemption and the salvation of mankind through a new ordering of society.

Marx, born in 1818 in the Rhineland city of Trier, son of a lawyer, came from a long line of rabbis. His father, to escape restrictions upon Jews in the practice of law, became a Christian and in 1824 had young Karl and his five sisters baptized. After completing *gymnasium*, Karl became a university student and during those years, became an atheist and a Young Hegelian. In 1841 he took his doctorate in philosophy and looked forward to a career as a university teacher. His political and religious views, however, foreclosed any chance for an academic appointment. Instead, in 1842 he joined the staff and soon became the editor of the *Rheinische Zeitung*, a new newspaper started by some liberal businessmen in Cologne. Under Marx's direction, the paper quickly won reputation and circulation for its spirit and daring. Inevitably, its liberalism and its social criticism put it in bad odor with the government. The censors reported that Marx was the source of the paper's dissident views, and in 1843 Marx resigned in a fruitless effort to prevent the suppression of the journal.

In June of the same year, Marx married. In 1836 at eighteen, he had fallen in love with Jenny von Westphalen, daughter of one of Trier's leading citizens. Both families raised objections to the match. The young couple took seven years to overcome family opposition and to reach the point where Karl seemed ready to earn a living. The marriage was a happy one, though marred by illness, poverty, deprivation, and by the deaths at birth or in childhood of four of their seven children. Stephen Born, one of Marx's earliest disciples, years later wrote that he had seldom met a wife so harmoniously attuned to her husband in every way. Yet, though she lived for the ideas of her husband, she never forgot her upbringing. In matters of marriage and morals, she was particularly intransigent.[59]

In appearance, Marx was a sturdy figure, alive with energy, with large, piercing eyes, a thick mop of black hair, and so dark-complected that family and friends called him by the nickname of Moor. Those who knew him found him uncommonly intelligent, indeed brilliant, and uncommonly disagreeable. There was a nearly universal consensus that he was arrogant, impatient, intolerant, obstinate, petty, treacherous, and vain. Moses Hess, a leading early socialist, in a letter to Herzen, complained bitterly about Marx's vanity and his insistence that others submit to his will. When the Russian Pavel Annenkov met Marx in 1846, he commented that Marx seemed convinced that he had a mission to control men's minds, to legislate for them, to lead them in his train. "Before me stood the personification of the democratic dictator incarnate," he continued, "just as might be pictured in one's imagination during times devoted to phantasy." Carl Schurz, who knew Marx in 1848, recalled that he had never met a man who was so provoking and intolerable.[60]

After he resigned from the *Rheinische Zeitung*, Marx and his new wife emigrated to Paris where, with Arnold Ruge, he founded the short-lived *Deutsch-Französische Jahrbucher*. Save for a few months in 1848–1849 and brief visits in the 1860s, he never returned to Germany. Yet he remained always a German, always an exile. He spoke and wrote almost exclusively in German, his few friends were fellow German radicals, and he made no effort to assimilate with the people and the culture of the lands in which he lived. He had stayed in Paris a little more than a year when the French government, at the request of the Prussian government, ordered him to leave. He moved to Brussels, but the Belgians expelled him in 1848. He went first back to Paris, then to Cologne, where he and Engels edited the radical *Neue Rheinische Zeitung* during the 1848 revolution. When the revolution collapsed, he was arrested, tried for sedition, acquitted, and expelled from Prussia in May 1849. On August 26, 1849, he and his family arrived in London and lived a hard life there until his death in 1883. He was supported by subsidies from Engels (who after the revolution returned to his family's textile business in Manchester), from small inheritances, and from the little that he earned from his writings and from newspaper articles. He took no regular employment and spent his days writing at home and doing research in the British Museum.

When Marx arrived in Paris in 1843, he became familiar with the writings of French socialists and became intimate with French and foreign radicals. He attended meetings of the League of the Just, a radical German secret society that was started in Paris in 1836. When Marx had to leave Paris and moved to Brussels, he and Engels, whom he had met in Paris, decided to form an international communist party with Marx as its head, using the League of the Just as their vehicle. In 1847 the League of the Just became the Communist League and commissioned Marx and Engels to draft a party program. That program was published as *The Communist Manifesto*. Written in German and printed in London, it appeared early in 1848, shortly before the outbreak of the February revolution in Paris. The *Manifesto* was a masterpiece of propaganda—short, clear, hard hitting, closely reasoned, and replete with ringing phrases.

The *Manifesto* encapsulated the theories that Marx, with Engels's assistance, had worked out in the preceding year. Marx borrowed heavily from the ideas of contemporaries, but that does not lessen his great achievement. By using the dialectical method, by stressing the importance of the methods of production in material life, and by introducing the concept of class conflict as the motor force of history, he created a dynamic revolutionary doctrine that appealed to reason and not to emotions. The *Manifesto* declared that socialism was the inevitable, unavoidable consequence of historical development. Using the Hegelian dialectic, the *Manifesto* argued that history advanced through an evolutionary cycle of thesis, antithesis, and synthesis. In each of history's successive epochs, the method of production and exchange in material life determined the structure, political and legal systems, ideas and culture of the society. In each stage of history—first slavery, then feudalism, and now capitalism—the history of mankind had been the history of struggle between the exploited and the exploiter, the oppressed class versus the ruling class. The bourgeois capitalists had triumphed over the feudal lords and had created a new synthesis. Their victory had simplified class antagonisms by splitting society into only two hostile classes, the bourgeois capitalists and their antithesis, the proletariat. The clash between the two will bring forth the new synthesis of a classless society. That will end for all time the oppression and exploitation of a ruling class. Man will at last be free, acting as an equal and cooperating member of a community, and controlling his own destiny. The state, which the *Manifesto* labeled "an executive committee for administering the affairs of the whole bourgeois class," would disappear. The *Manifesto* ended with the famous challenge: "The proletarians have nothing to lose but their chains. They have a world to win. Workers of the world, unite."

Marx and Engels of course knew that the proletariat was still relatively small in size and that the peasantry far outnumbered it. But they excluded peasants from the revolutionary force that would usher in the classless society. The authors of the *Manifesto*, repelled by the individualism of the peasant who wanted his own piece of land and repelled, too, by small-scale production, lumped the peasantry with shopkeepers, small manufacturers, and artisans in the lower middle class. By their efforts to preserve their occupations, the peasants tried to hold back the course of history. The *Manifesto* urged the expropriation of the land and its cultivation by "armies of laborers."

In 1840 another new chapter opened in the history of radical thought when a book titled *What Is Property?* appeared in Paris. The book began dramatically by answering the question in its title with the statement, "Property is theft." In the book's preface, the author declared that his purpose was to show how to improve the physical, moral, and intellectual condition of the most numerous and poorest class. The book's author, Pierre-Joseph Proudhon, has been called the intellectual father of modern anarchism. Though he wrote copiously in the years that followed, this first and best-known book contained the kernel of his thought and his contribution to radical ideology.

Proudhon was one of the few radical theorists of plebeian origin. Born in 1809 in Besançon in eastern France into a working-class family, he had little formal education. As a youth, he was apprenticed to a printer, and with a passion for books and for learning he became a self-educated man. He also developed a contrariness and a hostility to the established order. He had strong opinions about almost every subject and he wrote voluminously (his complete works filled thirty-three volumes in the 1861–1875 edition). Much of his writing was ambiguous and inconsistent since he often contradicted himself and changed his ideas as time went on. As a consequence, he is not only called the father of anarchism, out to destroy all existing institutions, by violence if need be, and to establish a society where everyone is equal in power and wealth. He has been tarred with many brushes. The Marxists called him a petty bourgeois who was an enemy of the working class. French reactionaries of the Third Republic hailed him as one of their own because of his attacks on democracy, his support of the peasantry, and his ardent nationalism. In our own time, he has been seen as a forerunner of fascism because of his anti-Semitism, his racism, and his extreme nationalism.

His perversity revealed itself in his first book, *What Is Property?* His reply that property is theft rendered him suspect to bourgeois society and to the French government, and won him the admiration of the young radicals who flocked to Paris. In fact, he did not want to abolish property. He wanted only to get rid of landlords, whom he called thieves because they drew income from the land without working it. His ideal society was one of small peasant households with holdings of more or less equal size. The right to own the land should belong to the individual peasant family who tilled it.[61]

In *What Is Property?*, Proudhon called himself an anarchist. Before his time the word had meant someone who advocated lawlessness and social disorder. Proudhon used the term to describe those who seek social order without a ruler or sovereign who made the laws that ruled society. "Although I am a strong supporter of order," he wrote, "I am in the fullest sense of the term an anarchist." He saw government as an instrument of oppression to protect the unjust economic system and the hierarchical structure. "Just as man seeks justice in equality, society seeks order in anarchy." He was as opposed to democracy as he was to autocracy. The oppression of an autocrat and the oppression of a majority differed only in degree. Religion was another instrument of oppression, employed by the masters to hold down the masses.[62]

Though they had talked and written about the coming of revolution, Europe's radicals were as surprised as everyone else by the outbreak of real revolution in 1848. They hastened to the scenes of the risings but they played insignificant parts. None of the self-styled spokesmen of the workers took over leadership in any of the risings. Marxist historians have labored diligently and at length to build up the significance of Marx and Engels and their followers in the 1848 revolutions, but without success. The chief effect of their agitations, like those of other radicals, seems to have been to drive moderate liberals into the arms of the reactionaries.[63]

The failure of the revolutions made radicals realize that they could not hope to triumph over the forces of the existing order. Some of them reacted bitterly. Mikhail Bakunin, the fiery Russian revolutionary, in a letter to Georg Herwegh at the end of 1848, wrote, "I remember what you said to me so often in Paris, before the revolution. 'The first revolution in Germany will have no encouragement for us, for it will be a victory of bourgeois baseness.' How great this baseness of the German philistine is I've now seen for the first time in full measure. Nowhere is the bourgeois worthy of love, but the German bourgeois combines baseness and smugness. . . . Even the way these people revolt is revolting." Others took the defeat of the revolutions more philosophically. Whatever their reaction to the disappointments of 1848, the radicals realized that they had to think and plan in terms of practical politics. In the years after 1848, they abandoned the idealism and utopianism and the heady dreams of revolutionizing society. They began to forge political movements that could operate within the bounds of the established order and ultimately achieve their goal of a socialist society. Meanwhile, the cooperative movement, born of Owenite socialism, from small beginnings spread through the years to many lands.

Not every partisan of socialism welcomed the thought of its ultimate triumph. Heinrich Heine predicted that the materialistic communists would have no use for art and literature. He said they would use his books to wrap coffee and snuff. Yet he supported communism because of the iniquities of existing society and because he hated its German nationalistic opponents. Communists, he declared, love all races and believe in equality and fraternity among all men. Herzen, like Heine, feared the victory of socialism because he, too, thought it would destroy the culture and art of the civilized elite. "The new barbarians will raze to the ground the edifices of their oppressors, and with them all that is most sublime and beautiful in Western civilization." Yet he believed that this same Western culture had offered nothing but suffering, and life without meaning, to the vast majority of mankind.[64]

CHAPTER THREE

Romanticism, Nationalism, Realism

"Romanticism is the star that weeps, the wind that wails, the night that shivers, the flower that flies, and the bird that exudes perfume. Romanticism is the unhoped-for ray of light, the languorous rapture, the oasis beneath the palm trees, ruby hope with its thousand loves, the angel and the pearl, the willow in its white garb. Oh, sir, what a beautiful thing! It is the infinite and the star, heat, the fragmentary, the sober (yet at the same time complete and full); the diametrical, the pyramidal, the Oriental, the living nude, the embraceable, the kissable, the whirlwind."[1]

That was how in 1836 Alfred de Musset, a leading figure in the Romantic movement, defined romanticism in one of the earliest attempts to explain the meaning of the term. Small wonder that the word has been the despair of those who have struggled through many decades to spell out its meaning. As long ago as 1925, an industrious Belgian scholar counted 150 definitions, and the number has continued to mount in the years since then. Arthur Lovejoy, famed historian of ideas, dismayed by the many incongruous and often opposing meanings that the term had acquired, suggested that the word by itself was useless as a verbal symbol. Lovejoy's suggestion, inspired in part by his noted distaste for scholarly humbuggery, fell on barren soil, though as a later historian put it, many cannot now face the term without wincing.[2]

Wince though one may, the word serves to describe an era in Western cultural history that ran from the last quarter of the eighteenth century to the

1840s. It was an age—to some a Golden Age—of idealism and sentimental-ism. Romanticism owed its genesis to the reaction against the reason, cos-mopolitanism, classicism, and search for the universal laws of nature of the eighteenth-century Enlightenment. Among its progenitors, Jean-Jacques Rousseau, who proclaimed the natural goodness of man and the supremacy of the emotions over reason, held first place. Rousseau sowed the seeds for a harvest of new ideas that profoundly altered the outlook and the values of an ever growing number of literate Europeans. It was a reaction, too, against the neoclassicisms of the French Revolution and against Robespierre's "Republic of Virtue" that lasted from 1792 to 1794. That was when Christianity was replaced by a "Cult of Reason" and when, in the name of saving the revolu-tion from its "internal enemies," twenty to forty thousand people were guil-lotined in the Reign of Terror.

Romanticism made its first appearance in England and especially in Germany and spread to other lands as the years went by. In Germany, as in no other land, Romanticism pervaded the entire culture from the mid-1790s until the 1830s. As the quotation from Alfred de Musset indicates, the Romantics had a penchant for obscurantism and multiple meaning; they took delight in contrasts and paradoxes; they yearned for secret and distant places; they prized the mystical and the emotional, and they sought to encompass and to synthesize all human experience.[3]

In sharpest contrast to the efforts of the Enlightenment to establish the uniformity of man as a rational being, the Romantics extolled the senses and the emotions. They denied that man lived by reason alone, but instead recon-ciled man's intellect with his emotions. They exalted individuality and sensi-bilities, and they rejoiced in human diversity. Man should no longer subject himself to old rules and conventions. Instead, they believed that man should seek to express himself in total self-assertion in order to achieve the highest attainments of which he was capable. They glorified nature and rhapsodized over its beauties. They saw the universe not as a great cosmic machine, as men of the Age of Reason believed, but as an organism in continual progress. In reaction against the Enlightenment's admiration of classical Greece and Rome, the Romantics looked back with nostalgia to Europe's Middle Ages and idealized everything medieval.

They celebrated the unlettered common man whose sensibilities, they claimed, had not been blunted by civilization. They panegyrized folk art and folk culture and eagerly collected folk tales and folk songs. The most famed of the collectors were the brothers Grimm, distinguished philologists. The Grimms rescued some two hundred tales from a dying oral tradition and made them part of Germany's and the world's literary heritage. Wilhelm Grimm wrote that "only folk poetry is perfect because God himself wrote it like the laws of Sinai; it is not put together from pieces like human work is."[4]

The Romantic emphasis upon tradition as the determinant of and guides for human behavior sparked a religious revival that stressed mysticism and pietism rather than rational exegesis. The Romantics saw themselves as possessing acute feelings that distinguished them from their less sensitive fellows. Some affected a fondness for solitude and thoughts of suicide and death. Others insisted upon the primacy of action, fostered the cult of the hero, and looked forward with confidence to the future. Romantic artists rejected classical models. Instead of placing the human figure in the center of their canvases, they turned to nature for their inspiration. Romantic poets abandoned the formalism of the classical revival of the eighteenth century. The verses of Wordsworth, Coleridge, Keats, and Shelley in England, Lamartine and de Vigny in France, and Pushkin in Russia bespoke a love of nature and of simple folk or expressed a fascination with faraway and exotic places, or told of great events and heroes in their nation's history.

Romantic novelists like Victor Hugo, Allesandro Manzoni, Alexandre Dumas, and Mary Shelley spun their tales out of nostalgia for times long past, told fanciful stories of heroic adventure and derring-do, recounted tales of love and romance, or wrote Gothic novels that involved demonic forces. Most of their novels belonged to the literature of escape, but some of them conveyed a message to their readers. Sir Walter Scott, the enormously popular master of the historical romance, and the novelists in other lands inspired by him, appealed to the conservatism of their readers. Their novels evoked a romantic longing for the hierarchical society of bygone days in which everyone knew and accepted his place in the social order, and when life was simpler and more direct. At the same time, they appealed to the new spirit of nationalism with their heroic tales of their nation's past and their accounts of lords and peasants standing united against the common foe. Other authors, reflecting the Romantic infatuation with the unlettered common folk, wrote stories of rural life, idealizing the peasant as the possessor of antique unspoiled virtues and of fundamental goodness.

The veneration of the traditional social structure remained typical of Romantic novelists until the early 1830s. Then a remarkable metamorphosis transformed Romantic belles-lettres. A new wave of writers, particularly in France, reacted against the conservatism of their predecessors. They believed that they had the obligation to strike blows for political and social reform. They portrayed men of the ruling class as evil-doers, or at best wastrels, while they reserved their sympathetic roles for people of the lower orders or even for outcasts of society. The contrast between a callous and exploitative elite and a virtuous commonality became a popular theme of Romantic fiction.[5]

The novels of George Sand (1804–1876) provided an even more striking departure from long-accepted standards. The author of scores of novels, plays, essays, political tracts, volumes of letters, and an autobiography, she either outraged or delighted hosts of readers from one end of Europe to the other. Feminist, socialist, and republican, she launched a headlong attack upon conventional morality in her writings and in her own life. Determined to shock her world—and to win attention to herself—she dressed like a man, booted and spurred, smoked cigars, chatted about such masculine interests as sports and clubs, and flaunted her unorthodox sex life that included liaisons with such well-known figures as Frédéric Chopin and Alfred de Musset, as well as with some women. Passionate love conquering all provided the leitmotif for most of her novels. Other of her novels took aim at Christianity, preached a single standard for men and women, portrayed the moral superiority of a man of the people to the spinelessness of decadent aristocrats, declared that her purpose in her pastoral romances was to show "what is good and beautiful in peasant life," or told how love bridged the chasm between social classes.

To a modern reader her novels seem awash in sentimentality and emotion, filled with convenient suicides, promises of everlasting love, stilted conversations, and remarkably improbable plots. In contrast, her contemporaries had great admiration for her work, and she enjoyed enormous popularity. Thackeray said of her book *Lelia* that it was "wonderful indeed, gorgeous in eloquence, and rich in magnificent poetry; a regular topsy-turvyfication of morality, a thieves' and prostitutes' apotheosis." Alexander Herzen's wife, Natalie, whose life would have made her an eminently suitable subject of a passionate and tragic romantic novel, in her diary wrote of Sand, "How profoundly she has penetrated human nature, boldly carried the living soul through sin and debauchery, and brought it unscathed out of the all devouring flame! Four years ago, Botkin remarked that she was a female Christ. It sounds comical, but there is much truth in it."[6]

Romanticism began as a revolution of aesthetes, many of them bohemians of the sort found in the vanguard of any new intellectual fad. Vaunting self-development, proud of their sensibilities, the Romantics found no interest in the world of affairs. Soon, however, as their numbers grew, their enchantment with folklore and folk culture, their empathy with the "common man," their emphasis upon the native language, and their fascination with the past engendered a new phenomenon: modern nationalism. This nationalism, which was destined to become a worldwide faith, began with the Romantics' reaction against the cosmopolitanism of the Enlightenment, the belief that man was everywhere the same. In place of universal law, the Romantics insisted that each nationality had its own unique qualities that distinguished it from all other nationalities. They singled out the differences in the history and cultural heritage of the separate nationalities of Europe. These differences, they said, shaped each people's national character. Scholars went to great and sometimes fanciful lengths to prove the independence, or even the existence, of their own nationality in the historical past, and to prove why each nationality should be united in the future. Every people, they asserted, had the God-given right to autonomous development and to fulfill its God-given mission. The state, the political unit that held each people together, was seen as a living organism, an individual like man himself, but infinitely greater and more powerful. The state was the creation not of man but of the will of God.[7]

From these beginnings in the late eighteenth and first part of the nineteenth centuries, there grew the modern creed of nationalism, the creed that each people should live as an independent nation in its own autonomous territory and with its own sovereign government. Prehistoric and primitive societies knew loyalty to family and tribe; citizens felt patriotism to city-states and empires that flourished in classical Greece and Rome; and peoples in late medieval and early modern times experienced glimmerings of national consciousness. But as one historian has cogently explained, those who trace modern nationalism back to earlier centuries "tear generic words like nation or nationalism from their historical context, read their contemporary substance back into the past, and thus see in the past the generalities and the universals evident actually in contemporary life."[8]

Before the dawning of modern nationalism, neither ethnic nor cultural nor linguistic diversity mattered to sovereigns or to their subjects. To the rulers, the lands over which they ruled belonged to their family dynasty, and dynastic considerations determined their policies. Their possessions changed hands with marriages, deaths, and conquests. The dynasts made no effort to establish the supremacy of one language or one culture. Loyalty to the dynasty was all the monarch demanded.

The subjects, for their part, thought of themselves as inhabitants of some specific region or province, or as members of a specific social group such as the nobility or the peasantry or townsmen, rather than as members of a specific nationality. They identified themselves as Bretons, or Catalans, or

Flemings, or Slovaks, or Wends, and so on, each with their own language, rather than as Frenchmen or Spaniards or Austrians or Germans. They made no protest when war, marriage, or inheritance transferred them from one dynasty to another. In any event, most of them were illiterate peasants aware of little beyond the borders of their villages. Intellectuals and members of the ruling elite were cosmopolitans. They moved easily from one land to another, holding high offices or enjoying the patronage of the ruler. They thought of themselves as citizens of the world. Goethe in 1772 wrote, "If we can find a place where we can rest with our possessions, a field to sustain us, a home to cover us, have we not there a fatherland?"[9]

The French Revolution, followed by the conquests of Napoleon, undermined this world that men had known and accepted for so long. The French Revolution proclaimed the idea of the nation with the people as sovereign. *The Declaration of the Rights of Man*, promulgated on August 26, 1789, declared, "The nation is essentially the source of all sovereignty; nor can any individual, or any body of men, be entitled to any authority which is not expressly derived from it." The outbreak of war in 1792 and the successes of the French against the powers aligned against them spread the idea of the sovereignty of the people and of nationalism to other peoples. Then Napoleon, to suit his own purposes of conquest, had promoted the new spirit of nationalism. To enlist support for his campaigns against the dynastic rulers of Europe, he had appealed to the national pride of subject peoples. In proclamations to the Hungarians, he told them that as proud possessors of their own national language and culture, they should have a king of their own choosing. He told the Poles to be worthy of their forefathers who had ruled over a united kingdom, and in 1807 he established the Grand Duchy of Warsaw. In 1805 he united most of Italy into a kingdom with himself as its ruler. In 1806 he grouped together sixteen states in central and southern Germany into the Confederation of the Rhine. In 1807 several western German states and western provinces of Prussia annexed by Napoleon became the Kingdom of Westphalia. These, like other Napoleonic creations, lasted only a few brief years, and the old rulers soon returned. But they had awakened hopes of national unification that never died.

The triumphs and conquests of the armies of the Revolution and of Napoleon contributed in another way to the growth of nationalism. The fiscal and military levies of the French in the lands they conquered angered the people of those lands. They had to pay taxes to the French and supply many thousands of soldiers for the armies of Napoleon. They had to submit to the laws and the administration imposed by the conquerors. They often had to admit French wares duty-free while their own wares were effectively excluded from France by high tariffs, and they had to join Napoleon's Continental Blockade of Britain, to their own considerable loss of revenue from goods they had previously sold to Britain. There was jealousy, too, of the military successes of the French, and resentment of French cultural domination. The result was that the Napoleonic conquests evoked a wave of national feeling, of national resistance to French domination, and enthusiasm for national independence.

When, after Napoleon's defeat in 1815, the victors met at Vienna, it seemed natural to the men gathered there to go back to the old ways. Under the principle that they called legitimacy, they restored old dynasties, and they parceled out Germany to some of its former rulers, accepting Napoleon's surgery that had reduced the number of German sovereignties from well above three hundred to thirty-seven, later increased to thirty-nine. The victors thought they had made a lasting settlement, but they failed to reckon with the effects of the French Revolution and Napoleon. Most of all, they failed to reckon with the handful of romantics—intellectuals, poets, and litterateurs—who fabricated the new creed of nationalism out of their imaginations. Men of obscure social origins for the most part, excluded from the ruling elite and from the world of action, they were convinced that they had the knowledge and the ability to play a leading role in their societies. Johann Gottfried Fichte, professor of philosophy and ardent nationalist, in 1794 in his *The Vocation of a Scholar* wrote that the scholar "sees not merely the present—he also sees the future: he sees not merely the point which humanity now occupies, but also that to which it must next advance. . . . In this respect the Scholar is the *Guide* to the human race." That seemed a preposterous statement, yet within a few short decades, scholars as creators of the creed of nationalism served indeed as guides to their fellow Europeans, and in the years that followed, as guides to the peoples of the world. They wrote histories that "proved" the greatness of their own nationality in bygone centuries. They celebrated their national heroes who were always victorious, strong, and courageous, and who struggled against the forces of darkness. They preached their doctrine in university lecture halls and in pulpits and in publications, and they foretold a glorious future once all those of their nationality lived in their own autonomous state.[10]

The fathers of nationalism laid great stress upon national language. Language seemed to them to include all the virtues of Romanticism. Each language had its origins in the distant past, it was a creation of the people themselves and not of any ruler or legislator, and it was the unique expression of the character and spirit of each people. Language was the basic determinant of nationality. That idea had been launched by Johann Gottfried Herder

(1744–1803), German critic, philosopher, theologian, and prolific writer on many subjects. Herder had introduced the vague and mystical concept of the *Volksgeist*, the metaphysical entity that, he said, binds together the people, the *Volk*, of the same nationality. The *Volksgeist* united and inspired all who spoke the same language; indeed, each nation's language is the guardian of its *Volksgeist*. "Has a people something more precious than the language of its fathers?" wrote Herder. "In it resides its whole intellectual wealth of tradition, history, religion, maxims of life, all its heart and soul." Each nationality, each *Volk*, had its own *Volksgeist*, and so each nationality had its own God-given language.[11]

Herder's work inspired scholars throughout central and eastern Europe to purify, or if necessary to resurrect, or even to invent their respective national languages. In what has aptly been called a lexicographic revolution, scholars studied philology, wrote grammars, compiled multivolumed dictionaries, wrote literature, and edited journals in their native tongues. Their aim was to create a standard language that would draw together people of a common stock who now spoke a wide variety of dialects. The native tongue was often the language of peasants, servants, and small shopkeepers, while members of the elite spoke a foreign language, such as French or German. A common language would make these people realize that they were indeed one people, independent of foreign domination. From the work of these intellectuals, there emerged during the first half of the nineteenth century modern Czech, Slovene, Serbo-Croatian, Slovak, Bulgarian, Greek, Hungarian, Ukrainian, and Finnish as the standard literary languages of their respective nationalities. The new languages differed from the dialects on which they were based in grammar, syntax, and especially in vocabulary in order to meet social, economic, and political needs unknown to the peasant communities who spoke the dialects. It was an astonishing accomplishment of literally a handful of devoted men who had a dream and saw it become a reality. These men, and others who shared their dream, wrote histories and epic poems that glorified their national past, and edited and published collections of documents that served as sources for the history of their people. Because of their work, the words nationality and nationalism first appeared and were quickly incorporated into most of the languages of Europe. Nationalists came in all shades of political opinion, but all believed that the nation-state provided the framework within which the individual realized himself. They insisted, too, that the nation-state must demand the loyalty and unquestioning obedience of all of its citizens.

František Palacký (1798–1876), pioneer of Czech nationalism, once remarked that if the ceiling of the room in which he had dined one evening with his fellow nationalists had collapsed, it would have wiped out the entire Czech nationalist movement.[12] But though they were few in number, the intellectual fathers of nationalism occupied pivotal positions in their societies. Their students and disciples became schoolmasters, professors, and clergymen, their books became texts used in schools and universities, and their poems, plays, and journals spread the word of the new creed. The ceaseless drumbeat of their propaganda reached ever widening circles, first the middle classes, then self-educated artisans and skilled workers.[13]

The growth of cities, the improvements in communications, the advances in popular education and the increase in literacy, and improvements in the manufacture of paper and in printing techniques exposed an always increasing number to the teachings of the nationalists. These teachings fell on fertile soil when more and more people experienced prejudice and lack of opportunity for social and economic advancement because of their ethnic origin, or because they spoke a language that differed from the language of the ruling class. In every land the peasants, living in isolated villages and bound by tradition, were the last to be converted. Jan Slomka, born in 1842 of Polish stock, wrote that the illiterate older generation of his youth had no consciousness of being Polish. Instead, they thought of themselves as the people of Masuria, a region of Poland, and called their language Masurian. Slomka did not know that he was a Pole until he attended the newly established village school and began to read newspapers and books. Polish nationalism advanced slowly among his fellow peasants. Even at the end of the nineteenth century, some of them still believed that the gentry wanted to reestablish an independent Poland so that the peasants would have to work for them as they had in the days of serfdom.[14]

As always with new ideologies that reject old patterns of thought, nationalism held a special appeal to the young. They seized upon it as a rejection of the adult world. They poured their youthful energies into secret nationalist societies organized especially for them. The Italian Giuseppe Mazzini, one of the great heroes in the story of nationalism, established the prototype of these societies in 1831. Exiled from his homeland and living in Marseilles, he organized his youthful fellow Italian exiles into the Federation of Young Italy. Only twenty-six himself, Mazzini said, "Set the young to lead the revolution, make them feel they have a noble part to play, fire them with praise, give them the word of power."[15] Young Italy had as its goal the overthrow of the sovereigns who ruled over a divided Italy and the establishment of a united republic. The creation of Young Italy inspired imitation by democratic youths of other nationalities. There was a Young Poland, Young France, Young Germany, and Young Ireland. There was a Young England, too, but it resembled its Continental counterparts in name alone. A friend of its members described Young England as "a kind of High-Church-divine-right-of-kings-philanthropic band of brothers, in which the working classes were to be looked after and elevated on the principle of everything for the people, but nothing by the people." The movement met with much ridicule and had a short life.[16]

The new creed of nationalism had its strongest impact in lands of central, eastern, and southern Europe that had not yet achieved nationhood. It had its effects, too, in long-established nations. In France, its most ardent advocate was the historian Jules Michelet (1798–1874). He devoted his work to the glorification of France, recounting its contribution to mankind and awakening his fellow Frenchmen to their country's mission as the interpreter and the medium through which new ideas in every field passed on to the rest of the world.[17] Many Frenchmen shared Michelet's vision of their country's unique importance, among them Victor Hugo. In his maiden speech on June 21, 1848, in the revolutionary National Assembly, Hugo said, "Paris is the actual capital of the civilized world. That which Rome was in past times Paris is today. Paris has a dominant role among the nations. Paris has the privilege to establish at stated epochs supremely, perhaps abruptly, *des grandes choses*. The intellectuals of Paris prepare them and the workers of Paris carry them out."

Lord Normanby, Britain's ambassador to France during the 1848 revolution, reported this speech and then drily noted that a few days later, "the workers of Paris who carry out *des grandes choses* sacked Hugo's house in the Place Royal while Hugo was in the Assembly opposing the workers' latest idea of *une grande chose*."[18]

In Great Britain, many among the Scots, the Welsh, and the Irish resented the domination of the English, and national movements began to develop, above all among the Irish (discussed in a later chapter). In England itself, with its long history of political unity, nationalism as a political movement did not become an issue of importance in political life. But it had a significant role in the thinking and writings of Englishmen and in their attitude toward other people. English Romantics like Edmund Burke, Wordsworth, and Coleridge thought of their nation as an organic, spiritual community that bound together all Englishmen, living and dead, throughout the ages. Other Englishmen, whether Romantics or not, were convinced of the natural superiority of their nation. "Why is it," asked the historian Thomas Macaulay in a diary entry in August 1849, "that an Irishman's or Frenchman's hatred of England does not excite in me an answering hatred? I imagine that my national pride prevents it. England is so great that an Englishman cares little what others think of her, or how they talk of her." (Obviously the "abroad is bloody" syndrome was already alive and thriving.) Ralph Waldo Emerson, visiting England in 1847, was struck by the nationalistic boasting. "The habit of brag runs through all classes," he wrote, "from *The Times* newspaper through politicians and poets . . . down to the boys at Eton. In the gravest treatise in political economy, in a philosophical essay, in books of science, one is surprised by the most innocent exhibition of unflinching nationality."[19]

To the Romantics who were the founding fathers of nationalism, the new creed meant the peaceful coexistence of the peoples of the world. God in His infinite wisdom had divided the human race into nationalities, each with its own language, culture, history, and traditions—its own *Volksgeist*. Each was intended by God to live in peace and harmony and cooperation with all other nations. Each had a role to play in the divine plan, and to carry out that role each must live free of interference or domination by another nationality. Like the utopian socialists, the romantic nationalists had faith in the nature of man and man's love for his fellow man, and they believed that the acceptance of their teachings would change the world.

In a few short decades, two new ingredients attached themselves to and changed the nature of romantic nationalism. One was the conviction that national unification could be achieved only at the price of revolutionary violence. Each nationality must be ready to fight for its freedom, and if need be, accept self-sacrifice and martyrdom as the price of that freedom. Only then could an oppressed nationality free itself from the yoke of its oppressor. By the 1840s revolutionary nationalism had become the dominant form of nationalism, reaching its crescendo in the revolutions of 1848.[20]

The other new ingredient had its origin in the Romantic belief that God had assigned a specific role to each nationality. This soon transformed itself into the belief that each nation was entrusted with a divinely inspired mission. That conviction often had messianic overtones in that it held out the promise of the fulfillment of mankind's destiny, the achievement of an era of universal peace and comity among the nations of the world. Soon the sense of divine mission became colored with the claims of the spiritual superiority of one nation's messianic mission over all the others. Peter Chaadayev voiced the Slavophil conviction that Russia "is destined for a great spiritual future; she will one day solve all the problems over which Europe is fighting." To Polish nationalists their country's partition among neighbors in the eighteenth century became the source of its superior virtues. Poles called their homeland the Christ among the nations. Crucified and martyred through no fault of its own, Poland by its struggles and sufferings would redeem and liberate all other nations. German nationalists claimed that the intellectual superiority and originality of thought of Germans gave them a creative power that, as J. G. Fichte wrote, "will open up new shafts and bring the light of day into the abysses, and hurl up rocky masses of thought, out of which ages to come will build their dwelling."[21]

Among the messianic nationalists none had greater fame than the Pole Adam Mickiewicz, and the Italian Giuseppe Mazzini. Both men lived in exile for most of their lives, driven from their native lands because of their nationalistic convictions. Both lived far from the realities of everyday life in their homelands. Both supported revolution to achieve their goals. They were both internationalists in the sense that they advocated national independence for all peoples, and they shared the faith that this would lead to an era of peace, justice, and the brotherhood of all people. Finally, and this was their great tragedy, both men outlived their time, overtaken by the tides of history.

Poland in early modern times had been a unified kingdom that reached from the shores of the Baltic to the Black Sea. As time went by, it was racked by political anarchy and revolts and threatened by its neighbors. Finally, in three successive partitions between 1772 and 1795, Poland disappeared as an independent nation, carved up by Russia, Prussia, and Austria. In prepartition Poland, only the nobility, bonded by the host of rights and privileges that they alone enjoyed, had considered themselves the nation. All others had been excluded from participation in the conduct of affairs. The great majority of the population were peasants, held in serfdom by the nobility, who treated them more like chattels than fellow humans.

After the partitions wiped Poland from the map and when it seemed that it would never again rise from its ashes, modern Polish nationalism was born. The nationalists held out their hand to all Poles. As in other lands, lexicographers, linguists, literary critics, ethnographers, and historians wrote about Polish national culture from its earliest—and sometimes imagined—beginnings, and celebrated the peasantry as the preservers of that culture. In 1830, encouraged by the success of the July Revolution in France, Polish nobles in Russian Poland, joined by intellectuals and students, revolted against the rule of the tsar. At first they scored surprisingly quick victories. Then, torn by disputes among the leaders of the rising and lacking hoped-for assistance from the West, the revolutionary forces fell before the fierce reprisals of the Russian army. Tsar Nicholas abolished the constitution granted to Russian Poland at the Congress of Vienna, which had provided for a measure of self-rule. He closed the Universities of Warsaw and Vilna, imposed martial law that continued for twenty-five years, began an intensive policy of Russification, established a vigilant and strict censorship, and introduced a program of land reform to win over the loyalty of the Polish peasantry. Many of the revolutionaries who escaped execution or imprisonment, about ten thousand of Poland's political, social, and intellectual elite, fled to the West in what came to be called "the Great Emigration." Over half settled in Paris, around 1,300 or so in Great Britain, and the rest scattered through other lands. In L. B. Namier's words, these people did not abandon Poland. They carried it with them. The center of Polish national life transferred itself to Western Europe, with Paris as its capital. Unfortunately, the refugees proved a fractious and faction-ridden lot, each with its own political agenda for the beloved homeland.

Despite the rivalries, Adam Mickiewicz, Poland's greatest poet and the leading figure in Romanticism in Poland, became the spiritual leader of the emigration and the spokesman of Polish nationalism. Born in Lithuania in 1798, he was the son of a minor nobleman. Lithuania, once independent, had merged with Poland early in the sixteenth century, and its nobility and bourgeoisie had become Polonized, adopting the language and culture of Poland.

After what he recalled as an idyllic childhood, Mickiewicz attended the University of Vilna from 1815 to 1819. There he published his first poetry and helped organize a secret student club called the Philomathean Society. True to their name, the Philomatheans loved learning and letters. They also involved themselves with nationalistic concerns. After leaving the University, Mickiewicz taught in a district school where he preoccupied himself with writing poetry in the Romantic style, then new to Poland. In 1823 he was arrested because of his continued involvement with the Philomathean Society, whose members were charged with plotting "to spread Polish nationalism." After six months in prison he was exiled to Russia. He never returned to his native land.

He had rather an easy time of it in his Russian exile. He published more poetry that was much admired, became the friend of Pushkin and other leading literary figures, was a favorite guest in the Moscow salon of Princess Zinaida Volkonsky, a member of the highest Russian aristocracy. He apparently got along well with the Russians, though in later years he expressed hatred of them and boasted that he had "duped the despot." In 1829 he received permission to leave Russia and he journeyed in Western Europe. When the Polish revolt erupted in 1830, he was in Rome. He felt it his duty to join the rebels, but he arrived at the frontier just as the revolt collapsed. His failure to join in the revolt filled him with guilt that haunted him for years. To expiate his failure at the moment when his nation needed him, he decided to devote himself to the cause of Polish nationalism. In August 1832 he arrived in Paris, and that remained his home for the rest of his life.[22]

Between 1832 and 1834 he wrote his two most famous poems, *Forefathers' Eve, Part III*, and *Pan Tadeusz*, and a small prose work of fifty pages that he called *The Books of the Polish Nation and of the Polish Pilgrimage*. The two epic poems and the small book recounted the sufferings of the Polish people, explained how a just God permitted the crucifixion of His beloved Poland, told of Poland's destiny as the Christ among nations upon whose resurrection depended the liberation of all of the peoples of the world, told of the genius of Poland's past, and held out the faith in an even more glorious future. These three works won Mickiewicz recognition as the teacher and leader of the Polish nationalist movement.

The mysticism and the messianic message of these writings became the dominant themes in Mickiewicz's life and in the lives of many of his fellow Polish émigrés. Alexander Herzen suggested that their frustration with the crushing of the 1830 rising and the consequent loss of hope for the liberation of Poland accounted for the mysticism and the messianism. Only such transcendental reveries, outcroppings of Romanticism, could sustain their faith that an independent Poland would live again.[23]

Mickiewicz wrote *The Books of the Polish Nation and of the Polish Pilgrimage* in biblical style as a collection of parables and aphorisms that suited its apocalyptic revelations. The first part, *The Books of the Polish Nation*, provided a brief sketch of European history from its beginnings to the partitions of Poland by "the Satanic Trinity, the rulers of Prussia, of Russia, and of Austria." But Poland did not die. "On the third day, the soul shall return to the body, and the nation shall arise and free all the peoples of Europe from slavery." Part one concludes with the words, "Just as with the resurrection of Christ, bloody sacrifices will cease all over the world, so with the resurrection of the Polish nation wars will cease in all Christendom." Mickiewicz began the second part, *The Books of the Polish Pilgrimage*, by identifying the exiles—he called them Pilgrims—with the soul of the Polish nation. Like Christ, who said, "Whosoever followeth me, let him forsake both his father and his mother and risk his own soul," the Polish Pilgrims said, "Whosoever followeth freedom let him forsake his Fatherland and risk his own life." Those who remained in Poland lived in slavery. The exiles must act like the apostles of their crucified nation, be pure of heart, love one another, and dedicate themselves to freedom. "Only then shall the nations be saved through the merits of the martyred nation."[24] Poland, reborn and purified by its torments, would lead the world in a spiritual revolution when all peoples will be united. Mickiewicz did not limit his messianic dream to his own land.

He urged a union of all Slavic peoples under the leadership of Poland. "The Slavic people," he wrote, "despite its misery and its poverty, is the most powerful instrument that God has destined for the achievement of good on earth in the future."[25]

A Russian who knew the youthful Mickiewicz during his years in Russia remembered him as "exquisitely courteous" in manner, having an attractive personality, and being at ease everywhere. Nine years later, when the French historian Michelet met him, he thought him "rather wild looking owing to the abundance of beard and hair" and with an abrupt and jerky manner of speaking. He was prematurely aged, with a heavily lined face and grizzled hair. Herzen, who met him at a dinner meeting in Paris in 1848, wrote that his face, with his weary eyes, "was suggestive of unhappiness endured, of acquaintance with spiritual pain, of the exaltation of sorrow—he was the molded likeness of the fate of Poland."[26]

In 1834 Mickiewicz married. At first all went well, but soon he was burdened by a household of six children, born in successive years, and by his wife's periodic spells of insanity, which required stays in asylums. His income from his writings was inadequate to meet his needs, and he had to depend upon gifts from friends and a pension of 1,000 francs a year from the French government, granted at the urging of Prince Adam Czartoryski, leader of the aristocrats among the Polish exiles. In 1830 the University of Lausanne appointed him as professor of literature. He spent sixteen happy months there, during which he wrote a cycle of lyric poems which proved to be his last creative writing. He tried to write more poems and plays, without success. Poland's greatest poet was not yet forty when his literary creativity ended.

In 1840 he left Lausanne to return to Paris. The French government had established a chair of Slavonic literature at the Collège de France and offered it to Mickiewicz as the premier poet of the Slavic world. Instead of talking about literature, he used his lectures to preach Polish messianism, to promote Pan-Slavism, and to criticize Western bourgeois society and the institution of the Catholic Church, though he counted himself a devout Catholic. The tone and virulence of his attacks persuaded the government in 1844 to dismiss him from his chair, though it continued to pay him half of his salary until the early 1850s.[27]

Mickiewicz owed the fervor and fanaticism of his lectures to a mystic named Andrzei Towianski, whom he met in 1841. Towianski reportedly established his ascendancy over Mickiewicz by curing his wife of her insanity. The mystic heralded himself as God's chosen instrument to save Poland and the world. Mickiewicz joined the circle of Towianski's disciples and took over its leadership when the French government, suspecting Towianski of being a

Russian agent, deported him. Mickiewicz's allegiance to Towianski's mysticism served to aggravate the divisiveness that plagued the exile movement, to strip Mickiewicz of his role as moral leader of the emigration, and to embitter him. In 1847 a longtime friend wrote of Mickiewicz that "he has become so petrified in sectarianism that no trace remains of the hearty, genial Adam of former times."[28]

Petrified sectarian though he may have become, Mickiewicz never abandoned his dream. When revolution broke out in Italy, he organized a legion of Polish émigrés to fight with the Italian revolutionaries against Austria. When the revolution collapsed, the legion, which never had more than 250 men, was disarmed and dispersed. Mickiewicz returned to Paris, where he worked in a library and edited a short-lived socialist newspaper. In 1854, when the Crimean War pitted Britain, France, and Turkey against Russia, Mickiewicz, like many other Poles, thought that liberation was at hand. In September 1855 he went to Constantinople, ostensibly on a mission for the French Ministry of Public Instruction. He hoped again to organize a Polish legion to fight against the hated Russians. Instead, in scarcely more than a month after his arrival, he lay dead, a victim of cholera.[29]

In 1834, in a letter to his mother, Giuseppe Mazzini called Mickiewicz "the greatest poet of our time." That was high praise, indeed, when Europe resounded to the poetry of giants like Pushkin, Heine, and Wordsworth, to name only three whom others might consider at least the equal of Mickiewicz. In time, Mazzini himself was to receive equally hyperbolic praise. One of his contemporaries recalled him as "the greatest man of the nineteenth century," and a noted modern historian wrote that he was "the most influential revolutionary of his century." Alexander Herzen provided a more temperate judgment when he wrote of Mazzini that, "in his ceaseless devotion to Italian freedom, in this faith which goes forward in defiance of facts, in the inexhaustible activity which failure only challenges and provokes, there is something of grandeur, and if you like, something of madness."[30]

The first stirrings of modern Italian nationalism occurred in the eighteenth century, when some educated Italians began to speak of their homeland as Italy instead of Tuscany or Venetia or Romagna, or some other part of the peninsula. The French Revolution and Napoleon stirred nationalistic fervor, but the illusion of unity that Napoleon created with his kingdom of Italy was short-lived. The victorious allies recreated a divided Italy. Lombardy and Venetia became parts of the Austrian empire. Bourbons or Habsburgs, under the protection of Austria, ruled in the duchies of Modena, Parma, and Lucca, in the Grand Duchy of Tuscany, and in the Kingdom of the Two Sicilies, whose capital was Naples.

The oppression of the restored reactionary regimes stifled liberal and nationalistic sentiments. Daring and fanatical radicals, drawn from all strata of society, formed secret revolutionary societies, of whom the best known called itself the *Carbonari*, the Charcoal Burners. These groups instigated unsuccessful risings in the twenties and thirties, aimed at the overthrow of existing governments and the attainment of vague dreams of liberty. Their failures transformed their movement into a liberal nationalism with the goal of a united, independent Italy. Three different approaches were proposed to attain that goal. Vicenzo Gioberti (1801–1852), a Catholic priest, advocated a federation of Italian states under the leadership of the pope. A second approach, championed by middle-class and noble Piedmontese, above all by Count Camillo di Cavour (1810–1861), looked to the Kingdom of Sardinia, the only truly independent state in Italy, to unify the country as a constitutional monarchy. Mazzini was the prophet of the third approach. He wanted a centralized democratic republic, to be achieved by a simultaneous mass uprising against all the existing governments.

Mazzini, born in Genoa in 1805, was the son of a successful physician and an intelligent and politically aware mother. He remained deeply attached to his mother, and made her his chief confidante in an unending stream of letters he wrote to her until her death in 1852. A nervous and intense child and youth, he read omnivorously and was reckoned as something of a prodigy. He early became a partisan of democracy and Italian unity. At fifteen, he became so obsessed with the brutal suppression of a Carbonari-led revolt in Turin that his mother feared he might commit suicide. Instead, in a typically Romantic gesture, he dressed himself in black in mourning for Italy. He kept to the wearing of black for the rest of his life.

He graduated in 1827 from the University of Genoa with a degree in law but practiced for only two years. His thoughts and his consuming interest centered always on plans for democracy, republicanism, and the unification of Italy. He recognized that the repressive regimes that ruled Italy made open activity to reach these goals impossible. The only alternative was conspiracy, the course he decided he must follow. Follow it he did, without interruption, from the age of twenty-two until his death forty-five years later. His was a life of assumed names, messages in code, false addresses, mail drops, clandestine meetings, underground networks, spies and informers, and always a stream of proclamations and manifestos. One can question the judgment that he was the greatest man of his century or its most influential revolutionary, but he certainly was his century's greatest conspirator.

He took his first step in 1827 when he joined the Carbonari. In 1830 the Genoese police, suspecting him of membership, arrested him. After a brief jailing, the government offered him the choice of rustication in an inland village far removed from any opportunity to conspire, or of leaving Italy. He opted for the latter. He chose a lifetime of exile and poverty so that he could carry on his chosen calling of conspirator. He lived in France and Switzerland until 1837 when he came to London. He made his home there almost to the end of his life. He made brief visits to Italy, usually clandestinely. As he confessed in a letter to George Sand in 1848, when he was there he never ceased to feel himself an exile.[31]

Not one of his conspiracies succeeded, but that did not daunt him. Ludwig Bamberger, himself a refugee from the 1848 revolutions in Germany, met Mazzini in London in 1849. "The slight, insignificant looking man," he wrote, "betrayed only through his fiery and flashing eyes the indefatigable conspirator that was imbedded in him. He was a true believer who moved mountains to reach his goal." Though Mazzini had only recently returned to London from Milan and Rome, where he took part in revolutionary actions that were crushed, he went on at great length to Bamberger about the next revolution in Italy. "In his head," Bamberger recalled, "everything was prepared down to the last detail."[32]

Mazzini sought not only the liberation and unification of his beloved Italy. He wanted all mankind to enjoy the blessings of freedom, equality, and national unification. "Humanity," he wrote, "is a collective and continuous Being, in which is epitomized the whole ascending series of organic creation, and in which, as the sole interpreter of the law, is most fully manifested God's thoughts on earth." True Romantic that he was, he rejected the rationalism and individualism of the Enlightenment in favor of an ethos of brotherly love and selflessness. He faulted the French Revolution's *Declaration of the Rights of Man* because it spoke to man's individualism and not to mankind's collective well-being. He replaced the Rights of Man with the Duties of Man, by which he meant men's obligation to become apostles of the brotherhood of man and of the unity of the human race. Man had the obligation to dedicate himself, and if need be to welcome sacrifice and martyrdom, for the welfare and the improvement of all humanity.[33]

But man alone, without the collective force of the millions with whom he shared the same language, customs, and culture, could contribute little or nothing to the enhancement of humanity. The nations into which God had divided all men provided the indispensable vehicle by which the individual could serve mankind. Nations, said Mazzini, are the citizens of humanity, as individuals are the citizens of nations. Without the nation there can be no humanity. Just as every individual should contribute to the power and prosperity of his nation according to his special capacity, so should every nation according to its special capacity contribute to the progress and prosperity of humanity. Humanity is the association of nations, joined in what Mazzini called the Holy Alliance of the Peoples. Before this messianic vision could be realized, each nation had to have an independent existence.[34]

Geography and history, wrote Mazzini, had marked out the boundaries of each nation, and no territory whose people spoke the national language should be separated from the nation. God has assigned each nation a task to fulfill for the progress of mankind. Italy united would have the supreme mission of leading mankind to moral unity and the realization of the brotherhood of nations. To Mazzini, the republic was the ideal commonwealth, where sovereignty belonged to the people, where caste and privilege were unknown save for merit and virtue, and where education, available to all, opened the door to advancement.[35]

Violence would seem alien to Mazzini, who spoke so often of peace and brotherhood. Yet the resort to violence had a principal place in his thinking and plans. The paradox of simultaneously advocating violence and the brotherhood of man did not disturb him. In his eyes, they were the two sides of the same coin. The Italians and the other "enslaved nations" must resort to force to gain their freedom. If one rebellion fails, they must continue to rebel, even for a thousand times, without becoming discouraged. In a letter to a friend, he called for "war to the knife" and wrote that "in our proclamations, our discourses, and above all in our deeds, we ought to inculcate the Italian hatred of the Teuton" by whom he meant the Austrians who dominated Italy.[36]

As mentioned earlier, in 1831 Mazzini founded Young Italy, the first of the many revolutionary conspiracies that he fathered. Members had to be under forty, had to arm themselves with a musket, fifty cartridges, and a dagger, and had to be ready to use their weapons when the signal came for a rising. He ordered all members of Young Italy to spread the principles of insurrection. Their organization would teach the public "that war is inevitable—desperate and determined war that knows no truce save in victory or the grave."[37] From a one-room headquarters in Marseilles, he and his associates poured out a steady stream of letters and propaganda sent into Italy. By 1833 Mazzini claimed a membership of fifty to sixty thousand scattered through the peninsula. That same year the French government, pressed by Italian rulers, expelled Mazzini. He went to Switzerland, where he organized an invasion by Young Italy of neighboring Savoy, part of the Kingdom of Sardinia. He planned to march in with a force of 800, but only 225 reached their destination. After a brief skirmish, the invaders retreated back to Switzerland. This embarrassing fiasco wrote a finis, for all practical purposes, to Young Italy. Its membership dwindled away though Mazzini and a few of his followers tried to keep the organization alive.

The failure of Young Italy did not discourage Mazzini. Foiled in his conspiracy against the tyrants of Italy, he decided to conspire against the tyrants of all Europe in what he called "the holy war of the oppressed." So he formed a new organization that he named Young Europe. On April 15, 1834, in Berne, seven Italians, five Germans, and five Poles signed an "Act of Brotherhood." That did not dissuade Mazzini from announcing that Young Europe "is a vast association of men from all countries who acknowledge one banner, that of the human fraternity, the solidarity of all suppressed, the alliance against the oppressors whoever and wherever they might be." In the succeeding two years, branches of Young Europe established themselves in Italy, Poland, Germany, Switzerland, and France. Disputes among the various national groups reduced Young Europe to ineffectiveness. Nonetheless, rumors of planned risings and invasions, reported by spies and *agents provocateurs*, alarmed governments. Diplomatic pressure from abroad persuaded the Swiss, in 1836, to round up and expel the members of Young Europe, bringing to an end its brief career.[38]

Mazzini undoubtedly owed his influence as much to his personal qualities as he did to his doctrines. From all accounts, he had a truly magnetic personality, possessed an enormous sympathetic nature, and had great compassion for the less fortunate. He had a sense of humor, was an excellent conversationalist and raconteur, and enjoyed companionship. He had a wide range of interests, especially in literature, art, and music; as one admirer put it, there was always something to be learned from him. His dedication, his gentle and gracious manner, and the nobility of his character won him the devotion and even the love of his friends, including those who disagreed with his views.[39]

Small and slight of build, with dark, flashing eyes and a pale olive complexion, he had been noted as a young man for his gracefulness and beauty. An Italian who met him in Marseilles called him "the most beautiful being, male or female, that I have ever seen." When Alexander Herzen met him in 1849, he found that Mazzini's features showed the effects of anxieties and disappointments. Yet, wrote Herzen, "even in Italy a head so severely classical, so elegant in its gravity, is rarely to be met with." Ill health plagued him all of his life, yet he refused to take medicines and claimed curative powers for the cigars that he constantly smoked. He had frequent nightmares, often hallucinated, and sometimes imagined that he heard voices calling to him. Sheer will kept him going, though in later years he wasted away until he was almost a skeleton.[40]

Despite the charm and the graciousness, Mazzini was not an easy person to get along with. Even in matters of small consequence, he exhibited what an English friend, the literary critic David Masson, charitably called "tenacity." In discussions of more serious matters, and especially those touching on politics, he was dogmatic and intolerant. His political views were to him articles of faith that admitted no questioning. He equated contrary opinions with immorality, and he measured the shortcomings of others by the degree of their incongruence with his own views. He thought of himself as the true prophet and found it difficult to share credit or to subordinate himself to others.[41]

Yet beneath this external show of confidence in himself and in his opinions, there lay a gnawing self-doubt and even self-pity that he revealed over the years in letters to friends. "My life is a continual strife," he wrote in a letter of 1837. "A continued alternation between an overpowering dejection . . . and a tension of mind which I seek to maintain with all my power, by the help in my beliefs in duty, in life being a mission, and in self-denial . . . I despair of ever having a ray of happiness, and of ever being able to give a ray of happiness." In another letter he lamented that "there is a fatality about me; where I touch I do harm . . . and I shall end by dying alone, accused and tormented—you will see." At other times he called himself "a sort of wandering, accursed Cain," "a Nimrod all hands against me, and I against all" or a John Huss, burned at the stake by those who did not understand.[42]

Mazzini had his brief moment of glory when, in 1848, the Italian peninsula exploded into revolution. At long last, he could emerge from the shadow world of the conspirator into the real world of open revolution. In early April he arrived in Milan where, on March 8, the first Italian revolution had erupted. The people of Milan, who had risen against their Austrian overlords, greeted him with rapturous acclaim. For a time, he became almost the dictator of the revolutionary regime. The euphoria born of the revolution's initial success was doomed to quick extinction, and by early August the Austrians had reestablished their rule. Mazzini returned to his calling of conspirator, plotting new risings and going from city to city in Italy to stir up a "People's War." Then in February 1849, the Constituent Assembly of the newly proclaimed Roman Republic invited him to come to Rome. In late March the Assembly elected him as the leading member of the Triumvirate, the new republic's executive. Suddenly Mazzini had been transformed into the ruler of a sovereign state, albeit a state that had little chance of survival. The Catholic powers of Europe had vowed to restore Rome and the Papal States to the pope. At the end of April, a French Army laid siege to Rome. On July 1 the city surrendered, and two weeks later, Mazzini slipped out of Rome and made his way to Switzerland and then back to London.

From then on, in the twenty-three years left to him, it was all downhill. He once again became a conspirator, the only craft he knew. During the years from 1849 to 1861, when the Kingdom of Sardinia, under the leadership of its prime minister, Count Camillo di Cavour, successfully created a united Italian constitutional monarchy, Mazzini stubbornly persisted in his struggle for republicanism. He planned and inspired insurrections in one city after another, succeeding only in inviting increased oppression from the government. His supporters fell away from him. The world had changed, but Mazzini had refused to change with it. Like Mickiewicz, and like all other Romantic nationalists, he had outlived his time. He could find no place in a world in which realism had triumphed over idealism. He died in 1872 in Pisa, a fugitive in his own land, disguised as an English businessman named George Brown.[43]

Mazzini died a worn-out and broken old man, his dream of a united and democratic republic in Italy unfulfilled. Yet his life was not a failure. For years, most Italians had firmly believed that the unification of Italy, whether as monarchy or republic, was a puerile idea. Mazzini's unending agitation, his ceaseless propaganda, and his conspiracies prepared the Italian popular mind for unification. "It was Mazzini and Mazzini alone," wrote the famed historian Gaetano Salvemini, "who imposed upon the Italian liberal nationalist groups the one dominating idea [Italian unity] to which through all the vicissitudes of the making of Italy, everything else was to become subordinated."[44]

During the years that Mazzini and his fellow Romantic nationalists dreamed and talked of a happy humanity of free nations living in peace and cooperation with each other, a new and baleful kind of nationalism emerged. There was a gradual renunciation of the commitment of the Romantics to peace and to brotherhood among the nations. Instead, by the middle of the century, the sovereign state became the supreme value and the final goal of history; not the freedom and welfare of all nations. Instead of man's duty to become an apostle of the brotherhood of man, the individual was obligated only to his nation. The state had the right—indeed, the obligation—to fight against other nations, to exist at their expense, and to assert its power and its ethnic superiority over other peoples. Instead of the Romantic dream of organic unity, nationalism and national unification led to international disunity and to the exaltation of war as an instrument of national policy. Instead of love and brotherhood, hatreds, rivalries, and xenophobia became the common currency of relations among nations.[45]

People began to think in terms of national conquests and annexations. In 1840 nationalist fervor in France became so intense that an attack on the Prussian Rhineland seemed imminent and was only narrowly averted. No shots were fired, but the threat of war inspired a "Battle of the Rhine" between French and German poets over whether the Rhine was French or German. Heinrich Heine, an exile in France since 1831 but always an ardent German nationalist, spoke disparagingly of this poetic combat, explaining that he was a friend of France but opposed war with Prussia. Both the French and the Germans were "the chosen people of humanity," but he vowed, "I will never yield the Rhine to the French for the very simple reason that the Rhine belongs to me." Varnhagen von Ense preened himself on his liberalism and cosmopolitanism. Still, when he visited the Netherlands in 1836, he confided to his diary that he was convinced that Holland must one day become a part of Prussia. That seemed to him almost a necessity for Prussia and a stroke of good fortune for the Netherlands. "Dutch culture and prosperity would gain immeasurably," he wrote. "We really have a lot to bring to these people."[46]

These were but a few straws in the wind that told of the rise of chauvinism behind the facade of Romantic nationalism. When nationalist revolutions convulsed much of Europe in 1848, the facade remained in place for only a few short months. In the early days of the revolutions, the nationalities, who for centuries had lived cheek by jowl as neighbors, fraternized with one another in their enthusiasm for the new freedoms they thought they had won. That euphoria soon dissipated, replaced by dissent and, finally, force when hard questions such as the demarcation of frontiers, the establishment of independent states, the rights of minorities, and apportionment of representation in legislative bodies came under discussion. The Romantic ideal of each nation's recognizing the right of every other nationality to establish its own sovereign nation, with its own language and culture, collapsed when the ideal ran up against reality. Instead, the majority in each nation did what it could to suppress the nationalistic ambitions of the minority peoples who lived among them. Romantic nationalism perished in the first few months of the 1848 revolutions, remembered only by a few lonely and anachronistic figures such as Mazzini and Mickiewicz.

In Germany the Romantic nationalists had long sympathized with the Polish yearning for independence. After the outbreak of revolution in Germany, the Pre-Parliament, which in April had preceded the summoning of the National Assembly in Frankfurt, declared the partitions of Poland a shameful injustice, adding that "the sacred duty of the German people [was] to do their utmost to achieve Poland's reconstruction." But when a Polish militia of some ten thousand men rallied in Posen, the Polish province taken by Prussia in the partition of 1772, the German minority there became mightily alarmed at the prospect of Polish domination. Fighting broke out and the Poles were soon routed. Posen was then split, with about two thirds of the province declared a German sphere that would be admitted to the German Confederation, sending twelve deputies to the Frankfurt Assembly. The arrangement set off a heated debate at the Parliament that ended with a fiery speech on July 24 by Wilhelm Jordan, a twenty-one-year-old leftist delegate from Berlin. Jordan began by asking, "Are half a million Germans to live under a German government and administration and form part of the great German fatherland, or are they to be relegated to the inferior position of naturalized foreigners subject to another nation less civilized than themselves and set adrift as aliens?" He called it "weak-kneed sentimentality" to restore Poland because of sympathy for its sad fate. Germany's right to Posen, he declared, "is none other than the right of the strong, the right of conquest." The conviction grew among the delegates that unless a nation put its own self-interest above moral considerations, it forfeited the right to exist. The historian F. C. Dahlmann, prominent liberal member of the Assembly, wrote, "Men are right when they dissuade nations from the cult of unlimited humanism."[47] The new hard line was made clear in the controversy over the Danish provinces of Schleswig and Holstein. The National Assembly voted to annex these provinces, populated largely by Germans. War broke out and Denmark was saved from defeat by the intervention of Russia, Britain, and France. That outraged most Germans, among them no less a supposed enemy of nationalism then Friedrich Engels. To Marxists, nationalism was a bourgeois device to distract workers from social issues. Nonetheless, in an article in the *Neue Rheinische Zeitung* of September 16, 1848, Engels declared that Schleswig belonged to Germany "by the right of civilization against barbarism, of progress against static stability."[48]

In Bohemia, Czechs and liberal Germans had rejoiced together when news came of the March revolution in Vienna. Before the month passed, the togetherness had ended when the Czechs proposed to Vienna a self-governing union of the provinces of Bohemia, Moravia, and Austrian Silesia. That would have meant Czech rule over the German minority. That was entirely unacceptable to the Germans. They insisted that Bohemia must become part of Germany, a proposal equally unacceptable to the Czechs. The Magyars wanted to establish an independent Hungary, but they refused to grant the Croats, Serbs, Slovaks, and Romanians who lived in Hungary the same freedoms they demanded for themselves. The Viennese who rebelled against the rule of the Habsburgs enthusiastically supported the Habsburgs' repression of their rebellious Italian subjects.

The revolutions of 1848 not only marked the triumph of chauvinistic nationalism over the Romantic variety but also revealed that the traditional regimes and the forces of reaction had far greater strength than the nationalists had anticipated. They realized that they needed power, backed by military might, to achieve their goal of national unity. In an address in the National Assembly in January 1849, Professor Dahlmann declared that the desire for liberty was not limited to liberty alone. "It thirsts much more for power," he said, "which so far has not been granted. Germany must at last become one of the great political powers of the European continent." The Romantic insistence upon freedom and the equality of all nations gave way to the conviction that nationality was more important than liberty.[49] Chauvinistic nationalism deepened national hatreds, filled men's minds with dreams of conquest, and bred opposition, discontent, and strife among rival peoples. Wars became semireligious crusades, conflicts between good and evil, instead of what they actually were—struggles for power and domination and the exaltation of national self-interest. Nations followed the policy called *Realpolitik*, "power politics," the hardheaded politics of expediency based on selfish national interests as distinct from moral objectives. Political morality bore no relation to private morality. Count Camillo di Cavour, the architect of Italian unification, recognized this when he said, "If we did for ourselves what we are doing for Italy, we should be great knaves."[50]

Only a few voices were heard warning of the perils of the new virus that was infecting Europe. In 1849 John Stuart Mill, in an article in the *Westminster Review* on the revolutions of 1848, condemned "the feelings which make men reckless of, or at least indifferent to, the rights and interests of any portion of the human species, save that which is called by the same name as themselves. . . . These feelings are characteristic of barbarians. . . . In the backward parts of Europe, and even (where better things might have been expected) in Germany, the sentiment of nationality so far outweighs the love of liberty, that the people are willing to abet their rulers in crushing the liberty and independence of any people not of their race or language." Nassau Senior in 1850, like Mill, identified nationalism with barbarism, and labeled it the curse of Europe.[51]

It was a short and easy step from chauvinistic nationalism to another pernicious modern ideology, racism. The roots of racism trace back to earlier centuries, but in the nineteenth century, thinking about race and about racial superiority became a widespread phenomenon that went hand in hand with chauvinistic nationalism. Like chauvinistic nationalism, racism emerged gradually and became prominent only in the second half of the nineteenth century. The Romantic conviction that God had entrusted each nation with a divine mission easily translated itself, as we have seen, into claims of a nation's superior mission and hence of its racial superiority. Nationalists like Fichte and Arndt wrote of the superiority of Germans over other peoples because they wanted to appeal to German pride and awaken the desire for national unification. In succeeding decades, others stressed the theme of racial superiority, as, for example, when Franz Schuselka, in a book in 1845, called the Germans the greatest and noblest of all people and identified Germany as the world's most important nation.

In England some writers in the eighteenth century expressed the belief that their constitutional system and their liberties owed their origins to their Germanic Anglo-Saxon ancestors. In the nineteenth century, the theory of the supposed Anglo-Saxon origins of English liberties won increasing numbers of adherents. By the 1840s they gained the name of Germanists or Teutonists. (An unfriendly critic later dubbed them Teutomaniacs.) They believed that the Anglo-Saxon invaders of Britain in the sixth century were a superior race who towered over the indigenous Celts. The invaders brought with them the primitive institutions of their Germanic homeland. To the Teutonists, the basic structure of the English nation—its laws, its parliament, the freedom of the individual—all were legacies from the Anglo-Saxon conquerors. Only the English were the true heirs of the freedom-loving Teutonic legacy. As time went on, the racism became more explicit and more sweeping. Charles Kingsley, cleric, professor of history, author of the beloved *Water Babies*, and racist, told an audience at the University of Cambridge that the Anglo-Saxon conquerors had been "the hosts of God" and that the "welfare of the Teutonic race is the welfare of the world."[52]

In France history was seen as a conflict between two races, the Franks and the Gauls. The Franks, a Germanic people, had conquered the indigenous Gauls and became the ruling class, the nobility of France. In the eighteenth century, spokesmen of the nobility had defended their privileged status by claiming descent from the Frankish conquerors. The theory took on new life in the first half of the nineteenth century, when the defenders of the Gauls went on the attack. The historians Guizot and Thierry also saw the Revolution as war between the Frankish rulers and the Gallic common people. To Guizot, the Revolution of 1830, which established the bourgeoisie as France's ruling class, confirmed that France owed its greatness to the Gallic race. But the debate did not end. In 1853 Count Joseph Arthur de Gobineau published his *Essai sur l'inégalité des races humaines*. Gobineau took up the cudgels for the Franks but transformed the thesis of Frankish superiority into a general theory of race. He created a racial hierarchy with whites of pure "Aryan" blood at the summit, the "race of masters" who merited their position as the elite. The rest of the white race followed them, then the yellow, and then the black race. In Gobineau's view, races have unfortunately constantly mixed with resulting degeneration. Miscegenation lowered the level of the superior race to the level of the less gifted race. That happened in France with the mixing of superior Frank and inferior Gaul, and that was happening everywhere.[53]

Europeans awakened on the morrow of the revolutions of 1848 sadder, wiser, less sanguine, and less idealistic. They abandoned their visions of freedom and liberalism and peace for a new *Weltanschauung* that came to be known as Realism, which became the prevailing intellectual temper of the second half of the nineteenth century. Like Romanticism, Realism was a broad and vague term that defies precise definition. Critics first used the term in 1850 to describe paintings by Gustave Courbet, who took scenes from everyday life and painted them without idealizing them and without telling a story. The term Realism quickly spread to literature and then to other parts of life, including politics and statecraft.

Realism placed its highest value upon action, power, success, and material progress. It glorified struggle and conflict and cared nothing for sentimentality, scoffed at Romanticism and idealism, and scorned mysticism and the supernatural. The firmness with which the conservative powers suppressed the revolutions of 1848, and the success of *Realpolitik* in unifying Italy and Germany, seemed to justify Realism in the world of practical statecraft. The advances in the physical and biological sciences and in technology, along with widespread economic growth and improvements in living standards, persuaded increasing numbers to approve of Realism's emphasis upon objectivity and materialism.

Revolutionary nationalism was made to realize its impotence and vulnerability. In Germany revolution lost its reason for being when Bismarck demonstrated the compatibility of nationalism, till now a liberal cause, with conservatism. He used the appeals of nationalism to legitimize the autocratic rule of the Hohenzollerns over a united Germany and to legitimize the persistence of the traditional social order.[54] In Italy the practical and hardheaded Camillo di Cavour succeeded in creating a unified Italian state. He set out with the goal of driving Habsburg rule out of Italy. Despite grave setbacks, which included the withdrawal of the French, he somehow managed to emerge victorious. On March 17, 1861, the first Italian parliament in history proclaimed the Kingdom of Italy with Victor Emmanuel, the ruler of Sardinia, as its king.

As if life were imitating art, Europe's novelists, poets, and artists foreshadowed the transition from Romanticism to Realism. Romanticism, of course, did not end abruptly at some fixed date. But by the 1840s, it had become clear that Romanticism no longer dominated European intellectual life. The changes that were transforming European life and culture made Romanticism passé. A new generation of novelists, who became known as Realists, or writers of the natural school, rebelled against the sentimentality, the exaggerated language, the heroic figures, the exotic settings and the idealism of the Romantics. George Sand had spoken for her fellow Romantics when she wrote in 1846 that "the mission of art is a mission of sentiment and love. . . . Art is not a study of positive reality; it is a search for the ideal truth." The Realists emphatically rejected that concept of art. The Realists wanted to describe life as it really was, to portray truthfully and accurately the actions and ambitions, the strivings and the disappointments, the kindnesses and the brutalities, the triumphs and the tragedies of everyday life. To achieve these aims, they wrote about commonplace people and commonplace events, and they did not shy away from the repugnant or the distressing. To reinforce their representations of reality, they included contemporary events and institutions and economic happenings and locales about which their readers knew. They believed that banal lives of ordinary people revealed the grain or the substance of what life is really like. They avoided romanticization and shunned both pathos and patronization. As a Realist of a later generation put it, they presented people without makeup. In a report of February 23, 1848, to Tsar Nicholas of Russia about two literary journals, the head of the Third Section, the tsar's powerful investigatory agency, wrote that the journals' contributors "attempt to portray nature and people as they are, without any ornamentation or exaggerations, therefore calling themselves writers of the *natural school:* and they express themselves with contempt concerning all former or contemporary writers who have described or who now describe subjects more ideal than those existing in nature."[55]

To lend verisimilitude to their novels, they paid close attention to the milieu in which the story unfolded. They painstakingly described the setting of the novel and the minutiae of the lives of their characters that seemed peripheral to the plot. Yet these details were of vital importance in providing the reader with the sense of authenticity and the sense of place that set the tone of the novel. The novelists thought of themselves as objective, impersonal, and careful reporters and analysts of contemporary life and manners: "as the secretary recording the history of a society," to quote Balzac, the master Realist of them all. They wanted to present a cross-section of contemporary life. Balzac explained that there were as many varieties of humans as there were of animals. Buffon, the great eighteenth-century naturalist, had sought to include the whole of the animal world in the forty-four volumes of his *Histoire naturelle*. Balzac wanted to do the same thing in the forty-six volumes of his *La comédie humaine*. Being mere mortals, however, the Realists could not free themselves of all subjectivity and didacticism. Their writings bore a message, whether reformist or radical, whether revulsion for the new commercial-industrial society or nostalgia for the traditional ways that had only so recently vanished, whether pity for the exploited or outrage at the oppressor.

Many authors could lay claim to the name of Realist. To mirror reality, however, was not enough. The great figures of Realism, like all great artists, possessed the extra dimension of genius. And has there ever been a generation that counted so many giants, so many immortals? Balzac, Dickens, Thackeray, the Brontës, Mrs. Gaskell, Flaubert, Dostoyevsky, Gogol, Goncharov, Turgenev—all of them born between 1811 and 1821, save for Balzac, born in 1799, and all of them lighting up the sky in the 1840s. Their genius endowed them with a vision to see and to understand far beyond the capacity possessed by the rest of mankind, and the power to capture the truth by weaving together reality and imagination. Even more remarkably, their gift gave them the power to transcend the spatial and temporal boundaries of their fiction and to provide the reader with revealing insights and new understanding of the human condition. Their books not only tell entrancing stories but are also invaluable sources for the social history of the period about which they wrote. Historians, economists, and sociologists, employing the methods of their respective crafts, can document the external manifestations, the facts and figures that they can dredge out of their sources. The novels of the great Realists go beneath and behind the external manifestations, the macrodimensions, as it were, to tell what life was like, what was changing and what was unchanged, and to provide an awareness of everyday existence.

The Realist style in literature spread swiftly from one end of Europe to the other. In earlier decades the writings of such Romantics as Walter Scott, George Sand, or Victor Hugo had been quickly translated into other languages and became enormously popular. Now translations of Balzac and others created a taste for Realism. Meanwhile, improvements in the printing press allowed an enormous expansion in the production of printed material.

As the decades went by, the reading public continued to grow. Reading rooms and lending libraries became common features of city life. Newspapers and periodicals proliferated, and all manner of books, and especially novels, poured from the presses. In Germany 4,012 titles had been offered for sale in 1800. In 1842 that number had risen to 14,309; the number of newspapers and periodicals rose from 780 in 1833 to 1,836 in 1846. The popularity of fiction skyrocketed when, in 1836, Émile de Girardin introduced the serialized novel in his new Parisian newspaper, *La Presse*. Serialization was an important feature of the revolution effected by Girardin in the newspaper business. Traditionally, newspapers had for their primary purpose the publicizing of a political or social point of view. Girardin's primary purpose was to make a profit. To do that, he had to attract readers of every opinion to buy his paper. He charged less than did the competition, he took no sides in political issues, and above all, he hit on the idea of running daily installments of a novel. The circulation of *La Presse* mounted, and other newspaper publishers quickly adopted his innovation.[57]

Readers waited impatiently for the next installment of the serial, and authors ground out chapter after chapter to meet press deadlines. Thackeray, Balzac, Dickens, Dostoyevsky, and other great figures, and lesser authors, too, published novels in parts, or fascicles, that appeared periodically and sold at a small price. The unquestioned kings of the serialized novels were the Frenchmen Alexandre Dumas and Eugène Sue. These two men churned out installment after installment, seemingly without effort, developing the plot as they went along. Dumas (1802–1870), who had many collaborators, produced a torrent of novels, plays, travel books, historical studies, and memoirs. When Sue's *Les Mystères de Paris* appeared serially in Paris's *Journal des Débats* in 1842 and 1843, queues of people of all classes formed outside of the newspaper's plant, waiting to buy the next installment as soon as the paper came off the press.[58]

To the modern reader, Sue's book seems a potboiler with a plot full of improbable coincidences, written to shock its readers with its sensationalism. The book started as a tale of the Paris underworld, but as the installments moved on, Sue, an avowed socialist, added a humanitarian and socialistic message that told of the sufferings of the masses and the evils of wealth. The enormous popularity of the book inspired many foreign imitations. In some thirty-six German cities similar mysteries appeared, including two *Mysteries of Berlin*, one in four volumes and the other in twelve, and there were mysteries of Vienna, Amsterdam, and St. Petersburg.[59]

Most of the literary Realists came from the middle class, but with the notable exception of some German authors, they were harshly critical of materialistic bourgeois values. In their novels men of business often appear as avaricious, narrow-minded hypocrites deserving only of contempt. Dickens was especially unrelenting in his strictures, peopling his novels with vicious characters such as Uriah Heep, Ralph Nickleby, Mr. Dombey, Jonas Chuzzlewit, Josiah Bounderby, and a host of lesser men of the same stripe. Balzac was even more relentless than Dickens in flaying the bourgeoisie, but unlike Dickens, Balzac (who added "de" to his name) admired aristocratic society and identified with it. His novels lament the triumphant advances of the vulgar materialistic world of the capitalists at the expense of the social elite. His villains, who include dishonest financiers, conniving industrialists, misers, and usurers, are heartless manipulators with an insatiable greed for money and power.

Many Realists addressed themselves to the exposure of the ills of their societies in the hope of persuading their readers of the need for reform. No one among them seemed more committed to this than Charles Dickens. In novel after novel he told of the unequal treatment accorded to the rich and the poor, and of the abuses and iniquities of England's legal and penal systems. In his zeal he tended often to exaggerate, so that characters in his stories often seem more caricatures than real people. But the moral of his tales came through clearly: the government and the ruling class were obligated to assume responsibility for the well-being of the less fortunate of society. This was the same benevolent paternalism that inspired the new philanthropic movement and the beginnings of the welfare state, discussed in the preceding chapter. The common people lacked the ability and the knowledge to improve their conditions. They had to be led by their social superiors.

Some writers warned of worker revolt. Mrs. Gaskell had firsthand knowledge of the sufferings and discontents of the factory workers of Manchester, where she made her home. In the preface to *Mary Barton*, her powerful novel of working-class life that appeared in 1845, she told of the bitter complaints of the workers about their employers, and of the sufferings and frustrations they had to bear. Some advocated socialistic solutions. Eugène Sue attacked the inheritance of wealth, supported the organization of labor, and advocated insurrection as a remedy for society's injustices. Other novelists, too, such as Frédéric Soulie and Émile Souvestre in France and Luise Otto, Georg Weerth, and Ernst Willkomen in Germany carried the message of social revolution. They apotheosized the proletariat in contrast to the decadent nobility and the corrupt bourgeoisie, who deserved only to be overthrown. In Russia writers of the natural school, alienated by the repression and corruption of their society, wanted to bring about a new era of justice and civil equality for all of their countrymen.

The impact of the Realists' novels of social protest can only be a matter of conjecture. Clearly, reform movements did not originate with these novels. Their authors took up causes that already had constituencies. Nonetheless, the novels must have served as an effective means of making their readers aware, and possibly even convincing them, of the need for reform. At least some contemporaries thought so.[60] Other contemporaries allowed that the novels of social protest had influence, but acknowledged this grudgingly and with a decidedly jaundiced eye. In a letter of 1845 to Sir Robert Peel, Thomas Hood warned of the dangers of a literary movement (of which he himself as author of the "Song of the Shirt" and "The Bridge of Sighs" had contributed) that aggravated "the existing repulsion between classes" and made wider the "moral gulf between the rich and the poor, with hate on one side and fear on the other." Harriet Martineau called the characters in Dickens's novels "profoundly unreal" and said that they gave foreigners a mistaken idea of English life. The historian and superpatriot Jules Michelet had the same criticism of French Realists. He complained that they painted France and its people in too dark colors. Because of their skill as writers, the world accepted their books as a true picture of France and the French. He took special aim at Balzac's *The Peasantry,* which he condemned as a slanderous attack "against the People and democracy." Balzac himself had harsh words to say of the novelists of social protest, but for reasons antithetical to those of Michelet. In the preface to *The Peasantry,* he spoke of "an attack of democratic vertigo to which so many blind scribes have fallen victim. . . . We behold something like an apotheosis of the proletariat. Sects have risen among us, every pen among them swells the chorus of 'Workers arise' even as once the Third Estate was bidden to rise."

Sometimes the reproaches were *ad hominem.* Harriet Martineau charged that Dickens was ignorant about the facts of economic life and so should not have attempted to write about them. The Baden diplomat Franz von Andlaw expressed an opinion of Eugène Sue that was doubtless shared by many of his fellow noblemen. He accurately described Sue as a sybarite who affected an aristocratic style of life. Yet, wrote Andlaw, in his novels, he could not find sighs and tears enough to lament the fate of the working class and to stir it up against the higher ranks of society. Nor did Sue escape criticism from the opposite pole. In 1845 Marx and Engels wrote *The Holy Family*, a diatribe against the Left Hegelians, who were led by Bruno Bauer. Marx went to great lengths to assail a favorable review of *The Mysteries of Paris* that had appeared in Bauer's journal and to denounce the book and Sue himself. He mocked the philosophical profundity of the review, and instead of viewing the book's hero as a benevolent reformer, Marx saw him as a hypocrite and the advocate of social theories that would not work.[61]

Not all of the Realists did battle with the social ills that beset their societies. Instead, they wrote novels of manners and morals. The stories of authors like Balzac and Thackeray, to name the two greatest masters of this genre, told of the vices and affectations and arrogance of the characters who people their pages. Their novels had neither resolute heroes nor melodramatic villains, nor did they have sentimental scenes that played upon the heart strings. Balzac, in the foreword to his collected works, wrote, "I thought I might succeed in writing the history of human manners that has been forgotten by so many historians." He explained that he wanted to write the social history of the France of his time "by assembling the principal facts about passions, by portraying character, by selecting the chief happenings of social life, by creating typical characters through combining the traits of homogeneous characteristics. . . . " In short, he sought to describe what might be called the physiology of French society.[62]

Thackeray, like Balzac, wrote of the effect upon people of their social environment. David Masson pointed out that Thackeray showed people in their customary surroundings "with that mixture of good and evil, and of strength and foibles which is to be found in their characters, and liable only to those incidents which are of ordinary occurrence. He will have no faultless characters, no demigods—nothing but men and brethren." Thackeray took special aim at the snobbery among classes that marked and marred English life, and at the unending struggle of middle-class social climbers to become accepted as members of the social elite. In a letter of March 1848, Thackeray said of Becky Sharp, who epitomized that world of follies and abominations that John Bunyan called Vanity Fair, that "it was only a question of money and fortune which made the difference between her and an honest woman. If Becky had 5,000 a year, I have no doubt that she would have been respectable, increased her fortune, advanced her family in the world, laid up treasures for herself in the shape of 3 per cents, social position, reputation, etc."[63]

Only thirty years separated crafty and scheming Becky Sharp of Thackeray's *Vanity Fair* from sheltered and gentle Lucy Ashton of Scott's *The Bride of Lammermoor*, but they inhabited worlds apart—the world of Romanticism and the world of Realism. Melodrama that included apparitions, ancient prophecies, and noble heroes surrounded the life and the tragic death of poor Lucy. Becky, cynical and wise in the ways of the world, wound up as a wealthy widow who busied herself in works of piety and who always had stalls in fairs for the benefit of the destitute and the distressed. This transformation of fictional heroines had its parallel in the movement during the 1840s from Romanticism to Realism, and from Romantic nationalism to chauvinism. "Nationalism," as one historian put it, "begins as Sleeping Beauty and ends as Frankenstein's monster."[64]

CHAPTER FOUR

The World of Learning

For half a century, Alexander von Humboldt was the world's most acclaimed scientist. In the early 1800s, when he was in his thirties and living in Paris, it was said that after Napoleon, he was the most famous man in the Empire. Some years later Napoleon, who disliked Humboldt, suspected him of being a Prussian spy and ordered him expelled from Paris—whereupon J. A. Chaptal, one of France's leading scientists and Napoleon's Minister of the Interior, persuaded the emperor that he was making a grave mistake. Humboldt was too valuable an asset to lose. He was so knowledgeable, said Chaptal, that "when he travels, it is like an entire Academy of Sciences on tour." Many years later in a letter to a friend, Charles Darwin wrote, "I shall never forget that my whole course of life is due to having read and re-read as a youth [Humboldt's] *Personal Narrative*." In 1852 Benjamin Silliman, Yale professor and leading American scientist, said that of all living men, Humboldt "belongs not so much to his country as to mankind [and] when he departs will leave no one who can fill his place." Everywhere he went, he met with a special consideration. The diaries and letters of his contemporaries resounded with his praises. Yet by the 1840s, science had passed him by. A new era had begun, an age of specialization and mathematization. Humboldt was the last universal savant. His kind of science had become obsolete.[1]

Humboldt was born in Prussia in 1769 into a recently ennobled family of landowners. He and his brother Wilhelm, older by two years, studied at the Universities of Frankfurt and Göttingen. Wilhelm was to gain fame as a philologist, educational reformer, and founder of the University of Berlin in 1809. Alexander developed an interest in science and in his twenties gained recognition for his studies of plant life, galvanism, and mineralogy. In 1796 his widowed mother died, and the sizable fortune that he inherited gave him the means to embark upon the great adventure that catapulted him to fame. In 1799 he and a friend, A. J. A. Bonpland, set off for Central and South America on a voyage of exploration and scientific investigation that lasted for five years. Traveling by foot, pack horse, canoe, and sail ship, and exposed to all manner of hardships and dangers, they journeyed through Venezuela, Colombia, Ecuador, Peru, Mexico, and Cuba. Equipped with a panoply of scientific instruments, they took notes and made measurements of everything animal, vegetable, and mineral that they encountered. They collected 60,000 plant specimens, 6,300 of them unknown in Europe. Humboldt measured the temperature of the Pacific current since known by his name. He drew up isothermic charts and he climbed mountains to study the relationship between temperature and altitude. His findings helped lay the foundations of the sciences of physical geography, meteorology, and cartography. In addition, he amassed exhaustive data on ethnography, linguistics, and history. It was an amazing record of accomplishment.

When Humboldt came back to Europe in 1804, he met with universal acclaim for the depth and breadth of his findings. He was hailed as "the scientific discoverer of America." He settled in Paris, then the scientific capital of the world, where he began to publish the journals of his travels. Between 1805 and 1834, he published thirty-four volumes, illustrated with handsome copper plates, dealing with zoology, astronomy, plant geography, botany, history, politics, and economics. In addition, he wrote a number of monographs drawn from his findings. These publications established his reputation as the master of all knowledge, a "modern Aristotle" as some called him, able to show the relationships between all learning.[2]

In 1827, after long and happy years in Paris, Humboldt returned reluctantly to Berlin. The costs of his travels and of his publications had bankrupted him. The generous pension offered him by Prussia's King Frederick William III, on condition that he live in Berlin, drew him eastward. His heart always remained in Paris, and he made an agreement with the king that each year he would spend four months in that city. Frederick William III used him as his cultural advisor and treated him as a friend. Then, in 1840, Frederick William IV, who had intellectual pretensions, came to the throne and converted Humboldt into a courtier. He required Humboldt's daily attendance at court and had rooms readied for him for overnight stays. Humboldt was unpopular with his fellow courtiers, who resented his liberal political views and his religious skepticism, and feared that he might deflect the king from his conservatism and religiosity. That never happened; the king simply enjoyed and was flattered by having the Great Man as his companion and engaging in intellectual discussions with him.[3]

Humboldt accepted his role as courtier with outward grace. Court life seemed to become a necessity to him, and reportedly he was resentful when left out of important matters and was said to envy those to whom the king turned for political advice. Praises of his royal master and of his deeds filled his letters to the king and to other members of the royal family. Inwardly, he seethed at the role imposed upon him by royal command. He complained that he had only the late hours of the night to study and write—fortunately he needed only three to four hours of sleep. He unburdened himself in conversations with and letters to his friend Varnhagen von Ense, who relished malicious gossip about those in high places. Humboldt spared no one, including the king, mocking, satirizing, and backbiting in a display of venom, pettiness, and ingratitude that revealed a dark and unexpected side of his character.[4]

On the other and far more important side of the ledger, Humboldt used his position and his influence to promote knowledge. Indeed, he made his most lasting contribution to science by his sponsorship and encouragement of young scientists. Through these efforts and his patronage, he played an important part in the rise of German science to world leadership, an ascent that began in the 1840s. He possessed the gift of being able to recognize talent in fields in which he had little or no expertise. Because of his great reputation, his recommendation of these gifted young men sufficed to win them university appointments. Young scientists turned to him as a father figure. As one of them, Émile Du Bois-Reymond, put it in 1849, "Every industrious and ambitious man of science is Humboldt's son; we are all his family." In an address in 1869, in observance of the centennial of Humboldt's birth, the famed geologist Louis Agassiz, another of Humboldt's protégés, recalled that "there was hardly a prominent or aspiring scientific man in the world who was not under obligation to him. His sympathy touched not only the work of those in which he was interested, but extended also to their material wants and embarrassments."[5]

Soon after his return to Prussia in 1827, Humboldt began to write a book that, as he put it, "would describe in one and the same work the whole material world" and that would be "instructive to the mind and at the same time be attractive by its vivid language." He decided to call the book *Cosmos* because it would encompass heaven and earth and every existing thing. The first two volumes appeared in 1845 and 1847, were enormously successful despite their labored and ponderous style, and were quickly translated into other languages. The fifth and last volume appeared soon after Humboldt's death in 1859. It was the last time anyone would try to bind all science together into a single integrated whole. The onrush of scientific knowledge had outdated the book before it was ever finished. Its critics pointed out its superficialities and its inadequacies, and Humboldt himself in his last years seemed to realize that the world of science had overtaken him.[6]

A new era in the history of science had begun. So much new was being uncovered that no one man could hope to master all science. The new kind of science first rooted itself in Germany in the 1840s. When Humboldt returned from America in 1804, he settled in Paris because it was the center of the scientific world of that day. In the years that followed, French scientific activity had declined and even stagnated. Joseph Henry, Princeton physicist and later first Secretary of the Smithsonian Institution, visiting Paris in 1837, found that the leading scientists there spent too much of their time in teaching (many of them held several teaching posts to augment their incomes) or in political activity or in posts in the civil service and not enough time in research. By 1850, when the young German physiologist Du Bois-Reymond visited Paris to lecture, he reported in a letter to a friend that "the ignorance and limited view of even the best men here is incredible."[7]

By that time Germany had become the undisputed leader of the scientific world. During the years of the French preeminence, there seemed little reason to expect that to happen. During the first forty years of the century, the most important sciences were poorly taught in Germany or were not taught at all. Germany did have some scientists of the first rank, but they were few in number. Typically they supported their own researches and rarely had an affiliation with a university. In the universities individual professors taught a mélange of subjects. Only a few professors had advanced degrees. In Prussia over half of the university professors taught at two or more institutions to increase their incomes. Not surprisingly they had little time and less interest in research and scholarly publications, nor was it expected of them. New fields of investigation opened up by scientists in other lands remained largely unknown in Germany.[8]

The largest part of the explanation for this disregard of scientific inquiry lay in the domination among German intellectuals of the doctrines of *Naturphilosophie*. This "philosophy of nature" sought for a single unifying principle for all of nature. Its adherents thought that they could discover God's hand in the universe and could demonstrate the process by which the

"Absolute Mind" achieved realization in the natural world. Limited almost exclusively to Germany, *Naturphilosophie* held a special attraction for intellectuals of that land; as a skeptical Englishman observed, they "loved those long and vague meditations on the attributes of the Deity." They believed that intuition and logic enabled them to comprehend natural phenomena without the methodology of science. They considered experiment and careful observation and measurement unnecessary interferences with nature. They viewed mathematical formulations of physical behavior as destructive of man's awe and wonder before the mysteries of the universe. In their philosophy science created a rift between man's emotions and his intellect. To add insult to injury, the humanists who dominated the universities and who were the stoutest defenders of *Naturphilosophie* scorned science as a utilitarian discipline. They thought that it corrupted its students, turning them toward materialism and away from the idealistic ends that they believed were the purpose of the university. Small wonder, then, that the teaching of science was only grudgingly accepted as a proper university discipline.[9]

Not all German scientists accepted this disparagement of their discipline. Individual scholars continued in their work in disregard of *Naturphilosophie*. Others, and above all Humboldt, actively opposed it. Humboldt had long protested against its doctrines, and lectures on physical geography that he gave at the University of Berlin in 1827 and 1828 proved the turning point. In these lectures he attacked *Naturphilosophie* and insisted that science must base itself upon patient observation, accurate experiment, and careful measurement. From then on the influence of *Naturphilosophie* waned as a new generation of scientists emerged. But many years were to pass before all scientists agreed to exclude providential implications as part of their findings.

The new generation became the prototypes of the modern scientist. Young men in their twenties and early thirties, their names still ring as great pioneers of their respective disciplines: names such as Hermann Helmholtz, equally famed in physics, physiology, pathology, and chemistry; Carl Ludwig, Émile Du Bois-Reymond, Ernst Brucke, and Theodor Schwann in physiology; Matthias Schleiden in botany; Rudolf Virchow in pathology; and the oldest of the lot, Justus Liebig, a chemist, who in 1840 was all of thirty-seven. These men, and others like them, had rebelled against the training they had received as students. Instead, they taught themselves, often learning mathematics and physics from French books. They rejected out of hand the speculations of *Naturphilosophie*.

A few had the good fortune to study at the University of Berlin's medical school in the 1830s and early 1840s with Johannes Müller, a great anatomist, physiologist, and teacher, who himself was in his thirties. Others were not that lucky. Carl Ludwig, famed physiologist, complained that in six years as a medical student at Marburg, Erlangen, and Bamberg, he never saw a distilling apparatus and had only seen a microscope from afar. At twenty-three, with a medical degree in hand, he realized that what he had learned was, as he put it, "inherently unfounded." He began to study the natural sciences on his own, eking out a living from minor academic posts. After a few years, "by means of untiring industry," as he explained, "I could make an organic analysis, manipulate the microscope and read Fischer's physics [a text published in France in 1797]." Justus Liebig remembered the chemistry lectures given by Professor W. G. Kastner at Bonn and Erlangen universities as illogical, disorganized, and a mélange of misinformation. Liebig cited examples of Kastner's explanation of natural phenomena, such as "the influence of the moon on rain is clear, because as soon as the moon becomes visible the rain stops." When Franz Neumann studied at the University of Jena, his zoology professor began his course by saying there were so many varieties of fish that he did not know how else to begin but by talking about the tastiest. His mineralogy professor told stories about his travels in Switzerland, and instruction in botany consisted of memorizing names and classifications.[10]

The young trailblazers broke away from the old methods and values of scientific inquiry. They created new standards, new techniques, and a new emphasis upon research, analysis, inductive reasoning, and a rejection of metaphysical concepts that became the model of the modern world of science. Within a few years their work and achievements became known, and in succeeding decades they attracted students to Germany from every part of the world. These students took the new kind of science with them when they returned to their homelands. Unlike the generalists of earlier generations, the new scientists became specialists in specific disciplines. Science in Germany, and ultimately in other lands, became a profession to which the scientists devoted all of their efforts and from which they earned their livelihoods. They published the results of their researches in newly established scholarly journals, and they formed professional societies for their disciplines.

New, too, was their full-time affiliation with universities. In earlier times scientists had usually been private scholars supported by their own wealth and working in their own laboratories and libraries. Now, young scientists won appointment to salaried university posts and worked their way up the academic ladder with commensurate increases in pay. For the first time a poor man could devote himself to a life of science, assured of financial security and provided with time and facilities for his researches. Scientists no longer worked in isolation. As professional men and university teachers, they formed a community of scholars. Each member of the community focused upon his own discipline, but each shared his knowledge with other members and so advanced the scientific knowledge of the entire community. The new scientists did much of their teaching in seminars that they introduced as a method of instruction, and in laboratories where they worked together with their students. The growth of universities and of research institutes affiliated with universities, first in Germany and later in other lands, and the always increasing importance of scientific research in industry, provided abundant employment opportunities to the young men who came out of their seminars and laboratories.[11]

The most striking of the differences between the new science and the old concerned the use of mathematics. The older generation believed that scientific knowledge depended upon empirical evidence and saw mathematical description as unnecessary. The new kind of scientists realized that ordinary language often failed to describe their findings about physical phenomena and the relationship of individual phenomena to one another. They turned to the language of mathematics to describe in accurate and concise terms what they had learned. That allowed them to be understood by scientists everywhere to whom mathematics became a common language. The use of mathematics and mathematical reasoning allowed scientists to examine theories and hypotheses without experimentation and observation. Mathematics also served to build bridges of understanding among the different branches of science.

Another difference between the old and the new science concerned the role of experiment. The older generation, when they did experiment, tended to satisfy themselves with superficial research. The new scientists used experiments to test hypotheses, insisted upon precision and exact measurement, and developed exhaustive research programs.[12]

One of the first problems addressed by the new breed was one of the oldest concerns both of philosophy and science. What is life? What makes living things different from the nonliving? Men had debated those questions for centuries, and though the grounds of the debate had changed as men gained increased understanding, the debaters had divided into two opposing camps, vitalists and mechanists. The vitalists believed that something they called a vital force, a *vis vitalis*, gave the organism life, that is, power possessed by no inanimate body. The *vis vitalis* was distinct from the chemical and physical forces working within the organism. It controlled the physical and chemical forces. When death came, the vital force vanished, releasing the chemical and physical processes that brought on the physical putrefaction of the body. The mechanists denied the existence of a vital force. They insisted that both the living and the nonliving conformed to the same laws of physics and chemistry. The elements that made up the living substance, themselves inanimate, combined in a complex pattern that gave life to the organism.

In the early decades of the nineteenth century, the Romanticism and the religiosity that appeared in reaction to the eighteenth-century Enlightenment alienated scientists from the mechanistic view. Many of them found its materialism morally repugnant. Then, in the 1840s, a small group of young physiologists, headed by five men of remarkable talent and even genius, by their researches forcefully advanced the mechanistic view. The future lay with them, though it took many decades before nearly all scientists accepted their position.

The leaders in this crusade were Émile Du Bois-Reymond, Hermann Helmholtz, Ernst Brucke, Carl Ludwig, and Rudolf Virchow. All of them had been medical students in the thirties and early forties. Each devoted himself to banishing the concept of a hypothetical vital force in the branch of physiology that each made his own. Each explained all living processes solely in terms of physical, chemical, and atomic mechanisms. In 1848 Du Bois-Reymond wrote the manifesto of their crusade in the introduction of his book *Untersuchungen über tierische Elektrizitat* (translated in 1852 as *On Animal Electricity*). "The vital force," he wrote, "is a comfortable bed where reason falls asleep on the pillow of obscure qualities. . . . In a word, the so-called vital force . . . is an absurdity." Not all of their great contemporaries agreed with the young mechanists. Justus Liebig believed in a vital force that was not immaterial and that could be studied experimentally. He compared this force to gravity and magnetism, forces that we know exist but cannot explain—yet scientists can determine the laws by which these unseen but indisputably real forces operate.[13]

The revolt of the young scientists was an important part of the intellectual and social currents of the forties. Their attack on vitalism reflected the growing materialism of German society, and their scientific findings reinforced the philosophy of materialism. Discontent with absolutism and criticism of established religion became widespread among the educated middle class, and almost without exception the scientists came from that class. The growing importance of the middle class, the expansion of factory industry, the unrest among the lower classes, and a new awareness of the "social question" introduced instability into the society and a questioning of long-accepted institutions and values. Inevitably, these evidences of crisis in the social order affected scientists. Some of them played active roles in the revolutions of 1848. Even those cloistered in their laboratories became ecstatic about the risings.

When the fervor of revolution withered, the scientists turned toward conservatism, like most of their countrymen.[14]

Politics, however, was of minor importance to men of science. Scientific research was their passion and their life. The many years' correspondence between Carl Ludwig and Du Bois-Reymond reveals the kind of men they were, and their devotion to science. Du Bois-Reymond, born in Berlin in 1811, was an outgoing person who early set out to make a reputation for himself. He was absorbed in his research, but he found time for academic politics, he cultivated other outstanding scientists, and he made it his business to know who received appointment to what post and how and why. As a scientist, he was a giant in his time. He devoted himself almost exclusively to experimental analysis of animal electricity and was the founder of modern electrophysiology. As much a physicist as a physiologist, most of his work has stood the test of time.

Carl Ludwig, born in 1816, the son of a Hessian bureaucrat, was cut from different cloth. Destined to become one of the greatest experimentalists in the history of physiology, he was a proud but retiring man. He hated to ask favors for himself. Du Bois-Reymond had to pressure him to ask Humboldt in 1849 for help in gaining an increase in salary at the University of Marburg. "You deserve to be rebuked," Du Bois-Reymond wrote, "for being too proud to have yourself recommended by a man as incomparably good and great minded as Humboldt." He further instructed Ludwig to be sure to say something complimentary about Humboldt who, said Du Bois-Reymond, was "susceptible to appreciation." He even instructed Ludwig to write in large and meticulous script because Humboldt had poor vision. For his part, Ludwig admired and envied Du Bois-Reymond's savoir faire. In his own "narrow middle-class circles," he wrote, he did not have the opportunity to meet sophisticated women such as Du Bois-Reymond knew. "Such rich gifts of intellect and education would be inconvenient rather than desirable to most men of my acquaintance," he continued, "as they themselves hardly send out into the world any spiritual feeler not related to their field, and in most cases only step into the circle of their loves tired and worn out, to converse there by smoking a cigar, while their spouse's contribution is a cup of coffee."[15]

Most of them sons of the lesser bourgeoisie, these young scientists had no money of their own. They started at the bottom of the academic ladder and their inadequate salaries left them chronically short of funds. In 1845 the twenty-four-year-old Rudolf Virchow, a house physician in a Berlin hospital, wrote to his father that a man of his age working on the railroad made as much in a day as Virchow made in a month. To add to their hardships, there were almost no laboratory facilities. They had to work in makeshift quarters or set up laboratories in their cramped apartments. There were hardly any instruments of the kind needed for their experiments, and so they had to invent their own instruments. Carl Ludwig was especially talented in this regard, designing or inventing devices that became standard laboratory equipment. The best known of his innovations was the kymograph, the revolving drum covered with smoked paper that allowed the graphic recording of the results of experiments. The introduction of that instrument into physiology has been called comparable to the introduction of the telescope into astronomy. Ludwig's pioneering experiments and his treatise on the structure of the kidneys became the foundation of all renal physiology. He attracted students from all over the world, and by the time of his death in 1895, almost every active physiologist had studied with him at some point in the man's career.[16]

The achievements of Ludwig and his fellow physiologists made Germany the world's leader in that branch of science. That supremacy in physiology had its parallel in chemistry. Justus von Liebig (he was ennobled in 1845) almost single-handedly made Germany the great center for chemistry, and Liebig himself became one of the most widely known and influential chemists of all time. There is hardly a branch of chemistry to which he did not contribute. His greatest achievement was in organic chemistry. His researches and writings did much to make organic chemistry an exact science capable of mathematical treatment. He introduced great improvements in analytical methods that enabled organic chemists to determine the composition of organic compounds.

Liebig, born in Darmstadt, Hesse, in 1803, knew from childhood that he wanted to be a chemist. At seventeen he entered the University of Bonn to study chemistry with Professor Kastner. He followed Kastner to Erlangen, where in 1822 he received his doctorate. As recounted on an earlier page, he found Kastner's instruction profoundly disappointing. A grant from the Grand Duke of Hesse enabled him to go to Paris, then the center of European science, to study with Gay-Lussac and other leading chemists. He spent two years there and for the first time was exposed to rigorous, quantitative experimental chemistry. He also met Alexander von Humboldt, still living in Paris. Humboldt was so impressed by the young man's ability that he decided to do something for him. So he wrote to the Grand Duke of Hesse and persuaded him to appoint the twenty-two-year-old Liebig as Extraordinary Professor of Chemistry at the University of Giessen without getting faculty approval. As might be expected, the Giessen faculty did not take kindly to their new colleague, but in two years Liebig overcame all opposition and was promoted to a full professorship.[17]

Giessen, where Liebig taught until 1851, when he left for the University of Munich, was a small and obscure provincial university. Yet in later years Liebig said that it was his great good fortune that he started his career there. Had he begun at a larger institution, he explained, he might have diverted and dissipated his energies in efforts to extend his influence and authority. At Giessen he concentrated all of his effort in his work. The first thing he did was to start a teaching laboratory. In Paris he had worked together with Gay-Lussac in the latter's personal laboratory. He decided to replicate that experience for his students at Giessen, so that he could be for them what Gay-Lussac had been to him. Other universities offered laboratory instruction in chemistry, but for all practical purposes, Liebig's laboratory was the world's first laboratory for the teaching of chemistry. The laboratory consisted of one unheated and unventilated room, with barely space enough for twenty students and Liebig. That small laboratory became the model on which the modern teaching of chemistry is based. Liebig transferred the teaching of chemistry from the lecture platform to the laboratory bench. He worked out a program in which the student, always under the supervision of the professor, progressed systematically from elementary chemistry to independent research. Word spread quickly of the value of the program, and students flocked to study with Liebig. He made little Giessen the premier school of chemistry in Germany and, indeed, the world. His success inspired other and greater universities to follow his lead, establishing teaching laboratories not only in chemistry but in the other experimental sciences as well.[18]

The revolution in teaching methods was only one aspect of Liebig's record of spectacular achievements. His ingenious technical innovations made the analysis of organic substances, hitherto a tedious process that demanded much skill, a simple, routine operation. Now he could entrust analyses to his students. His researches involved him in cooperation with other chemists and sometimes in bitter controversy with them, for Liebig was never one to shy away from a professional dispute. By 1839 the thirty-six-year-old Liebig was supreme in his field and head of the largest scientific laboratory in the world. But Liebig was never content to rest on his laurels. Instead, he explored new fields, including the application of organic chemistry to agriculture and physiology. In 1840 he published the book (called in its English translation) *Organic Chemistry in its Application to Agriculture and Physiology*. Time showed that the book had shortcomings and errors, but it won quick recognition as a work of extraordinary value. Liebig drew upon his own researches and deductive reasoning, and from the work of predecessors in the field. He pointed out that improvident agriculture had desolated once fertile lands. Now, utilizing the knowledge provided by chemistry, man could replenish the soil and preserve its strength in perpetuity. If man did not follow this practice, Liebig presented an apocalyptic vision of the future.[19] After writing his treatise on agriculture, Liebig turned to the study of animal chemistry and nutrition. In 1842 he published *Animal Chemistry in its Application to Physiology and Pathology*. Like his book on agriculture, this work had far-reaching effects. He described the complementary relationship between respiration and nutrition. "All vital activity," he wrote, "arises from the mutual action of the oxygen of the atmosphere and the elements of the food." Actually, he went far beyond the proofs available to him and made generalizations for which he gave no reliable evidence. In succeeding years, further research repudiated much of what he wrote. Nonetheless, despite its many failings, the book stimulated scientific interest in animal metabolism and provided the foundations for its study. Liebig's great reputation inspired others to follow the lines of research that he had laid down and, in the process, to correct or abandon much of what he had written. As a modern scholar has noted, "Seldom has a book written with so little regard for scientific standards of objectivity and caution wielded such demonstrably important scientific influences."[20]

In addition to his scientific achievements, Liebig gained great public esteem by his popular writings on chemistry. In 1841 he began a series of essays in the form of letters on chemistry in the *Augsburger Allgemeine Zeitung*. In 1843 the articles appeared in book form, first in English called *Familiar Letters on Chemistry*, and then in German in 1844. The book went into fifty-one editions in these and other languages. Liebig decided to take advantage of his popular fame and especially his work on nutrition. He concocted and manufactured a beef extract, held to be uncommonly high in protein. Called Liebig's Extract and certified to meet his exacting scientific standards, each jar bore his name in large letters. The extract enjoyed a wide sale and added much to Liebig's income for many years.[21]

The importance of Liebig's contributions equaled and perhaps more than equaled his high opinion of himself. He was an arrogant and conceited man with a very short fuse. He either dismissed or scorned those who disagreed with his findings, or else he plunged into bitter arguments with them, sometimes turning against erstwhile close friends. He was reluctant to give credit to other scientists upon whose findings he drew and elaborated. He could be duplicitous, too. In his long correspondence with the famed Swedish chemist J. J. Berzelius, which began in 1832 when Liebig was twenty-eight and Berzelius fifty-two, he repeatedly referred to himself as Berzelius's son in chemistry, and in 1842 he planned to write a flowery and fawning dedication to the older man for his book on animal chemistry. But in letters to his friend Friedrich Wöhler, he called Berzelius a lion whose teeth had become blunt and whose roar could not frighten a mouse. He suggested that Berzelius should leave the arena to those who had something to contribute.

These distasteful attributes did not diminish his status as a chemist. He was passionately devoted to his students and to their subsequent careers. In 1851 Hermann Helmholtz, no admirer of the man, wrote that "in spite of his vanity, Liebig is the greatest of living chemists, and his renown as a teacher has spread far and wide."[22]

Helmholtz, who became Germany's most revered scientist of the second half of the nineteenth century, as Humboldt had been in the century's first half, was a very different person from Liebig. As a young man, he had been shy and awkward in company. In the 1840s the perceptive and sophisticated Du Bois-Reymond took him under his wing, as it were, though he was only three years older than Helmholtz. As he matured, Helmholtz became a warm and serene man, thoughtful always of others, and careful in his controversies with other scientists to remain always in the bounds of good taste. He was a master of many fields. His interests included medicine, the physiology of optics and acoustics, physics, mathematics and the arts, and above all music. He had an extraordinary gift for experiment combined with an outstanding ability at the mathematical formulation of his findings. His researches, especially on the sensory organs of the eye and the ear, impelled him to the philosophical problems of epistemology, that is, how we have knowledge of the external world. At seventy, he explained that from his youth on, he had spent his life in the search for an understanding of the underlying principles that unified all of nature. He could not rest, he said, with apparent solutions "so long as I felt there were still dark places."[23]

Helmholtz was born in Potsdam in 1821, the son of a poorly paid teacher at the local *gymnasium*. He had hoped to study physics at a university, but his parents could not afford the expense. At his father's suggestion, and with the help of an influential friend, he was awarded a stipend to pay his living costs at the tuition-free royal medical college in Berlin. In return for his education there, he was obligated to serve for eight years as an Army doctor after graduation. While at medical school, he studied physiology and anatomy with Johannes Müller who, as mentioned earlier, taught and inspired other bright young men. He took no courses in mathematics, but read on his own and developed a mastery of that subject. A bout of typhus put him in the hospital for a time, and because students did not have to pay hospital charges, he saved enough money from his stipend to buy a small microscope. He used the instrument in the research for his doctoral thesis. This study, on the structure of the nervous system of invertebrates, became a basic contribution to histology. Awarded his medical degree in 1842, the twenty-one-year-old Helmholtz became an Army surgeon, serving in Potsdam. His scientific achievements won him the support of Humboldt, with whose help he gained his release from military service in 1848. Again with Humboldt's patronage, he became an assistant at the anatomical museum in Berlin, and the next year an assistant professor of physiology and anatomy at the University of Königsberg. In 1855, once more with the help of Humboldt, he became a professor of anatomy and physiology at Bonn. Three years later, he went to Heidelberg, where he remained until 1871, when he took over the chair of physics at the University of Berlin.[24]

Helmholtz's outstanding abilities and vast learning won him the early attention and admiration of his peers. By the time he left Königsberg for Bonn, he had become one of Germany's most renowned scientists.[25] His rise to national recognition began with a brochure of some sixty pages that he published in 1847. He called it *Über die Erhaltung der Kraft* (*On the Conservation of Force*). It turned out to be one of the most famous scientific papers ever written. In it he showed that there is in nature an indestructible force that goes from one form to another and is never lost. No matter what form it took, whether chemical or mechanical or electrical energy, or heat, and no matter what the circumstances, energy is the one entity that is imperishable. After a couple of preliminary essays he laid down in his paper of 1847 the principle of the conservation of energy, or force, as he called it, that became known as the First Law of Thermodynamics. He always insisted that he had written the treatise primarily for physiologists, but it became one of the pillars of modern physics and, indeed, of all natural science. The principle of the conservation of energy is recognized as one of the most important breakthroughs of nineteenth-century science.[26]

Helmholtz was surprised by the reception accorded to the paper. Years later he said that he expected the experts to say, "That's all well known to us. What does this young medical man think when he feels he has to spell it out for us in such detail." Instead, to his astonishment, the scientific establishment, offended by the assault on their prized vital force, denounced the essay as speculation and fantasy. But Helmholtz found enthusiastic approval among his own generation, and Du Bois-Reymond mustered the support for the paper of the recently founded Physical Society of Berlin.[27]

Actually, Helmholtz was not the first to determine the principle of the conservation of energy. In one of the most remarkable instances of simultaneous discovery in the history of science, three other men, widely scattered and working in ignorance of one another, published papers between 1842 and 1847 announcing the discovery of the principle. Julius Robert Mayer, who was the first, was a German physician, A. Colding was a Danish engineer, and James Joule was a wealthy English "gentleman scientist." Helmholtz knew nothing of the work of Mayer and Colding, and learned of Joule's contribution only when he had completed his own essay. Helmholtz, then, was not the first, but as C. C. Gillispie elegantly observed, "He couched his discussion in the most sophisticated language known to physics, not all weighted down by lumps of data like Joule's heavy-handed reports, nor confined to the primitive numerical equivalents of Mayer, but on the graceful, taut, and lissome differential equations of classical dynamics."[28]

The coincidence of four men working independently of one another discovering the principle of the conservation of energy, though remarkable, was not overly surprising. The way had been readied by earlier scientists who had found that heat and light were quantitatively interchangeable, or had suggested the existence of an "imperishable force" that manifested itself in many forms. The ever-increasing use of steam engines in industry and transport, showing the conversion of heat into mechanical work, turned inquiring minds to attempt to find out why that happened. Similarly, new discoveries in electricity, magnetism, and chemistry, showing, for example, that electricity produced by chemical interaction in a galvanic battery could produce heat and light, provoked speculation among scientists seeking an explanation.[29]

Soon after settling in at the University of Königsberg, Helmholtz in 1850 turned to the investigation of sensory physiology. The next year, he invented the ophthalmoscope as a tool for use in his research on the eye. In 1854 he devised the ophthalmometer. These two instruments made it possible for the first time to observe the interior of a living organ and to measure its mechanism. In the years that followed, up to his death in 1894, a steady stream of articles, books, and addresses poured from his pen. They dealt with all manner of subjects, scientific and humanistic. After his death, his old friend Du Bois-Reymond, in his memorial address at the Berlin Academy of Sciences, concluded with these words: "We will never see his like again. Indeed, it is questionable whether such a man as he can ever appear again."[30]

In contrast to the scientific ferment in Germany, Britain lagged far behind. In 1837 the British Association for the Advancement of Science invited Justus Liebig to visit England. On his return home, Liebig wrote to Berzelius that he "had seen much and learned little. England is not the land of science. There exists there only a widely cultivated dilettantism."[31] Science in Britain was, indeed, pursued mainly by amateurs who worked in isolation and for whom science was a hobby. Most of these amateur scientists were men of private means, retired businessmen or clergymen. A handful among them made significant contributions. For example, Francis Bailey, after making a fortune as a London stockbroker, retired at fifty to devote his full time to astronomy. Though he had only an elementary education, he became a leading astronomer, and through his findings and his organizing abilities, he became a major figure in the advances of astronomy. James Joule, son of a wealthy brewer in Manchester, carried on his researches in a laboratory in his home and his father's brewery. He won lasting fame as a physicist, especially for his recognition of the law of the conservation of energy. And of course the greatest and the most famous of these British amateur scientists was Charles Darwin.

A few Britons recognized and publicly deplored the low state of science in their homeland. Charles Babbage, a mathematician of great power, who also happened to be an exceedingly irascible and contentious man, in 1830 published *Reflections on the Decline of Science in England and on Some of its Causes*. In it, he accused the Royal Society, Britain's oldest and most prestigious scientific organization, of failing in its supposed purpose of promoting the advancement of the sciences. He demanded reforms in education that would give science a more important part in the curriculum. He complained that the ruling elite held science in low regard and did not consider it a proper profession for a gentleman.[32]

Nowhere was the apathy toward science more evident than in Oxford and Cambridge, the finishing schools, as it were, for the ruling elite. Indeed, foreign visitors found that all education had a low priority in these ancient institutions. An American college president wrote that at Cambridge there was "more *form* than *study*" and that the university functions "are more suited to the purpose of external pomp—to public display—to the pampering of an overgrown aristocracy—to the sustaining of a defective church establishment, than to the great purpose of intellectual and moral elevation." Robert von Mohl, a distinguished German scholar and a visiting professor at Oxford and Cambridge in 1844, found that "there was hardly any talk of the study of sciences, law and medicine, as well as most subjects with which our . . . faculties so rightly concern themselves" and that the task of the students "to accomplish the least possible with the most possible means was served in an astonishing manner." Lecture hall in the sciences stood empty or nearly so. In the early 1840s, lectures at Oxford in chemistry, botany, and anatomy each had only three to seven students out of a student body of 1,500. The story was much the same at Cambridge.[33]

A relatively few men did earn their living as professional scientists. Their number included teachers of science at the universities. Of these academics, Sir David Brewster, himself a Scottish professor of physics, wrote in 1830 that none of them engaged in any original research.[34] That was something of an exaggeration, but not by much. In contrast, a handful of scientists not affiliated with universities, like the physicists John Dalton and Thomas Young, the chemist Humphrey Davy, and the astronomer William Herschel, made contributions of great consequence. Above all, the genius of Michael Faraday made him one of the greatest figures in the history of science.

Faraday (1791–1867) was not only a great scientist, he was also an admirable human being, a simple, kind, and gentle man, without pretensions, who triumphed over great handicaps. Born in Surrey, he was the son of a poor and sickly blacksmith who could provide only the barest of livings for his family. Fortunately, Faraday's mother, a woman of great inner strength, provided emotional security and love for her four children. She was sustained by her deep fundamentalist faith that she passed on to Michael and that he never abandoned. The boy had almost no education, learning only the rudiments of reading, writing, and arithmetic. At fourteen he was apprenticed to a London bookbinder and spent the next seven years, required by the law of apprentices, in that trade. He hated the work, but bookbinding helped him develop the manual dexterity that later distinguished his experimental researches. More important, the apprenticeship gave him the opportunity in his leisure hours to read the books on the store's shelves, and he became an omnivorous reader. A chance reading of an article on electricity and a book, first published in 1805 by Jane Marcet, titled *Conversations on Chemistry*, awakened and focused his interest in science. He joined the City Philosophical Society, a group of young men who met every Wednesday evening to listen to lectures on science. It was there that Faraday learned his basic science.

In October 1812 Faraday finished his apprenticeship and faced the seemingly certain prospect of a life as a bookbinder, instead of the scientist that he longed to be. Chance gave him the opportunity to make his dream come true. A customer of the binder gave him tickets to lectures by the famed chemist Humphrey Davy at the Royal Institution, a private scientific society of which Davy was the director. As was his custom, Faraday made careful notes of the lectures. He made a copy of the notes, bound them, and sent them to Davy, whom he greatly admired, along with a letter asking for employment at the Institution in any capacity. At first Davy had no place for the young supplicant, but in February 1813 an opening appeared. Faraday became a laboratory assistant at the Royal Institution. There he spent the rest of his long scientific career. He became Davy's protégé and ultimately his successor as director of the Institution. In later years, Davy boasted that of his many discoveries in science the greatest was Michael Faraday.

Faraday knew no mathematics. Instead, he depended upon intensive and interminable experimentation, careful and full notes, acute perception, great powers of concentration, and remarkable technical ingenuity. Most important of all, he possessed an instinctive ability to understand the workings of physical nature. After Faraday's death, Helmholtz said of him that "it is in highest degree amazing how without using a single mathematical formula he discovered a large number of comprehensive theorems whose methodical proofs demand the highest powers of mathematical analysis, by a kind of inner intuition and instinctive assurance."[35]

Faraday did his first work in Davy's field of chemistry and soon established a reputation as an analytical chemist. He pioneered in applying chemistry to technology. He also began the highly original researches in electricity that occupied him for the rest of his career. His studies of electrical and magnetic phenomena provided science with some of its most fundamental principles. They also had an important impact upon technology. His investigation of electromagnetic induction led him to the invention of the dynamo, the precursor of modern dynamos and generators. He showed that a simple machine could convert mechanical energy into electrical energy. That discovery was one of the earliest applications of basic research to industry. His studies of electrolysis (he gave that process its name) also had important results for technology. He made a systematic study of the manner in which electrical charges passed through a conducting solution, or electrolyte, as he called it. He capped his career of enormous achievement by providing what Albert Einstein a century later called "the first great fundamental advance in theoretical physics since Newton." After much experimentation, he concluded that fields of force, or "lines of force" as he called them, filled the space around a magnet or an electrified object. By 1850 he determined that these lines of force filled all space and explained magnetic and electrical phenomena, radiation, and gravitation. His theory opened up a vision that in the next generation James Clerk Maxwell transformed with mathematical exactitude into a new concept of the physical world.[36]

Despite the achievements of a Faraday and his fellows, British science remained a large untilled field. By the 1840s, however, evidences of an awakening interest in science manifested themselves. Most significantly, in 1826 University College, London, opened its doors. A private institution, its founders intended it as an alternative to the Anglican orthodoxy of Oxford and Cambridge, which admitted only communicants of the Church of England. The new college charged much lower fees than did Oxford and Cambridge, thereby providing students from middle- and lower-class families the opportunity for higher education. Its curriculum emphasized the study of science; in its first decade, it appointed seventeen professors in science, engineering, and medicine. In 1845 the newly established Royal College of Chemistry began to train professional chemists. In 1850 the School of Mines, England's first institute for technical training, began instruction. In addition, an increasing number of young Britons studied science at German universities.[37]

Meanwhile, an interest in science attracted the public's attention. It became a fashionable interest for the elite and a more serious concern for the working class. By 1850 Britain had several hundred so-called Mechanics Institutes, where artisans and workmen received instruction in practical science and technology. Lecturers, most of them of limited competence, toured the provinces, earning a precarious living from the modest admission fees which they charged. In major cities lectures by important scientists drew large audiences. Faraday, for example, gave over one hundred of these lectures to help support the Royal Institution and to supplement his own small income. The listeners did not always understand what they had heard, but that did not seem to deter them from attending.[38]

The one science that held the greatest attraction for British public and scientists alike was geology. It was easily comprehensible and at the same time highly controversial; it did not require special training to discover fossils; and it appealed to the British love of the out-of-doors. Britons took a leading role in the development of the science. They established a national geological society in 1807, and in 1835 the government set up the world's first national geological survey. Both British and continental geologists had developed theories about the history of the earth's crust. Some, called Neptunists, claimed that one or more great floods had formed the face of the earth. Others, called Vulcanists, attributed it to natural catastrophes such as volcanic eruptions and earthquakes. Then, in 1795, James Hutton, a Scottish geologist, argued that forces still in operation had created the earth's mountains and valleys and rivers and seas over the course of countless ages. His theory, called uniformitarianism, made few converts at first. It contradicted the Bible's story of the flood and the widely held belief, based upon the chronology of the Bible, that God had created the earth in 4004 B.C. As the years went by, uniformitarianism gained adherents. After the publication of Charles Lyell's *Principles of Geology* in the early 1830s, it became widely accepted, though many, including well-known geologists, disputed it on religious grounds. Gradually, educated men saw the biblical account as a symbolic story and not a literal one, and recognized the immense age of the earth.[39]

The uniformitarianism of Lyell's book, with its depiction of the geological evolution of the earth over vast periods of time, almost inevitably raised thoughts of biological evolution. Not that it was a new idea. The possibility of the mutation of species had occurred to some scientists and philosophers from at least the middle of the eighteenth century. Now, more and more people became intrigued by the idea. When, in 1844, a book called *Vestiges of the Natural History of Creation* appeared, it became an immediate best-seller. It went through four editions in its first six months and a total of eleven editions by 1860. Its author, knowing that his book would arouse the fury of theologians and many scientists, chose to remain anonymous. Not until the twelfth edition in 1884 was it revealed that Robert Chambers, a Scottish author and publisher who had died thirteen years earlier, had written the book.

Chambers was an amateur geologist and widely read in scientific and philosophical literature. He argued in his book that at the beginning the Creator had set off evolution by a single event and at the same time had ordained the uniform laws that evolution would follow through all time. Chambers's book was full of errors, misstatements, and unfounded and wild speculation, so that even scientists favorable to the theory of evolution ridiculed his efforts. Nonetheless, the book had an enormous influence. It popularized the idea of biological evolution and so prepared the way for its acceptance. Charles Darwin thought that Chambers's geology was "bad" and his zoology "far worse," yet he said that the book "has done excellent service in calling attention to the subject and removing prejudices."[40]

In the same year that Chambers's book appeared, Darwin had written an essay of over two hundred pages. In that essay he outlined the essentials of his theory of evolution that he finally published in 1859 as *On the Origin of Species by Means of Natural Selection*. Born in 1809 into a prosperous and intellectual family, Darwin studied medicine briefly at Edinburgh, then went to Cambridge to study for the ministry. There he became a friend of J. S. Henslow, professor of botany. He attended Henslow's lectures but did not study botany. Such was the academic preparation for his career as a scientist. In 1831 Henslow recommended Darwin, then twenty-two, for the Admiralty survey ship *H.M.S. Beagle* as unpaid naturalist. The Beagle set off to survey the coasts of Patagonia, Tierra del Fuego, Chile, and Peru; to visit some Pacific islands; and to continue around the world. The journey took five years. Darwin's observations and experiences, and a close reading of Lyell's *Principles of Geology*, convinced him of the great age of the earth and the slow action of natural forces. On his return to England, the concept of the mutation of species by natural selection began to take form in his mind. He revealed his ideas only to a few friends, and his essay of 1844 remained unpublished. Finally, in 1856 at the urging of Charles Lyell, he started writing *The Origin of Species*.[41]

Until the middle of the nineteenth century, science did not contribute significantly to the advances in technology. Inventors and engineers knew little or nothing of scientific theory. They were empiricists guided by trial and error. As for the scientists, many of them, and above all in Germany, viewed the practical application of science as unworthy and even morally corrupting. Science must be pursued for its own sake and not be polluted by utilitarian relevance. The new generation of German scientists were more flexible. They, too, insisted upon the study of science for its own sake and not for any utilitarian purpose, but they did not object to the application of their findings to practical ends, contending only that "pure science" preceded the application. In contrast, British scientists had no reservations about the practical uses of science. Most of them took an active part in the application of their researches to industry and agriculture. Justus Liebig found this attitude disturbing. In a letter to Michael Faraday in February 1845, he wrote, "What struck me most in England was the perception that only those works that have a practical tendency awaken attention, and command respect, while the purely scientific, which possess far greater merit, are almost unknown. And yet the latter are the proper and true source from which the others flow."[42]

The egotistical Liebig doubtless assumed that his own work could serve as the model for the progression from pure science to practical application. His book on *Organic Chemistry and its Application to Agriculture* represented the first time that a distinguished German scientist had applied his science to the uses of industry. By calling attention in the book to the need for rigorous scientific study of agriculture, Liebig stimulated the establishment of agricultural experiment stations in Europe and the United States, where continued research produced improvements in the techniques of agriculture. His emphasis on the need for fertilizers led to the exploitation of the great guano deposits of the Peruvian coast. His own efforts at the commercial production of artificial fertilizer failed, but others, inspired by his teachings, proved successful and created a new and gigantic industry.

Another great industry had its origins in Liebig's laboratory in Giessen. August Wilhelm Hofmann (1818–1892) took his Ph.D. with Liebig in 1841 with a study of the chemical properties of coal tar. In 1845, at twenty-seven, he became head of the newly founded Royal College of Chemistry in London. There he continued his researches and published papers on derivatives of coal tar, especially aniline. In 1848 one of his students devised the method for the fractional distillation of coal tar and thereby provided the foundation for the artificial dyestuffs industry. That industry took off in 1856 with the discovery by W. H. Perkin, another Hofmann student, of aniline purple, or mauve, the first artificial dye.[43]

The popularity of science, and especially of geology, led to some remarkable frauds. A Dr. Albert C. Koch perpetrated one of the most imposing hoaxes. He constructed a 114-foot-long skeleton that he said was a fossil sea serpent. Charging an entrance fee, he exhibited it first in New York and then in Europe. One of the visitors, Professor Jeffries Wyman, an anatomist, proceeded to show that Koch had fabricated the monster from bones of various animals. The undaunted Koch continued to exhibit his creation. In 1847 he took his "serpent" to Germany, where a German anatomist declared it authentic. With that cachet, it made a great impression upon a gullible public. Koch crowned his deception by selling his monstrosity for 1,000 *thalers*.[44]

In the early nineteenth century, F. J. Gall, an Austrian anatomist, and his disciples developed the pseudoscience of phrenology. They claimed that the contours of the human skull corresponded to the contours of the surface of the brain and that each human characteristic or faculty had its seat in a specific area of the brain. They charted thirty-seven of these characteristics, such as combativeness, veneration, benevolence, amativeness, and so on. Measurements of the contours of the skull would reveal an individual's mental abilities, traits of character, and personality. In succeeding decades, phrenology attracted great public attention. Practitioners and devotees in Europe and the United States organized phrenological societies and published journals devoted to the "science." Responsible scientists scoffed and published attacks, but to little avail. Prominent people, including such men of considerable intellectual distinction as Karl Marx, Auguste Comte, Herbert Spencer, and Richard Cobden became confirmed believers. People passed judgment on others by observing the shape of their skulls. Some even judged the character of the dead from statues. The American historian W. H. Prescott wrote of Sir Walter Scott that "his cranium, to judge from his busts, must have exhibited a strong development of the organ of veneration."[45]

Some progress was made in medical science during the first decades of the century. Frenchmen made most of the advances, taking the lead in medicine as they did in natural sciences. Paris became the Western world's leading medical center, and students flocked there for medical study. Despite these advances, the theory and practice of medicine remained enchained by tradition, by unproven and arbitrary theories, and by metaphysical concepts. Years were to pass before there were any significant changes. Doctors treated all diseases by bloodletting and purges that were supposed to cure the patient by a process of "depletion," that is, exhaustion. The sick consumed vast amounts of purges on the theory of "cure constipation and cure all." In 1850 a contemporary account reported that St. Bartholomew's Hospital in London, with an average occupancy of 500 patients, used annually 1,352 gallons of "black draught," a mixture of salts and senna, 2,000 lbs. of castor oil, twelve tons of linseed meal, 2,700 lbs. of salts, and 1,000 lbs. of senna.

Rival "schools" of medicine arose, each advancing its own therapy. Some proposed a single cause for all maladies. The German Samuel Hahnemann, the founder of homeopathy, claimed that something he called *psora* was responsible for nearly every chronic disease. *Psora*, literally "itch," he described as a morbid material in the body that also produces a variety of skin diseases. Schools in central Europe reached their extreme with the "therapeutic nihilism" of the so-called New Vienna School. One of its gurus proclaimed that a doctor could describe and diagnose a disease but could not cure it. "To do nothing," he said, is the best medicine. Given the level of medical expertise of that era, that may well have been the soundest therapy of them all.[46]

Many physicians became advocates of hydrotherapy. Doctors had known for centuries of the values of this treatment, but a new variety began with a seventeen-year-old peasant in Austrian Silesia named Vincent Priessnitz. In 1816 he was run over by a wagon and suffered severe injuries. He had seen the peasants of his mountain village cure contusions and sprains of their animals by cold water compresses and had himself become skilled in that therapy. He decided to try the treatment on himself, applied water compresses for a year, and recovered completely. He went on to develop a program of draughts of cold water, cold showers, cold sitz baths, wet cold sheets, and enemas. News of Priessnitz's remarkable recovery started a craze for this treatment. By the 1840s the enthusiasm had spread across Europe and the United States. Priessnitz himself opened an enormously successful establishment at Graefenberg in the mountains of his homeland, where he practiced his cold-water therapy.

Elsewhere mineral springs became the rage, and spas large and small opened for business. Central Europe, where they were most common, had over three hundred of these establishments. Part sanitarium and part resort, people from kings to commoners came to "take the cure" and enjoy the relaxed atmosphere of the hotels and gardens and casinos that sprang up around the waters. Stories spread of miraculous recoveries of apparently hopeless invalids crippled in body or mind, of the banishing of repulsive skin diseases, of the restoration of sexual vigor, and whatever else ailed people. Doctors at the spas supervised the people taking the cure, usually seeing them informally at the waters. At Marienbad in Bohemia, the most popular physician saw around three hundred people each morning.[47]

The obvious shortcomings of professional medicine left the field open to all manner of healing cults and cures. One of the most popular originated with Franz Anton Mesmer in the latter part of the eighteenth century. Mesmer called it "animal magnetism," others gave it the name of mesmerism. Mesmer, a Swiss-born Austrian physician, claimed that every individual has a magnetic fluid with which he can "magnetize" another person. Using passes of the hand, the individual could induce a somnambulistic trance in another person and draw pain and disease from the other person's body. A later follower of Mesmer discovered that he could induce the trance by having the subject stare at a bright object and called the technique hypnotism. By the 1840s mesmerism had gained wide acceptance among all classes, despite often sharp criticism and mockery from many physicians. Tales were told of even more astounding cures than those claimed at the most renowned spas. George Mifflin Dallas, American Minister to Russia and later vice-president of the United States, told of a woman thrown from her horse. Severely injured and unconscious, her doctor "magnetized" her, and though apparently lifeless, she prescribed in Latin, a language unknown to her, the medicines and applications needed for her recovery. A widely traveled German mesmerist reported that he saw cures as miraculous as those of the earliest days of Christianity. Animal magnetism became the rage among the elite. In Britain luminaries of the literary world, among them Dickens, Wordsworth, Browning, Thackeray, Carlyle, and Harriet Martineau, became convinced believers.[48]

The breakthrough in medical science, as it did in the physical sciences, came in Germany in the 1840s. Many of the young men who, in the forties, led in the creation of a new kind of science, had studied medicine and had become thoroughly disenchanted with their training. The backwardness of medicine and its rejection of research in chemistry, biology, and physics dismayed the new science-oriented generation of the 1840s. Years later, Hermann Helmholtz, who graduated from medical school in 1842, recalled those days. "My education," he wrote, "fell within a period in the history of medicine in which utter despair reigned among thoughtful and conscientious minds. It was not hard to recognize that the old, predominantly theoretical methods of practicing medicine were completely untenable. . . . We need not wonder that many straightforward and thoughtful men turned from medicine in dissatisfaction, or resigned themselves to an excessive empiricism."[49]

A beginning was hardly made in the forties. Yet a brief half century later, Germany had become the world's leader in medical science. Students came from every corner of the globe to study medicine in Germany, to carry back to their homelands the science that they had learned there, and to establish medical schools on the German model. In 1897 T. W. Engelmann, professor of physiology at the University of Berlin, wrote to his friend Johannes Brahms that "in the short span of the last fifty years—or even thirty years—medicine has become a truly natural science that avails itself of the strictly scientific method of observation, namely the experiment. . . . By contrast, all the work done during previous millennia must be considered insignificant."[50]

A principal founder of modern medical science was Johannes Müller (1801–1858), who was professor of physiology and anatomy at the medical school of the University of Berlin. His own contributions and those of his students, and above all, his and their insistence upon research, experimentation, and rigorous scientific method, were destined to transform the teaching and practice of medicine. Müller, a man of commanding presence and graced with rare personal charm, inspired the young men who studied with him by his ability, his knowledge, and his dedication. Rudolf Virchow remembered him as "an abiding priest of nature; the culture which he served also bound his students to him, as if by a religious bond; and the earnest priestly manner of his speech and movements completed the impression of reverence with which everyone looked up to him. . . . So stood this man before the altar of nature, freed by his own strength from the fetters of training and tradition, a witness of personal independence."[51]

During the same years that Müller helped lay the foundations of modern medical science, his contemporary Johann Lukas Schönlein (1793–1864) performed the same service for modern clinical medicine. In his clinic Schönlein restructured the program of treatment. Among other innovations, he introduced the examination of the blood and urine of patients by microscope and by chemical analysis, and the use of percussion and the recently discovered stethoscope for examination of the chest. Schönlein innovated in another way, too. In 1840 he is said to have become the first doctor in Germany to use German instead of Latin when he made his clinical rounds.[52]

In 1845 Rudolf Virchow, twenty-four years old and barely two years out of medical school, in two addresses at the Friedrich-Wilhelm Institute of Medicine and Surgery at Berlin, pronounced the manifesto, as it were, of the new generation of medical men. Medical progress, he said, came from three principal sources: careful clinical observation of the patient with the aid of knowledge provided by physics and chemistry; animal experimentation to determine the causes and cures of disease and to study the effects of therapeutic drugs; and pathological anatomy, especially with the aid of the microscope.

Virchow's emphasis upon microscopy reflected the improvements made in that instrument in the 1830s. The new generation made intensive use of it. They concentrated especially on investigation of the cell, which they gradually recognized as the structural and physiological unit in all living organisms.

Through their microscopic studies, they related disease to cellular structure and determined intimate details of the tissues of the body. Virchow himself began his career of discovery with the identification of leukemia in 1845, and between 1846 and 1856 made major studies of thrombosis and embolisms. These were the earliest steps in a record of astounding achievements that continued for decades. His researches laid the foundation of cellular pathology and contributed to nearly every other branch of medical science.

The new generation of medical scientists spread the word of their findings and their emphasis upon research and experiment through the medium of three journals founded in the forties. Each was started by men who became leaders in their respective fields. They insisted that the articles they published were based upon careful and exact research, and their journals had great influence upon medicine and its practice. Virchow and another young physician started one of these journals. They called it *Archiv für pathologische Anatomie*, but it became known and is still known as *Virchows Archiv*. Its first issue announced that the journal had as its point of view and its purpose the close union of clinical medicine, physiology, and pathological anatomy. That was the ideal that German medicine adopted and that influenced medicine throughout the world.[53]

In these same years in France, Claude Bernard (1813–1878), another great pioneer of medical science, began his career. Like so many of the new generation of scientists, he came from a modest family background. He received his medical degree in 1843 but never practiced. Instead, he engaged in research under the direction of François Magendie (1783–1855), France's premier medical authority of the preceding generation. Bernard busied himself in research in two fields. One, the subject of his dissertation in 1843, was the chemical and physiological study of gastric digestion, tracing what happened to food from its entry into the body until its assimilation or excretion. He concentrated especially on the pancreas, and his investigations prepared the way for later studies of diabetes. His other field of research concerned the function of nerves. By experimentation on animals, he had a series of remarkable successes that later culminated in his discovery of the vasomotor nerves. In these early years of his researches, he also experimented with toxic substances. He found that they and other drugs act on a particular part of the organism and not on the entire body as hitherto assumed. Once the locale affected by the drug was known, the researcher could study the drug's effect on diseased tissue, and the physician could prescribe it.[54]

The decade of the forties also saw the introduction of what Charles Greville hailed as "the greatest blessing ever bestowed on mankind. All the great discoveries of science," he declared, "sink into insignificance when compared to this." The German diarist Varnhagen von Ense was scarcely less hyperbolic. Their paeans were for the discovery of ether and of chloroform as anesthetics. They had reason for these hosannas. Patients had suffered horribly on the operating table. To minimize the torture, surgeons, greatly disadvantaged by the struggles and suffering of the patient, had to work at breakneck speed. Obviously, under these conditions, surgeons had no time for precautionary methods or for precise surgery. The relief from pain was only part of the blessing of anesthesia. Even more important from the viewpoint of the advance of medical science, it gave the surgeon the gift of time to work carefully, perform more complicated operations, devise new techniques, and make new discoveries.[55]

Ether had its first use as an anesthetic in the United States. Dr. Crawford Williamson Long of Danielsville, Georgia, had noticed the anesthetic effect of ether. In March 1842 he began to use it in operations, but he published no report of his findings. In 1844 a dentist in Massachusetts, Dr. William T. G. Morton, used ether to fill a tooth and then to extract a deeply rooted bicuspid. Pleased by his success, he persuaded Dr. John Collins Warrens of the Massachusetts General Hospital in Boston to use ether in an operation on October 16, 1846, for the removal of a superficial tumor from the neck of a patient. The next day, another surgeon used it to remove a large tumor from a patient's shoulder. On November 18, 1846, an article in a Boston medical journal printed the story of these operations. Word spread quickly and ether came into wide use.

On November 4, 1847, almost exactly a year after the announcement of the use of ether as an anesthetic, Dr. James Simpson, an obstetrician in Edinburgh, used chloroform for the delivery of an infant. Dr. Simpson had been the first obstetrician to use ether in childbirth, but he found chloroform more satisfactory. He quickly published his findings, and chloroform came into wide use in obstetrics as well as in general surgery. With a few whiffs of chloroform, a lying-in woman was spared the fearful pangs of childbirth. That did not sit well with some clerics and even some physicians. They disapproved of the use of chloroform because it allowed women to escape the curse pronounced on Eve.[56]

The success of natural scientists in presenting a new conception of physical reality inspired efforts to achieve similar triumphs in what later came to be known as the social sciences. Already in the seventeenth century and increasingly in the eighteenth, men sought to apply the findings of the natural sciences to human behavior. In the nineteenth century, the attempt to relate natural science to social phenomena received explicit form in the writings of Auguste Comte. Comte, born in Montpelier in the south of France in 1798, had been a pupil and later an examiner in mathematics at the famed École Polytechnique in Paris, and had also been a lecturer there in astronomy. He had an extensive knowledge of the physical sciences, but he maintained that they alone could not provide the synthesis needed as a guide to the understanding of intellectual and social conduct. He therefore formulated a system that he called Positivism. He claimed that this system provided a scientific methodology to determine the natural laws which governed social behavior. He assumed that human thought and the phenomena of social life were analogous to the phenomena of the physical world, and so could be analyzed and reduced to quantitative terms by the methodology of the natural sciences. Man could then achieve the objectivity and the exactitude of the physical sciences in his search for the natural laws of human behavior.

Comte began to lecture on his philosophy in 1826 to a private group. From these lectures there evolved his two major works, the *Cours de philosophie positive,* which appeared in six volumes between 1830 and 1842, and the four volumes of the *Système de politique positive,* published between 1851 and 1854. He wrote these fat volumes without notes, without revisions, and without regard for literary grace and style. The results were dull, pedantic, involved, and repetitious treatises. Despite their opacity, these and his other writings demonstrated that Comte possessed vast erudition and an exceptionally powerful intellect. That explained his appeal to many intellectuals who believed that he had opened up new vistas of human understanding. Adopting ideas expressed earlier by Turgot and Saint-Simon, he postulated his Law of the Three Stages through which mankind had progressed. Each stage determined how men thought and acted during that stage. In the first stage, the theological men thought that the world was determined by the will of God and His intervention. The second stage, the metaphysical, replaced theology with philosophy and explained the world in terms of metaphysical abstraction. In the third and final stage, the positive stage, upon which the world was only now entering, men renounced philosophical musings about origins and final purposes, and instead explained the world in terms of observable phenomena and clearly established scientific truths.

Comte classified all sciences into a hierarchy of increasing specificity and complexity, associated and interdependent with the Law of Stages. Mathematics, with its self-evident maxims and abstract theorems, formed the base of the intellectual pyramid. Astronomy, physics, chemistry, and biology followed in that order. Finally came sociology, the science of society, the most complex of the sciences, dealing, as it did, with human relationships, and including economics, anthropology, history, and psychology. Each science depended for its positive content upon the science that preceded it in the hierarchy. Sociology, which embodied the intellectual unification of society, capped the pyramid. It was the supreme science, the interdisciplinary social science whose laws could guide mankind. This ultimate science had not entered on its positive stage. Once it had reached that stage, people would accept its laws without questioning them, just as they accepted the laws of astronomy and physics and the other natural sciences. People would then forsake their disputes about religion and politics and the other controversies that now divided them and live rationally and peacefully in compliance with the laws of the science of sociology. Comte first called this final science social physics, but when the statistician Quêtelet borrowed that term, Comte in 1838 gave his new science the name of sociology.[57]

Comte had as his ultimate aim nothing less than the regeneration and reorganization of human society. He insisted that mental and moral change had to precede social and political change. Early on, even before he embarked upon the writing of the *Cours*, he saw the need for a spiritual force, a new church, that would serve not some fictional Supreme Being but humanity itself. In the 1840s, having completed his scientific synthesis, Comte established his Religion of Humanity, as he called it, and declared himself as its High Priest. The founding of this new religion was enmeshed with Comte's obsession with a woman that he met in 1844 and with whom he fell madly in love. Their romance, which apparently was never consummated, lasted eighteen months, ending with the woman's death. The devastated Comte incorporated his love for her into his Religion of Humanity. He assigned her the role of the Virgin Mother, superior to himself, who was only the High Priest. He prayed to her and made her grave a place of sacred pilgrimage.

T. H. Huxley (1825–1895), famed as scientist and agnostic, called Comte's Religion of Humanity "Catholicism without Christianity." Indeed, it bore many resemblances to the faith that Comte had abandoned in his youth. He insisted that the spiritual power be independent of and superior to the temporal power. He drew up a Positivist catechism and devised a multitude of rituals for his religion, with sacraments for each stage of life from birth to death. In the last year of his life, he announced that he would call himself the Grand Priest of Humanity and that he was more sacred than the pope because he had discovered the fundamental laws of human evolution and was therefore the personification of the Great Being.[58]

Comte's retreat into religious fatuity—and his suspicion and even rejection of the rational analysis that he had formerly praised—repelled many who had become his disciples. Some of them abandoned his philosophy. Others rejected Comte's religiosity as extraneous to the principles of Positivism and continued as supporters of his teachings. Positivism attracted people who shared Comte's conviction that traditional society had become obsolete and that a new order had to be constructed. Its claim to be scientific at a time when science began to enjoy a special cachet added to the appeal of Positivism. Within a few decades, important figures in French intellectual and political life became his disciples. John Stuart Mill observed in 1866 that when Comte's philosophy was scarcely mentioned in France it was "already working powerfully in the minds of many British students and thinkers." In Russia in the sixties, Comte's works became widely known among the intelligentsia. As James Billington explained, Comte brought "the young rebels' emotional belief in progress into harmony with their intellectual attachment to the scientific method."[59]

By the end of the century, the confident philosophy of Positivism had been eclipsed by new currents of thought that undermined the naive belief in scientific or mechanistic determinism. Comte's Positivism faded away, but his legacy lives on in sociology, the social science of which he was the father, and which retains his insistence upon regarding social phenomena as subject to scientific investigation.

Adolphe Quêtelet (1796–1874) was another great pioneer of the social sciences. He, more than anyone else, became the founder of modern statistics—in short, the founder of modern quantitative social science. Statistics was, of course, not a new discipline. The effort to describe social phenomena numerically reaches back into earlier centuries. The word *Statistik* first appeared in print in Germany in 1672. In England it was called Political Arithmetic and had as its purpose the providing of information for the use of state policy. Quêtelet's work marked the debut of the modern era in statistics. He used mathematical formulae applying the normal or Gaussian distribution, the familiar bell-shaped curve, to the analysis of social data. In 1835 Quêtelet published *Sur l'homme et le développement de ses facultés, essais d'une physique sociale,* which quickly won him international fame. The book owed much of its impact upon his presentation of the concept of the "average man." That man was an abstract being, constructed by Quêtelet from statistical data that he drew from the range of human activities. Quêtelet maintained that the behavior of the average man could be foretold because of the regularity of the occurrence of events when they are statistically analyzed as mass phenomena.

Quêtelet was not content with describing the average man and his behavior as a statistical phenomenon. Like Comte, he set a higher goal: the advancement of human welfare. In the same passage in which he spoke of the regularity of human misdeeds, he accused society of being responsible for the crimes men commit. "The observation," he wrote, "which seems discouraging at first sight, is comforting at closer view, since it shows the possibility of improving people by modifying their institutions, their habits, their education, and all that influence their behavior."[60]

History, too, developed pretensions to achieve an exactitude that rivaled that of the physical sciences. That belief appeared in the later stages of a renaissance in the writing of history that began in the early years of the nineteenth century. The renaissance began when authors started writing a new kind of history that was infused with the spirit of Romanticism. As noted earlier, the writings of these historians had an important part in the propagation of the ideology of nationalism. The new spirit of nationalism not only motivated historians to tell of the glories, past and present, of their respective nations. It also inspired the collection and publication of documents that reached back to the origins of the nation and so provided the material for the writing of national history. The publication of these documents and other collections of local, regional, and national sources continued into the twentieth century and amounted to many hundreds of volumes.

Remarkably enough, the Romantic historians drew much of their inspiration for their kind of history from the novels of Sir Walter Scott. It was a debt that historians everywhere readily and gratefully acknowledged. Thomas Carlyle, one of the greatest of the Romantic historians, in 1838 explained that Scott's novels had taught historians that "by-gone ages of the world were actually filled by living men, not by protocols, state papers, controversies and abstractions of men. Not abstractions were they, not diagrams or theorems, but men in buff or other coats and breeches, with colors in their cheeks, with passions in their stomachs, and the idioms, features, and vitalities of very men." A twentieth-century successor to the Romantic tradition, George Macaulay Trevelyan, thought that Scott did more than any professional historian to present a true conception of history because he was the first to realize that history was not simple but was complex and never repeated itself. He showed, wrote Trevelyan, that "history must be living, many colored and romantic if it is to be a true mirror of the past." Scott's novels, translated into many languages, had a deep influence upon the reading public, too, persuading them to think historically and to value the past.[61]

Romantic historiography had another characteristic that distinguished it from earlier historical writing: its enormous popularity. The Romantic emphasis on tradition and folklore and local color helped create the popular interest in history. More significantly, the rapidly evolving realities of social, economic, and political life had more to do with the attraction of history. The rise of nationalism, the impact of industrialization, the growth of cities, the growing unrest among the middle and lower classes, and the sometimes kaleidoscopic changes in political life kept the times in ferment. The rapid and dramatic transitions that they could see occurring about them made the educated public, increasing always with the growth of the middle class, wonder about the origins and background from which these changes had emerged. They wanted their history in fullest detail, so that multivolumed works became the order of the day. The poet Lamartine's *Histoire des Girondins*, published in 1847, filled eight volumes and became a literary sensation. The first two volumes of Thomas Macaulay's *History of England Since the Accession of James II* came out in 1848. The first printing of three thousand copies of the two volumes, each of over seven hundred pages, was sold in six hours. The two volumes reached a fifth edition in six months and were translated into almost every major European language. The history began in 1688, and Macaulay had planned to bring it down to the death of Queen Anne in 1714. Five volumes had appeared, each hugely successful, and Macaulay had not yet reached the end of the reign of William III in 1702 when he died in 1859. A ten-volume *History of Europe*, written by Archibald Alison, Sheriff of Lanarkshire in Scotland and part-time historian, appeared between 1833 and 1842. It was marred by multiple shortcomings and defects, and knowledgeable contemporaries scorned it as an inferior work. Yet it sold in the hundreds of thousands; went into numerous editions; was translated into French, German, and, surprisingly, Arabic (in which language two thousand copies were published); was "epitomized" in a children's edition; and made Alison a wealthy man.[62]

Histories not only enjoyed popularity, but their authors did as well. Through their work, historians had an influence on political life unparalleled since that time. They wrote their books with a political purpose in mind. German historians preached the gospel of nationalism and glorified the Hohenzollern rulers of Prussia as the hoped-for unifiers of Germany. In 1848 Gustav Droysen, professor of history at the University of Kiel, wrote to F. C. Dahlmann, a fellow historian at Bonn, about a plan to write a cooperative history of Germany. "We Germans can't be helped," he wrote, "so long as we don't know what we had [he meant the medieval Holy Roman Empire] and what we lost. . . . We live as if we have no past, as if at every moment we are just beginning, as if every root of our historical existence has been severed." The first requisite for the cooperative history, he continued, was to have the right people contribute. The second requisite was to make Prussia the focus.[63]

In Britain in 1827, Henry Hallam published a three-volume treatise on constitutional history that has been called the first work on modern England of national and international importance. Despite its careful scholarship, the book amounted to a Whig manifesto that exalted the principles of the "Glorious Revolution" of 1688. Hallam became the first authoritative advocate of the so-called Whig interpretation of British history.

If Hallam was the first authoritative advocate of the Whig interpretation of history, Thomas Babington Macaulay was its most popular and most eloquent. Macaulay's interest in people and events and, above all, his sparkling prose, made his volumes a pleasure to read. In the first pages of the first volume, he said that he planned to write the history of the people as well as of the government, to trace the progress of the arts, the rise of religious sects, changes in popular tastes and manners, and even dress and furniture. Above all, his history would show how England owed its prosperity, its position as a great power, its sound public credit, its supremacy in world commerce, its maritime power, and just about every other blessing to the effects of the Revolution of 1688. "The history of our country during the last hundred and sixty years," he wrote, "is eminently the history of physical, of moral, and of intellectual improvement." As Lytton Strachey observed, "A preposterous optimism fills his pages. The Revolution of 1688 having succeeded, all was well: Utopia was sure to follow, and it actually had followed—in the reign of Victoria."[64]

The impact of historical writing upon political life was particularly marked in France. In the 1820s a number of young men made their debut as historians, among them Thiers and Guizot, who disliked one another and who later held high office in the government of the July Monarchy. They wrote what might be called the Whig interpretation of French history. They supported liberalism, greatly admired Britain for the liberties its people enjoyed, and in their writings compared France unfavorably with Britain. Thiers wrote a ten-volume history of the French Revolution that appeared between 1823 and 1827. The famed critic Charles-Augustin Sainte-Beuve said that Thiers's volumes had the effect of the Marseillaise and made its readers love the revolution. Not surprisingly, in view of their mutual dislike, Guizot did not share Sainte-Beuve's high opinion. In a letter to his confidante Princess Lieven (who had enjoyed Thiers's volumes), Guizot said that book showed talent and art but was wrong because it drew no conclusions: no one was right, no one was wrong, nothing was true, nothing was false.[65]

No one could accuse Jules Michelet of not reaching conclusions. In his multivolume *History of France,* which he began in 1831 and completed only in 1859, the year of his death; in his *History of the French Revolution*; and in his other writings his hero was always the common people of France. He wanted to trace their history through the centuries and tell of their oppression by kings and nobles and the church. Their moment of triumph came in the first years of the French Revolution, before self-servers subverted the Revolution to their own purposes. Michelet, through his histories, wanted to reconstruct French society so that the people—the plebeians—would at last gain the rights that belonged to them. Michelet's history of the Revolution, Lamartine's history of the Girondists, and a history of the revolution by Louis Blanc contributed importantly to the popular discontent with the July Monarchy that led to the February revolution in 1848. Their books glorified the revolution and implied that its work was unfinished. Actually, only Lamartine had completed his book before 1848. Michelet's seventh and final volume appeared in 1853, and Blanc did not complete his twelfth and final volume until 1862. But the volumes that appeared before 1848 were perfectly timed to stimulate the revolutionary ardor that was building up in the French public.[66]

In the thirties and especially in the forties, in the waning years of Romanticism, historians, attuned to the changing spirit of the times, began to write history in a new realist manner. They wanted to analyze and explain and not simply to narrate. Inspired by the successes of the natural sciences, they thought they could arrive at equally scientific—that is, accurate—accounts and conclusions by careful and exact research. The roots of this kind of history lay in the study of classical philology. In 1786 Sir William Jones, in his book *Asiatic Researches*, called attention to the similarities among Sanskrit, the ancient language of India, and Greek, Latin, and other European tongues. German scholars seized upon the idea, testing it by comparison of grammatical structures and by the study of ancient classical texts. They critically examined the ancient manuscripts to establish their authenticity, to determine whether they had a single author or were a compilation of different sources, to establish the primitive forms of the language in which they were written, to trace their origins to myths and folklore, and to gain an understanding of the life and thought of ancient peoples. It was a short step for men trained in the rigors of philology and its concern for sources to turn to the writing of history.[68]

The greatest figure among these realist historians was Leopold von Ranke (1795–1886). George Peabody Gooch, himself one of the masters among twentieth-century historians, wrote of Ranke, "He was beyond comparison the greatest historical writer of modern times, not only because he founded the scientific study of materials and possessed in an unrivalled degree the judicial temper, but because his powers of work and length of life enabled him to produce a larger number of first-rate works than any other writer. . . . No one has ever approximated so closely to the ideal historian." Caveats have been raised to Gooch's panegyric, but no one can question the high quality, the depth, and the breadth of Ranke's work and his amazing record of achievement. His collected works fill sixty-three volumes.

In 1885, when he was ninety, Ranke recalled that as a youth, the novels of Sir Walter Scott had enchanted him. He decided to learn more about the Age of Chivalry that Scott had described and so turned to the sources that Scott had used. He discovered that Scott's fiction often controverted the history related in the sources. He also discovered that the sources were far more interesting and, as he put it, "more beautiful." So Ranke turned away from Romantic fiction and with it turned away from the Romantic historians whom Scott had inspired. Instead, Ranke insisted upon realism in the writing of history. In a famous and often quoted phrase from one of his early writings, he stated that the historian's duty was "only to tell how it really was." The historian must treat his sources with the same objectivity and impartiality with which the natural scientist studied the phenomena of nature, without imposing value judgments of his own. Ranke went to the contemporary sources, the diaries, letters, diplomatic reports, charters, and the accounts of eyewitnesses, using other writings only if they were drawn from contemporary materials. He wrote history authenticated by the documentary evidence and then explained its meaning.[68]

This, said Ranke, was scientific history. In truth, Ranke, like all historians before and after him, could not escape the human frailties of biases and predilections. Ranke, who thought himself an objective historian and free of value judgments in his consideration of history, believed that history revealed the intentions of God. He wanted to seek God's purpose, to find the hand of God in the continuities that he believed underlay all human history. He wrote what he called universal history, history from a universal viewpoint rather than from a parochial perspective, because he wanted to show the diversity of God's design for mankind and, at the same time, its interconnectedness.[69]

In addition to his religious predilections, Ranke had a nationalistic and politically conservative bias. In university lectures on German history, Ranke told his students that while all national histories had importance, German history was the most important of all. German historians, he said, should strive "to provide body for an otherwise vague historical consciousness, to reveal the content of German history, and to experience the effective, vital spirit of the nation in it." He supported the status quo, agreed with conservative political thought, was an advisor of King Frederick William IV of Prussia, and wrote political memoranda for his guidance.[70]

Like their peers in the natural sciences, Ranke and his fellow German historians—many of them his students—established history as an academic discipline and made Germany the world's leader in historical scholarship. Ranke himself founded the historical seminar (he called it his *exercitationis historiae*) that set the pattern for the historical seminars that became the standard method of training professional historians. Ranke's seminars met weekly in his home. A student presented a paper at each meeting, and his fellow students criticized the paper and its use of sources. Ranke himself showed the relationship between the seemingly disparate reports and their common historical theme. A student in one of the seminars remembered with admiration the calm objectivity with which Ranke drew historical phenomena out of the totality of their causes, put them in a living picture, and made clear the connection between the past and the root of future development.[71]

Like the study of science, the professional study of history in England lagged far behind that of Germany. At Oxford in 1850, out of 1,600 students only eight had enrolled in modern history. Cambridge in 1847 offered no lectures in history. In 1849 Prince Albert, as chancellor of Cambridge, wanted to appoint a man of distinguished ability to the chair in history. He hoped this would create a student interest in historical study. He offered the post to Macaulay, who declined; and then the Prince settled on Sir James Stephens as the man best qualified after Macaulay. Stephens had served for many years in the Colonial Office, where he had made many enemies, and had frequently written articles for the *Edinburgh Review*. That apparently was the sum of his qualifications for the post. After talking with Sir James, the Prince appointed him to the chair. In a letter to Baron Stockmar, his longtime mentor, Albert explained (if that is the word) the appointment. "Never have I seen an Englishman," he wrote, "with a mind more open and free from prejudice. I understand now why he was unpopular; for he hits hard at the weak points of his countrymen."[72]

Though Britain lagged behind Germany in the professional study of history as well as in science, British theories of economic behavior reigned supreme. In the midst of the Romantic era, with its devotion to sentiment and emotion, the so-called classical school of economics continued the rationalism of the Enlightenment all but unchallenged until the 1840s. Adam Smith and his successors proclaimed that natural law ruled economic life. A natural harmony and the famed "invisible hand" allowed each individual in a free, competitive market to contribute to the welfare of all society by pursuing his own self-interest. The state should remove all barriers to individual enterprise and trade between nations and restrict itself to the maintenance of public order and the administration of justice. Later economists of the classical school, notably Thomas Malthus and David Ricardo, cast a dark shadow over Smith's optimism. They concluded that the population, if unchecked by natural causes or man-made calamities, would exceed the food supply and that wages would always sink to the level of bare subsistence; such notions seemed to undermine the beneficent effects of natural law on human welfare and persuaded Thomas Carlyle, in 1850, to call economics the "Dismal Science." Nonetheless, the theories of the classical school, albeit nuanced and modified, commanded wide adherence as orthodox economic theory well into the twentieth century.

In Germany scholars regarded classical economics as canonical until Friedrich List decided to challenge the tenets of the Smithian doctrines. List, as described in an earlier chapter, had spent seven years in the United States. Here he had become an advocate of the "American system" that called for high tariffs to protect infant industries from imports from more developed nations. After his return to Germany in 1832, where he took up the career of journalist, he wrote a steady stream of articles on economic subjects. Again and again he attacked the theories of the classical school. He denied the existence of natural laws of economic behavior. Instead, he insisted that historical circumstance and the stage of a nation's economic development should determine its economic policies and interests. The state must not be a bystander but should take a leading hand in the development of the national economy as an integral part of national life and culture. Only Britain, with its superior industrial establishment, could afford the policy of free trade, selling its manufactured wares in return for the raw materials of less-developed lands. Germany should adopt protective tariffs so that its industries could grow and compete successfully with British manufacturers. That would strengthen Germany as a nation and provide its people with a higher standard of living.[73]

In 1841 List published *The National System of Political Economy*, the culmination of his campaign against the teachings of the classical school. In that book he developed his doctrine of economic nationalism and introduced the theory of the stages of economic growth. All societies, he wrote, passed through three economic stages: first agricultural, second, the establishment of new industries, and third, the developed industrial economy. The government at each stage should adopt appropriate economic policies. In the first stage free trade should prevail so that people should acquire the skills needed for economic growth. In stage two, the state could impose protective tariffs and encourage industrial growth by subsidies and monopolistic privileges. In the third stage, which only Britain had entered, nations could afford to return to free trade.

List's advocacy of economic nationalism met with the derision of many who labeled him, among other things, a hireling of German manufacturers. Supporters of his doctrines were on the defensive until the revival of protectionism in Europe in the last quarter of the nineteenth century. That led to a revival of interest in List's writings. His book was reprinted in Germany and translated into other languages, and List assumed the status of a seminal figure in the history of economic thought.[74] List's opposition to the classical school and his theory of stages were mirrored in the academic world when in 1843 Wilhelm Roscher (1817–1894), the young, newly appointed professor at the University of Göttingen, published *Sketch for Lectures on the National Economy, According to the Historical Method*. That book laid the foundations for the Historical School of Political Economy, which lasted well into the twentieth century. List had used history selectively to support his theories. The Historical School, like List, denied the validity of deducing natural laws of economic behavior. Unlike List, they applied the new inductive methodology of history to describe objectively the totality of human relations entered into during the production and distribution of goods, and the historical and natural phenomena that gave form to these relations. They disparaged theory and extolled historical research. Each nation had its own distinctive economic, political, and social life, shaped by such factors as climate, topography, race, and *Geist*, the cultural, moral, and spiritual factors that were essential in historical development. Yet each nation passed through the same successive stages of growth, with institutions appropriate to that stage—with institutions such as slavery acceptable and, indeed, necessary in one stage, but reprehensible in a later stage.[75]

The uses of history by List and by Roscher became the model for the study of economics, a model soon taken over by other social scientists. The realist, objective history of the school of Ranke seemed to offer the instrument to probe the meaning of the past of a nation and to point the way to its future destiny. In later times that view of history as a sufficient explanation of a people's experience and present condition, and the conviction that history permeated intellectual life, was called historicism. Time has shaken this reliance on history. But in the course of their researches and writings, these German social scientists and historians, like their brethren in the natural sciences and medicine, made German scholarship and German methodology supreme in all the world into the first decades of the twentieth century. German universities and German research institutes drew students from every corner of the globe, and they carried back the spirit, methods, and accomplishments of German scholarship to their native lands. This global impact on the pursuit of knowledge represented Germany's greatest contribution to the understanding and well-being of all mankind.

PART TWO

CHAPTER FIVE

Great Britain: A New Era

In 1837, after an unusually cold spring, William IV, king of Great Britain and Ireland, passed to his reward. His crown went to his eighteen-year-old niece, Alexandria Victoria, daughter of the Duke of Kent. Named Alexandria after Tsar Alexander of Russia, she was always called Victoria. To some, her succession to the throne seemed to fulfill an old prophecy for the year 1837 that went, "The year will be without a spring, and Great Britain without a king."

The throne that she inherited was a badly shaken one. Some of its most loyal supporters feared that its days were numbered. In the eighteenth century, the throne had used public moneys, honors, and above all else, appointments to government offices, many of them sinecures, to create a "king's interest," or the "King's Friends," in Parliament. The placemen voted the way that the king wanted them to vote, and no ministry could survive without the votes of the "king's interest." Then, from 1780 on, reforms slowly undermined the influence of the crown. Controls upon the expenditure of public funds gradually restricted their use for political purposes. Most important, the patronage at the king's disposal was increasingly curtailed until by the mid-1830s many of the sinecures had been abolished. Those that survived became targets of censure. "A placeman is in these days an odious animal," wrote Charles Greville, clerk of the Privy Council and grandson of a duke who held two sinecures, "and as a double placeman I am doubly odious."

The long succession of reforms had ended the crown's ability to sustain the "king's interest" in Parliament and severely reduced the authority and influence of the throne.

The waning of the influence of the monarch during the early years of the nineteenth century was vastly accelerated by the character and behavior of the rulers of the House of Hanover who sat in Britain's throne, and, indeed, the character and behavior of the entire royal family. George III had early shown signs of mental instability. In 1788 he suffered a spell of madness from which he never fully recovered. In the succeeding years, his mind grew dimmer, and in 1811 he lost all contact with reality. In the remaining nine years of his life, his eldest son served as Prince Regent and in 1820 succeeded his father as George IV.

Sad as was his illness, George III's greatest misfortune was the children whom he sired. He had fifteen, of whom seven sons and five daughters reached adulthood. Charles Greville characterized the unsavory brood as "rogues, blackguards, fools and whores." They were self-indulgent, dissolute, irresponsible, reckless with money, in heavy debt from gambling, constantly in and out of disgraceful and sometimes appalling scrapes, begot illegitimate children, and seemingly lacked any sense of moral restraint.[3] The death in 1817 of Princess Charlotte, the Prince Regent's only child, left open the succession to the throne in the next generation. To fill the gap, three of the Prince Regent's brothers, the Dukes of Clarence, Cambridge, and Kent, broke off long liaisons, and each hastened to wed a suitable spouse in an effort to produce an heir to the crown. Time proved Kent the winner of the sweepstakes.

George IV, who reigned from 1820 to 1830, was a remarkably inept ruler. Greville, who knew him well, called him "a contemptible, selfish, unfeeling dog" and said that "there was nothing false and base he would not have been guilty of if he had dared, only he was such a coward." His misrule, his dissolute life, and his failed attempt to divorce his long-estranged wife, Queen Caroline (herself no role model of morality), brought the throne into popular ridicule and disrepute. William IV, who succeeded his brother in 1830, was a dim-witted and vulgar man. He had lived for years with a Mrs. Jordan, who bore him ten Fitz-Clarences. When the death of Princess Charlotte left open the succession, he threw over Mrs. Jordan, proposed marriage in quick succession to three English heiresses who rejected him, and then married a German princess. Despite his successes in fathering bastards, he failed in one of the primary duties of a monarch, namely to produce a legitimate heir. That left the way open for the only child of the next generation, the young Victoria, daughter of the Duke of Kent.

The insanity, immorality, and ineptitude of Victoria's immediate predecessors strained the traditional allegiance of the British people to their sovereign. The royal family was held in contempt, and the crown had never been
lower in popular esteem. A long downswing in economic life and growing
resentment among the underprivileged against the inequities of Britain's
class structure aggravated the discontent that roiled national life. Though a
wave of public rejoicing—and probably relief—greeted Victoria's coronation
in 1837, there seemed small reason to believe that the future held much
promise for improvement in the quality of the nation's sovereign. Victoria
was, after all, a Hanoverian. Her father, Duke of Kent, fourth son of George
III, was a sadist, a hypocrite, a liar, and an intriguer. Greville, with perhaps
pardonable hyperbole, called him "the greatest rascal that ever went
unhung." For over twenty-five years he lived with a French-Canadian
woman. Then without ado or regret he turned her out and in 1818 married
Victoria of the German House of Saxe-Coburg and the widow of Carl
Leinigen, a minor German prince. The fastidious Austrian diplomat Count
Rodolph Apponyi once described her as "a big woman with the manners of
a housemaid."[4]

In 1819 the new duchess of Kent fulfilled her function by giving birth to
the future Queen Victoria. Eight months later the infant's father died, and
soon thereafter her mother formed a close personal relationship with an
adventurer named Sir John Conroy. It was not a happy environment for a
sensitive child, as Victoria was. She grew up dominated and bullied by her
mother and by Conroy, and with few friends. Her mother did keep her away
from her father's family. She feared plots against herself and her daughter by
Victoria's uncles, who resented the child because she stood between them
and the throne. Her line of royal succession had the unforeseen benefit of
insulating the young Victoria from the manners and morals of her paternal
kinsmen.

Her subjects often called their new ruler "the little Queen." Less than five
feet tall, she had a slim and girlish figure, bright blue eyes, the sloping chin
and forehead and the fair skin that marked many of the Hanoverian line, a
small and unattractive mouth, and a lovely voice. Britons vied with one
another in praising her appearance.[5] She was not a clever or bright person.
She could be stubborn, resentful, thoughtless, and even heartless. She
enjoyed remarkably good health, was physically strong, bore nine children
without great travail, and never had a serious illness. Poorly educated, she had
little or no taste for literature or the arts or sciences, and sometimes displayed
a startling ignorance about everyday subjects. She knew scarcely anything and
seemed to care little about the social and economic problems that plagued

her less fortunate subjects. On a visit to Germany in August 1845, the Sunday costumes of poor peasants there so impressed her by their cleanliness that she wrote, "This is because they are peasants, and do not aspire to be more. Oh! If our people would only dress like peasants, and not go about in flimsy silk bonnets and shawls!"[6] Reared almost in isolation by her German mother and her German governess, Baroness Lehzen, in a German-speaking home, she was in many ways more German than English, and always showed a predilection for anything German.

Her youth, her sex, her sheltered life, the fact that, as someone put it, she had transferred at once from the nursery to the throne, persuaded wise men that she would be lost in her high office. In very short order she proved them wrong. Less than a month after her accession, Princess Lieven, Russian-born cosmopolite and shrewd observer of the great world, wrote in letters to a friend that the young queen has a strong will, knew her own mind, and with a childish smile and a clear, soft, and silvery voice, had everyone cowed. "Everyone has been taken in by her; she has secretly prepared herself for a long time for her destined position. . . . Her self possession is incredible. . . . The Queen is outstanding. . . . With so much power at 18 what will she be like at 40?"[7]

Not surprisingly, the immature Victoria, carried away by her new power and determined to have her way, overstepped the bounds. The end result of her transgression was a serious diminution of the already weakened authority of the throne and the onset of a new era in the history of the British crown and the unwritten British constitution.

It all began with Victoria's attachment, indeed her infatuation, with Viscount Melbourne, leader of the Whig party and the Queen's Prime Minister. The often told story of the bond between the eighteen-year-old queen and the fifty-eight-year-old prime minister is one of the most endearing episodes in the long history of the British crown. For the first time in her life, Victoria met a handsome and worldly man of great personal charm, with wide experience and sophistication, who was a lady's man to boot—he had been cited in two well-publicized matrimonial suits. He was a learned, wise, and entertaining conversationalist, and that, too, was a new experience for her. All in all, she was overwhelmed. Melbourne, for his part, responded warmly to the young queen and quickly acquired a paternal love for her. Like a wise father, he devoted himself to ridding her of the narrowness and prejudices of her upbringing, of strengthening her character, and of preparing her for the role she had to play. He spent long hours with her every day. He never used his influence with her to promote himself and his party. He even abandoned personal habits of long standing, such as sprawling at ease in his chair, spicing his language with expletives, affecting an air of ennui, and enjoying sophisticated and clever conversation with his peers. In the presence of the queen, he sat bolt upright, carefully guarded his language, and endured without protest the trivial and dull chitchat of the court.[8]

Then, in May 1839, catastrophe struck for which Victoria was entirely unprepared. Melbourne's government lost on a major vote in Parliament and resigned. When Lord John Russell came to tell her that the Tories would form the new government under Sir Robert Peel as prime minister, she dissolved into tears and retreated to her bedroom. She had been a partisan of the Whigs, but her tears were not for their defeat. She wept for the departure of Melbourne from her side. She dreaded that without him she would relive the dark days before her accession, without friends and with kinsmen who resented her and bore her ill will. When she sent for Peel, she told him that she much regretted losing Melbourne and his cabinet and strongly approved of their policies, but that she bowed to her constitutional duty. Peel must have been surprised at the queen's frankness, but doubtless he respected her honesty.

Things went along well enough, and Victoria agreed with his suggested cabinet members, though she detested some of them and in fact disliked Peel. Then Peel noticed that three or four Ladies of the Queen's Bedchamber were closely related to certain Whig politicians whom Peel regarded as his principal political enemies. He asked the queen to replace these women with ladies of Tory connections as a public demonstration of her full support and confidence in her new government. He told her that it was impossible for him to administer public affairs without that demonstration.

That small request, concerning positions of no recognized political importance, tripped off the explosion famed as the Bedchamber Crisis that led to a major constitutional confrontation. The indignant Victoria chose to believe that Peel, as a matter of constitutional principle, wanted to dominate her entire household. In a letter to Melbourne, she wrote, "They wished to treat me like a girl, but I will show them that I am Queen of England." She insisted that the offices in her household were exempt from ministerial control. Peel pointed out that every appointment, including those in the Royal Household, was a public office, since the office and its stipend were authorized by acts of Parliament.

In the collision of emotion with principle, emotion won. The queen saw in the impasse the opportunity to keep Melbourne. Peel for his part refused to form a government. There seemed no way out save to restore Melbourne as prime minister, though his party was in the minority in the House of Commons. The will of the young queen had prevailed over the will of Parliament, the elected representatives of the people.[9]

By reason of her youth and, not least, her obstinacy, Victoria had over-reached herself and thereby had accelerated the decline of the royal preroga-tive. Her misstep and stubbornness soon transformed the enthusiasm that had attended her accession to either indifference or opprobrium among the ruling elite of the realm. She outraged the Tories by her partisanship for the Whigs and by refusing advice given her by the Duke of Wellington, a Tory hero and national idol, calling him an "old rebel." Whigs, too, joined in the censure. Charles Greville confided to his diary, "The willful obstinate child of twenty deserves the severest apprehension, but the castigation she merits cannot be administered without impairing the authority, the dignity, the sanc-tity of the Crown she wears, and it is necessary to spare the individual for the sake of the institution."[10]

In insisting upon keeping Melbourne as her chief minister, Victoria had followed royal precedent. No rule of constitutional law declared that earlier monarchs had gone beyond their proper authority in keeping favorites in office in defiance of votes in Commons. Although Victoria had imposed her will upon Parliament by being stubborn, her triumph proved short-lived. It was the last time that an English monarch dictated who would hold the high-est offices in his government. In 1841 Parliament adopted a resolution declaring that "for a minority to continue in office without the confidence of the House" violated the spirit of the Constitution. The queen could no longer keep Peel from becoming her prime minister. Only then did Melbourne and his cabinet leave office. To save face for the queen, it was arranged that if asked by the prime minister to make changes in the Ladies of the Bedchamber, the queen would have the affected ladies "retire" of their own volition and would personally tell the ladies suggested by the prime min-ister that she intended to appoint them.

The era of personal rule had ended forever. Though by law and precedent Victoria still possessed the theoretical right to appoint and dismiss, she could no longer exercise that right. The neutrality of the throne with regard to polit-ical parties had become an axiom of that remarkable unwritten code, the British Constitution. The throne became separate from and above political parties, giving its support to any government that had a parliamentary majori-ty. The government, supported by and answerable to the House of Commons, had annexed the power included in the phrase "the Royal Prerogative." The throne could not overrule the policies of its ministers, nor act independently of them in matters of state. If it tried, Commons could cut off the money needed to run the country. So complete was the subjugation of the crown that in 1867 Walter Bagehot, in his classic study of the English Constitution, said that the monarch would have to sign his own death warrant if the Commons and Lords unanimously sent it up to him.[11]

The power of the throne, already weakened before Victoria's accession, had suffered a further dramatic decline. In 1841 the French ambassador to London reported, "In reality the sovereignty of the queen of England is only that of submissiveness. The constitution of the country leaves no place for the exercise of her will in politics." John Stuart Mill in 1849 wrote that the very essence of Britain's constitutional monarch was that "the so-called sovereign does not govern, ought not to govern, is not intended to govern; but yet must be held up to the nation, be addressed by the nation, and even address the nation, as if he or she did govern." Nassau Senior, economist and political commentator, in 1847 wrote to his friend Alexis de Tocqueville that the English had reduced the crown to a mere ceremony. "Our Queen is a phantom, put there not to act, but to fill space, to prevent anyone else from being there."[12]

Senior went too far. The throne had not become a nullity. Its political neutrality did not prevent it from expressing its opinions, sometimes in the strongest terms, in both foreign and domestic matters. As Bagehot explained in a famous passage of his book, the crown had three rights: the right to be consulted, the right to encourage, and the right to warn.[13]

Victoria's stubbornness in May 1839 had kept Lord Melbourne in office, but his place in her heart was soon supplanted when, on October 10 of that same year, her first cousin, Albert of Saxe-Coburg-Gotha, came to visit her. It was love at first sight, at least on Victoria's part. In a letter to Leopold, King of the Belgians, her uncle and Albert's uncle, too, she gushed that "Albert's beauty is most striking, and he is most amiable and unaffected—in short, fascinating." Four days after their first meeting, she told Melbourne that Albert had conquered her heart. The next day she asked Albert to marry her. She told the duchess of Gloucester that she had been very nervous when she proposed. When the duchess expressed surprise that the queen had done the proposing, Victoria, who never forgot who she was, explained that Albert "would never have presumed to take such a liberty with the Queen of England."[14]

Actually the match had been arranged years earlier. Almost from his birth in 1819, Albert's family, and especially his Uncle Leopold, had decided that the infant boy would be the future consort of Victoria, also born in 1819, the presumptive heiress to the British throne. Albert was the second son of Duke Ernest I, who was the brother of Victoria's mother. That Victoria fell head over heels in love with the handsome young prince was a bonus and not a requirement for a royal marriage. Albert, something of a cold fish, was more loved than loving, but the marriage proved very happy and successful. The morning after the wedding in February 1840, the newlywed couple surprised onlookers when they rose very early from their wedding bed to take a walk. The ever observant Greville, for whom royalty watching vied with horse racing as his favorite hobby, thought it strange that a bridal night should be so curtailed. He told Lady Palmerston that "this was not the way to provide us with a Prince of Wales."[15] Greville need not have feared. The royal couple had their first child ten months after their marriage and had eight more children in the succeeding seventeen years until Albert's death.

Before her marriage Victoria had written in her journal that it would be a "dreadful thing" if Albert opposed or thwarted any of her wishes or "meddled with affairs." Victoria quickly forgot her premarital resolves as her love for Albert became idolatry. She referred to him as her "dear master," called him her "beloved Angel" in letters to Uncle Leopold, could not bear to be separated from him, and could use only superlatives to describe whatever he said or did. She gained enormous respect for his intelligence and his opinions—not always a corollary of conjugal love. She depended upon him in every way, from taking his advice on matters of state and drafting her official letters to asking his approval of the clothes that she wore. Albert, for his part, took upon himself the task of making a different woman of the queen. In a memorandum of June 8, 1843, George Anson, Albert's private secretary, reported that "The Prince is systematically going over the Queen's education and reforming her mind and drawing out her Powers, and the progress he has made . . . has been quite wonderful."[16]

Albert firmly established himself as the queen's political advisor by the important part he played in the negotiations that ended the Bedchamber Crisis and in accustoming Victoria to her reduced status. Political figures generally recognized that to have the good will and the support of the sovereign was always helpful and at times important. Albert's trusted unofficial advisor, Baron Stockmar, writing from his home in Germany, warned Albert that the monarch should not become a mandarin figure that has to nod his head in assent or shake it in denial as his minister pleases.

Victoria and Albert sought to follow that advice, sometimes successfully and sometimes unsuccessfully. Their principal failures concerned the conduct of foreign affairs by Lord Palmerston, who served as foreign minister from 1835 to 1841 and again from 1846 to 1851. Palmerston was a master of the dangerous art of diplomatic brinkmanship. His actions, like those of all ministers, were in the queen's name. She and Albert disapproved of almost everything he did but were powerless to stop him. She complained that she often only knew what Palmerston chose to tell her or what she read in the newspapers. She and Albert hated the man, openly expressed their aversion, and argued unsuccessfully that Victoria had the right to dismiss him because he had altered dispatches after she had approved them. Palmerston remained unperturbed by the protestations and the enmity of the royal couple. When, in April 1841, the Whig politician John Hobhouse, later Lord Broughton, spoke to Palmerston of Victoria and Albert's opposition to his foreign policy, Palmerston said, "To be sure, it does not signify a pin, after all."[17]

The protests of the throne against Palmerston's policies, like all of the throne's pronouncements, were always in the name of Victoria. Actually, she adopted Albert's views as her own. She had no special taste for the work that went with the office of sovereign, while he relished it and became king in everything but name. Indeed, as Lord Ashley told Albert in a conversation in April 1848, he could accomplish more than a crowned king because he was not burdened by the necessary and inevitable restrictions that bound a king.

An able and even a gifted man and a prodigious worker, Albert was also something of a busybody. There seemed no subject affecting Victoria's realm that did not attract his attention and draw from him exhaustive memoranda suggesting changes and improvements. In 1845, at age twenty-six, he did not hesitate to tell the newly appointed Bishop of Oxford, an experienced and talented churchman, what a bishop should do. He offered gratuitous advice on German politics to the king of Prussia. That proved even too much for Albert's beloved old mentor, Baron Stockmar, who politely told Albert that he did not know what he was talking about.[18]

He made other gaffes (such as his saying that no tailor in England could make a coat), but he had a remarkable record of achievement.[19] His contributions ranged across the spectrum from curbing duels among army officers, restructuring the Royal Household, curricular reform at the University of Cambridge, promoting the arts, sciences, and industry, to taking the lead in the planning of the great International Exhibition in 1851. His greatest contribution and his most lasting one was to carry through the fundamental transformation in the political role of the crown. Through his influence with Victoria, he saw to it that the throne accepted and adjusted to its greatly diminished political power.

His host of talents, as well as his model family life—apparently he never looked at another woman—won him general if sometimes grudging admiration. Unfortunately, his qualities of mind and character did not win him popularity. The plain fact was that he was too German for British tastes. He spoke flawless English but with a German accent; his stiff manner and his inability to unbend in public, his pedantry, his air of superiority, his way of thinking, and even his appearance were German. At his suggestion the royal family spoke with one another in German, and he introduced German customs into the royal household, including the delightful tradition of the lighted Christmas tree. Though he was entirely loyal to Britain, he thought of himself always as a German prince who, as he himself put in a letter to King Frederick William of Prussia in 1847, was incidentally the husband of the queen of England. He never lost the feeling that he lived among a people who thought of him as a foreigner. He told his brother Ernst, who visited him in 1840, that when Ernst left, he would have no one to whom he could talk candidly and critically. "An Englishman," he said, "cannot grasp or understand such matters, and only sees in words like those I have just uttered an arrogant desire to blame on the part of the foreigner." His unpopularity worried him, but he lacked the personal warmth and the simple humanity—the common touch—to overcome it.[20]

Despite his unpopularity, Albert made a deep and lasting imprint upon English life. His moral earnestness, his straitlaced propriety, and his prudery helped set the tone of what history has labeled the Victorian Age. Albert, of course, was not alone responsible for the emergence of this new system of values. The growing importance of the middle class, with its emphasis on work, discipline, personal responsibility, respectability, family life, and strict religious observance, played a far greater role. So did a sea change in the personal deportment of the elite. The profligacy, the frank language, the frivolous spending, and the indebtedness that had characterized the preceding generation had vanished. The Regency rake had become an extinct species. Now a new generation of landowners, fortified by evangelical zeal, attended church regularly, spent their money carefully, were faithful husbands and watchful fathers, and personally attended the operations of their estates to insure a maximum return. Not every lord, of course, became a model of propriety. The elite had its share of wastrels like Richard Greville, Duke of Buckingham and Chandos, who in a few short years went through a great fortune, or notorious debauchees like the 3rd Marquis of Hertford (whom Thackeray portrayed as the odious Lord Steyne in *Vanity Fair*). But most of the landed elite apparently had a strong sense of responsibility and took seriously their role as the leaders of the nation and as landlords of their tenants.

Albert contributed importantly to the new age by raising the moral tone of the court to hitherto unknown heights. That made the court serve as both sanction and model for the moralism, the prudery, the earnestness, and the sense of rightness that became the hallmarks of the Victorian era. His influence became evident within months of his marriage to the queen. A few days after leaving office at the end of August 1841, Melbourne described Albert as "extremely strait-laced and a great stickler for morality," whereas Victoria was "rather the other way and did not much care about such niceties of moral choice." Peel, now the prime minister, shared Albert's views on morality and cooperated with the Prince in vetoing for court appointments individuals of whose personal lives they did not approve. The Duke of Wellington agreed with Melbourne that Albert insisted upon spotless character for court appointments, while the young queen could not have cared less.[21] Victoria's lack of concern about morality lasted only a short while. As with everything else, she soon wholeheartedly adopted Albert's standards of morality and rectitude and for the rest of her life served as the embodiment of the age that bore her name.

Increasingly in recent decades, careful studies, girded with detailed scholarly apparatus and searching analysis, have revealed, with the air of great discovery, that many Victorians succumbed to the sins of the flesh. For this reason they have portrayed the Victorian age as an era rife with hypocrisy. Perhaps these scholars might have been less stringent in their judgments had they recalled the words of Sir Walter Scott: "There is a certain hypocrisy of action, which, however it is despised by persons intrinsically excellent, will nevertheless be cultivated by those who desire the good repute of men."[22]

An exercise in so-called counterfactual history, the "if only" rewriting of the past, would be to imagine that Albert had been born the elder brother, instead of Ernst, and so the heir to the duchy of Saxe-Coburg-Gotha; Victoria would then have married Ernst. The two brothers, separated in age by only a year, were devoted to one another. Though subjected to the same education and discipline, they could scarcely have been more different. Ernst was a dilettante whose interests flitted from one field to another, a spendthrift whom Albert bailed out on several occasions, and a royal who had only a passing interest in politics. Above all else, in contrast to Albert's stress on personal morality and to his prudery, Ernst thoroughly enjoyed the life of a rake. In their correspondence Albert, who took on the role of stern parent, constantly chided Ernst for his escapades, but to no avail. Ernst joyfully followed in the footsteps of their father, a notorious libertine. He punctuated his long life—he survived Albert by thirty-two years—with an unending series of liaisons. In 1883 Lieutenant Colonel Arthur Haig, in Coburg for a festive anniversary celebration, in a letter to Victoria's private secretary called Ernst "the Father, nay the Grandfather now, of many of his subjects." He wrote that "the Grand Duke's Consort and all his other consorts will be there—all those that have been—that are—and that are going to be—all."[23] Had Ernest married Victoria it seems quite possible (especially in light of Victoria's

Hanoverian genes) that the Victorian age might have turned out to be a much different and much livelier epoch.

The erosion in the authority and prestige of the throne sharply accelerated after Albert's untimely death in 1861 at forty-two. The grief-stricken queen entered upon long years of mourning and became almost a recluse. Meanwhile, her son, the Prince of Wales, whom she would not trust with any royal duties, became the object of much unfavorable attention because of his "fast" style of life. "To speak in wide and general terms," Prime Minister Gladstone confided in a private letter in December 1870, "the Queen is invisible and the Prince of Wales is not respected."[24] Some people began to talk about making Britain a republic. Then in the 1870s, when Britain entered upon its greatest years, when British power and British wealth circled the globe, the tide turned. A great wave of patriotism swept across the nation, speeded in no small part by the new "popular press," and by a literature of adventure and violence that apotheosized Britain's imperial conquests. Victoria emerged from her seclusion, and though still clad in her widow's weeds, took center stage in great and colorful imperial ceremonies that had enormous popular appeal. In the thoughts of her subjects, she became the matriarch of her people and the symbol of the nation's greatness. The badly shaken throne that she had inherited a half century earlier had become a revered, albeit politically powerless, institution, cherished by the millions of her subjects scattered across the globe.

The ebbing in the political power of the throne that began in the late eighteenth century left a vacuum that had been quickly filled by an oligarchy of great landowners and their kin who became the true rulers of Britain. Already in 1810 Thomas Jefferson had written of Britain that "the real power and property in the government is in the great aristocratical families. . . . The nest of office being too small for all of them to cuddle into at once, the contest is eternal, which shall crowd the other out. For this purpose, they are divided into two parties, the Ins and the Outs, so equal in weight that a small matter turns the balance."[25] The famed Reform Bill of 1832, once represented as transferring the domination of the government to the middle class, left the landed elite still in command of the state. The right to vote remained hedged by substantial property qualifications. The number of electors rose from less than 500,000 to 813,000, leaving over 85 percent of Britain's adult male population still disenfranchised.[26] The end result of the reform was that the men elected to the House of Commons differed scarcely at all from those who sat in prereform Parliaments. Of the 815 men who sat in the House of Commons from 1841 to 1847, 247 were heads of families of the baronetage or gentry, 116 were the sons of such families, 180 were the sons of peers, and

115 were the relatives of peers, baronets, or gentry. Only 157 members during these years had no ties of kinship to the peerage, baronetage, or gentry. The votes of many of the members were controlled by peers who sat in the House of Lords and to whose support they owed their seats. That included members who had no familial connection with the landed elite. William Ewart Gladstone, son of a wealthy Liverpool merchant, began his Parliamentary career in 1833 at age twenty-four, when the Duke of Newcastle used his "influence" in the borough of Newark to have Gladstone elected. Years later Gladstone, who served four times as prime minster, in a speech to Parliament in 1859, defended the designation of M.P.'s by great noblemen. Populous constituencies, he said, would not elect young, inexperienced men. "If you want a succession of men trained to take part in the government of the country," he argued, "you must have a great proportion of them elected to the House while they are boys."[27]

The House of Lords was the preserve of the peerage. In the late 1830s the peerage had 353 members, ranging from three dukes of the blood royal down to 182 barons. They were joined by sixteen Scottish lords elected to each Parliament by the Scottish peerage, twenty-eight Irish peers elected for life by their fellows, and thirty Anglican bishops, twenty-six of them from England and four from Scottish sees. In past times the House of Lords had been seen as the balancing force between king and Commons, thereby protecting the liberties of Englishmen from attacks by the throne or by the lower house. That conviction still lingered and lent support to the authority and prestige of the nobility. The peers still had extensive legislative power, but their sessions were poorly attended and their debates conducted in a desultory fashion. When Alexis de Tocqueville visited Lords in the mid-1830s, he found only about fifty members present, sitting around a large table or lounging on the cushions of the benches. Tocqueville, himself a noble and something of a snob, found himself charmed by the scene. "There was nothing pompous," he wrote in his journal, "but a general air of good manners and easy good taste, and so to say an *aroma* of aristocracy." Both Commons and Lords held their sessions in the evening, after the long dinners fashionable in the London of that time. Not unexpectedly, many members, sated with food and wine, fell asleep, while others lay back in their seats and barely managed to keep their eyelids open.[28]

The landed elite continued in its long-held monopoly of membership in every cabinet, no matter which party held power. Sir Robert Peel's Tory cabinet of 1841 had two dukes, three earls, three barons, four baronets, the heir of an earl, and one lone commoner. The Whig cabinet of 1846, headed by Lord John Russell, a younger son of the Duke of Bedford, included two marquesses, four earls, two barons, an Irish viscount, the heir to an earldom, three baronets, and two commoners. Of the 103 men who held cabinet rank between 1830 and 1868, only three were middle-class politicians who represented the specific aims of their class. To make matters even cozier, many members of the ruling elite were related to one another by blood or marriage, which made it almost impossible to avoid nepotism, even if the prime ministers wanted to. "Damn the Whigs!" Peel once exclaimed. "They're all cousins." He could have said much the same of Tory cabinets.

If they were not related, they all knew one another and were knit together by a strong group feeling and by shared values. As boys they went to Eton or Harrow. There, according to Lord John Russell, the same rough treatment experienced by all of them created a "democracy of the aristocracy" and at the same time provided a common intellectual climate that prepared them for public careers. They rode and hunted together; they had London houses in the same neighborhoods; they met one another at dinner parties, at their clubs, and on long weekends at the great country houses; and they talked freely and openly to one another. When Guizot served as France's ambassador to London in 1840, he found that he had no need for spies or informers. "What can't be learned from the newspapers or in fashionable gatherings," he wrote, "is not worth the trouble of being sought after." It was a male-dominated society, but women held a significant place in it and were much admired. Mothers saw to it that their daughters made marriages that added to the prestige and connections of the family, a matter of grave importance to these people. Dowagers, always respected and often feared, were formidable figures in the social world around which the world of the landed elite revolved.[29]

The domination of the landed elite, the four thousand or so families of the nobility and gentry, reached out beyond London to the farthest corners of the kingdom. The central government, lacking both the means and the will, depended upon the landed elite to carry out its domestic policies and to preserve internal order throughout the realm. In each of England's forty counties, a great peer always held the highest office, that of lord-lieutenant. Justices of the peace, chosen by the lord-lieutenant from the gentry and Anglican clergy of the county, had judicial powers over most criminal offenses. They also ran local government, and at quarterly meetings, with the lord-lieutenant in the chair, they settled the administrative affairs of the county. They served without pay. A sense of *noblesse oblige* persuaded them to devote time and effort to the interest and welfare of the people who lived in their counties. Their paternalism toward their social inferiors served to justify their superior status to themselves and to the public. One of their number warned that if they relinquished their duties to paid employees of the government, they would degenerate into idle and useless members of society and forfeit the respect now justly paid them.

Their control of local affairs extended to the parish church. The vicar owed his appointment to the local magnate who, as the expression went, "presented him with a living." Birth, upbringing, and political connections determined who was chosen. The bishops formed the elite of the Anglican church. Half of them came from families of the nobility, and the other half had formed close personal ties with important families, often after once having served in their households as tutors. In short, the Church of England, the kingdom's established church, was very much an integral part and an agent of the ruling elite.[30]

The nobility and the gentry not only ran the national and the local governments of the country. They also owned most of it. The so-called *New Domesday Book*, compiled in the 1870s, estimated that the United Kingdom had about one million proprietors. Of these one million, about seven thousand individuals owned 80 percent of the realm. In England alone, 363 proprietors, nearly all of them peers, and each with estates of over ten thousand acres, owned 25 percent of the land. Another three thousand with holdings of one thousand to ten thousand acres owned 30 percent. There is good reason to assume that these estimates held true for the earlier years of the century. Some of the wealthiest proprietors also owned much land in London and other cities. In addition to the rents they drew from their lands, the elite had income from other sources that included mines on their properties, canal and turnpike tolls, investments in commerce and industry, and payments from the new railroad companies for rights of way across their lands.[31]

The greatest proprietors probably were rivaled in their wealth only by the great serf owners of Russia. They lived in a magnificent style. They had enormous country houses, some of them truly palaces, with vast gardens and deer parks, and with hosts of servants and gardeners. They also had great London houses where they lived during "the season," where they entertained in princely manner, and where they engaged in their political wheeling and dealing. Visitors, unaccustomed to life on this scale, found themselves overwhelmed. When the American Henry Colman visited Althorpe, the ten-thousand-acre seat of Earl Spencer, he reported that the house had bedrooms for seventy guests, plus servant quarters, a hundred-foot-long gallery hung with paintings by masters, and a library of over fifty thousand volumes, reputedly the largest private library in the world. Lord Hertford invited a French friend to stay in one of his houses. "I have a place in Wales," he said, "which I have never seen but they tell me it's very fine. A dinner for twelve is served there every day, and a carriage brought around to the door in case I should arrive. It's the butler who eats the dinner. Go and settle there; as you see it will not cost me a farthing." A peer without wealth was considered an anomaly; as a contemporary put it, "A mendicant peer is very unmonarchical."[32]

The elite preserved the integrity of its landed property from generation to generation by primogeniture and a form of entail called strict family settlement. Only the eldest male inherited. He had to pass the property on intact to his eldest male heir. About 50 percent of England's land lay under strict settlement. Dowries large enough to attract suitable husbands provided for the daughters of the house. When de Tocqueville asked Henry Reeve, a knowledgeable man of letters, what happened to younger sons, Reeve told him that their fathers bought them commissions in the army, or they became clergymen and received an appointment to a well-endowed "living" from some great landowners, or qualified as members of the bar, an expensive procedure for which the father paid, or took posts in India. Because of the unhealthy climate of India, the odds were three to one that the appointee would die there. Thus, India always had a large number of vacant positions, and all of them were always in demand. Reeve should have added the diplomatic corps and the civil service to his list. A prime reason for a peer to involve himself in politics was to find appropriate positions for his offspring and other kinsmen, and to gain promotions for them. In the early 1850s Sir Charles Trevelyan, himself a longtime civil servant in India and in Britain, characterized the civil service as a refuge for aristocratic failures and "the incompetent, the habitually idle, the imperfectly educated and the unhealthy."[33]

The elite especially prized the sinecures that still existed, not only for their relatives but also for themselves. In what the visiting American professor George Ticknor called an example "of the pleasant abuses with which England abounds," the Duke of Wellington received a sizable stipend as Governor of the Tower of London but had nothing to do with its operation. Lord William Bentinck, Governor of Bengal, also held the office of Clerk of the Pipe, one of whose duties was to hold the train of the Lord Chancellor. Charles Greville, grandson of the 3rd Duke of Portland, as mentioned earlier held two well-paying sinecures as Clerk of the Privy Council and Secretary of the Island of Jamaica. The first post had minimal duties and the second apparently had none.[34]

These men of the elite who stood at the pinnacle of their society were not possessed of any special faculties of mind or of natural abilities that distinguished them from the rest of their countrymen. One of their own recognized that when he wrote in his journal, "What great men are Lord Lonsdale, the

Duke of Rutland, Lord Cleveland, etc., but strip them of their wealth and power, what would they be? Among the most insignificant of mankind; but they all acquire factitious consideration by the influence they possess to do good and evil." Unlike the nobility of continental lands, the British nobility did not form a legally privileged order of society. Aside from the right to sit in the House of Lords, the British titles of nobility were, as the earliest volumes of Burke's *Peerage* put it, "very unimportant, and minister much more to the pomp than to the power of the possessor." Their privileges included the right to trial by a jury of their peers when indicted for high treason or a felony, exemption from jury duty, personal access to the sovereign, and immunity from arrest for debt. Unlike most of the continental nobility, they had to pay the same taxes and obey the same laws as all other Britons. And again unlike the Continent, where all descendants of a nobleman were themselves noble and bore their parent's title, in Britain only the eldest in the male line inherited the title of nobility. All other family members were commoners. That was why the English peerage was so small in number, compared with the continental nobility.[35]

Their wealth, their domination of location and national government, and above all else, the deference shown them by their fellow subjects marked the peerage and other members of the landed elite off from the rest of society and made them supremely self-confident and certain of their superiority over the rest of mankind. The unquestioning acceptance of that superiority provided the most remarkable aspect of the ascendancy of the landed elite. A centuries-old consciousness of hierarchy persisted everywhere. Each stratum of the social pyramid deferred to the stratum above it and felt superior to those beneath it. No one expected any indulgence from those above him and, indeed, the superior lost face if he exhibited forbearance. A few lonely voices, among them that great tribune of the middle class, Richard Cobden, protested against the demeaning and even groveling submission to the privileged landed few. "We are a servile, aristocracy-loving, lord-ridden people," he complained in a letter of 1849 to John Bright, "who regard the land with as much reverence as we still do the peerage and the baronetage. Not only have nineteen-twentieths of us no share in the soil, but we have not presumed to think that we are worthy to possess a few acres of mother earth."[36]

During this period, a septuagenarian with an oversized head on a frail and bent body, whose high-arched arrogant nose seemed to reach out to his jutting chin, toothless, deaf, with the tremulous voice of old age, served both as public symbol and justification of the preeminence of the elite. His name was Arthur Wellesley, conqueror of Napoleon, first Duke of Wellington, known simply to everyone in Britain as "the duke," as if there were no other dukes in the realm. When he died in 1852, Charles Greville wrote, "The Crown never possessed a more faithful, devoted, and disinterested subject. . . . He never for a moment considered that his great position and elevation above all other subjects released him from the same obligation which the humblest of them acknowledged." The royal family turned to him constantly for advice. So did countless other people, and it was said that in the uppermost strata of society, no marriage nor family matter was arranged without consulting him. The Duke of Argyll recalled that in the House of Lords Wellington's vote carried more weight than a majority vote of the members. In Commons, too, he had great authority. His contemporaries did not content themselves with calling him merely a great man. Queen Victoria, who had once inveighed against the duke, called him the greatest man ever produced in Britain. Earl Grey, an unremitting political opponent of the duke, went the queen one better. He declared that "in every circumstance of public life, the Duke of Wellington is the greatest man that ever lived."[37]

This hyperbolic adulation was not restricted to Britons. In 1847, when the king of Prussia came to England for a royal christening, the duke, dressed in a Prussian field marshall's uniform and wearing the Prussian Order of the Black Eagle, met him at the dock. The king rushed to him with open arms, and expressed his delight by announcing that it was the proudest day of his life. Philipp von Neumann, an Austrian diplomat with long service in London, wrote that Wellington's moral qualities, nobility of character, elevation of mind, in addition to his military genius, put him in the ranks of the greatest leaders in all of history. Guizot proved more restrained. In his memoirs, he recalled that the duke had most impressed him by his "wonderful good sense and sagacity. He had not a spark of imagination, but he did not want it. . . . He was not forced to conjecture; he could see every part of his subject."[38]

Admiration of the duke was no less extravagant among the general public to whom he had become a sort of demigod. When he walked or rode through the streets of London, clad in old-fashioned style in a buttoned-up long blue coat, white duck trousers, and a stove-pipe hat with an extremely narrow brim, passersby on foot and in carriage raised their hats. The duke acknowledged the reverential salutes, whether he saw them or not, by repeatedly raising two fingers to his hat brim. In his youth, he had cut a wide swath with the ladies, and to his death he retained an antique gallantry which in anyone else would have been ridiculed. The diaries and memoirs of his contemporaries repeatedly told of dinner parties and country weekends at which the duke recounted stories of his victorious campaigns against Napoleon. Apparently he never tired of retelling these tales, and apparently his admiring audiences never tired of hearing them.[39]

The duke did have his shortcomings. Despite his great influence in Parliament, he cut a poor figure as a speaker. Nor was he a good horseman. Robert Smith Surtees, knowledgeable about such matters, said that he had seldom seen a man with less idea of riding than the duke, and that he knew of few men who had more falls in the course of the year.[40]

His death in 1852 at age eighty-three became the occasion for great public displays. His body lay in state for six days. When, on the third day, the doors opened to the general public, the crowds were so enormous that three people were crushed to death. At the funeral procession, an estimated 1.5 million people lined the streets. The diplomatic corps turned out *en masse*, though the French ambassador had hesitated to attend the funeral of the man who had conquered France's national hero. The Russian ambassador dispelled his doubts by telling him, "If this ceremony were intended to bring the duke to life again, I can conceive of your reluctance; but as it is only to bury him, I don't see that you have anything to complain of."[41]

The elegance, the domination of political life, the deference shown by the rest of society, and above all, the supreme self-confidence of the English landed elite, made it both the envy and the model for the nobility in the rest of Europe. They patterned themselves on what they considered the concept of the "English gentleman." They emulated the manners, dress, country mansions, gardens, and deer parks of the English elite. They founded gentlemen's clubs on the English model and took over the word "club" unchanged in every major European language. The attachment of the English to tradition held a special appeal for the elites of other lands. No other people seemed to hold on to its past by so many ties. The English justified reforms by identifying them not as innovations, but as the restoration of rights and privileges to people to whom they rightfully belonged.[42]

The aggrandizement of the political power of the landed elite at the expense of the throne brought about a remarkable transformation in the organization of politics. In the eighteenth century and the early decades of the nineteenth, political parties in the modern sense did not exist. People called themselves Whigs or Tories, but that meant only that they felt bound together by family ties, by friendship, and by patronage—and not by allegiance to certain political principles. The government had really been the king's government, and, as mentioned earlier, no ministry could survive without the confidence and support of the king. When the political power of the throne dwindled, parliamentary groupings took on increasing importance. The modern party system came into being, albeit rudimentary in structure, loosely organized, and years away from crystallizing into national organizations.

A speech by Sir Robert Peel, then prime minister, in December 1834, heralded the new ordering of politics. In form, it was a campaign speech for Peel's reelection to Parliament from the borough of Tamworth, in Staffordshire. In fact, Peel and his supporters intended it as a statement of Tory principles directed to the entire nation, and had copies of it widely distributed. It became famed as the Tamworth Manifesto. The Manifesto promised a careful review of civil and ecclesiastical matters, and "the correction of proved abuses and the redress of real grievances," but always without infringing on established rights. Peel mentioned a number of specific matters on which he promised action, always limited and never in advance of public opinion.[43]

The publication and distribution of the Tamworth Manifesto, an unprecedented action in itself, marked the beginning of what became known as the Conservative Party. The Whigs followed suit in February of the next year when, in the so-called Litchfield House Compact, Whigs joined forces with radicals and Irish nationalists. Intended initially as a temporary alliance to drive Peel's government from office, it became the "point of origin" of the Liberal Party. By the early 1840s members of Parliament identified themselves as members of one of these two parties. Usually they voted with the leaders of their party, but as Viscount Melbourne explained in a letter to Victoria in 1842, the leader could not always hold them in line. This was especially true, he explained, when the party was out of office and so could not threaten dissidents with serious political consequences.

Party discipline reached out from London through provincial associations and party agents. Despite often bitter personal and political animosities, only small differences distinguished the two parties. They easily coalesced in the effort to smother, or at least retard, reforms proposed by so-called radicals. These radical members were too diverse and too divided on their pet projects to form a unified party with its own leader and platform. They urged legislation that would make government more responsible to the needs of the society and that prepared the way for the emergence of the modern welfare state.[44]

One man, Sir Robert Peel, dominated the politics of the new party structure. Contemporaries, including those who differed from him in their political views, recognized him as the outstanding politician—they said statesman—of his time. He mastered the ways of the House of Commons, which he had first entered when he was only twenty-one, and had gained recognition as its most powerful member. Always knowledgeable of his subject no matter what it concerned, he spoke in a measured and passionless tone. With faultless logic and in clear and forceful language, he made his case and refuted his opponents. He lacked eloquence but he always held the close attention of his listeners. He led his party for almost twenty years and served twice as prime minister, briefly in 1834–1835 and then from 1841 to 1846. He was a cold and unconfiding man. Daniel O'Connell, the famed Irish leader, once said that "Peel's smile was like the silver plate on a coffin." Lord Ashley, who sat next to Peel at a dinner in 1841, reported that, "It was the neighborhood of an iceberg with a slight thaw at the surface."[45] Always formal and even pompous in manner, more admired and respected than liked, he seemed an unlikely master politician. However, his qualities of mind and character, his administrative abilities, his skills as a debater, and his ability to recognize and to adjust to the changing opinions and sentiments of his fellow Britons more than compensated for the lack of warmth in his manner and personality.

Born in 1788, Peel was the eldest son of a wealthy cotton manufacturer who vowed to have his son become prime minister and trained the boy from early youth for a political career. In 1809, as soon as he became twenty-one, his father bought him a seat in Parliament, where he quickly gained recognition for his abilities. He served as Home Secretary for most of the 1820s. In that post, he carried through a reform of the criminal law and established the London police force, still called bobbies or peelers in recognition of their founder. By the early 1830s, he had become the acknowledged leader of the Tories.

He was a handsome man, tall and well built, with a fair complexion, reddish hair, a strong and pleasant face with high forehead, and a long and slightly aquiline nose. Always elegantly dressed, he carried himself well, though he had a certain awkwardness in his movements. Very much the devoted family man, he had a charming and lovely wife and seven children. He wrote an affectionate letter to his wife every day that they were apart, addressing her with such phrases as, "My own dearest love, or "My dearest life," and the like.

In social gatherings he sometimes seemed distant and at other times could be lively and full of stories. Possibly the difficult social position he occupied among the elite explained his guarded manner. Apparently, he never forgot that he was the first man of recent middle-class origin to become prime minister—nor was he allowed to forget it. He seemed overly sensitive to the difference between his family background and that of his high-born Tory colleagues. The duc de Broglie, scion of the old French nobility, in London in the mid-1840s, noticed that at social functions, as Peel passed, some people exchanged mocking glances or whispers, indicating that they did not consider him of their own kind. Broglie proved himself a keen observer. Charles Greville, grandson and cousin of dukes and a Whig by birth and conviction, grudgingly recognized Peel's ability. He called him *facile princeps*, easily the first, in the House of Commons. But he wrote scornfully of him as a "vulgar man." "In all his ways, his dress, his manner," Greville wrote in 1835, "he looks more like a dapper shopkeeper, than a Prime Minister. He eats voraciously, and cuts creams and jellies with his knife. [The Earl of] Jersey pointed this out to me. And yet he has genius and taste, and his thoughts are not vulgar though his manners are to such a degree." The Duke of Wellington liked to say, "I have no small talk and Peel has no manners."[46]

Peel, a proud and thin-skinned man, undoubtedly sensed and resented the snobbery of men inferior to him in every way save social standing. In private letters, he revealed his low regard for titles. He advised a friend to "retain the distinction" of not having a title, and he felt strongly that the heirs of peers should win honors by their own merits rather than by inheritance. This attitude underlay his refusal to accept the Order of the Garter from Queen Victoria, who had become his devoted admirer. In a letter to a friend, written in the starchy style that seemed natural to him, he explained that he sprang from the people and was essentially of the people, so that the highest honor would be misapplied if awarded to him. His reward, he continued, lay in the confidence of the queen and not in titles of honor or social distinction. He left instructions that after his death no member of his family should accept a peerage or any other distinction as a reward for his services. Broglie called it "a somewhat affected disdain for the highest honor of his land." Some even suggested that his support for the repeal of the Corn Laws in 1846, a measure anathema to most of the landed elite, revealed his latent middle-class antagonism to these people.[47]

The repeal of the Corn Laws crowned Peel's remarkable record as a reformer. By heritage, education, religion, and personal bearing and manner, he seemed the very model of a conservative. Yet his integrity and his intelligence made him recognize that new times and new forces in society demanded new policies. He did not hesitate to change course by vigorously supporting reforms that he had once opposed, if he was convinced that they were in the nation's interest. Once a foe of Catholic emancipation, he came to recognize its necessity and voted for the 1820 act that allowed Catholics to vote, to sit in Parliament, to hold public office, and to attend Oxford and Cambridge. An opponent of the Reform Bill of 1832, he defended it after its passage. When he became prime minister in 1841, he set out on a program that included the restructuring of the British banking system, the requirement that joint-stock companies register and publish their balance sheets, the introduction of an income tax, legislation regulating the labor of women and children in mines and factories, the reduction of many tariffs on imports and ending tariffs on exports, and finally, the abolition of the Corn Laws.

Parliament in 1815 and 1828 had renewed the Corn Laws, centuries-old regulations governing the import and export of grain. The laws were to protect British producers of grain from foreign competition. They established a sliding-scale tariff on imported grain that rose when grain prices in Britain fell because of bountiful harvests, and declined when domestic grain prices rose because of poor harvests. Their net result kept up the price of bread, then a major component in working-class diets. To the advocates of free trade, the Corn Laws were the keystone of Britain's system of tariff protection and allowed, they argued, the landed interest to enrich itself at the expense of the rest of society. The Corn Laws, they said, also severely retarded the growth of British industry and commerce. Other nations could not buy manufactured goods from Britain, the world's leading industrial power, unless they could pay in food and raw materials.

The agitation against the Corn Laws reached a crescendo in the second half of the 1830s when an economic downturn, widespread unemployment, and poor harvests racked Britain along with most of the rest of Europe. The price of grain soared, and the possibility of a shortage threatened. That was when seven men in the industrial city of Manchester, stronghold of free traders, organized a local anti–Corn Law association. It quickly attracted members, and early in 1838 it became the National Anti–Corn Law League. Two remarkable men, Richard Cobden and John Bright, emerged as the League's most prominent and most forceful leaders. Cobden, born in 1804, one of eleven children of an unsuccessful farmer, knew poverty and privation as a youth. He had some schooling but essentially he educated himself. A compelling speaker, he spoke in a conversational tone, without rhetorical flourishes or emotional appeals, and in simple language, but with a sincerity and earnestness that his listeners found difficult to resist. He was elected to Parliament in 1841, where, as he himself said, his fellow M.P.'s regarded him as a "Gothic invader." He quickly assumed a leading role in the struggle against the Corn Laws. Victory in this controversy did not end his appetite and enthusiasm for reform. He was a man who took to causes that included the adoption of free trade by other nations, world peace, the extension of the franchise, public education, diminution of the prestige and influence of the landed elite, and temperance.

John Bright, born in 1811 into a wealthy Quaker family of cotton manufacturers in Rochdale, near Manchester, had early entered the family business. He showed no special interest in public affairs until the death of his wife in 1841. Cobden, who knew Bright, happened to be visiting nearby and dropped in to pay his respects. To console the grieving husband, he told him (with considerable but doubtless unintended exaggeration) that in thousands of English homes people were dying of hunger and that he should join Cobden in the campaign to repeal the Corn Laws. Bright took up Cobden's proposal, for as he explained years later, "I felt in my conscience that this was a work that somebody must do." So was formed a political partnership of two gifted men who worked together in a relationship so close that the name of one is rarely mentioned without the name of the other.

Bright gave up the family business to work full time for repeal. In 1843 he entered Parliament and spent the rest of his active career as a leading politician. He was a burly man, with a square jaw, deep-set eyes, and a severe, even grim mouth. A journalist wrote that he was "the most English-looking man I ever saw." Indeed, he looked remarkably like the mythical John Bull, albeit a dyspeptic one. He was a no-nonsense sort of man. Above all else, he was a magnificent orator, acknowledged as having few if any peers in an age and a land that prized oratory. He had a powerful and resonant voice that he used with artistry to lend effect to selected passages. He had a sense for the rhythm of words and sentences and a gift for the choice of the right words that gave his speeches a special quality.[48]

With advocates like Cobden and Bright, the Anti–Corn Law League quickly motivated the opponents of the laws, most of them from the urban middle class. The League became the most effective political pressure group that Britain, and indeed the world, had yet seen. It was a new phenomenon, the first of its kind anywhere, the model for all future pressure groups. Its leaders literally invented the modern technique of the political education of the public. They organized local branches throughout the country, published a newspaper, turned out pamphlets that were distributed by the millions of copies, set up a successful fund-raising operation, persuaded over six hundred nonconformist ministers attending a conference to preach and pray for repeal when they returned home, and engaged in campaigns to elect the League's candidates for seats in Parliament. Above all, the League held hundreds of meetings, large and small, throughout the kingdom, where speakers spread the word for repeal. Their rhetoric usually included condemnations of "aristocratic tyranny," "hereditary opulence," and "social injustice" and the declaration that "trade shall no longer pay a tribute to the soil." They stressed the insensitivity of the landed oligarchs to the sufferings of the people, repeating over and over again the remark of the Duke of Norfolk that the poor should allay their hunger by taking an occasional pinch of curry in a little water.

The aroused members of the League made large cash contributions to support its work. In 1840 the organization raised between £7,000 and £8,000. By 1845 that figure had risen to £250,000. When the League dissolved after the repeal of the Corn Laws, a public subscription raised £75,000 to £80,000 for Cobden, who, because of his absorption in the fight for repeal, had wound up a poor man.[49]

The League left a legacy that had enduring effects upon British national life and politics. For the first time in British history, people hitherto excluded from the national councils made their voices heard. The League educated them in a problem in economics, and united them in a demand for reform. Already in 1841 a wise Scottish lawyer pointed out that the controversy about tariffs and free trade could be seen as merely a conflict of one interest group against another. He saw it, however, as striking evidence of the advance in the public's understanding of the functioning of the economy. No discussion on such matters, he wrote, could now take place without public knowledge and understanding of the facts and doctrines of economics. Moreover, under the guise of the demand for repeal of the Corn Laws, the League was attacking the entire Establishment, the men and the institutions that governed Britain. Conservatives recognized this and saw the specter of democratic revolution if the government yielded to the League's demands. If that happened, how could the government resist other popular movements for change? In any event, the odds seemed all against repeal.[50]

Fears of democracy and predictions of certain defeat did not daunt Peel, nor did his own longtime support of protection for agriculture keep him from arguing for repeal. In a letter to Lord Aberdeen, he explained that by 1845 he had decided that the welfare of the public had necessitated the abolition of the Corn Laws. He had intended to proceed slowly, but the potato disease and bad weather forced his hand. The potato blight appeared in Ireland in August of 1845 and spread rapidly, bringing famine and death to the Irish peasantry whose diet depended almost exclusively upon potatoes. Simultaneously, heavy rains flooded fields and ruined harvests in England and Scotland, and heavy taxation followed to pay for the feeding of the hungry poor. Peel and his supporters offered the alternative of ending the Corn Laws and allowing imported grain to flow freely into Britain.

After much political maneuvering, the repeal bill came before the House of Commons. Outraged Tories who felt that Peel had betrayed them flayed the prime minister. A truly Odd Couple led the attack. One was the exotic Benjamin Disraeli, flamboyant in dress and manner, with glittering chains around his neck and his hair in ringlets, the outsider who yearned after the English aristocracy. The other was Lord George Bentinck, a duke's son, the archetypical English milord, who until 1845 had devoted his adult life to racing and hunting, and whose sole and unfulfilled ambition had been to win the Derby. He entered into the controversy over repeal only because he wanted "to rally the broken and dispirited forces of a betrayed and insulted party, and to avenge the country gentlemen and landed aristocracy of England upon a minister who presuming on their weakness, false flattered himself that they could be trampled on with impunity." Disraeli, gifted, witty, and a talented speaker, led the fight on the floor. Despite the stinging rhetoric of Disraeli and the politicking of Bentinck, the bill, supported by a coalition of Whigs, Radicals, and Tories loyal to Peel, passed the House in mid-May. The Lords passed it in late June. The queen signed the bill on June 25, and it became law. That same night Bentinck and Disraeli had their revenge. To get even with Peel, they led a successful fight over a bill that concerned Ireland. Peel and his government fell to a coalition of Tory protectionists seeking revenge and Whigs seeking office.[51]

In his last speech to Parliament as prime minister, Peel paid handsome tribute to Cobden, attributing to him the success in the battle for repeal. Peel was too generous. His decision to support repeal, and his ability to win the votes of the so-called Peelite Tories and the Whigs, enabled repeal to carry the day. After he left office, Peel became the nation's senior statesman. The press and the public generally assumed that one day he would again head the government as prime minister. Tragically, in 1850 his life was cut short by a fall from his horse when riding home from a courtesy call at Buckingham Palace. Word of his death set off a wave of mourning throughout the kingdom.[52]

The repeal of the Corn Laws marked the beginning of free trade in Britain that lasted until after World War I. The tariff on grain was phased out gradually by the end of 1849. Other tariffs remained, but successive governments abolished them, and by 1860 Britain had virtually free trade. Meanwhile, in 1849 Parliament had repealed the Navigation Acts that reached far back in British history, and thereby opened Britain to the shipping of all nations. Historians long viewed the repeal of the Corn Laws as the triumph of the middle class over the landed elite. In recent decades, historical revisionists have hacked away at this interpretation with so much energy and enthusiasm that one of them even claimed that the struggle for repeal was "much ado about nothing." Their studies have shown, among other findings, that contemporaries overestimated the need for imported wheat, that the price of wheat did not fall after repeal, and that English agriculture, far from declining, boomed and entered a "Golden Age" that lasted until the final quarter of the nineteenth century.

Despite the revisionists, the struggle over repeal was far from much ado about nothing. The phenomenon of men of the landed elite supporting legislation contrary to the interests of their class certainly lent historical significance to the repeal. Contemporaries suggested explanations for what seemed to many of them a sacrificial act. Peel himself believed that by supporting the repeal of the Corn Laws, he saved Britain from revolution. In a letter written soon after he left office, he wrote, "I am a Conservative and the most Conservative act of my life was that which has caused the sacrifice of power."[53] Peel's home secretary, Sir James Graham, put it more bluntly when he wrote that repeal would provide "some hope of surviving the din of this odious and endless topic of democratic agitation, and would give increased security to the aristocracy by improving the condition and diminishing the discontent of the great masses of the people." In short, these men and others like them, convinced that the nation was best served by the rule of the landed elite, realized that they had to make concessions to stave off the threat to their domination. Events proved that their strategy worked, for they continued to govern Britain for many decades to come.[54]

They remained in power, but in a drastically changing nation. An amazingly rapid growth in population from around 15 million in 1801 to over 27 million in 1851, an even more startling increase in urban population, great advances in industry, increase in the wealth and self-confidence of the middle class, increasing restiveness among the lower classes, urban and rural alike, and the shrinking of the agricultural sector in the national economy were continuing to create a new kind of society. A once predominantly rural nation was transforming itself into the world's first industrial society. As that unprecedented transformation proceeded, new pressures and demands emerged, and long-accepted values and traditional patterns of behavior came increasingly under question and attack.

The greatest beneficiaries of the transformation were men of the upper middle class. Owners and investors in the new factories and mills and trading companies and banks and railways, and rightfully proud of their achievements, they pressed for an appropriate share in the conduct of public affairs. The landed oligarchs, fearful that these men might ally with the rest of the middle class and bring about a social and political revolution, decided to make concessions that would win over the upper middle class. A French visitor to England suggested that the bourgeoisie used the principle of free trade to raise their status and power in the same way that the barons of the thirteenth century had used the principle of political liberty against King John to aggrandize their position.

The middle class ranged from people of great wealth and economic power to small shopkeepers, artisans, and tenant farmers who were scarcely distinguishable from the proletariat. The middle class was an anomalous classification, yet society recognized its existence and easily identified those who belonged to it. Partly a matter of rank and station in life, partly a matter of self-identification, the middle class followed the principle of meritocracy in sharp contrast to an aristocratic social structure in which birth and kinship determined status and power. Each individual rose or fell by reason of his own abilities and accomplishments.[55]

A long article in the *Edinburgh Review* in October 1840, a leading journal of criticism and opinion, mirrored the new self-confidence and air of triumph of the upper middle class. The government of England, wrote the anonymous author, "is progressively changing from a government of the few, to a government, not indeed of *the* many, but of many—from an aristocracy with a popular infusion, to the regime of the middle class." Ralph Waldo Emerson, in England in 1834 and again in 1847–1848, observed that many Englishmen, university graduates and born to wealth, "are every day confronting the peers on a footing of equality, and outstripping them, as often, in the race of honor and influence." Lord Stanley, 15th Earl of Derby and a Tory leader, lamented that "the monied interest is now all in the ascendant" and believed if it gained control of the legislative power, England would be well on the way to becoming a republic.[56]

These men and others who expressed like opinions went too far. Strikingly few men of the middle class sat in Parliament or held leading posts in government. Britain's upper bourgeoisie seemed content to leave the conduct of the affairs of state in the hands of the landed elite so long as the oligarchs responded, however grudgingly, to their pressures. The latter cooperated because of the threat to their domination by public opinion, mobilized by men of the upper middle class. It was a reciprocal relationship that historians have named the Victorian Compromise, a tacit understanding between oligarch and plutocrat, that each should respect and protect the other's interests. The arrangement served both factions, but with the landed elite holding the upper hand.

The respective attitudes of landed elite and upper bourgeoisie for each other reflected this unequal relationship. People of the upper middle class deeply resented the fact that in Britain's social hierarchy they were the inferiors. They portrayed themselves as energetic and hard-working paragons whose unceasing efforts brought wealth and progress to the nation. Richard Cobden, in a speech at Covent Garden in 1845, told his listeners that the elite had for ages robbed, plundered, and bamboozled the people. He portrayed the aristocracy as a subtle and powerful enemy of the middle class.

Thomas Carlyle thought that England was fortunate in having "another aristocracy, that of wealth, nay, in some measure that of wisdom, piety and courage—an aristocracy not at all of the 'chimerical or do nothing' sort."

Two American visitors reported scarcely less harsh condemnations from distinguished English personalities of the era. In April 1838 George Ticknor had breakfast with Sydney Smith, a leading figure in London's literary and social life, and Henry Hallam, the historian and critic. To Ticknor's considerable surprise both men, who, as Ticknor pointed out, were "to a singular degree petted and sought by the aristocracy," spoke bitterly and forcefully of what they termed the noxious and oppressive influence of the elite. Charles Dickens aired his contempt for the nobility by the names and traits of character that he gave them in his novels. There was the nepotist Lord Decimus Barnacle, head of the Circumlocution Office in *Little Dorrit,* the vicious Sir Mulberry Hawk and his patron and dupe Lord Frederick Verisopht in *Nicholas Nickleby,* the fatuous Lord Mutanhead and the haglike Dowager Lady Snuphanuph, whom Mr. Pickwick met at fashionable Bath, or Lord Boodle, the self-important political leader in *Bleak House,* who as a dinner guest pontificated about his fellow distinguished party leaders, Lords Coodle and Doodle and Foodle and Goodle, and so on.[57] An attack on the elite from another level came from the scurrilous newspapers that became popular during these years. An American visitor perceptively observed that these scandal sheets had social and political significance. This kind of journalism, he wrote, "could only live in the shadow of an Aristocracy. . . . The Peer is dragged through a horse-pond for the sport of the plebeian. The artisan chuckles to see Princes and Nobles wallowing in dirt, in print."[58]

Deep as the resentment went, under it lay an envious admiration for and a hankering after the life-style of the landed elite. Though many successful men of the middle class were content and took pride in their status, many others coveted a higher position in the social hierarchy. Leon Faucher in 1845 wrote that the English middle class loved liberty but had little taste for equality, sharing with the nobility a passion for social distinction. Successful businessmen purchased country estates at a cost of many thousands of pounds, bought the right to have a coat of arms on their table silver and the doors of their carriages, and sent their sons to exclusive boarding schools and to Oxford and Cambridge, where the young men adopted the manners and ways of their elite classmates. Once having wrested the franchise and free trade from the reluctant oligarchs, these social climbers lost interest in further reform. Their one-time adherence to dissent in religion and liberalism in politics gradually gave way to adherence to the Church of England and to political conservatism. "The snobbishness of the moneyed classes in the great seats of commerce," Cobden told Bright, "is a fearful obstacle to any effectual change in the system."[59]

The landed elite for its part affected a scorn of "trade" as crass and materialistic and unbefitting a gentleman. Trade was considered demeaning. A young orphaned woman of good family, frequently at Court, married a merchant, and as she recounted, was immediately made to feel inferior "as though I had become a Pariah to them, because I was connected with Trade." The orphaned daughter of the Earl of Lindsay married an ironmaster and immediately lost social status, though as she put it, she came "of the best blood of England." Charles Greville, who disliked C. E. Poulet-Thomson, later Baron Sydenham, put him down by noting that he was originally a merchant and had "a quantity of counting-house knowledge."[60]

The landed elite's lofty disdain of trade was actually one of the myths by which men live. Members of the peerage and gentry who had coal and iron deposits on their lands took an active part in exploiting these resources. They participated, too, in many other enterprises that included canals, railroads, turnpikes, and the development of urban property. In the Parliament of 1841–1847, at least a third of those members who belonged, or were related, to landed families engaged in business activity, either as direct participants or as directors. There was nothing new in this; participation of the English elite in business enterprise reached back to much earlier times.

The political and social domination of the landed elite seemed unimpaired by pressures that came from the middle class. In 1858 Cobden lamented that in his experience, the ruling oligarchs never stood so high in relative social and political rank, with the middle class content with the crumbs from the table of the elite.[61]

Despite its continued domination, fissures began to appear in the elite's monopoly of power in the 1830s and increased in the 1840s. In local government salaried bureaucrats and elected town and county councils replaced the unpaid local gentry who for so long had run local affairs. The process began when the increase in population, industrialization, urbanization, and a new concern among the upper classes about public welfare compelled a reluctant Parliament to take remedial action. Between 1833 and 1854 Parliament established sixteen new agencies empowered to supervise the activities of local authorities and institutions and to enforce new welfare legislation. Agencies such as these needed salaried engineers, doctors, and other specially trained men who would devote all their time and energies to their duties. Most of these new bureaucrats came from the upper ranks of the middle class. Only a few had aristocratic connections, a small number came from the lower middle class, and none from the proletariat. Well educated, intelligent, industrious, and filled with reforming zeal, they took leading parts in the efforts to correct social abuses, to enforce new welfare legislation, and to reorganize and provide new ideas and new vigor to government departments.[62]

The working arrangement between landed elite and upper middle class excluded the great mass of the people of Great Britain—the middle and lower strata of the bourgeoisie and the workers in field and factory. The upper middle class, having gained a measure of political power, was content with the status quo. They bitterly opposed legislation that regulated conditions of labor in mines and factories as infringements upon individual liberty. They believed that the government had no right to interfere in the contract between employer and employee. When H. S. Tremenheere, civil servant and an architect of mine and factory reform, met Cobden and Bright at a private dinner, they assailed him as one of the "humanitarians who will ruin the manufacturing industries of the country," as a theorist who did not know what he was creating, and as a self-styled philanthropist whose ideas would lead to the pauperization of the people.[63]

Both landed elite and upper middle class vigorously opposed the extension of the suffrage to the lower classes. They maintained that government belonged in the hands of the educated few and not in the hands of the uneducated many. To these men the word *democracy* was a term of opprobrium, much as the word *communism* is to many people of our own time. Their condemnation of democracy reflected their fear that the working classes would rise and overthrow the existing order. That fear, and their alarming visions of social revolution, were not without cause. Hungry, ill-fed, ill-clad, ill-housed, and overwhelmed by the dull misery of poverty, workers in town and country often turned to direct action to give voice to their discontent. They called strikes, kept nonstrikers from going to their jobs; they rioted, set fires, attacked policemen, broke machinery, and sometimes pillaged and extorted money from the well-to-do. Economic downturns, mass unemployment, poor harvests and the rising cost of food, agitation against the new Poor Law of 1834, with its workhouses for the indigent, the emergence of radical ideologies, growing resentment of the hardships and injustices of proletarian life, and unanswered demands for a greater voice in government—all of these factors stoked their discontent.

Disturbances began around 1830 and continued on through the 1840s in the longest period of continuous social disorder in modern British history. Britain was closer to revolution than at any time since the civil war of the 1640s. Major outbreaks of violence erupted in South Wales in 1839 and in 1842, starting in Staffordshire and spreading to Wales, the Midlands, and industrial towns in Scotland. They had to be put down by troops, sometimes

with deadly force. Similar but less turbulent outbreaks continued in the succeeding years and persuaded Britons and foreign visitors alike that the kingdom faced a troubled and perilous future.[64] Lord Melbourne shared these
forebodings. In August 1842 he told Queen Victoria that the discontent
engendered by unemployment and destitution, aggravated by political
rhetoric and demagogues, was driving England into near if not actual revolution. In September of that year, Charles Greville wrote in his diary that "those
who are best informed look with great anxiety and apprehension to the
future." Thomas Carlyle in his *Past and Present*, published in 1843, warned
that unless England could correct the wrongs done to its workers and end
their grief and rage, England would perish. Similar gloomy forecasts came
from all quarters of the political and social spectrum and included such notables as Sir Robert Peel, the Duke of Wellington, Lord Aberdeen, Matthew
Arnold, and the Lord Chancellor, Baron Campbell. In 1842 Heinrich Heine
thought it possible that British workers "will rise and thirst for blood"; and
Friedrich Engels, in 1845, confidently prophesied that Britain faced violent
class warfare.[65]

The disturbances in towns and cities attracted most of the attention of
contemporaries and of later historians. But the countryside, too, knew serious, and in some districts, almost unending turmoil that the authorities
found difficult or impossible to prevent. Small tenant farmers and farm
laborers, who in the best of times lived at the margin of subsistence, now
found themselves reduced to paupers. The growth of population produced
increased pressure on the land, many were unemployed or underemployed,
and alternative employments were not available out in the countryside.
Repeatedly peasants poured out of their mean dwellings, broke down fences
that enclosed land once held in common, and set fires. In 1843 a kind of
guerrilla war erupted in Wales. Peasants there, oppressed by poverty, and outraged by the tolls on highways and lesser roads imposed by local landowners,
came out at night to smash the toll gates and sometimes to burn the house of
the collector of the tolls. Often disguised in women's clothes, they called
themselves Rebecca and her Daughters, after the passage in Genesis 24:60
that reads, "And they blessed Rebecca and said unto her . . . let thy seed possess the gates of those which hate them." Local sympathy with the vandals
made it impossible to stop the disturbances. No one would inform and no
jury would convict. As time went on, the Rebeccas grew bolder, lawless elements reportedly began to take over, the depredations became more serious,
and some lives were lost. At last soldiers and the police succeeded in putting
down the movement. The authorities dealt lightly with those Rebeccas who
had been captured and wisely ordered the end of most of the tolls. In his

memoirs William James Linton, famed wood engraver and one-time fiery radical, called the insurgence of the Rebeccas the only successful uprising in England since the great rebellion of the 1640s.[66]

Unrest among the oppressed and the exploited of town and country and sporadic outbursts of violence reached far back in the history of Britain and every other European land. Whether the sudden eruptions of people who had reached the breaking point or whether the result of conspiracy and agitation, these outbreaks did not offer a worked-out program of reform. Instead, they addressed themselves to specific grievances and injustices. Whatever the cause, they lacked ideological content. Then, in this era of unrest in Britain of the 1830s and 1840s, a new phenomenon appeared. For the first time an open, organized, and militant working-class movement with a program of reform came into being: the National Chartist Association. This development marked the entry into political life of a class that had till now been excluded, denigrated, and unrepresented.

The history of the Chartist movement began with a small group of highly skilled London artisans who formed the London Working Men's Association in July 1836. They announced as its purpose the attainment of equal rights for all Britons. The missionary zeal of its members soon succeeded in establishing 150 similar organizations in other towns. In 1838 six members of the London Association met with six liberal members of Parliament and drew up a platform for the Association. The document was heralded as The People's Charter, a title certain to win popular attention and support. First published in May 1838, it was presented and hailed at large mass meetings throughout the land.

The Charter was an entirely political document. Its famed "Six Points" (already familiar in Radical circles) advocated universal male suffrage, annual Parliaments, the secret ballot, abolition of the property requirement for election to Parliament, payment of members, and the division of the country into equal electoral districts. The government could adopt these measures—and ultimately did adopt them many years later—without earthshaking social and economic consequences. But to the men who drew up the People's Charter and to the untold thousands of workers for whom the Charter became a talisman, the political reforms were only a necessary first step. Their adoption, they believed, would enable the common people to replace the oligarchs who ruled England and the plutocrats who controlled its wealth. That would result in a social and economic regeneration of society and would provide justice and a decent wage to the working man.

A national organization came into being in July 1840 when twenty-three delegates met in Manchester and formed the National Charter Association.

Soon many local groups affiliated with the new organization. The hard times of those years mustered loyalty and support from working men everywhere. Many shades of opinion, ranging from left radicalism to mild reformism, evidenced themselves among and within local Chartist associations.[67] Whatever the differences among the views of the local associations, Chartism held out the promise of a brighter future for workers with its pledge of "a fair day's wages for a fair day's work." In addition, it gave them a realization of their own worth, a sense of purpose, and an excitement that made them forget for a moment the meanness and monotony of their lives. They turned out by the thousands to demonstrate and to listen to overheated oratory, to march and sing Chartist songs in torchlight parades, to luxuriate in a new feeling of camaraderie with their fellow workers, and to bask in the knowledge that their activities threw fear into the hearts of their "betters." Their enthusiasm was maintained at high pitch by frequent local meetings, membership on committees, social events, major conferences at urban centers, local and regional newspapers and circulars, and by monster petitions to Parliament urging the adoption of the Charter. In 1839 the first of these petitions had over a million signatures. In 1840 another petition had 3,317,202 signatures on a roll of paper six miles long, carried into Parliament on the shoulders of sixteen men. Parliament rejected both petitions by huge majorities.

Meanwhile, lack of strong central direction and disagreements among competing local leaders about ideology and tactics severely weakened the movement. The most damaging schism, between the so-called "physical force" and "moral force" Chartists, appeared almost from the outset of the movement. The advocates of physical force believed that only violence, or the threat of violence, would persuade the government and the middle class to yield to the demands of the Chartists. The supporters of moral force argued that success could come only with the support, or at least the respect, of the upper classes. The use or threats of physical force would antagonize the Establishment and destroy all hopes of its cooperation.

The prophecies of the "moral force" advocates that violence would irreparably damage the movement soon came true. Nearly all of the rioters in South Wales in 1839 were Chartists, and Chartists rose in three other towns. Public outrage swept through the kingdom, and whatever support Chartism had among the upper classes evaporated. The government moved swiftly against the leaders of the Welsh rising, condemning three of them to death. The sentence was later commuted to transportation for life to Australia, then a prison colony, and in 1856 the government pardoned them and allowed them to return to Britain. All over the country, hundreds of leaders were arrested and some of them sentenced to jail terms of one to two years. Many

moderate workmen, shocked by the violence, left the movement. Chartism
went into decline. A worsening in economic life in 1842 brought about a
brief revival, but once again Chartists turned to direct action and once again
met with defeat, repression, and decline.[67]

The movement was kept alive through the efforts of a man named Feargus
O'Connor, born in Ireland of a prominent family. Blessed with a powerful
baritone voice, he was one of Europe's greatest demagogues in an era that
knew many such men. A giant of a man with great physical strength, he
abounded with personal charm. He possessed that special quality that attracted
and held the blind loyalty of his followers who, as one of them remembered
years later, would have gone through fire and water for him. He gained his
leadership and wielded his influence by his inspiring oratory and by the
Northern Star, the weekly national newspaper that he founded in 1837 and
edited. The paper reached a circulation of fifty thousand in 1839, the heyday
of Chartism, and then entered upon a steady decline, so that by the end of
the 1840s, it sold less than five thousand copies. Still, at a time when many
could not afford the price of a newspaper, each issue passed through many
hands and was read aloud to those who could not read, so that the paper's
audience exceeded by many times its circulation. O'Connor filled it with
inflammatory editorials, news stories, his own speeches, letters, and unending
encomiums to himself.[68]

The last great flare-up of Chartism came in the spring of 1848. The revolutions on the continent, beginning with the February Revolution in France,
had spurred radical activity in Great Britain and had stirred up a frenzy of
fears among the upper classes. O'Connor decided that the moment had
arrived to strike a decisive blow for Chartism. He planned a giant demonstration in London for Monday, April 10, after which the Chartists would
present a new petition to Parliament. When London learned of these plans,
panic gripped the city. The government, acting as if a horde of Visigoths
were about to descend on the nation's capital, took extraordinary measures.
It swore in between one hundred and two hundred thousand volunteers as
deputies to act as the first line of defense. The defenders were organized by
parishes into some semblance of military organization. Shops closed, all
government offices were garrisoned by soldiers, and a sandbag parapet with
openings for muskets surrounded the Bank of England. Troops and artillery
were brought in during the dead of night and stationed out of sight, to be
used only if the volunteers failed to repulse the demonstrators. The government entrusted the command of the defense of London to the nation's most
famed warrior, none other than the Duke of Wellington. The seventy-nine-
year-old duke, deaf and frail but full of spirit, was elated once more to be in

command. His old eyes, reported Lord Monteagle, "sparkled like a girl's at her first ball." The government commandeered the new telegraph network for the exclusive use of official messages and to prevent news of a possible Chartist triumph going to other parts of Britain. The Duke of Wellington, itching for action, could smell the smoke of battle. "Only tell me where they are," he said, "and I'll stop 'em." To Charles Greville, the readiness of Londoners to face danger and the excessive preparations seemed "either very sublime or very ridiculous."[69]

The latter proved to be the case, though not through the fault of the Londoners. The dreaded demonstration proved a colossal and even farcical failure. A crowd of twenty-five to thirty thousand Chartists, many of them from out of town, assembled under a cloudy sky on Kensington Common, on the bank of the Thames. A contingent of policemen, under the command of Richard Moyne, London's Commissioner of Police, stood nearby. When O'Connor arrived, Commissioner Moyne told him that the meeting could go on at the Common but warned him of the forces facing the demonstrators if they marched on Westminster. O'Connor, instead of protesting, thanked Moyne and insisted upon shaking his hand. He proceeded to give a rambling speech to the demonstrators, and then told them to disperse. Most did, save for some fiery young men who clashed with the police and special deputies. Before matters could get out of hand, a drenching rain began to fall and washed away the resolution of the would-be rioters. O'Connor meanwhile went by cab to the office of Home Secretary George Grey to tell him that the demonstration had ended and to thank the government for its forbearance. According to Greville, the Home Secretary asked O'Connor if he planned to return to the meeting. O'Connor said no, complaining that his pocket was picked and his toes trodden on until he became lame. The petition was brought to Westminster in the afternoon. The Chartists claimed that 5.7 million people had signed it. Clerks counted the signatures and found only 1,975,496, and many of them obviously spurious, such as "Queen Victoria," "the Duke of Wellington," and the like. Simultaneous demonstrations in Glasgow and Manchester faded away when the telegraph brought the news of the fiasco in London.[70]

The collapse of the demonstration in London proved especially heartening to Britain's ruling class. It was a revelation, according to the *Morning Chronicle,* of "how deeply and solidly are the foundations laid upon which the vast fabric of our social state silently reposes. Commerce and shop keeping have not taken the manhood out of us." Not surprisingly, Marx and Engels had a different, indeed, an apocalyptic view of the significance of the failure of the Chartist demonstration. In an article of November 30, 1848, in their Cologne journal, the *Neue Rheinische Zeitung*, they claimed that the "victory of order" on April 10 in London was the first important blow against the pan-European revolutionary movement, the first memorable date in the ultimate victory of the European counterrevolution.[71]

Chartism never recovered from the London disaster. From being a force that inspired dread and hostility in the upper classes, it became an object of contempt and ridicule. The government, employing spies and *agents provocateurs*, arrested and jailed leaders and ordered transportation for some of them. In 1850 left-wingers gained control of the National Association and converted what remained of Chartism into a socialist party.[72]

Discontent with the established order did not confine itself to the working class. In addition, dissenters opposed the privileged status of the Church of England. The Oxford Movement within that church and a schism that rent the Church of Scotland roused strong emotions among a people to whom religion was of the greatest importance. But no challenge reached the proportions of the quandary of Ireland. After centuries of turmoil and insurrection, Ireland remained an intractable dilemma for its English overlords.

The terrible poverty in which most Irishmen lived proved the most dismaying aspect of the problem. English and foreign visitors alike were appalled by the wretchedness they saw on every hand. An American visitor wrote that the filth and squalor of Irish peasant life was beyond all conception and had to be seen to be believed. Much of the blame for the overwhelming poverty and wretchedness lay in what came to be called the "Land Question," a dilemma brought about when in earlier centuries the English conquerors confiscated Catholic-owned land and granted it to Protestant and mainly English landlords. These often absentee proprietors showed scant consideration for their Catholic peasant renters. Most of the peasants held their land on short-term leases or at the will of the landlord. The uncertainty of these tenures discouraged the renters from making improvements to their holdings. Most of them lived at the margin of subsistence. Yet they did not lack for food and fuel. Easily grown and high-yielding potatoes, their principal food—the adult male ate an estimated twelve pounds a day—provided them with most of their nutritional requirements. Peat, nearly ubiquitous and easily dug up, afforded an abundance of fuel for heating and cooking. Contemporaries complained that this easily obtained food and fuel made the Irish peasant lazy and kept him from making any sustained effort to raise his standard of living. The landlords, for their part, seemed an equally feckless lot. Unlike their fellows in England, the typical Irish proprietors showed no interest in introducing innovations that would increase the productivity of their lands. They seemed content, to quote Sir Robert Peel, "to drink, smoke, attend horse races, and lead a life of idleness and dissipation."

The attitude of the English added to the dimensions of the Irish problem. To the usual Englishman, no matter what his status, the Irish were a lower order of mankind, lazy, ignorant, priest-ridden, lawless by nature, and incapable of ruling themselves. Knowledgeable Englishmen despaired of the value of any reform imposed by the British government. "You can't make people dig the ground instead of scraping it," wrote Lord Lieutenant Clarenton, "or go out to fish, or rely upon some other food than the potato, or prefer a slated house to a thatched cabin, or having a desire to better their condition. . . . Nor will an Act of Parliament inspire the gentry and middle classes with the love of truth, nor make them live within their means, nor spend their money to the best advantage for themselves and those dependent upon them."[73]

The reciprocal ethnic and religious distrust and hatred had produced centuries of turmoil, violence, and repression. On a few occasions the Irish had risen in full-scale revolt, but typically they protested by acts of violence against the person and property of their landlords or their agent. By the early 1840s rural unrest reached a new intensity. It was aggravated by increased population and a resulting increase in the numbers of landless or nearly landless peasants, by unemployment, and above all else, by a new wave of political agitation led by a man named Daniel O'Connell.

To the English, who detested him, Daniel O'Connell was a cross they had to bear. To the Irish, who loved him, he was "The Liberator." A leading barrister in Dublin, he was a big man with a strong face, careless and disorderly in his dress, with a brown, ill-fitting wig on his long head, and possessed of enormous charm and personal magnetism. He had a sharp mind, a determined will, and had about him an air of strength and shrewdness. He was a magnificent orator, with a bass voice, flexible and rich, that he used to great advantage. He placed no restraints on his tongue, never hesitating to use outrageous abuse. He dwelt relentlessly on the age-old enmity between Celt and Saxon, as he always called the English. Nor did he hesitate to use outrageous flattery, knowing that his Irish audiences, quick though they were to recognize blarney, could not resist his appeal to their vanity.[74]

From his earliest youth, O'Connell had harbored a deep antagonism toward Britain. Yet he did not want independence for his homeland. Rather, he wanted equality for Ireland and always declared himself a loyal subject of the crown. He reasoned that the only way that the English would make concessions was by the use of threats of disorder and even insurrection. So he devoted himself to arousing the simmering discontent of the Irish peasantry. After the passage of the Catholic Emancipation Act in 1829, O'Connell was elected to Parliament, where he quickly became a powerful figure. He had a large measure of control over those who came to Parliament from Ireland. O'Connell threw his support behind the Whig administration of Lord Melbourne who, in return, made some concessions to Irish demands.

When Peel and the Tories took over power in 1841, O'Connell put all of his energy and ability into a drive for the repeal of the Act of Union of 1800. That act, which united England, Scotland, and Ireland into the United Kingdom, had ended the limited autonomy that Ireland had enjoyed since 1782. O'Connell envisioned repeal of the act as the first step in a series of reforms that included universal male suffrage and improvement in tenures. In 1840 he founded the Loyal National Repeal Association. He made it a grass-roots movement by enlisting parish priests as the local leaders, knowing the influence that they had with their parishioners. Their response to his call was overwhelming—and frightening to English officialdom. The lord-lieutenant of Ireland complained to Prime Minister Peel about the "direct and powerful action of unprincipled priests upon the minds of an ignorant population."[75]

O'Connell's supporters formed local repeal associations and enrolled "associates" who paid a so-called "Repeal rent" of one shilling a year. So great was the appeal of the movement that by 1843 the income of the Repeal Association had risen to over £48,000. O'Connell, flushed with his success, announced that 1843 would be the "Repeal Year." He held huge open meetings at places associated with great events in Irish history, and with himself as the principal speaker. Thousands thronged to the meetings, held usually on Sunday. People went first to mass and then, led by their parish priests, came from miles around.[76]

At a meeting on October 1, O'Connell and his lieutenants talked openly of military preparations. They set the next meeting for the eighth at Clontarf, where in 1014 King Brian Boru led the Irish in a famous victory over Danish invaders and where Brian himself was slain. It was to be the last and biggest meeting. Great crowds had already gathered when the lord-lieutenant of Ireland, on instructions from London, ordered the cancellation of the meeting. O'Connell, who, despite all of his bluster, had always opposed violence, immediately declared that the lord-lieutenant's order must be obeyed and told the crowd to return to their homes. That they obeyed showed the enormous power he had over his followers. But O'Connell's capitulation to the lord-lieutenant's ultimatum lost him the confidence of his followers and marked the waning of the repeal movement. O'Connell himself and seven of his associates were arrested and charged with a variety of offenses. The trial was a travesty of justice. The court sentenced O'Connell to a year of imprisonment and a fine of £2,000. The other defendants received lesser sentences. O'Connell spent scarcely three months in prison. The House of Lords heard his appeal and the Law Lords reversed the lower court's decision.[77]

The Irish greeted O'Connell's release with great enthusiasm. But the Liberator's day was over. Nearing seventy, tired and defeated, and perhaps already suffering from the brain disease that soon would kill him, he tried to reestablish his leadership. Abandoning repeal, he now favored a federal arrangement in which Ireland, Scotland, Wales, and England would each have its own legislature, with the Parliament at Westminster in charge of foreign affairs and colonial policy. He found little support for this among the younger men now emerging as Ireland's new leaders. Meanwhile, O'Connell, knowing that death was near, wanted to end his life in Rome, where he would receive the blessing of the pope. He set out for Italy but reached only Genoa, where in May 1847 death overtook him.

O'Connell's last years were darkened by a catastrophe of unprecedented proportions that overwhelmed his beloved Ireland: the potato blight. The disease appeared in other European lands, too, but in no other land did the people depend so heavily upon the potato as did the Irish. Ireland faced starvation, and the suffering of the people went beyond description. Everywhere people in rags begged for crusts, ate carrion, and tried to satisfy their hunger with grass and field herbs. No one knows how many died of starvation or of famine-induced pestilence. Perhaps as many as two hundred thousand fled the island for the New World, but the horror pursued them. Disease went with them on the vessels into which they crowded, and many died during the voyage on what the emigrants came to call "the coffin ships."

The British government made efforts to provide some relief for the Irish, but without much conviction or sympathy. Government officials and most English taxpayers believed that care of the poor was the responsibility of the local propertied classes through the payment of appropriate tax levies. Meanwhile, the English continued to import meat and grain from Ireland (the blight affected only potatoes) while Irish peasants starved. Nor did the government make any genuine effort to stay either the eviction of starving tenants who could not pay their rent or the conversion of their holdings into pasture to raise meat for export to England.[78]

The horrors of the famine erased all thoughts of autonomy, much less rebellion, from the minds of most Irishmen. A fortunate few who did not face starvation continued the agitation. A group of young men, most of them from well-off families, had launched the Young Ireland party, dedicated to the awakening of Irish national consciousness. In 1847 they formed the Irish

Confederation, initially advocating moral suasion rather than force, to achieve its goal. The success of the February Revolution in France in 1848, and Britain's continued insensitivity to the sufferings of the Irish people, persuaded the leaders of the Confederation that the time had come to use force. They began to plan an armed insurrection. The revolt came in Tipperary on July 29. Several hundred poorly armed insurgents marched on the town of Ballingary. After a brief skirmish with the police, the rebels fled in confusion. After the defeat at Ballingary the movement for Irish autonomy faded away, not to be revived until the last quarter of the century under the name of Home Rule.[79]

The scuffle at Ballingary was the closest that Britain came to armed insurrection in a year when revolution convulsed other European lands. That their country was spared the turmoil of revolution did not surprise some Britons of that day. For instance, Judge Henry Cockburn, observing the world from his haven in Edinburgh, thought that except for the Chartists and "the crazy Irish repealers," no one thought that Britain needed a revolution. That, he said, made him prouder than ever of his country.[80]

Not all Britons of the 1840s shared the complacency of people like Judge Cockburn. For some years many had faced the future with fears of revolutionary conflict, and in the spring of 1848, revolution seemed to them on the verge of erupting. On April 2, 1848, Charles Greville wrote that although Britain seemed undisturbed in the midst of the universal hubbub, there was plenty of cause for apprehension. Those who shared Greville's fears were concerned that the excitement among all classes at the news of the February Revolution would spark revolution in Britain as it had in Continental lands. Those who belonged to the traditional elite opposed it, while, wrote Dickens, "All the intelligence and liberality . . . are with it tooth and nail." Working men greeted the news with great enthusiasm. Chartists seized upon it as an opportunity to give aided life to their movement. Major disturbances broke out in early March in Glasgow and other cities. In London on March 6, a crowd of some fifteen thousand, some shouting *"Vive la République!"* fought with police. That evening a mob, led by a young man who wore epaulets, marched on Buckingham Palace. The Palace guard turned out and the mob scattered.[81]

In other lands that seemed as troubled or even less troubled than Britain, the news from France was enough to light the fires of the revolution. Yet Britain came through unscathed. Surely one important reason, perhaps the most important one, why Britain was spared was the resolution shown by its rulers. Had they been as indecisive as Louis Philippe in France, as unwise and erratic as King Frederick William IV of Prussia, or as purblind and unprepared as the tired old men who ruled Austria, history might have had a different story to tell. Instead, the leaders of the British government lost neither their nerve nor their wits. They did not hesitate to make a show of force, and if need be to use force, when confronted with threats to public order wherever they occurred. The six thousand miles of new railroads made possible the dispatch of troops when local authorities could not handle dangerous situations. The new telegraph helped, too, by providing the government rapidly with news about troubles in the provinces.

Nor did the government hesitate to abrogate famed British liberties when it believed that danger to the state outweighed the preservation of traditional rights of Britons. The most notorious of these infringements came in response to the revived Chartist agitation and the upsurge in Irish activism. In April 1848 Parliament passed an act that ordered severe punishment for anyone advocating such actions as the establishment of a republic, the secession of Ireland from the United Kingdom, or urging the rebellion against the crown, making such acts felonies. Another act gave the government the power to deport aliens suspected of coming to Britain to stir up discontent. In June Parliament suspended the writ of habeas corpus in Ireland to hold persons whom they suspected of conspiring against the government. These and similar repressive actions, which included packing juries and shutting down newspapers, made an American visitor think that England was fast becoming as despotic as Russia.[82]

The attitude of the middle class provided another reason for Britain's avoidance of revolution. In continental lands middle-class businessmen, professors and other intellectual types, and students, all demanding liberal reforms, led in the initial risings against their governments. In Britain the middle class, satisfied with the concessions made to it by the landed oligarchy, and especially the adoption of the principle of free trade, remained steadfast in its loyalty to the throne. They did not trust the lower classes and did not want to extend domestic reforms to them. And so, unlike their counterparts on the Continent, they did not press their own demands by encouraging the lower orders to mount the barricades (an action that the bourgeoisie of the Continent quickly came to regret). Sir Robert Peel understood the attitude and reaction of the British middle class. In a speech in Parliament on July 6, 1849, he said that the government had gained the confidence and the good will of the powerful middle class "by parting with that which was thought to be directly for the benefit of the landed interest [the Corn Laws] . . . which in no small degree enabled you to pass triumphantly through the storm that convulsed other countries during the year 1848."[83]

Britons preened themselves on the way in which their country had come through that year of revolution. Heads throughout the kingdom must have nodded in agreement when they read the *Annual Register*'s review of 1848. It began, "The security which under the protection of Providence this country derives from its free and popular constitution was never more signally exemplified than during the year of political agitation and disorder of which the memorable events are commemorated in this volume. While almost every throne on the Continent was emptied or shaken by revolution, the English monarchy, strong in the loyal attachment of the people, not only stood firm in the tempest but appeared even to derive increased stability from the events that convulsed foreign kingdoms."[84]

The political and social turbulence and the hard times of the 1840s were followed by the stable and prosperous years of mid-Victorian Britain. The good times brought about a relaxation of social tensions. The expansion of markets, increased profits, and Britain's position as the world's leading economic power brought new wealth and increased self-confidence to the middle class and confirmed its belief in the blessings of free trade and laissez-faire. They were good years, too, for the landed proprietors. They not only retained their grip on political power but, as mentioned earlier, for twenty-five years agriculture flourished as it never had before. The working classes, too, shared in the prosperity and optimism of these years, though to a far lesser degree. The slow improvements held out the promise of better times to come.

The symbol, and it was an inspired one, of the opening of this new era of prosperity, peace, and understanding was the London Exhibition of 1851, or to give its full name, The Great Exhibition of the Works of Industry of All Nations. A remarkable man named Henry Cole, a civil servant who was also an editor, artist, music critic, and a promoter and enthusiast of British industrial design, first advanced the proposal. When Prince Albert heard of it, he seized upon the idea, and a Royal Commission was appointed to plan what became the world's first great international exposition. It was housed in the famed Crystal Palace in Hyde Park, a vast, beautiful structure of four-foot plate glass panels, framed in cast-iron girders painted red and supported by cast-iron columns painted green. Joseph Paxton, who had built a great glass conservatory for the duke of Devonshire, was chosen in July 1850 to design the building. Through standardization and prefabrication, it took only months to construct. More than a third of a mile in length, its center rose to 140 feet, and the structure covered nineteen acres. The exhibitors came from many lands of East and West, but half of the exhibits were British, and it was clear for all to see that Britain led the world in industry and transportation.

The Palace also contained exhibits of art, including what was described as "a forest of nudes," which occasioned censure from clerics and shocked the prudish sensibilities of others, but was viewed with much interest by most visitors. The Great Exhibition opened on May 1 and closed on September 15. It had drawn more than six million visitors, most of them British, brought from all corners of the island by the new railroad lines. The visitors paid £356,000 in admission fees, and the Exhibition made a profit of £86,000. The profits were used for helping to build Albert Hall and the complex of museums and colleges of art and music in London's South Kensington.

Victoria, in a letter to her uncle Leopold, called the opening of the exhibition "the *greatest day* in our history . . . and the triumph of my beloved Albert." Not everyone shared her enthusiasm. The curmudgeonly William Albert Shee admitted that the Exhibition was a great show but lamented that all manner of relatives who used to vacation at Torquay or at German spas came to London and inflicted themselves on kinsmen, who suffered from excess family affection. The Exhibition, said he, had "ruined the 1851 season and embittered the lives of the upper classes."[85]

After the Exhibition closed, the Crystal Palace was disassembled and reerected in 1854 in another part of London, where, with some alterations, it served as an exhibition and entertainment center. In 1936 fire damaged it, and in 1941 it was torn down because it served as a guide for German bombing planes. Ninety years earlier it had stood as a symbol of Britain's greatest era. Now its destruction symbolized the beginning of a sadder and far less glorious chapter in Britain's long history.

CHAPTER SIX

France Comes Full Circle

In 1830 Louis Philippe, duc d'Orléans, cousin of the Bourbon kings, ascended the throne of France after another of the dizzying series of revolutions that had roiled France since 1789. This revolution took only three days at the end of July and so bore the name of the July Monarchy. Prince Metternich insisted that the July Revolution of 1830 had been an accident that no one had expected. When, in February 1848, another revolution brought down the curtain on the July Monarchy, Lord Brougham, like Metternich a man who laid claim to omniscience, called *that* revolution an accident, "an unexpected change, without preparation, without pretext, without justification."[1] Metternich and Brougham each overstated his case, but there was more than a little truth in what they said. The July Monarchy played out its brief life between two revolutions that did not have to happen.

After the defeat of Napoleon in 1814, the victorious allies had restored the Bourbons, in the person of Louis XVIII, to the throne of France. The new king, brother of Louis XVI, whom the revolutionaries had executed in 1792, issued a constitution, called the Charter, that created a constitutional monarchy similar to that of Britain. Louis XVIII was succeeded in 1824 by his brother Charles X. The new king, who epitomized the apothegm that the Bourbons learned nothing and forgot nothing, tried to introduce a series of repressive measures. As it happened, his reactionary policies coincided with an economic downturn and poor grain harvests. Still there was no outpouring of public resentment and opposition until agitators stirred up restless crowds in Paris. On July 27, 1830, violence erupted, barricades went up in the streets of Paris, and rioters looted gun shops to get weapons. Most of the street fighters were small shopkeepers, artisans, and skilled workers. Few came from the middle class or from the dispossessed of the Paris slums. By the morning of July 29, Paris was in the hands of the revolutionaries. A few days later, Charles X abdicated. Paris had carried out the revolution by itself, almost before word of it reached the rest of France. "We dispatched our revolution to the departments by coach," a contemporary boasted. "They had only to acknowledge its receipt." News of the revolution spread quickly to other lands and triggered unrest and uprisings.

In Paris the radicals, who controlled the streets, wanted to establish a republic. The moderate and liberal bourgeoisie, remembering the excesses of the republic of 1792–1795, wanted a constitutional monarchy that would unite a hereditary crown with a parliamentary government, which they would dominate. They turned to the fifty-seven-year-old Louis Philippe, who had endured exile from 1793 to 1814, because he belonged to France's royal family and because, as François Guizot, one of his strongest supporters pointed out years later, he was "a French constitutionalist, a French liberal, a Frenchman of our generation of 1789." On the morning of July 30, Paris awakened to find the city placarded with posters calling on Louis Philippe to become king. The next day he came to the city hall, where the Marquis de Lafayette, veteran of both the American and French revolutions, carrying the tricolor flag beloved by republicans, embraced Louis Philippe and called for a throne "surrounded by republican institutions." The Chamber of Deputies reconvened, approved revisions of the Charter, and on August 7 elected Louis Philippe, not as king of France, but as "King of the French, by the grace of God and the will of the nation." The amended Charter, which Louis Philippe swore to support, among other provisions confirmed freedom of the press by declaring that censorship could never be reestablished.[2]

Years later the Prince de Joinville, third son of Louis Philippe, said in his memoirs that his father had only associated himself with the revolution to avoid being exiled as a member of the royal family. He reluctantly yielded to the entreaties of those who wanted him to become king.[3] If there had ever been reluctance, the new king speedily overcame it and set up a determined course to establish himself as the ruler of France. His actions proved a disagreeable surprise to the republican radicals, who had seen him as a figurehead whom they could easily throw out should the occasion demand it.

He was a complicated man, shaped by his family's heritage, by revolution, and by exile. Head of the House of Orléans, his was the junior branch of the royal family of France, descended from Louis XIV's brother, Philippe. For nearly two hundred years the dukes of Orléans had to play second fiddle to their cousins, the Bourbon kings of France—a hard lot for proud men. They struggled against it and thereby gained the reputation of intriguers who sought popularity with the people. Understandably, the Bourbons never gave them their complete trust. The rivalry reached its climax when revolution came in 1789. Philippe, duc d'Orléans, father of Louis Philippe, who now called himself Philippe Égalité, supported the revolution. His moment of truth came on January 16, 1793, when, as a member of the revolutionary assembly, he voted for the death of Louis XVI (the vote was 361 for and 360 against). He declared that duty compelled him to vote for the death of his cousin, but some believed that he sought to ingratiate himself with the leaders of the revolution in the hope that they would give him the throne. Whatever his motive, it stood him to no avail. Within a few months, the revolutionary tribunal of the Reign of Terror sent him to the guillotine—in November of 1793.

Young Louis Philippe shared his father's enthusiasm for the revolution. He early had joined the Jacobin Club and fought with the national army in the war against Austria and Prussia that began in 1792. Then in 1793, disenchanted, he deserted and went into exile. In 1809 in Naples, he married Marie Amélie, one of the five daughters of King Ferdinand. Meanwhile, he had managed a reconciliation with his Bourbon cousins. When the victorious allies restored the Bourbons to France's throne in 1814, Louis Philippe regained his title as well as the great fortune of his family. He also followed the tradition of his family by seeking popularity.

When he became king, he wooed popular support by acting the role of a bourgeois Frenchman, a gesture that invited criticism. Alexis de Tocqueville, scion of a noble family and disdainful of the bourgeoisie, thought that the king, despite his high birth, had the mind and soul of a bourgeois. He described the king as polite, but without discrimination or dignity, the politeness of a tradesman rather than that of a prince. He was enlightened, subtle, and tenacious, but all his thoughts turned to the useful. He was moderate in his tastes, an enemy of any excess. Charles Greville, monarchist to the core, thought that Louis Philippe's bourgeois affectations demeaned the majesty that should surround a king. Writing soon after Louis Philippe had ascended the throne, he said that the new monarch "need not affect the manners of a citizen and the plainness of dress and demeanor very suitable to an American president, but unbecoming a descendant of Louis XIV."[4]

In the first years of his reign, the king walked along the streets of Paris dressed in ordinary clothes, looking, as someone remarked, like an honest grocer, and always carrying a big umbrella under his arm. Passersby stopped him to shake his hand or even to invite him into a nearby cafe for a glass of wine. Sometimes he walked out with his queen on his arm, their children trailing behind, like any middle-class family out for a stroll. He played the role of "Citizen-King" with good humor and great skill, but he never forgot that he was a prince of the blood royal. When the occasion demanded it, as when he visited Queen Victoria in 1844, he became royal to his finger tips, full of dignity and grandeur of manner.[5]

Of medium height, he was full in figure and face, with a narrow forehead, fat cheeks, a prominent nose, and large, expressionless eyes. He wore side whiskers and a black wig with a high pompadour. A man of regular habits, he rose each day at seven and, after a simple breakfast, settled down to a long workday. At night he held a reception until ten, and then retired to his study and worked until the small hours of the morning. He had a prodigious memory upon which he constantly drew in his conversation. He loved to talk but tended to monopolize the conversation. Tocqueville found that out when, in a conversation in early 1848, the king asked him to talk about the United States and then proceeded himself to talk about America, with total recall of the places and men he had known when he lived there himself for two years during his exile. The monologue went on for forty-five minutes, with Tocqueville not having said five words. The king then rose and dismissed the vastly irritated Tocqueville.[6]

An excessive interest in acquiring wealth was a less attractive characteristic of the king. He had recovered much of the Orléans fortune with the restoration of the Bourbons, but that did not satisfy him. In the succeeding years he added to his wealth with a zeal that seemed unbefitting a royal personage. A reputation for avarice and corruption pursued him throughout his reign.[7] In actual fact, he was neither miserly nor corrupt.

Unlike many monarchs, and very much like a bourgeois *paterfamilias*, Louis Philippe was happiest in the intimacy of family life. His wife, to whom he was devoted, possessed all the graces that one could ask of a queen, save beauty. Prince Talleyrand called her the greatest of great ladies. Her air of natural grandeur commanded the immediate respect of all who approached her. The royal couple had eight children of whom it was said that all the daughters were chaste and all the sons valiant. Of all his family, Louis Philippe was closest to his sister Adelaide. A spinster, plain in appearance and brusque in manner, she lived only for her brother. She was his closest friend, his confidante, his adviser. He concealed nothing from her. She read every document and entered his study whenever she liked. She so resembled her brother in her ways of thinking that, as one of the king's ministers explained, she had influence with him because she reacted to a problem in the same way he did.[8]

Apart from being objects of parental love, Louis Philippe's children figured importantly in his policies. Above all else he was a dynast, determined to establish his line on the throne of France. He knew that to achieve that goal he not only needed the support of his subjects but also the acceptance as an equal by the rulers of other lands, evidenced by their willingness to provide spouses for his children. He ran into difficulties on that score. Major royal houses vetoed such marriages because of the instability of both the French throne and the Orléans dynasty. It was understandable for the founder of a new ruling house to ensure the continuation of his line, but Louis Philippe seemed to have gone too far. That was the opinion of a canny Russian diplomat and also of Prince Albert and the latter's mentor, Baron Stockmar, who after the king's fall believed retribution overtook him because he thought more about dynastic interests than about the well-being of his people.[9]

France itself during the years of the July Monarchy was a society in transition. During the 1840s France entered a new era of economic development. The pace of change was neither sudden nor dramatic. France remained overwhelmingly a peasant land. In 1851 three quarters of its people lived on the land or in towns and villages of fewer than two thousand inhabitants. Still, evidences of change abounded. New or improved roads, bridges, and canals added thousands of miles to the transport network. River steamboats, first introduced in the 1820s, came increasingly into use. A fledgling railway system grew from 255 miles in 1840 to 1,811 miles in 1850, though construction lagged badly compared with that of other lands. The improvements in transportation and the growth of towns and cities opened new markets for agricultural production. Large-scale mechanized factory industry still barely touched the lives of most Frenchmen, but industrial production had begun an upsurge. In banking, innovators introduced new and more flexible institutions. Joint-stock companies, organized to build the railroads, canals, gas works (for street illumination), and heavy industrial enterprises, raised capital by selling shares to the French public and to foreign investors.[10]

The leaders of the bourgeoisie who, in July 1830, chose Louis Philippe to head the state, had every reason to be satisfied with their choice. Under his benevolent guidance they became the masters of France. The triumph of the French bourgeoisie ushered in a new era in the history of Europe. For the first time the middle class, or more precisely the upper strata of the middle class, became the rulers of a great power and supplanted the older rulers, the aristocracy of birth. One of their number, recalling a royal reception at

Versailles in 1837, called the throng that filled the great hall "the new France, mixed, bourgeois, democratic, invading the palace of Louis XIV . . . peaceful but sovereign invaders, conquerors somewhat astonished in the midst of their victory, ill constituted to enjoy it, but determined to keep what they had won. . . . "[11] The value system of the old noble society, the concern with lineage and the inordinate pride of ancestry, the scorn of trade, the cavalier attitude toward money, the prodigality and love of display that was called "living nobly," and, above all, the conviction that they were superior beings possessed of qualities that merited the respect and deference of the lesser mortals among whom they lived—all was swept away by the ascent of the bourgeoisie. France was the first European nation to experience that revolutionary change.

In a way the French bourgeoisie had gained power by default. Most of the old nobility who supported the Bourbons at first refused to accept the July Monarchy and deliberately withheld their support from the government. The urban masses and the peasantry, for their part, had little interest in or understanding of constitutional government. As Guizot, in London in 1840 as France's ambassador, explained to Lord Palmerston, Britain's foreign minister, "Another class, that of the great manufacturers, the masters of forges, and merchants, is, on the contrary, attached to the king's government, and brings to it, on all occasions, the support of its activity, its intelligence, its wealth, and its influence in society."[12] Actually, Guizot had too narrowly listed the membership of the new ruling class. He should have included important officials of the central and local governments, doctors, lawyers, academics, and landowners who drew their large incomes from urban and rural properties that they owned and from government securities.

Scholars have struggled mightily, and often in wearying detail, but never successfully to arrive at a definition of the middle class that would meet with the universal acceptance of the scholarly community. Frenchmen of the mid-nineteenth century found the task much less difficult. In a speech in the Chamber of Deputies, Guizot explained that in France "there exists a class not devoted to manual labor, not living by wages, which has the freedom and the spare time that enables it to dedicate a considerable portion of its time and abilities to public service; possessing not only the necessary wealth for such an undertaking, but also the knowledge and independence without which such work could never be accomplished." To the historian Jules Michelet, a sense of security was the essential distinction of the bourgeois. That sense involved a way of life and a seemliness that set the bourgeois apart from the masses and that won him the respect of his peers.[13]

Bourgeois society, like any other social agglomeration, formed a hierarchical structure. The *haute bourgeoisie*, the wealthiest bankers, merchants, industrialists, and landowners, stood at the top of the pyramid, with descending strata determined by wealth and occupation, down to the petty bourgeoisie, the small shopkeepers, clerks, artisans, and minor employees of the government. Though it seemed rigid, the structure remained always in a state of flux and renewal. "The doors of the bourgeoisie are open to all the world," said the *Journal des Débats*, "to leave as well as to enter." Increasingly, people no longer accepted their inherited social position. Upper mobility became more possible than it ever had been before.[14]

Though important, wealth was not the only avenue that led into the ruling elite of the July Monarchy. Careers opened up to talent of every kind. Guizot, whose own life story bore witness to the upward mobility possible to the outstanding individual, told the Chamber of Deputies in May 1837, "You live in a society completely open to progress and the expectation of equality. There has never before been a like concentration of individuals, raised by their own efforts, to the highest rank in every kind of career. Nearly all of us have won our rank by the sweat of our brow and on the field of battle." Nowhere else in the Europe of that day was it easier—or in many lands even possible—for a man of humble origins to rise by virtue of his abilities far above the station into which he was born. Journalists, authors, and professors took their places as members of the ruling elite.[15]

The aristocracy of wealth, and above all the *haute bourgeoisie* of Paris, displaced the aristocracy of birth as the leaders of the fashionable world. The center of the social world shifted to the town houses of the great bankers. The palatial home of Baron James de Rothschild on the rue Laffitte became an especially favored rendezvous for the elite. "*Tout le monde* flocks to his home," wrote Countess Nesselrode to her husband, Russia's foreign minister, while visiting Paris. The countess, whose letters to her husband were often diplomatic reports laced with the latest gossip, had dinner with Rothschild one evening in December 1840. He must have known that everything he told her would get back to Saint Petersburg. Perhaps that is why he spoke so freely to her and possibly exaggerated his own importance, great though it was. He told her that he saw all of the king's ministers every day, and when he thought they followed policies he believed contrary to the interests of the state, he called on the king, whom, he said, he could see whenever he wished. "Since the king knows I have much to lose," he told the attentive countess, "and that I desire only tranquility, he has complete confidence in me and takes into account what I tell him."[16]

The bourgeoisie served in the National Guard, the citizen militia first organized in 1789 to preserve public order and protect private property. In 1827 the Bourbon King Charles X disbanded the Guard because of its liberal leanings. Reconstituted on the second day of the July Revolution with Lafayette as its commanding general, the Guard helped ensure the accession of Louis Philippe to the throne. With only few exceptions, all able-bodied citizens from eighteen to sixty who paid direct taxes had to serve. They paid for their own arms and uniforms, had to turn out when called, and had to report as often as once a month for guard duty. In 1837 a new law opened membership in the Guard to the petty bourgeoisie, that is, those who did not pay direct taxes and did not have the suffrage. The Guard served the regime well during the 1830s, helping to put down unrest and insurrection. The king, in his annual address from the throne to the Chamber of Deputies, called the loyalty of the National Guard his strongest support. In the forties discipline became lax and absence from duty became common, especially among those who considered themselves above such commonplace activity. Lower ranks of the bourgeoisie began to take over as officers, and the Guard increasingly became an organization of the lesser bourgeoisie, men unhappy with the existing political system in which they had little or no voice. The king no longer lauded the Guard in his annual address from the throne, and he discontinued his reviews of the Paris National Guard.

The rise of the bourgeoisie to dominance and their materialism invited attacks and satire. They became favorite targets of the caricaturists of the time, including Honoré Daumier, the greatest master of that art. Novelists delighted in what has been called "celebrated and unremitting castigation" of the bourgeoisie. Flaubert, son of a prosperous upper-middle-class family whose money allowed him to live a life of self-indulgence, defined a bourgeois as "anyone who thinks basely." Balzac filled the pages of his great novels with tales of the ambitions, jealousies, deceits, social climbing, dishonesty, and materialism of men and women of the middle class. Tocqueville told Nassau Senior that the Orléans dynasty had "rested on the most selfish and grasping of plutocracies . . . looked up to with envy and dislike by the multitude below it, and looked down on with scorn amounting to disgust by the better born and better educated above it." John Stuart Mill said much the same thing when, in his defense of the February Revolution of 1848, he wrote that the July Monarchy had never appealed to any noble, elevated, or generous principles of action, but instead appealed almost exclusively to the meaner and more selfish impulses of mankind.[18]

Contemporaries and later writers alike seized upon the phrase *enrichissez vous*, or "get rich," spoken by Guizot in a debate in the Chamber of Deputies. The phrase seemed an affirmation of the materialism of the bourgeois regime, but this misrepresented what Guizot meant. The debate concerned the extension of the franchise that was based upon the size of the individual's income. Guizot opposed the extension. He pointed out that anyone could attain the suffrage by gaining wealth through work and saving; *"enrichissez vous par le travail et par l'épargne"* was the way he put it. The Protestant Guizot was expressing the work ethic of his Calvinist heritage; wealth as the reward for hard work and thrift and as a sign of personal merit and intelligence.[19]

The government of the July Monarchy did not lock out the nobility from participation in the government. A few members of the old nobility loyally served Louis Philippe from the outset of his reign, and as the years went by, a steadily increasing number became active in the regime. They held posts in government offices, in the diplomatic corps, and in the military, though not in the numbers of the past. In 1831, less than one tenth of the 459 members of the Chamber of Deputies had been of noble birth. By 1848 nobles made up one third of the deputies. Most of them came from the old nobility, whose patents of nobility antedated the Revolution of 1789, the rest from the nobility created by Napoleon. Few of these men, however, held high posts in the Chamber—most were backbenchers.[20]

Still, the nobility was but a shadow of what it had once been. It had long before lost the privileges guaranteed by law and tradition. Now nobles lived under the same laws as everyone else in the kingdom. The Bourbons, restored in 1814, had accepted the principle of equality before the law but had restored the nobility to their titles, had compensated them for their property confiscated during the Revolution, had created a hereditary aristocracy in the Chamber of Peers, and had restored the nobility to their social and political power. All of that ended with the July Monarchy. The new regime adopted the principle of careers open to talent and an elite based upon individual accomplishment and not birth. The office that dealt with the registration of titles and with letters patent of nobility was abolished, and the law ended all penalties for assuming a title without letters patent. Anyone was now free to take any title that he wanted.

All that remained to the nobility was pride in their lineage and the deference still paid them. Many of them withdrew to their country estates, where the local people recognized them as *grande notables* and where they took leading roles in local and provincial political and intellectual life. Others lived in Paris, where they enjoyed an active social life that often intersected with the *haute bourgeoisie*. In imitation of the English, horse racing, and especially the steeplechase, became a passion of Parisian high society. Elaborate balls provided special opportunities for gaiety and display. Weddings, too, were grand social occasions.[22]

Whether in Paris or in the provinces, the nobility, despite their dwindling

importance, held fast to their sense of caste. The distinction between nobleman and commoner persisted unabated in their way of thinking. In a conversation with Nassau Senior in 1849, Tocqueville explained that although he
may not have had two thoughts in common with a fellow nobleman, when he
spoke with him he felt that they belonged to the same family, spoke the same
language, and understood one another. "I may like a bourgeois better," he
continued, "but he is a stranger." When Senior visited Tocqueville at his
chateau in Normandy, he learned that a friend of Mme. de Tocqueville had
proposed to invite the local nobility and bourgeoisie to a ball. The wives of
the nobles sent word that their husbands would attend but they would not.
Unlike England, where younger sons became clergymen, doctors, or lawyers
without losing caste, these professions were considered beneath the dignity of
a noble and suited only for the sons of the bourgeoisie. The sons of the
nobles, all of whom inherited the title of their father, found their callings
principally in public service, whether civil or military.[23]

The bourgeoisie and the nobility held center stage in the July Monarchy,
but they formed only the thin top layer of the society. In the 1840s something
like 27 million, or three quarters of the 35.4 million people of France, lived
out in the country, most of them peasants who drew their livings from working the land. In 1851 the economist Adolphe Blanqui, like Disraeli who a
few years earlier had written of two nations within Britain, said there were two
within France. Disraeli's two nations were the rich and the poor, as ignorant
of each other as if they inhabited different planets. Blanqui's two nations were
the people of the city and the people of the country. In a report commissioned by the Academy of Moral and Political Sciences, Blanqui, after extensive research and field trips, wrote that the line of demarcation between city
people and rural people was so deep and their lives so completely different,
that it was "as if two alien races, strangers to one another, lived in the same
country."

Like peasants everywhere in underdeveloped lands, most of France's peasants lived hard lives, engaged in an unending struggle to make ends meet.
They lived often in one- or two-room huts, strung along an unpaved village
street, or in isolated farmsteads. Their diets comprised a dreary repetition of
a few items.[24] The family provided the core of peasant life, the social and economic unit upon which the well-being and security of each family member
depended. They lived and ate together, worked the land together, and pooled
their resources. The father ruled the household, assigning each member to
specific tasks. No special affection was shown to children, nor were they
mourned when they died in infancy or early childhood, as they often did.
They could be easily replaced. At the age of five to seven, they were put to

work, guarding sheep or cattle, collecting firewood, or frightening birds from the newly sown fields. They worked at their jobs from dawn to dusk, they suffered abuse and beatings from their elders, they were given the poorest and the least amounts of food, and no one paid attention to their emotional needs.

Behind the facade of the peasant family's apparent solidarity, there often lay disloyalty, dissatisfaction, quarreling, ill will, and even hatred. The crowded dwellings in which most peasants lived must have had much to do with the unhappiness of family life. Privacy was impossible. Physical violence was a constant, with the stronger beating on the weaker. Expressions of love and consideration for one another were rare. Instead, children and the sick and the aged became unwelcome burdens on the family.[95]

Most peasants lived in villages, isolated from the rest of society and viewing the outside world as essentially hostile. Surrounded by forces natural and man-made that they did not understand, they, like peasants everywhere, turned to witchcraft, sorcery, and spells. They believed that this black magic explained events and was the source of such calamities as crop failures, animal diseases, and personal misfortunes. Their poverty, their primitive way of life, and their ignorance left them so culturally deprived that people of the time called them savages and barbarians. To add to their distinctiveness, many of them did not speak French or even know the language. Instead, they had their own local dialects, scarcely or entirely incomprehensible to outsiders, or they spoke Provençal in the south, Breton on the Atlantic coast, Catalan near the Spanish border, Flemish in the north, and German dialects in districts along the Rhine.

Whatever their language and wherever they lived, French peasants craved land. Unlike agriculture in England, where the elite owned the land and peasant tenants and farm laborers tilled it, agriculture in France was predominantly a peasant economy. Land, whether owned by the peasant, or rented on lease or shares, guaranteed the maintenance of the family and also brought social status. The amount of land held by a household determined the importance of its members in the village community. The consuming passion for land combined in varying proportions love of the land for its own sake, attachment to it because it was the only form of economic security that the peasant knew, and unashamed and unvarnished greed. So important was land to them that they borrowed from local money lenders at usurious rates to purchase land.

Stagnation, barbarism, and misery remained the norm for many decades for much of France's peasantry. But breakthroughs began to evidence themselves in the 1840s in the less isolated parts of France. Construction of roads and canals, the first beginnings of the railroad, and the slow acceptance of the compulsory education law of 1833 brought the world to the doorsteps of more and more villages. The peasantry came increasingly into contact with the bourgeoisie of nearby towns and began to participate in national life. Studies of local regions show that peasants began to have the means and the desire to live better. And in increasing numbers they left their villages to go to the cities, above all to Paris.[26]

Paris dominated the nation to an extent unparalleled by the capital city in any other land. As the sometime prime minister Adolphe Thiers put it, "Every pulsation of the heart of Paris is instantly felt in the Pyrenees and on the Rhine." The banks of Paris dominated the financial life of the country, its factories accounted for one third of France's total industrial production by value, and its exports amounted to almost one quarter of the nation's total exports. Second in size only to London in all of Europe, its population had almost doubled between 1801 and 1851, from 547,756 inhabitants to 1,053,262. More than half of the increase had taken place after 1830. So great was the influx from the provinces that in 1851 half of Paris's population had been born outside the department of the Seine. Not only Frenchmen flocked to Paris. The city drew visitors from many lands. All of them were drawn to Paris by its reputation as the center of elegance, of culture, and of gaiety. Even sober-sided Methodist preachers like John Price Durkin, D.D., president of Dickinson College in Carlisle, Pennsylvania, and a leader in missionary effort, succumbed to its spell. Visiting Paris in 1842, he wrote, "The French capital strikes you as the seat of human enjoyment. You find the art of life, so far as mere physical good is concerned, in perfection there." And after a paragraph celebrating its delights, he concluded, "When you leave Paris you have just begun to enjoy it, and desire to return again."[27]

The Paris that enchanted visitors like Durkin was still a medieval city. Before the great rebuilding that began in 1850, its streets, except for a few main thoroughfares, were narrow lanes and alleys, intended for pedestrians, horsemen, and sedan chairs, not for carriages and wagons. Often without sidewalks, they were muddy and covered with what one visitor described as "slimy, slippery filth." Private companies had recently installed gas lighting, but in most of the city flickering oil lamps, suspended by cords, barely lit the streets and were extinguished at midnight, plunging the streets into inky darkness. The five- to seven-story houses that lined the streets were divided into apartments, all served by one generally filthy staircase. Most houses lacked individual drainage and domestic filth piled up everywhere. The houses seldom had water pipes and water had to be brought in from public fountains in the streets. In 1850 Paris had only sixty-eight of these fountains, or one for every fifteen thousand inhabitants, so that many Parisians had to depend upon water from the Seine and from wells. The flood of newcomers and the failure to build new housing drove up rents and forced people to live in cramped and shockingly unsanitary quarters.

The government made some effort to introduce improvements. Among other projects it built new streets and sidewalks, extended the system of underground drains, increased the number of water lines and the volume of water delivered, and provided that special feature of Paris, street urinals for the male Parisian. But by far the chief new construction project of the July Monarchy was a twenty-four-mile-long stone wall some twenty feet high that encircled Paris, with ninety-four bastions and girdled by seventeen forts scattered along its perimeter. Built between 1841 and 1845, it cost about 145 million francs. The government said that it was vital to the defense of France, for if Paris fell to an invader France would fall, so closely linked were capital and country. It also offered the benefit of providing work for the unemployed and restive proletariat of Paris. Opponents argued that it had for its real purpose the containment of possible revolution within Paris, in order to prevent its spread to the rest of the nation. Whichever side had the right of it, the wall was never used, whether to repel an invader or to contain a revolution and deserves high rank among the major boondoggles of history.[28]

Early in his reign Louis Philippe spelled out the two guiding principles of his reign in foreign affairs and in internal matters. He told a delegation from the provinces that "we must not only cherish peace; we must avoid everything that might provoke war. In respect to domestic policy, we will seek a *juste milieu*." By *juste milieu* he meant the golden mean between absolutism and clericalism, on the one hand, and republicanism on the other. Louis Philippe felt certain that these two principles, peace and the *juste milieu*, expressed the will of the people of France. Scarcely two weeks before revolution drove him from his throne in February 1848, he told a Russian diplomat that after thirty years of studying the mind of the French people, he had arrived at the conclusion that there were two things that they did not want: a republic and a war. "The task of my reign," he continued, "is to keep them in that frame of mind."[29]

Louis Philippe had seriously misread the mind of his people. As one of them put it after the king's flight, "What a misfortune that he did not love *la gloire*." Supporters and opponents alike said that Louis Philippe's love of peace lessened the greatness of France, lowered respect for her in the rest of Europe, and humiliated all Frenchmen. Victor Hugo, who otherwise admired the king, wrote that he would have ranked among the most illustrious of rulers "if he had loved glory a little and had a feeling for what is grand." Adolphe Thiers, twice premier and then leader of the opposition in the Chamber of Deputies, thought that the king's great fault lay in his timidity. "He was personally a hero but politically a coward," said Thiers, who had dreamed of war against other powers but who had failed to persuade the king to take up arms.[30]

Both instinct and political calculation inclined Louis Philippe to the policy he called *juste milieu*. To him, the concept meant the maintenance of the status quo established by the July Monarchy. He and his supporters seemed indifferent to the problems and the sufferings of the poor. The only important piece of progressive legislation in all of the eighteen years of the July Monarchy was the law on public education in 1833, which ordered the establishment of primary schools in every commune, secondary schools in certain cities, and a normal school in each of France's eighty-six departments to educate teachers.

The resistance of the regime to any extension of the suffrage proved an especially serious misreading of the mind of the public. The electoral law of 1831 provided that only those men who paid a property tax of not less than 2,000 francs could vote for deputies to the Chamber of Deputies, and only those who paid a property tax of not less than 5,000 francs could stand for election. In 1831, 165,583 and by 1846, 240,938 men, out of a population of 35 million, met the qualifications to serve as electors, and of these men a much smaller number met the qualification to serve as deputies. In short, the law considered only the wealthiest men of France qualified to represent the rest of the nation. In 1846 over four fifths of the deputies won their seats in elections in which less than four hundred ballots were cast.[31]

At first those who wanted to broaden the franchise made moderate demands. The refusal of the government to accede to this moderate demand served to increase discontent with the electoral system, encouraged more far-reaching proposals, and fueled a campaign for reform that won ever wider public support, and finally led directly to the February revolution.

The efforts to reform the suffrage and the regime's resolute opposition to these efforts reflected the dilemma that confronted Louis Philippe from the outset of his reign. The competing forces that had momentarily joined in successful revolution in 1830 differed in their views of the powers and functions of the new regime, so that Louis Philippe had no clear mandate from the people who chose him as their monarch. He resolved to abide by the constitution, but the implementation of that resolve presented great difficulties. His government lacked the strengths and loyalties offered by legitimacy. Many among those who had supported the July Revolution wanted the king to reign but not to rule. Louis Philippe refused to accept that role. He was determined to govern. His determination roused resentment and exasperation. Adolphe Thiers complained that the king always seized the rudder and tried always to have a ministry so weak and so heterogeneous that it became his tool. The number of important political figures who withdrew from public life because of disagreement with the king's policies lent substance to Thiers's charge.[32]

The demands of the dissatisfied and the regime's rejection of compromise introduced an instability that haunted the July Monarchy from its inception. The republicans and the radicals who had manned the barricades of the July Revolution had fought for a republic, only to have the fruits of their victory stolen from them. They had accepted the monarchy because they assumed that the new king was a figurehead whom they could depose if the occasion demanded it. They did not know their man. It took them a year to recognize the magnitude of their miscalculations. The property qualifications established by the electoral law excluded most of the republicans and their partisans from the vote, even as they had been excluded during the Bourbon restoration. Concentrated in the cities, and above all in Paris, they vigorously resumed their agitation for revolution and republicanism. The clubs that they established and the propagation of their demands persuaded the government in 1834 to place severe restrictions on the right to form associations, to abolish trial by jury for offenders against the security of the state, and to put 164 republican leaders on trial before the Chamber of Peers.[33]

To evade the new restrictions, republicans and other disaffected people formed secret societies that became centers of agitation and conspiracy. Except for a handful of leaders, the secret societies consisted in largest part of working men. Their unrest, exacerbated by the regime's indifference to their deprivation and manipulated by republican and radical agitators, found expression in sporadic eruptions of strikes and of violence. The worst outbreak occurred in 1834 among the silk workers of Lyons. Soon after the suppression of the rising in Lyons, rioting broke out in Paris and was put down with a ferocity captured for all time by Daumier's haunting lithograph of a slain man in a nightgown lying beside his bed in a pool of blood, with two other bodies nearby. Other risings nearly always required the use of the military to put them down. Louis Cass, the American minister in Paris, writing in 1840, was struck by the large number of troops stationed in or near Paris. The military presence was necessary, he wrote, or else "the peace of the capital and the safety of the kingdom could not exist twenty-four hours."

Louis René Villermé, in his study published in 1840 on the condition of the still small but growing urban industrial proletariat, vividly documented its exploitation and its misery and prophesied the inevitability of a revolution. In that same year Heine reported that in his visits to factories, he found workers reading new editions of radical writings of the French Revolution that "smelled of blood." And in 1840 three books appeared, Étienne Cabet's *Voyage en Icarie,* Louis Blanc's *L'Organisation du Travail,* and Pierre Proudhon's *Memoire sur la Propriété,* which preached the gospel of socialism to a wide and increasingly receptive audience.[34]

The republicans, the radicals, and the disaffected workers formed the left wing of the regime's opposition. A part of the nobility, and especially those whose patents of nobility antedated 1789, stood at the other end of the spectrum. They had loyally supported the restored Bourbon dynasty and regarded Louis Philippe as a usurper. The legitimists, as they came to be called, kept scrupulously aloof from the new regime. The legitimists faithfully awaited another restoration of the Bourbon dynasty. Some favored armed revolt to speed the process, but most advocated patience. In time, they said, the Orléanist regime would succumb to its own failures and the nation would call upon the Bourbon pretender, the count of Chambord, to be its savior. The legitimists had as their allies on the right the ultramontanists, who looked "beyond the Alps" to Rome for guidance, and who were appalled by the July Monarchy's indifference to religious matters and its secular educational policy.

Liberal monarchists who supported the overthrow of the Bourbons were dismayed by the conservatism of the new regime. They joined the loyal opposition, and a few went over to republicanism. Among the latter were Armand Carrel, editor of the influential newspaper, *Le National*; Félicité Lamennais, the liberal Catholic priest and intellectual; and another famed priest, the Dominican Abbé Lacordaire, whose eloquence drew as many as five thousand people to the Cathedral of Notre-Dame to hear him preach what one listener in 1841 called "pure republicanism." Writers, too, struck out against the conservatism of the regime, telling of the sufferings of the poor and the forgotten, and attacking privilege and inequality.[35]

The press—by 1845 there were about 520 dailies, weeklies, and biweeklies of which nearly half were political—bore primary responsibility for the denigration of Louis Philippe and his government in popular esteem. Rarely, if ever, have a monarch and his counselors been so viciously and scurrilously assailed and lampooned. The onslaught began almost immediately after the July Revolution, when the new monarch announced the end of the censorship. At first the deposed Bourbon ruler and the Catholic church served as the butts, but soon Louis Philippe and his government became the favored targets. Editors and caricaturists sought to outdo one another in the malice and vindictiveness of their censures. The journalists and cartoonists found something either sinister or gross in almost everything that the king and his ministers did. The caricatures proved especially devastating.

The campaign began in November 1830, when Charles Philipon, artist and republican, put out the first issue of *La Caricature*, with two pages of text and two caricatures. In 1832 he started *Charivari*, a daily with three pages of text and one drawing. Philipon, convinced that Louis Philippe had betrayed the revolution, resolved to get revenge through his publications. He assembled a small remarkable band of artists that included the youthful Honoré Daumier and inspired them with his genius for malignity. The best-known and most lasting caricature of the king appeared in 1831 when Philipon, accenting Louis Philippe's narrow forehead and bulging cheeks and jowls, portrayed the king's head as a pear. The drawing caught on immediately with the public. It not only mocked the king's looks. The French word *poire*, "pear," has the colloquial meaning of "simpleton." Anyone could draw a pear, and soon walls and fences everywhere in Paris bore pears drawn with chalk or coal.

Louis Philippe reportedly for a time endured the attacks and lampoons philosophically and even with good humor. But soon patience wore thin and the government initiated prosecutions, seizures, and fines against the offenders. Philipon was arraigned for contempt for the king's person by his drawing of the pear. Thackeray, living in Paris at the time, reported that Philipon escaped punishment by drawing a picture of a large Burgundy pear for the jury. Then he drew a second pear and with a few strokes made it bear a ludicrous resemblance to the king. Next he drew a careful portrait of Louis Philippe. He then turned to the jury and said, "Can I help it gentlemen of the jury, if His Majesty's face is like a pear? Say yourselves. . . . Is it or is it not like a pear?" "Such eloquence could not fail of its effect," Thackeray reported, "the artist was acquitted and *La Poire* is immortal." Others were not as fortunate as Philipon. Between 1831 and 1835, the editors of the most influential republican newspaper were put on trial 114 times, found guilty twenty-three times, sentenced to a total of forty-nine years in jail, and fined a total of 159,000 francs, or an average fine of 7,000 francs. Finally, the paper was suppressed in May 1835.[36]

Punitive actions such as these did not stem the flood of journalistic criticism. Then on July 26, 1835, a savage attempt to assassinate the king led by a man named Giuseppe Fieschi shocked public opinion and gave the government the excuse for more severe repression. The Chamber of Deputies, called into special session, passed the so-called September Laws, most of them directed against the press. To circumvent the Charter's prohibition of censorship, the new legislation hedged the press with prohibitions designed to restrict its freedom of expression. It now became treason to advocate overthrow of the monarchy or publicly to recommend another form of government, thereby outlawing open support of republicanism. The legislation took direct aim against the caricaturists by forbidding the publication of drawings of any sort without the authorization of high government officials. The caricaturists, no longer able to hold the king up to contempt, found ready targets in everyday French life and especially in bourgeois society, and so continued in their mission of ridicule. The September Laws did bring on the demise of some thirty republican newspapers, but in general the legislation was not rigorously enforced. A Russian who lived in Paris in the early 1840s found that the press enjoyed a freedom unmatched anywhere on the Continent save in Belgium and a few Swiss cities.

The unceasing political opposition to and criticism of Louis Philippe by republicans, liberal monarchists and legitimists, and by the press—and his misreading of the minds and wishes of the French—had an inevitable result. Almost from the outset of his reign, Louis Philippe was hounded by an unpopularity that grew steadily with the years. Foreign visitors were struck by it.[37] The disaffection did not restrict itself to words and drawings and lack of respect for the monarch. The talk of regicide that spread among radicals in the first years of Louis Philippe's reign infected others who nourished grudges, real or imagined. Between 1832 and 1846, would-be assassins tried eight times to kill the king, and other plots to murder him were uncovered before they could be carried out. Even more striking than the number of attempts at assassination was the fact that none of them succeeded. Sometimes others were killed or wounded, but Louis Philippe went all but unscathed, escaping death each time by a hair's breadth.

Ideology and politics apparently had little or no part in the motivation of some of the assassins. One penniless man blamed the king for his family's misfortunes. Another assassin, a Paris laborer, seemed to hate kings in general and Louis Philippe in particular. When asked his occupation (he scrubbed floors), he replied, "Exterminator of tyrants." Ideology did have some part in the best-known and most bloody of the attempted assassinations. In 1835 a Corsican named Giuseppe Fieschi and three accomplices planned to kill the king as he rode in a parade to celebrate the fifth anniversary of the July Revolution. Fieschi, a corrupt and vicious man who had served time in prison and in the galley for a variety of crimes, had no sincere political convictions. His accomplices, however, a saddle maker, a grocer, and a workman, were republicans.[38]

As could be expected, the repeated attempts at assassination deeply concerned the royal family. A stream of anonymous threatening letters heightened their alarm. In 1835 the king, who in the first year of his reign had strolled through the streets of Paris, rode out now in an armored carriage and with a heavy guard. A detachment of dragoons preceded his carriage, mounted aides surrounded it, and a second detachment of dragoons brought up the rear. The king showed a wry humor about his need for protection when, in 1837, he offered to take a visiting nobleman to see the museum at Versailles. "You need not be afraid, my Lord," he said, "my carriage is bulletproof." In 1840 John William Croker, who had a talent for putting things in the worst possible light, in a letter to Lord Brougham wrote, "Poor Louis Philippe lives the life of a mad dog, and will soon, I fear, suffer the death of that general object of every man's shot." In 1846 a friend of the scholar and translator Sarah Austin wrote, "It has become kind of a pastime to shoot at the king. . . . The royal person, if not the royal office, has fallen into contempt."[39]

Louis Philippe's unpopularity in France had its analogue in the coolness, indeed, the aversion shown him by his fellow monarchs of the Continent. He seemed pathetically grateful when Victoria and Albert consented to pay him a state visit in 1843. He thanked Albert over and over again, telling him that he and his family felt that the courts of Europe treated them like lepers. They scorned him as a usurper raised to the throne by a revolution, a violator of the principle of legitimacy upon which their authority rested. Most of the lesser states followed the lead of the powers in showing little regard for France's king.[40]

Besieged by his unpopularity at home, bedeviled by would-be assassins, and rebuffed by his fellow rulers, the hardest and most irreparable blow of all came on July 13, 1842. On that day Louis Philippe's eldest son and heir, the duc d'Orléans, died in an accident. When his horses suddenly bolted, he jumped from an open carriage and hit his head on a curbstone. His death had a devastating impact upon the fortunes of the House of Orléans. The young duke was truly a beau ideal. Handsome, elegant, recklessly brave, intelligent, dignified yet approachable, he was immensely popular with all levels of society. He kept a close watch on affairs, and his father paid attention to his views, which often differed from those of the king. All of France had looked to him as the *chef de demain*, the leader of tomorrow. His brother Joinville called him the chief prop of the July Monarchy. His death left an enormous void. When word of it spread through Paris, it was met with dismay and grief. The public recognized that the regime had suffered a blow which could become mortal. "God has removed the only obstacle which existed between the monarchy and the republic," said Alexandre Dumas. In March 1848, after the fall of the July Monarchy, the British ambassador in Paris wrote in his journal that had Orléans lived, history would have taken a different course. Many others agreed with that opinion.[41]

The death of their beloved eldest son overwhelmed Louis Philippe and his queen. They both aged perceptibly. A year after Orléans's death, in a conversation with Franz von Andlaw, Baden's minister in Paris, the king said that he was tired of living. With tear-choked voice he told Andlaw that the much-gifted Orléans had been the strongest support upon which he had built his plans for the future. His death left everything in question. He had good reason for his concern. He was nearing seventy when Orléans died, and Orléans's son and heir was a child of four. A long regency seemed inevitable. Louis Philippe's second son, the duc de Nemours, who would have presumably acted as regent, lacked the ability, the personal charm, the warmth, and the popularity of his elder brother. "Orléans had a noble manner," explained Heinrich Heine in a dispatch to a German newspaper, "Nemours has the manners of the nobility." The king himself, after apologizing for his immodesty, said, "Nemours has my good sense but not my talents." The chances for the continuation of the dynasty after Louis Philippe, with a child on the throne and without a strong and popular regent in command, were indeed slight.

Even family unity began to disintegrate after Orléans's death. The younger sons each went their own way, and one of them, Joinville, openly criticized royal policies. In 1847 Louis Philippe lost his closest friend and most trusted advisor when his sister Adelaide died suddenly. The king himself, now in his seventies, became increasingly irritable and threatened to abdicate and retire with his wife to his chateau at Eu. These family frustrations were an augury of the catastrophe soon to engulf the House of Orléans.[42]

Next to the king, the political life of the July Monarchy revolved around two men, François Guizot and Louis-Adolphe Thiers, and their incessant rivalry. Heinrich Heine wrote that people spoke and argued so much about these two that it became tiring. He marveled that the French still had the patience to keep discussing them year after year. The rivalry began soon after the death, in the cholera epidemic in 1832, of Casimir Periér, the king's chief minister, wealthy banker, and man of the *haute bourgeoisie*. In contrast, both Guizot and Thiers were men of modest means whose origins lay in the lower ranks of the middle class. In their competition for high office, Guizot was clearly the winner. He served in eight of the seventeen ministries of the July Monarchy, and from October 1840 to February 1848, he was the effective chief minister, if not always in name. The Revolution of 1789 and its excesses still fresh in his memory, he believed that republicanism would lead inevitably to anarchy. France must have a king to survive as a nation, and the king must have the power to rule and not merely reign. The extension of the suffrage would introduce radical and dangerous changes. Above all, like his master, he wanted the order and balance of the *juste milieu,* and believed that the political system of the July Monarchy was admirably suited to achieve that end.[43]

Guizot was distinguished in appearance and manner, with a sensitive yet strong face, a pale complexion, an aquiline nose, a firm jaw with thin lips, and piercing and haughty eyes that, according to one observer, "were veiled with melancholy." He was of slight, almost puny, stature, though in later life he put on weight. He often made an unpleasant impression at first meeting, but many found him lively and agreeable. A reserved and grave man, he became transformed when he mounted the tribune of the Chamber of Deputies. The flowing and fiery eloquence, the studied gestures, the sonorous and confident voice enthralled his audience. After hearing him speak, the famed actress Rachel said, "I would love to act in a tragedy with that man."[44]

Born in southern France in 1787 of Protestant parents, educated in Geneva (his family moved there in 1799), Guizot came to Paris at eighteen. There he devoted himself to literary pursuits and in a few short years won recognition for his writings. Such was his success that in 1812 he became professor of modern history at the University of Paris. In succeeding years he wrote and edited multivolume histories, edited collections of historical sources, translated Shakespeare and Gibbon, and contributed to journals and newspapers. This prodigious torrent of productivity, written with style and elegance, gained him recognition as one of Europe's preeminent historians and finest writers. In 1830 he won election to the Chamber of Deputies and in July of that year helped to bring Louis Philippe to the throne.

Superior women played an important part in Guizot's life. When he was only seven his father, a liberal lawyer active in politics, perished under the guillotine. His mother, a stern Calvinist and a woman of great inner strength, made it her mission to shape the mind and character of her son. She continued as an important influence on him until her death at eighty-four in 1848. In 1812 he married an accomplished writer, fourteen years older than he, who worked with him and with whom he enjoyed great happiness. She died in 1827, and the next year Guizot married her niece, who was seventeen years younger than he. Like her aunt, she helped Guizot in his research and writing. After only five years of a happy marriage, she, too, died.

In 1837 Guizot, at the age of fifty, became the constant companion of Princess Dorothea Lieven, two years his senior. Surely this was the most unexpected turn in the career of this no-nonsense, puritanical, and very bourgeois Calvinist. Princess Lieven, daughter of a distinguished family of Baltic Germans, estranged wife of a Russian diplomat (who died in 1839), sister of the head of Russia's infamous secret police, intimate of the courts of tsars and kings, was a leading figure in Europe's high society. One-time mistress of Prince Metternich and Russia's Grand Duke Constantine, disdainful of all who lacked a noble pedigree, she would seem to have been the least likely woman to attract Guizot, and even more improbably, to be attracted to him. Yet for twenty years, until her death in 1857, they were deeply in love. They wrote constantly to each other, and neither could bear a long absence from the other. In their twenty years of companionship, they wrote a total of 3,958 letters and 1,287 notes to each other. Most people believed that they had married secretly, but they had not. A few days after her death, Guizot told the duc de Broglie that he would have married her if she had agreed to take his name. Ultimate snob that she was, she could not bear to give up her title. Riding one day in her carriage with Countess Nesselrode, Princess Lieven remarked, *"Ma chère,* can you imagine me being announced as Madame Guizot!" and fell back laughing against the cushions.

Though Guizot did not gain a wife, he did gain prestige by his close association with the princess. His political status and his amour-propre required a salon in a city of salons presided over by grande dames. He wanted a salon in which he could hold forth, one that clearly outshone the salons favored by his political rivals. The salon of Princess Lieven provided him with a setting hard to equal. Her status as a leader of international society and her personal acquaintance with the social and political leaders of most European lands drew the most important people of the day to her salons.[45]

Guizot's unrelenting support of the interests of his own class and his disregard for the working class, his opposition to the extension of the suffrage and his tolerance of corruption to maintain his power in the Chamber of Deputies branded him as an unsuccessful and even dishonest—or at least disingenuous—politician. Guizot himself knew the perils of his profession. Long after he left office, he wrote that in politics, "where under the eyes of the world, men risk their self-respect and their reputations, as well as their fortunes, life is severe and hard, the combat is without caution or respite, success is endlessly contested and precarious, failures are widely known and galling."[46]

The career of Guizot's archrival, Louis-Adolphe Thiers, bore many resemblances to that of Guizot. Like Guizot, Thiers, who was ten years younger, came from the south of France. Born of bourgeois parents, his father deserted his family, and Thiers was raised by his mother and an aunt. Both men had good educations and both came to Paris as young men to earn their livings as litterateurs. Both quickly established their literary reputations and promoted their political ambitions. Thiers, between 1823 and 1827, published a ten-volume history of the French Revolution. It became immensely popular, contributed significantly to the growth of French nationalism, and made Thiers a national figure.

Like Guizot, too, a remarkable woman played an important role in his career. In 1820, when he was twenty-three, the socially ambitious Madame Dosne, the twenty-six-year-old wife of a wealthy stockbroker, became his patroness and his closest companion until her death in 1869. She cemented their alliance in 1833 when her sixteen-year-old daughter married Thiers. He then moved into the palatial Dosne home, where Madame Dosne started a salon and received the social and political elite of France. She became celebrated for the clarity of her thought and speech as well as for her tart tongue and biting remarks. Monsieur Dosne? In 1830 he received the appointment of collector of taxes in Brest and then in Lille, possibly through Thiers's influence. He died in 1849 in his sixty-eighth year.[47]

Thiers became a leading figure of the new regime, sitting in the Chamber of Deputies from 1830 to 1848 and serving briefly as chief minister, in 1836 and again in 1840. He and Guizot served together as ministers from 1832 to 1836. Neither man was willing to accept the leadership of the other. It was not only a matter of incompatibility and personal dislike. More important, they clashed over the role of the king in a constitutional monarchy. Unlike Guizot, who supported the active participation of the monarch in the government, Thiers wanted to limit severely the royal power. He argued that ministers responsible to the electorate should govern and that it should not matter whether the king approved or disapproved of their actions. Unlike Guizot, who saw no need for reform, Thiers wanted gradual change that would extend the suffrage to the middle and lower ranks of the bourgeoisie. He disagreed with the pacific foreign policy of Guizot and Louis Philippe. Not surprisingly, the king thoroughly disliked Thiers and never felt at ease with him.[48]

Thiers, like Guizot, was a small man, barely five feet tall. Homely and very nearsighted, he had an ungainly figure, and a shrill, unpleasant voice. The American historian, J. L. Motley, visiting Paris in 1842, thought he looked and sounded like a small screech owl. All that was forgotten when he spoke from the tribune of the Chamber of Deputies. Motley reported that "his style was so fluent, so limpid, and so logical, his manner so assured and self-possessed, that . . . I thought him one of the most agreeable speakers I have ever heard. . . . His consummate brass, added to his ready wit, makes every one of his speeches gall and wormwood to his enemies." Unlike other great orators of his day, Thiers did not use gestures nor ornate language. Instead he affected a conversational style that gave the impression of a dialogue between Thiers and his listeners.

The "consummate brass" that Motley noted reflected the consummate self-confidence of the man. Certain that he was always right, he could not abide interference nor share authority. In 1836, when he served briefly as chief minister, he told Count Apponyi, attaché at the Austrian embassy in Paris, that he and Metternich held the reins of all European politics in their hands, he for the west and Metternich for the east. They could arrange all the affairs of Europe by having a conversation. Metternich, Thiers continued, would quickly be for Thiers's way of thinking, and the result would be the greatest good for Europe.[49]

Corruption and bribery, with Guizot named as the chief culprit, became the most frequently repeated charge against the July Monarchy. Stories were told of deputies (who received no salaries) always on the alert to sell their votes for a few hundred francs. The government, well supplied with money, could always win the support of the Chamber of Deputies for its policies. In addition, there were around 677,000 salaried government slots, nearly all of them at the disposal of the government. The small size of the electorate made it easy to win support by the distribution of these jobs, as well as by favors, and by contracts for public works or for supplies. Though Guizot was scarcely the originator of the corruption, it reached its zenith in the 1840s, when he held power. Though personally incorruptible, he did not scruple at preying on the moral weakness of others to gain their support.

In 1847 a series of scandals that involved men who held high office seemed to confirm the popular belief in the prevalence of governmental corruption. Lesser incidents that in other days would have attracted little attention were blown up into major crimes. The press, nearly all of it now in opposition to the regime, took full advantage of this new opportunity to assail its favorite target. Fair-minded people recognized that the public's perception grossly exaggerated the facts. Modern studies have in fact shown that electoral corruption was far less common than people of the time believed.[50]

Crimes and scandals in the highest social circles added fuel to the public's distrust and alienation. These crimes and scandals, fully and colorfully reported in the press, convinced the public that vice and depravity held sway among the ruling elite of France. Then, in August 1847, other scandals were eclipsed by the savage murder of his wife by the duc de Praslin-Choiseul. Praslin, scion of an important and very wealthy noble family, had married the only daughter of Marshal Sebastiani, a hero of the Napoleonic era and a major political figure of the July Monarchy. The duke reportedly had affairs with a succession of governesses of his young children. On the night of August 17, Praslin and his wife argued heatedly about the latest governess and struggled with each other until the maddened duke stabbed his wife repeatedly. After a brief investigation he was arrested and jailed. Three nights later he committed suicide by drinking poison that, mysteriously, he had been able to procure. The brutal murder created a sensation and sent a chill of horror not only in Paris but throughout Europe. Then, even before the first shock had dissipated, came the news of the duke's suicide. The rumor quickly spread that the government, to avoid a public trial for so prominent a figure, had provided the duke with the poison. Still another rumor—that many believed—insisted that the suicide had been a hoax, that the king had allowed the duke to escape, and that he was living in England under an assumed name.

The belief that the government had supplied Praslin with a poison, or had allowed him to escape, persuaded many that justice for the elite differed from justice for the rest of society. That conviction, abetted by the press, which reveled in the details of the crime, and by fiery orators of the left, worsened the malaise that afflicted the French people. Alienation and disaffection, centering in Paris, pervaded much of society. The London *Economist* reported that the crime was "brought to bear, by the journals, against the government, against the aristocracy, against the whole system of political society. It is spoken of as one of those mournful presages which overwhelm men with a presentiment of a great coming calamity."[51]

Supposedly responsible politicians, seeking political advantage, contributed to the unrest by charging that the regime had sold out to the capitalists, or that it was the pawn of foreign courts, or, like Thiers, joined with extremists to claim that Protestant and Jewish bankers ruled France. The economic downturn that began in 1846, which included poor harvest, rising prices of food, banking and commercial failures, and unemployment, heightened the discontent. A remarkable flowering of socialist doctrines, attracting many urban workers and bourgeois intellectuals, fueled social discontent. Most were apostles of utopian socialism who thought that change could come by peaceful persuasion, without violence. They fostered a belief among many that a new order of society, free of the inequities of the present, lay just over the horizon.

The fire was laid. All that was needed was a match, which the government itself provided by a foolish and unnecessary act. In the spring of 1847, the Chamber of Deputies had defeated bills for electoral and parliamentary reform. The leaders of the reform movement decided to seek public demonstrations of support for their program. The September Laws forbade overt political meetings, and so the reformers decided to sponsor public banquets with speakers. The first banquet was held in Paris in July 1847, and the idea spread quickly to other parts of the country. Some fifty banquets were held in twenty-eight departments, with about twenty-two thousand paid subscriptions plus three or four times that number who heard the speeches. The speakers urged electoral reform, an end to corruption, and social reforms including improvements in the condition of the working class. Despite their popularity, the banquets failed to persuade the government to introduce reforms, and the movement lost momentum. In an effort to revive it, its promoters decided to hold a monster banquet in Paris on February 22, 1848, to bring together all shades of opinion. To avoid possible trouble, they decided to hold the banquet near the Champs-Elysées rather than in the crowded neighborhood first chosen, and agreed that police would be present to halt the proceedings if necessary. Despite these concessions and despite the obvious failure of the banquet campaign, the government, fearing a disturbance, on February 21 forbade the holding of the banquet.[52]

That turned out to be a fatal mistake. Most of the banquet's organizers accepted the ban, but a few activists announced that they intended to hold it. On the morning of the twenty-second, a cold and rainy day, a crowd of around three thousand, made up largely of students and workers, gathered in the Place de la Madeleine, and demanded the adoption of reforms and the dismissal of Guizot. There was much milling about but no serious disturbances. The next day, despite the continued bad weather, a larger and more aggressive crowd gathered. The king called on the National Guard to restrain the crowd, but many of the guardsmen joined in the demand for reform. The king could have called in troops stationed in or near Paris to restore order but decided against it, perhaps because he feared it would bring on street fighting and spill blood. With great reluctance he decided to appease the demonstrators by announcing the dismissal of Guizot as his chief minister. The news set off rejoicing with people singing revolutionary songs and shaking hands with one another in the streets. But Guizot's dismissal did not satisfy the demonstrators, who had now formed into an uncontrollable mob. Disorders increased, and that evening some of the mob marched to Guizot's official residence. One of the soldiers guarding the building accidentally fired a shot. His comrades apparently panicked and fired a volley into the crowd, killing fifty-two and wounding many more. Soon a huge wagon, lit by torchbearers, carried the slain through the streets of Paris.

After dismissing Guizot, the king could not bring himself to appoint Thiers as chief minister. He asked Count de Molé to form a government, but by midnight of the twenty-third, Molé gave up the attempt. The king realized he had to turn to Thiers. But it was too late. By the morning of the twenty-fourth, with the rain still pouring, the city was in turmoil. Felled trees and barricades of paving stones blocked the narrow streets. The mob controlled Paris. An angry mob gathered at the Tuileries, the royal palace, threatening the safety of the royal family. Fighting broke out nearby. The king rode out to review the troops guarding the Tuileries and was greeted with shouts demanding reform. He returned to the palace and had hasty consultations with people offering all manner of advice. He decided to abdicate in favor of his eldest grandson, the Comte de Paris, the nine-year-old son of the dead duc d'Orléans. Then word came that the mob was pouring into the palace. The royal couple, in fear for their lives, with family members and a few faithful followers, fled through a rear entrance, crowded into three carriages, and rode off into exile.

Meanwhile, that same day the duchess of Orléans, leading her two small sons, made a dramatic appearance at the Chamber of Deputies to ask the deputies to accept her eldest son as king and herself as regent. The deputies seemed ready to consent when a mob invaded the hall, driving out the duchess and her sons and some of the deputies. Under the leadership of republican speakers, the mob compelled the remaining deputies to form a provisional government. That evening a republic was proclaimed.

And so without plan or even intention, France abandoned constitutional monarchy and embarked upon the Second Republic. The First Republic had lasted from 1792 to 1799. The Second had an even shorter life, ending in 1851. France paid a small price in human life for the February Revolution—72 soldiers and 289 insurgents—but the political and social costs were incalculable. The February rising in Paris gave the signal for the tidal wave of revolution that swept through much of Europe in the spring of 1848, and for the reaction and repression that followed, developments which influenced European history for decades to come.

Prophecies of revolution by both Frenchmen and foreigners had become common currency during the July Monarchy. The outspoken opposition and the virulence of the attacks on the king and his policies seemed to insure that the regime would sooner or later be overthrown. Yet the outbreak of the revolution and its quick success seemed to fill nearly everyone with consternation. Observers could scarcely believe that the revolution had happened and that Louis Philippe had been driven from his throne so quickly and easily. John Stuart Mill wrote of the February Revolution that it "stands almost alone among revolutions, in having placed power in the hands of men who neither expected nor sought it, nor used it for any personal purpose."

The fact was that despite all the criticism and all the discontent and all the ridicule, no one had planned to overthrow the monarchy. Someone once said that the February Revolution was an effect without a cause. The legitimist politician count de Falloux amended that to say that the revolution was an effect out of proportion to its cause. "There was no tyranny to overcome," he wrote, "no provocation to repulse, no real culprits to punish." The easy victory of the revolution baffled contemporaries. They pointed out that the king had a large army loyal to him, that he had a majority in the Chamber of Deputies, and a ministry of able men. Yet monarch, monarchy, and dynasty crumbled without a struggle before what a Russian diplomat called "the canaille of the faubourgs."[53]

After the event it is easy to tick off a series of causes that led to revolution. It is easy, too, to recognize that the ultimately decisive factor in the quick victory of the revolution was the king's failure to use the army. Had he called out the troops they would have suppressed the tumult before it became a revolution. Why did he not take that obvious step? Was it because of a reluctance to use the army against his subjects—a reluctance not shown by him in putting down the risings in Lyons and Paris in 1834? Or was it because of a failure of nerve? This remarkable man, who had endured so much and had won admiration for his personal courage, panicked. So did those close to him, with the striking exception of his queen. "My dear," she said, "do not ever abandon your office, sooner die as king." Perhaps the suddenness of the storm took him so much by surprise that his courage deserted him. Perhaps Duke Ernst of Saxe-Coburg-Gotha helped explain the king's loss of nerve when he wrote that "Louis Philippe was far more tired of reigning than incapable of doing so." The years had taken their toll of the seventy-five-year-old king. A few days after the revolution Guizot, who like Louis Philippe had fled to England, told Lord Aberdeen that in the preceding two years he had noticed a change in the king, who at times evinced his former strength of mind and acuteness, but who on the whole had much declined.[54]

The royal couple had fled in such haste that the king had only the money in his pocket—fifteen francs. After a hazardous flight, the couple arrived at Le Havre, the king disguised as an Englishman named William Smith, wearing thick glasses and minus the famous side-whiskers and wig. They set sail for England, and arriving there, settled in Claremont, an estate owned by their son-in-law, Leopold, the Belgian king. There the old king lived until his death in 1850.

After the demise of the July Monarchy, France never tried constitutional monarchy again. But the July Monarchy proved to be the seedbed for the development of the political institutions of modern France. For the first time in its history, France had a cabinet responsible to the Chamber of Deputies, the elected representatives of the people. As could be expected of a new kind of government, the system had frequent breakdowns. In the eighteen years of the July Monarchy, France had seventeen ministries, fifteen before October 1840, but only two thereafter. Many of the same names appeared time and again in the succession of ministries. Party organization and party discipline were lacking. Louis Philippe, new to the system of constitutional monarchy, was unwilling to efface himself from the business of governing. He insisted on choosing and dismissing ministers and influencing policy decisions. Nonetheless, the principle of a ministry composed of members of the legislative body and responsible to the elected representatives of the people established itself. That perhaps was the greatest legacy of the July Monarchy. When the Second Empire collapsed in 1870, the French looked back at their experience with parliamentary government and chose that kind of government, albeit without a monarch.

The provisional government of the newly proclaimed Second Republic had seven members, only one of them a radical. The others were moderate republicans, some newly converted from constitutional monarchy to the republican creed. Later, four radicals were added. During its first days the provisional government, under pressure from the left, enacted a series of reforms that included the establishment of a work-relief program called the National Workshops, freedom of the press and of assembly, and universal male suffrage. At one stroke of the pen, the provisional government increased the French electorate from 240,000 to 9,000,000.

These and similar measures did not satisfy the demands of the radicals. In some provinces the news of the revolution in Paris set off waves of violence, especially among peasants who overran lands of large proprietors, sacked châteaus and attacked moneylenders. To worsen matters, the February Revolution precipitated an economic crisis with resulting widespread unemployment. By June over half of the workers in Paris had no jobs. To raise the money needed to pay wages in the National Workshops, the government introduced a series of draconian measures that alienated property owners and taxpayers.

Massive street demonstrations in March and April reflected radical dissatisfaction with the provisional government. The dissatisfaction intensified after April 23, when Frenchmen went to the polls to elect delegates to the Constitutional Assembly, which had as its primary task the drafting of a constitution for the Second Republic. Eighty-four percent of the electorate cast ballots. Only 55 radicals won seats; 285 others had been republicans before February, and 566 were former monarchists newly converted to republicanism.

In the Beginning

The convening of the Constituent Assembly on May 4 formally ended the provisional government. The Assembly chose an Executive Commission of five men, all of them opponents of radicalism, to run the government. Radicals and workers, dismayed by the results of the elections, staged violent demonstrations. Troops put down the disturbances. The Executive Commission ordered the arrest of radical leaders, suppressed clubs, forbade street gatherings, and began to plan the dissolution of the National Workshops because of the strain they placed on government finances. The reaction had begun. On June 21, the government announced its decision to close the Workshops.

Crowds immediately gathered in the streets, and barricades rose in eastern Paris, cutting the city in two. On the twenty-third, the Executive Commission put General Eugène Cavaignac, the Minister of War, in command of the government's forces and turned over full executive power to him for the duration of the crisis. Thousands of workers—estimates run from fifteen thousand to fifty thousand—joined the rising, famed as the June Days. The revolt was a spontaneous outburst, without plan or organization or leadership, of a destitute and despairing people, infuriated by the failure of the government to provide work for them. The insurgents fought desperately, but the outcome was never in doubt. By the morning of the twenty-fourth, it was all over, the rebels surrounded and defeated. They had lost four to five hundred men in the fighting. The worst, however, was yet to come. Youths of the government's newly formed *Garde mobile*, recruited from the working-class districts of Paris, in mindless savagery slaughtered insurgents—some said as many as three thousand—in cold blood. About twelve thousand rebels were arrested, of whom about two thirds were imprisoned without trial. Most were released in succeeding months, but about 4,300 were transported to penal colonies in Algeria and French Guiana.[55]

Had the government moved more gradually in its dismantling of the National Workshops, and had it provided some alternative program of employment, the June Days might have never happened. Instead, frightened by the threat of revolution by workers disappointed in the hopes raised by the February Revolution, the government acted precipitously. The result was to aggravate the antagonism between workers and the bourgeoisie and to push France further along the road of repression and reaction.

After the defeat of the insurgents in the June Days, General Cavaignac laid down the dictatorial powers given him by the Executive Committee. The Constituent Assembly then chose him to become president of the Council of Ministers. The Cavaignac government introduced a number of repressive measures but also sponsored some mild social reforms. The regime's most significant accomplishment was a new constitution, overwhelmingly approved by the Assembly and promulgated on November 12, 1848. Among its provisions the new constitution guaranteed freedom of the press and of assembly, ordered free primary education for everyone, and ended all civil distinction between classes. It provided for the election of a president instituted for a four-year term and forbade his reelection, and instituted a unicameral legislature of 750 deputies elected to three-year terms.[56]

Three weeks after the promulgation of the constitution, the French went to the polls to select their president. Five men ran for the office. Nearly 7.5 million, or three quarters of the electorate, cast ballots. An overwhelming majority chose a man named Prince Louis Napoleon Bonaparte. He received almost three quarters of the vote. General Cavaignac, in second place, had less than 20 percent, and the rest was scattered among the other three candidates.[57]

The story of the man who won by such vast proportions and who soon went on to still greater triumphs seems so incredible that it can only be believed because it really happened. He had only one thing going for him. He was the nephew of the great Napoleon Bonaparte—and there was reason to doubt even that. Born in 1808, he was the third son of Napoleon's younger brother, Louis, whom Napoleon had made king of Holland, and Louis's queen, Hortense de Beauharnais. It was an unhappy marriage, and a widespread and persistent rumor held that King Louis was not the boy's father. Louis Napoleon could not have been less Napoleonic in manner, personality, and appearance. He lacked the magnetism that the great Napoleon had possessed in abundance. Cold, reserved, and taciturn, he repelled people rather than drew them to himself. Except for six years in an isolated French prison, he had never lived in France and had visited that land only twice, briefly and uninvited.

He was the kind of man whom people constantly and understandably underrated. Richard Cobden, who met him in London, thought he was a weak man. Henry Greville, meeting him in 1847, thought he was "by no means *de l'étoffe dont les héros sont fait*." Even when he rose to great power, people still underrated him. Karl Marx called him a grotesque mediocrity, and Chancellor Bismarck of Prussia referred to him contemptuously as "a sphinx without a riddle." Yet this seemingly very ordinary man had a vision and an unshakable confidence that he would succeed. A stranger to doubt and discouragement, he had an absolute faith that it was his destiny to succeed the first Bonaparte as the ruler of France.[58]

When the Napoleonic empire collapsed in 1814, Queen Hortense left her husband and settled in Switzerland with her third son, Louis. Her eldest son had died in infancy, and the second one died in 1831. The next year the duke of Reichstadt, Napoleon's only son, died. Napoleon's surviving brothers refused to lay claim to the throne. That made Louis Napoleon the Bonapartist pretender. None of his kinsmen shared his enthusiasm or gave him any support or encouragement. Only his mother did not scoff at his ambition, and even she felt small hope for its fulfillment.

In 1836 he resolved to make his move. On October 30 he appeared in Strasbourg, near the German border, dressed in colonel's uniform and with a handful of adherents. He planned to win over the army garrison there, issue proclamations, march on Paris, and emulating Napoleon's triumphant return from Elba in 1815, take over as the new emperor. In short order the ludicrous enterprise collapsed and Louis Napoleon and his followers were jailed. Instead of a trial that would bring the young Bonaparte to public notice, Louis Philippe ordered him deported to the United States. He remained in the States until January 1837, when he learned of the serious illness of his mother. He hastened back to Switzerland and remained there until her death later that year. After her death he moved to London, where, using money inherited from his mother, he lived in grand style. He also acquired an English mistress, Elizabeth Howard (née Harryett) by name.

Unchastened by his harebrained "invasion" of Strasbourg, Bonaparte decided to try again. On August 6, 1840, he crossed the Channel to Boulogne on a chartered steamer, accompanied by fifty-five men, among them his chef, his butler, his tailor, and his fencing master, plus assorted hired hands, and one tame eagle (some claimed it was a vulture posing as an eagle). The invaders wore the uniforms of the regiment stationed in Boulogne, which Bonaparte expected to win over to his cause. As could be expected, the preposterous adventured proved a failure. Within five hours after he landed, Napoleon was captured. This time Louis Philippe decided to charge him with treason. The Chamber of Peers heard the case and sentenced Napoleon to imprisonment for life and his fellow conspirators to prison terms of from two to twenty years.

Louis Napoleon and several of his followers were imprisoned in the gloomy fortress of Ham, in northwest France, guarded by four hundred soldiers. Bonaparte spent his time reading, conducting a busy correspondence, seeing an occasional visitor, and in the evening playing whist with his fellow prisoners. He also fathered two children by the prison laundress and contracted rheumatism from his damp prison. His fellow prisoners were released in 1846 and Napoleon decided to escape. Workmen were repairing his building, and on May 25 the prince, disguised in workman's clothing, with a plank from one of his bookshelves across his shoulder, his moustache shaved, and his face rouged to hide the prison pallor, slowly walked out of the gates of his prison. Two days later he reappeared in London and took up his life where he had left it six years before, including his liaison with the compliant Miss Howard, who remained his companion until 1853, when he married the Spanish Countess Eugénie de Montijo de Guzman. He then rewarded the discarded Miss Howard by creating her the Countess de Beauregard.[59]

As part of his campaign to keep his name and his ambitions alive in the public's mind, Louis Napoleon wrote books and pamphlets and articles for newspapers and magazines on a wide variety of subjects. One of his best-known works, *Des idées napoléoniennes*, published in 1839, went through four French editions and was translated into six foreign languages. The tract argued that France's salvation lay in the restoration of the Bonapartist regime and identified Louis Napoleon as the man who could save France. Another widely circulated work, a thirty-nine-page pamphlet *Extinction du paupérisme*, appeared in 1844, denouncing the inequities of France's economic system that kept so many in poverty and that threatened the disruption of the social order. The pamphlet gave the prince the reputation of a man who had a genuine concern for the plight of the poor.

The whirl of London social life did not distract Bonaparte for a moment from his faith in his destiny. He thought his time had come when revolution drove Louis Philippe from his throne. Bonaparte departed for Paris, where he offered his services to the provisional government, which responded by giving him twenty-four hours to get out of France. Obediently, he returned to London. Meanwhile the disorders and demonstrations that plagued France made people long for order. Cries of "*Vive l'Empereur*" began to be heard in the streets. Then, in by-elections to the Constituent Assembly in early June, Napoleon was elected a deputy in four departments. That created great excitement and the government ordered the arrest of the prince on sight. Louis Napoleon, still in London, chose discretion as the better part of valor, resigned his seat by letter to the Assembly, and waited for a more propitious moment. That came in September with its by-elections to the Assembly. This time he was chosen as a deputy in five departments, and this time he took his seat. A poor and fumbling speaker, he cut an unimpressive and even slightly comic figure in the Assembly. Once again Louis Napoleon had been under-rated. Out in the streets of Paris and in the provinces, his performance and his reputation in the Assembly did not affect the rising tide of Bonapartism.

That tide crested for the first time when, on December 10, 1848, a huge majority of the electorate chose him to become the president of the Second Republic. His election came as no surprise to most observers, though his great margin of victory astonished them. With each passing day it had become increasingly clear that most Frenchmen had wearied of the existing regime. The Second Republic had been likened to an unwanted child, rejected by its parents almost from the moment of its birth. Throughout its brief life it was haunted by fears of revolt, by secret societies plotting new revolutions, by rural unrest and riots, and by endless rumors of impending violence.[60]

In the early days of his administration, the new president played his cards carefully, avoided conflicts with the Assembly until he consolidated his own political power, and accepted, sometimes reluctantly, measures passed by the legislature. In elections held in May 1849 for the new parliament—called the Legislative Assembly—a coalition of monarchists won over 500 of the 750 seats in the new body. The radical left made something of a comeback with 180 seats. The radicals, made overconfident by their gains, decided in mid-June to stage an insurrection. Their summons to the workers of Paris to revolt brought only a small response, and troops easily dispersed the would-be insurrectionists. Lyons saw a far more serious rising that cost two hundred lives, but it, too, was quickly suppressed.

The risings provided the government with the excuse for expelling thirty radical deputies from the Assembly and for a series of repressive measures in the succeeding months, including a revision of the electoral laws that disenfranchised about 30 percent of the electorate. Louis Napoleon disapproved of the disenfranchisement but signed the legislation because he was not yet ready to take a stand against the Assembly's majority. In the second half of the year, he decided he was ready. He wanted above all to revise the provision of the constitution that forbade the reelection of the president. The next election was scheduled for 1852, and Napoleon planned to succeed himself. He toured the country to win support, but the bill to revise the constitution fell ninety-seven votes short of the two-thirds majority needed for revision.[61]

There seemed no way to settle the issue by legal parliamentary action, so Louis Napoleon resolved on other means to reach his goal. Working with a small group of conspirators, he laid plans for a *coup d'état*. The conspirators settled on December 2, 1851, for their *coup*. Soldiers arrested leading opposition members of the Assembly in their beds and placarded the city with the announcement that Louis Napoleon had dissolved the Legislative Assembly, restored universal male suffrage, promised a new constitution that greatly lessened the power of the legislature, placed Paris under martial law, and summoned the voters to a referendum in the near future to give their approval to the new regime. During the next two days, barricades went up in the streets of Paris, troops moved against them, and by the evening of the fourth, resistance in Paris had ended.

It was a different story in provinces in central and southern France. In what turned out to be the last great popular rising of the era, an estimated hundred thousand rose against the *coup*. Large numbers of soldiers, dispatched quickly to quell the resistance, had successfully carried out their mission by the tenth of December. Something less than four hundred lost their lives in the rebellion; in its aftermath over twenty-seven hundred were arrested. Thousands were transported to French colonies, and other thousands were placed under police surveillance. These punishments were only part of the far-reaching repression of those accused of opposition to the regime. Civil servants lost their posts, teachers were discharged, and owners of shops and cafés were compelled to close.[62]

Eighty-two percent of the electorate cast ballots in the plebiscite held on December 20 and 21. Over nine tenths voted in favor of the new regime and authorized Louis Napoleon to draft a new constitution. The huge majority made it clear for all the world to see that most Frenchmen, wearied of parliamentary wrangling and constitutional impasses, fearful of street fighting and violence, and frightened by socialistic panaceas that threatened the right of private ownership, preferred the security and order of authoritarianism to the uncertainties of republican self-government.

The repressions that followed the *coup* continued until the end of March 1852, when the new constitution went into effect. The constitution gave supreme power to the president. Among its provisions, it ordered a ten-year term for the president, who would name his successor, and stipulated that only the president could initiate legislation, so that the legislature did little more than vote for or against the proposed law.

Almost immediately after the *coup* the Prince-President, as he was now called, began to assume imperial trappings. He moved his official residence to the Tuileries, where Napoleon had lived as emperor, added the imperial eagles to the standards of his army, had coins minted with his portrait on them, and restored titles of nobility. Bonapartists mounted an elaborate and successful campaign to muster popular support for the elevation of Louis Napoleon to emperor of France. The Prince-President convoked the legislature, and on November 7, it restored the empire and called for a plebiscite to ratify its decision. In the plebiscite, held two weeks later, 7,824,149 people voted for the empire and 253,145 against it. Over two million did not vote. On December 2, 1852, the appropriate legislative authority declared the empire reestablished. The new emperor called himself Napoleon III. Napoleon I had abdicated after his defeat at Waterloo in favor of his four-year-old son, who would have been Napoleon II and who died in Austria in 1832.[63]

France had once again come full circle. The restoration of the Bourbons in 1814, and then the reign of Louis Philippe, had restored monarchical government that had lapsed in 1792 with the execution of Louis XVI. The Second Republic sought to restore the democracy and symbols of the First Republic that had lasted from 1792 to 1799. Now France had a Second Empire. It had taken Napoleon I nearly five years to crown himself emperor of France in 1803. Napoleon III achieved the same eminence in a year, the only accomplishment in which the nephew exceeded the uncle—that and the fact that the nephew's empire lasted eighteen years while the uncle's survived for only ten.

The short-lived Second Republic accelerated the political and social transformation that had gotten under way in the years of the July Monarchy, and especially in the 1840s. As in Britain, the middle class had been the chief beneficiaries of these economic changes. Unlike Britain, where the landed elite retained its political and social supremacy, the bourgeoisie in France became the dominant class. For the first time in European history, the middle class, or more exactly the upper strata of the bourgeoisie, became the ruling class in a major state. And, more than at any other time in past European experience, merit, rather than birth or inherited wealth, became the key to entry into the ruling class.

Workers and peasants had been excluded from membership in the political community. Now, through the medium of universal manhood suffrage, introduced during the Second Republic, they became participants in political life. The improvements in transportation ended the isolation of many villages. They also made it easier for peasants to leave the land and seek employment in the growing factory and service industries in urban centers. In ever increasing numbers, peasants and workers entered into the mainstream of society, with all the social dislocations and perturbations that always accompany discontinuities of this magnitude. The workers expected great things from the February Revolution. They had made that revolution all but unaided. They heard the bold words of the radicals and socialists, who flourished in France as in no other land, and were entranced by their visions of a better and more just world. But almost from the first days of their triumph, the fruits of their victory were denied them. Men of the middle class took the revolution away from the workers. Leaderless and without a viable program, any hopes the workers had for gaining control were crushed in the June Days and then in the *coup* of December 2, 1851, and the cruel repressions that followed these events. Through it all the middle classes, fearful of an overturn of the social order, stood firmly against demands for social and economic reform. The conflict of interests between bourgeoisie and workers brought about a gulf between the classes that continued to widen as the years went by, a gulf that characterized and still characterizes the history of modern France.

CHAPTER SEVEN

Austria:
Empire of Silence
and Stagnation

The emperor was a sweet-tempered, retarded, misshapen epileptic called Ferdinand the Amiable by court panegyrists and Ferdy the Ninny by the common people of Vienna who loved him. A State Conference of three old men ran the government for the incompetent emperor. The emperor's uncle, Archduke Louis, who seemed incapable of making up his mind, presided. The other members were the deaf and garrulous Prince Metternich, who considered himself infallible, and Count Kolowrat, hypochondriac and intriguer, who constantly threatened to pick up his marbles and go home. The empire over which Ferdinand nominally ruled did not have a single official name, but was called variously the Lands Ruled by the House of Austria, the Austrian Imperial Hereditary Monarchy, the House of Austria, and the Austrian Monarchy. Austria or the Habsburg Empire served as names of convenience. No name was generally agreed upon because it was not a single state but instead a conglomerate of six kingdoms, two grand duchies, seven duchies, two earldoms with the rank of princedoms, and two margravates. In all, these lands covered 270,000 square miles (only Russia was larger) with a population in 1846 of 37.5 million people. The bond of this medley was that they all had the same sovereign, the head of the House of Habsburg, who ruled over them from Vienna. He was the King of Bohemia, the King of Hungary, the King of Galicia and Lodomeria, the King of Lombardy-Venetia, the King of Dalmatia, the King of Croatia-Slavonia, the Grand Duke of

Transylvania, the Archduke of Austria, and so on and so on. The so-called Grand Imperial Title listed over fifty titles claimed by the Habsburg ruler and wound up with "etc., etc.," in the event that some claim had slipped by. The Habsburgs had acquired much of their territories by skillfully arranged marriage alliances. They gained more power and fame by nuptial diplomacy than they ever won in battle.

In short, the Austrian empire was not a state. It was a personal possession of the Habsburg dynasty, a survival from earlier centuries before the emergence of the unified national state. Each of its lands had its own rights and privileges, its own language, its own traditions and culture, and sometimes its own dress. Each land had within it sizable ethnic minorities with their own languages and traditions who usually suffered discrimination at the hands of the majority. In all, the empire had eleven principal nationalities: Germans, Hungarians, Italians, Romanians, Czechs, Slovaks, Poles, Ruthenians, Croats, Serbs, and Slovenes, plus a number of minor ethnic groups, such as Sorbs, Szeklers, Saxons, Wends, and gypsies. Most of these nationalities did not get along with and even openly disliked one another, and all joined in an antipathy toward Germans and toward the Jews who were scattered throughout the empire. In the 1780s Emperor Joseph II, in the interests of efficiency, made German the official language of the empire and thereby aroused an increased aversion to Germans.

History has always counted the Habsburg emperor of those days among the absolute rulers of Europe. That was true of the German and Slav parts of the empire, where assemblies called estates, made up of representatives of the clergy, the nobility, and the royal cities in the eighteenth century, lost what little authority they had once possessed. In the Kingdom of Hungary, however, which covered a third of the realm, the Habsburg ruler had to share his power with the Diet. The Diet was divided into four estates. The lords spiritual formed the first estate; the titled nobility—the magnates—made up the second; representatives of the untitled nobility made up the third estate, and the fourth estate was composed of deputies of the royal free cities. The Diet had to give its approval to legislation proposed by the throne and could itself initiate legislation that became law when signed by the ruler.

Even with the most efficient and skilled administration, governing this gallimaufry of lands and peoples would have offered monumental difficulties. The Austrian government could have been charged with many things but never with administrative skill and efficiency. Each department went its own way, making decisions without consulting the other agencies. Most of the high posts in the bureaucracy, the army, the diplomatic service, and the church went to men of the great noble families, with little or no regard for their competence. Unfortunately for Austria, these men usually lacked the sense of responsibility and the political skills of the elite who dominated the government of Great Britain. They delegated their duties to nobles of lesser distinction or to commoners, and devoted themselves to the social life and recreations of their class.[1]

As could be expected, confusion, delay, and stagnation were the normal state of affairs. Many in Austria and in foreign lands called the empire an anachronism and prophesied that the antipathies of its nationalities for one another would tear it apart. Yet somehow, to the puzzlement of contemporaries and historians of later generations, this anachronistic and misgoverned agglomeration continued to hang together and to hold rank as one of the great powers of the world. Some found the key to explain this phenomenon in geography. They pointed out that the empire had formed around the basin of the Danube, the great stream that flowed through the heart of the realm. The Alps, Sudeten, Carpathian, and Dinaric mountain ranges form the natural boundaries of the basin. None of the many nationalities within this geographic perimeter had the resources or the military and economic power to stand by itself. The confederation provided by the Habsburg empire offered the only alternative to anarchy, or even worse in the minds of contemporaries, conquest by the dreaded Russian empire.[2] There was a mystique, too, that enveloped the Habsburgs, who had ruled for so long over the disparate people of their realm. Time had conditioned their subjects to the instinctive acceptance of the rule of the Habsburgs. Loyalty to the emperor seemed part of the natural order of things. Their devotion to the House of Habsburg was as unquestioning as their religious faith.

In any event, until the 1840s the great mass of the people of the empire had neither interest nor concern about the central government. Most of them were illiterate and unfree peasants living on the margin of subsistence; their horizons had rarely risen above the boundaries of their villages. They paid taxes, and some of their young men served as conscripts in the imperial army. That was as far as their relationship with the state went. Because of the low cultural level and the economic backwardness that prevailed in most of the empire, few demands were made of the central government. It could devote itself principally to the conduct of foreign and military affairs, to raising enough taxes to support these functions, and to pay for a relatively small bureaucracy and the glittering Imperial Court. Its presence was felt lightly, if at all, as a sort of patina. Its most common reminder was the appearance of the letters *k.u.k.* standing for *kaiserliche und königliche*, "imperial and royal," to indicate an official bureau or to show that an establishment had the sanction of the regime—sometimes in unusual places, as an English visitor discovered. He noticed a small wooden hut in a niche on a street in Vienna that bore the sign *k.u.k. privilegierte Retirade*, thereby authorizing an old woman to operate a public toilet.[3]

When Emperor Ferdinand succeeded to the throne in 1835, he announced to his subjects that he would maintain unchanged the policies of his father, Francis I, a prescription for stagnation and ultimately revolution. Francis, whose long reign began in 1792, was as much an anachronism as the empire over which he ruled. He resolved that new ideas and reforms should not disturb the peace and order of his realm. To achieve that end, he created a system of government whose primary function was to block all change. Any suggested action that had no precedent had to receive his personal approval, which he gave rarely. Instead, he procrastinated, demanding report after report, and using all manner of subterfuges to postpone a decision.[4]

How much of this inactivity was purposeful and how much of it was part of Francis's character is impossible to determine. Certainly the lessons of the French Revolution, during which his empire faced dissolution, had not been lost on him. He feared revolution above all else, and so he determined to checkmate any proposal that seemed to him to offer a threat to the status quo. His refusal to act, however, had deeper roots. When he was still a youth, his uncle, the childless Emperor Joseph II, said of Francis, who was his heir, that he was "undecided in thought, action, and opinion, and had a fear and an aversion for vexatious matters." His indecisiveness grew with his years. Lacking confidence in his own judgment, equally uncertain of the advice of his counselors, yet determined to exercise supreme authority, he took refuge in indecision. His fear of innovation prevented needed administrative reforms, and his deliberate postponement of decisions led to contradictions and confusions and ultimately to governmental impotence.[5]

As the years went by, some of his subjects grew discontented with his rule. But to the vast majority, Francis became a beloved figure. He possessed the "common touch" that enabled him to establish a personal relationship with his subjects. His seemingly kindly nature, his common sense and lack of ostentation in his public appearances appealed to ordinary people who felt that they could identify with him. They called him Francis the Good, and when he died in 1835, they mourned for him as for a beloved father. Two years later, when that indefatigable tourist Mrs. Trollope visited the imperial catacombs in Vienna, the grief, sobs, and tears of the throng who pressed around Francis's tomb astounded her.[6]

Perhaps the most telling judgment on Francis came from Francis Grillparzer, one of Austria's greatest literary figures. On the day of the emperor's death, Grillparzer wrote in his diary that "the Austrians loved the emperor as Desdemona loved Othello, for his misfortunes, when in the fearful events of the Napoleonic wars his people rallied behind him. They were inspired by him because in a difficult time he seemed to be inspired. In ordinary times his true nature reemerged, neither evil nor stupid nor weak nor mean. To call him common is too harsh. He was banal. There was no greatness in him."[7]

Francis was survived by two sons. Tragically, the eldest, Ferdinand, who succeeded to the throne, was weak in mind and body. From his childhood on, it was common knowledge that Ferdinand would be incapable of ruling the empire. Nonetheless, the principle of legitimacy, so important both in Austria's foreign and domestic policies, demanded his succession. In addition, change in the order of succession, or the establishment of a regency, would have required the consent of the Hungarian Diet. That would have given the Diet too important a role for the tastes of the policymakers in Vienna. There was fear, too, that the creation of a regency would have aroused dangerous rivalries and factions within the imperial family, with the archdukes, Emperor Francis's brothers, long excluded from active political life, contesting for power.[8]

A few days after Ferdinand's succession, Baron Kübeck von Kubau, a high official, who had just had his first audience with his new sovereign, reported that Ferdinand did not understand a word of the matter presented to him and unhesitatingly signed anything put before him. "We now have an absolute monarchy," wrote Kübeck in his diary, "without a monarch." Yet to the wonderment of foreign observers, Ferdinand's subjects accepted his rule for thirteen years. When the duchess of Orléans asked the French ambassador to Vienna why the Austrians were so obedient, the only answer he could think of was that "apparently the Austrians love obedience for its own sake." There was, of course, more to it than that. In 1847 an Englishwoman who had just attended a mass and *Te Deum* sung in honor of Ferdinand's birthday found "something touching, generous, self-forgetting" in the people's devotion to their ruler. "The trifle that the Emperor is a helpless idiot," she wrote, "makes no difference. Not that the people don't know it. But what then? He is *unser armer Herr* (our poor sovereign)."[9]

Those who knew him best reported that his intelligence fluctuated, but that even on his best days it did not equal that of a normal person. A small man, he had a disproportionately large head, a pasty complexion, and the pendulous "Habsburg lip." He had trouble holding his head erect, and most of the time his chin rested on his chest. His lusterless eyes roved so that he never looked at the person with whom he talked. He spoke rapidly and sometimes unintelligibly. On top of everything else, he suffered from epileptic seizures.[10]

His infirmities aside, he was a gentle and good man. He endeared himself to his future subjects when, in 1832, an attempt was made on his life. Slightly wounded himself, he held his would-be assassin in his arms to protect him from the crowd, who threatened to lynch him. Then he successfully implored Emperor Francis, who wanted to execute the man, to imprison him instead and to provide a pension to support the man's family. He loved music and flowers and enjoyed visiting factories and mines. He showed no interest in marriage until his late thirties. A pleasant story recounts that the duchess of Modena, visiting Vienna in 1830, so charmed Ferdinand that he gallantly told her that he would marry if he could find a woman like her. The quick-witted duchess replied that she had a twin sister who resembled her in appearance and personality. Actually, the sister was ten years younger. Before he could have second thoughts, negotiations began and soon Ferdinand found himself wed to Maria Anna of Savoy. It turned out to be a successful albeit childless marriage. Maria Anna, a deeply religious woman who once thought of becoming a nun, had limited knowledge and even less understanding of the world. Tall and stately, she made a fine appearance. She seemed genuinely fond of her husband and made every effort to cover his deficiencies. She wanted children badly, not to produce an heir to the throne but to know the joys of motherhood. With characteristic gentleness and lack of guile, she told the wife of the French ambassador that she would regret having a son because that would give pain to her ambitious sister-in-law, Sophie, whose son Francis was in the direct line of succession. "But," she continued, "if God answered my prayers with a daughter I would be very happy."[11]

Two days before he died, Emperor Francis had signed two letters to Ferdinand. One letter, drafted by the Court chaplain, instructed Ferdinand to free the Catholic Church from the remaining restraints imposed upon it by Emperor Joseph II a half century earlier. The other letter, that reproduced almost verbatim a draft composed by Prince Metternich, told Ferdinand to change nothing, to seek the counsel of Archduke Louis, Francis's youngest brother, in all important internal affairs, and to make no decisions in public affairs or concerning individuals without first consulting Prince Metternich, "my truest friend and servant." Francis's letter did not mention Count Franz Anton Kolowrat, long the emperor's principal counselor in domestic affairs, and Metternich's detested rival for power. Metternich, of course, had seen to the omission of Kolowrat's name when he drafted the letter. But he had over-reached himself. Kolowrat had too many allies at court. More important, Metternich had too many enemies, especially among Francis's brothers, the archdukes. Metternich had lorded over them during Francis's reign and now they had their revenge by supporting Kolowrat. In short order Kolowrat had joined Metternich and Archduke Louis in the so-called State Conference that ran the government for the emperor.

The State Conference soon proved itself remarkably ineffective because of the ineptitude of Archduke Louis, who presided, and, above all, because of the incompatibility of Metternich and Kolowrat. Louis dreaded responsibility. He once told an acquaintance that he had long been accustomed to obeying and preferred nothing more than to have someone over him. His favorite axiom was "the best way to solve a problem is to let it alone." Baron Kübeck, admittedly a partisan of Metternich but a man of great discernment, called Kolowrat weak in intellect and character, capricious, and a puppet in the hands of others. Metternich unburdened himself in a letter to Count Clam-Martinic. After protesting that no one appreciated Kolowrat's merits more than he, he proceeded to tear into his rival. Among other charges he said that Kolowrat "acts only by impetus from outside. He is one of those men who imagines that he is directing others when they are really directing themselves. . . . He was born to be an instrument and not an innovator." Kolowrat, not to be outdone, declared his great respect for Metternich's intellect and character. But one day in December 1839 he said to Baron Kübeck, "The Prince always takes a tone of instruction toward me, tells me that five *plus* three are only eight, but five *times* three makes fifteen, that between those little words, plus and times, there is a great difference, a fact that one should reflect upon in government. . . . And there is the intolerable vanity of the man, who in all his life has never been wrong, foresaw and still foresees everything that has happened and that has not yet happened. In short, I can't get along with the man."[12]

Each man tried ceaselessly to undermine the other's influence even though both realized that their rivalry paralyzed the government. In 1838 Kolowrat told Kübeck that the State Conference was a failure. "Prince Metternich suffers no one beside him and I am too proud to tolerate anyone over me. Only one man can rule—it won't work without a Richelieu." In 1850 Metternich, driven out of office by revolution in 1848, wrote that neither the European nor the Austrian public realized "the indeed scarcely conceivable fact that our empire had no government after the death of Emperor Francis." The State Conference rarely met after 1838, instead communicating with one another by memoranda and reports. Meanwhile the machinery of government clanked on in its traditional rut, impelled by its own momentum until the outbreak of revolution in March 1848 brought it to a standstill.[13]

By the 1840s Metternich's greatest days lay in the past. After the collapse of the Napoleonic empire in 1814, he had devoted his efforts to rearguard actions to preserve peace and the status quo. His defense of legitimacy, monarchy, and aristocracy against constitutionalism, liberalism, and nationalism made him the best known of Europe's leaders—so well known that historians have sometimes called the years from 1815 to 1848 the Age of Metternich. Born in the Rhineland in 1773 into an old family of counts of the Holy Roman Empire, Metternich early won attention for his outstanding qualities of mind and person. Engaging in manner, equally skilled as a master of the social graces and as a womanizer, as a young man he was the beau ideal of eighteenth-century aristocracy. In 1801 he entered the service of Emperor Francis and by 1809 he became Austria's minister of foreign affairs, the office he held for the next thirty-eight years. In 1813 his grateful sovereign made him a prince and in 1821 named him Imperial Chancellor. Far more important than these honors, the emperor accorded him a degree of trust and confidence that he gave no other person.

Metternich well merited that trust. Whatever successes Austria's foreign policy enjoyed and whatever international prestige and authority the empire had were due in large part to Metternich. An enormously skilled negotiator with an extraordinary sensitivity to nuance, he excelled at manipulating people and events. He dominated every diplomatic parley in which he participated. He always knew what he wanted to accomplish, and he never lost sight of his goal. He was a prodigious worker, spending long hours at his desk, writing thousands of letters and memoranda and keeping abreast of events and currents everywhere in Europe.

The favor and regard shown him by the emperor made Metternich the most important man in the empire, next only to the emperor himself. Wherever he went, he immediately became the center of attention and of unending flattery. The archdukes, the brothers of the emperor, feared him because of his influence with the emperor. Archduke John, possessing the most independent mind of Francis's brothers, called Metternich a "deified Prince" and prided himself that unlike other members of the imperial family, he did not crawl before him. But John was a special case. The emperor and Metternich had deliberately excluded John, who had married the daughter of a Styrian peasant, from the affairs of state. John, the most intelligent of the archdukes, deeply resented his exclusion, confiding to his diary his discontent and unhappiness.[14]

In his younger years Metternich had been a handsome man, with an aquiline nose, curly blond hair, pale blue eyes, and a fresh complexion. As the years passed, his good looks faded, and by 1840 a visitor found that nothing remained of the elegance of his youth. Now he was a dumpy old man with a graceless bearing. He had always talked a lot, and as he grew older he became ever more long-winded. He became increasingly hard of hearing, too, which made it all the more difficult to have a satisfactory conversation with him. As one visitor put it, he harangued rather than conversed. By far his most unattractive trait was his enormous, even grotesque, ego. Throughout his career he never tired of telling whoever would listen of his wisdom, his foresight, and his skillful leadership. Supremely self-confident, he had no doubts about the rightness of his opinions and his actions. In exile in 1848, he told the French statesman Guizot that error was foreign to his spirit. Doubtless other eminent men of past and present had and have the same overfull measure of self-confidence, but surely few have been so vocal about it as Metternich. Perhaps that explains the quiet glee of lesser mortals when they learned that four days before the outbreak of revolution in Vienna in March 1848, Metternich told Lord Hardinge, who was passing through Vienna en route home from India, that because of his policies, Austria stood unthreatened while other thrones tottered. One of the first persons Hardinge ran into when he reached London was Metternich who, forced out of Vienna, had fled to the British capital.[15]

Despite the conviction of his superiority to the rest of mankind, Metternich lacked the relentless drive and will to power that marks the great leader. He avoided direct confrontation whenever he could. He believed that he had time on his side and that until the right moment came, he had to make concessions. He told the visiting American George Ticknor that there was nothing more important for a man than to be moderate in his expectation and not wish to do anything that he could not accomplish. What Metternich called moderation others called weakness and irresolution. Tsar Alexander I of Russia had noticed that the moment Metternich saw the slightest difficulty, he hesitated, stopped, and looked for ways to escape. Guizot said that Metternich lacked the courage of impulse and enterprise, had no taste for a fight, and feared the risks more than he longed for success.

A serious illness in 1839 and other spells of ill health in succeeding years took their toll of Metternich. People who met him were shaken by the decline in his physical and mental powers. A young secretary of the Saxon legation in Vienna was shocked when he met Metternich in late February 1848. He found him a deaf and shriveled old man of seventy-five, preserved as in a cocoon, using old-fashioned language and "with a head no longer strong enough to brave the storm upon us."[16]

Though the fires burned lower, Metternich never abandoned the mission he had set for himself from the very outset of his career: to preserve the peace of Europe and, not incidentally, to preserve the Habsburg empire from collapse. He once told the Duke of Wellington that he thought of Europe as his fatherland, but he operated on the principle that what was good for Austria was good for Europe. He devoted his efforts to the creation of an international network that would involve other like-minded powers in the fate of Austria. A Frenchman put it succinctly in an open letter to Metternich in 1846: "You are the first politician," he wrote, "whose whole ambition has been to remove stones from the paths of others for fear they might throw you off balance if they fell." Friends and foes alike called the network the Metternichean system, though he objected. Calling it by that name, he said, suggested that it reflected only his views. To his way of thinking, the network was not a diplomatic system but rather a statement of the principles of conservatism.[17]

Metternich's method of preserving peace and order everywhere in Europe was by suppressing all threats to the status quo. To justify the continued sovereignty of hereditary monarchs, he advanced the concept of "legitimacy." Efforts to reduce the authority of these monarchs, who were the only lawful rulers of their lands, or to supplant them, would lead to anarchy. To thwart such efforts, the powers had to cooperate with one another, to employ censorship and espionage, and to intervene in other states when revolution threatened a "legitimate" ruler. Freedom of speech and press and freedom of association and assembly could not be tolerated. States unwilling to employ force to suppress dissent would not survive. As an Austrian statesman of that day described it, Metternich's system amounted to "the undiminished maintenance of the rights of sovereignty and the denial of every claim of the people for participation in those rights."[18]

Metternich's system was not merely an instrument created for purposes of policy. It reflected his deepest convictions. An aristocrat to his innermost being, he was appalled by the teachings and excesses of the French Revolution. He thought democratic revolution was a sickness that poisoned society, while monarchy alone united men and made them capable of the highest degree of culture and civilization. Representative government only tied the hands of those in power without unifying the hands of the people. He scorned the revolutionary watchwords *liberty* and *equality* as empty abstractions. "Liberty of what?" he asked. "Liberty to do good?—but all the world enjoys that right—or to do evil?" As for equality, men were equal before God and the law, but certainly not in their social, economic, and intellectual capacities. He condemned nationalism as a screen behind which revolution hid in its most brutal form.[19]

Metternich knew full well that nationalism and liberalism attracted an always increasing number of adherents. Time and again he spoke of living during an age of transition. Yet he deliberately chose to defy the tide of history because of his dark vision of the future. He believed that the French Revolution showed that violence and anarchy were the companions of great social and political change. His forebodings convinced him that he must do what he could to lessen the dangers that lay ahead. In 1819 he wrote, "Fate has laid in part upon me the duty of restraining, as far as my powers will allow, a generation whose destiny seems to be that of losing itself upon the slope that will surely lead to its ruin." In 1847 in a letter to a friend, he wrote, "The world is indeed sick. With each day the moral gangrene becomes more obvious. If you do not see me give way before the disease you will find the cause in a temperament which does not know how to bend in the face of difficulties. . . . " Many years earlier he had said that old Europe was nearing its end and that chaos would reign before the new Europe would emerge. He wished that he had been born earlier or later: if earlier he would have enjoyed the aristocratic world of the eighteenth century, if later he could have helped to rebuild society. "I wish I had been born in 1900," he said, "and have the twentieth century before me."[20]

Despite his dedication to the status quo, Metternich insisted that he did not oppose change, only its too hasty introduction. Actually, for Metternich the time for innovation never seemed to come. Like reactionaries of past and present, he was convinced that men of ill will secretly plotted revolution. The plotters, said Metternich, worked without respite to undermine the foundations of the political and social order and to prepare the ground everywhere for a universal *bouleversement*. When, in 1846, civil war broke out in Switzerland, Metternich sensed that this signaled a new era of revolution. With tears flowing down his cheeks, he told his wife, Princess Melanie, that an age of violence had begun, that his own role was finished, that he would rather die than see the evils that no one would be able to prevent.[21]

Princess Melanie, who was thirty-two years younger than her husband, had become Metternich's third wife in 1831 when he was fifty-eight. The couple had five children between 1832 and 1837 (only two survived). Melanie immersed herself in the life of her husband and soon became his closest confidante. A beautiful woman, with raven-black hair and striking eyes, she was the daughter of a socially and politically important Hungarian noble family. Melanie's combination of poise, self-confidence, and arrogance equaled that of her husband, but she sorely lacked his tact. A man who knew her called her "the undiplomatic wife of the allegedly chief diplomat of the world." She had a hot temper and a sharp and intemperate tongue. She made no effort to conceal her opinions of others, mocked people to their faces, and referred to them in uncomplimentary terms in a loud voice to insure that they would hear her. She was a ridiculous snob who never allowed anyone to forget her high social rank and her power. On the other side of the ledger, she was a devoted and admiring wife. She did what she could to ease the burdens of his office and consoled him in his time of defeat and exile.[22]

Posterity has given Metternich mixed reviews. Some writers have reviled him. One even called him "an evil genius" who knew that his policies would lead to disaster but followed them to satisfy Emperor Francis and thereby retain his own high rank. Others have grudgingly given him high marks for his diplomatic skills but condemned him as the archfoe of liberty. The most influential study, by Heinrich von Srbik, himself an Austrian of strong conservative bent, denied that Metternich was a self-serving courtier or a blind reactionary. He saw Metternich as a conservative European statesman who sought to preserve Austria as a rock of order in a sea of revolution. Others praise him for his effectiveness in preserving peace in Europe between 1815 and 1848, but fault him for his failure to make concessions to the new forces that demanded to be heard. They attribute this shortcoming in part to his lack of imagination and creativity, but mainly to his abhorrence of the kind of society that would have emerged. Henry Kissinger, in a penetrating study that appeared two decades before he himself became an international statesman, said that if Metternich never came to terms with the new age, it was not because he failed to understand it but because he disdained it.[23]

Metternich had faithfully reflected the obscurantist policies that Emperor Francis had established to prevent new ideas from disturbing the peace and order of his realm. Metternich followed these policies not only because it was his task, but also because he agreed totally with them. He paid special attention to the detection of threats, real and imagined, to public order. He worked hand in glove with Count Joseph Sedlinitsky, who became Police Minister in 1817 and who continued in that post until revolution in 1848 swept him out of office along with Metternich. Sedlinitsky proved himself a master of espionage, counterintelligence, and underground police activity. He built an organization that became famed among the practitioners of these black arts in other lands. He enlisted men and women of all classes and occupations, from brothels and low taverns to the highest reaches of society, who reported whatever they heard that seemed critical of the regime. He had files on everyone of importance, including Metternich himself, and on many lesser people who had somehow come to his attention. William Stiles, an American diplomat in Vienna in the later 1840s, felt that every other person whom he met was in the pay of the police. The public, he said, aware of the omnipresence of informers, realized that no one could be trusted. Stiles suggested that the creation of this climate of fear, and not the collection of information, may have been the primary purpose of the elaborate system created by Sedlinitsky.

Sedlinitsky's agency gained special renown for its skill in opening mail. A large staff intercepted the letters of selected individuals, including members of the imperial family, and even the wife of the emperor, high officials, and foreign diplomats accredited to Vienna.[24] Sedlinitsky presided, too, over a censorship rivaled only by that of Russia. Criticisms of the social and political order, of leading personages, and even the mention, much less the discussion, of nationalism, constitutionalism, and similar matters, fell immediately under the censor's ban. The censors forbade the performance of Shakespeare's plays that dealt with the dethronement or assassination of kings for fear they might give their audiences dangerous ideas. They banned *King Lear*, too, because they deemed it unfitting and unsettling to show how misfortune could cause a ruler to lose his sanity. Authors of the stature of Gibbon, Hume, Goethe, Schiller, Herder, and others were totally or partly suppressed and their creativity stifled by restrictions. Not surprisingly, the censorship kept an especially tight rein on newspapers.[25]

Despite its precautions and its elaborate organization, the censorship proved inadequate in its efforts to suppress the written word. Contraband literature entered Austria easily, either by smuggling or by bribing customs officials. Austrians published books abroad, anonymously or under assumed names, when the subject matter was prohibited. These works became readily available in Austria and reached a wide audience. A book published in Hamburg in 1843, entitled *Oesterreich und dessen Zukunft (Austria and Its Future)*, became the best known and the most influential of these works. It was written by Baron Viktor von Andrian-Werburg, by birth and wealth a member of the high circles of the nobility and holder of an important post in the government. The censors employed unusually severe measures to prevent the distribution of the book, but that only increased its popularity, and new printings quickly appeared. The book passed from hand to hand, even in the imperial court. Encouraged by the book's success, its author published a second part in 1847.

A number of liberal young men, unable to tolerate the oppression of intellectual and political life, fled to Germany. There, free of the Austrian censorship, they wrote political and literary articles for publication that were smuggled into Austria. Ignaz Kuranda, a thirty-year-old Jewish liberal from Prague, started the publication in 1841 of what became the best known and the most influential of the émigré publications. He called it *Die Grenzboten (The*

Border Messenger). Appearing weekly, it published outspoken dispatches from anonymous correspondents in all parts of the empire and somehow procured and printed full texts of important official documents. Those in opposition to the regime seized upon it as a source of information that fueled their discontents. Others read it closely and even in the presence of high officials and in the most public places spoke openly about the journal, if only to criticize it.[26]

Education did not escape the attentions of the government. An imperial commission supervised the entire educational system from the primary grades to the universities. The commission prescribed the course of study to ensure that students would not be exposed to knowledge or ideas considered dangerous. The secondary schools (the gymnasiums) prepared their students principally to become bureaucrats or to enter seminaries to study for the priesthood. The faculties taught by rote and made no effort to stimulate independent thinking or original work among their students.

The universities, too, had as their principal mission the training of young men for government service. Study abroad was banned lest the student become infected with revolutionary ideas. To their credit the universities, like the secondary and primary schools, charged no tuition. That gave the sons of the petty bourgeoisie and the peasantry the opportunity for an education that, despite its restrictive nature, allowed the development of a liberal and even revolutionary awareness.[27]

The repressive policies of the state had their inevitable result. In an era of change and movement, Austria stood still. Andrian-Werburg, in his book, called the empire "the classic land of routine, of custom that is followed today because it was followed yesterday." Even a man of strong conservative convictions, Count J. A. von Hübner, an important statesman close to Metternich, mourned the lack of movement. He called the 1840s a sad time. In a book on the coming of the revolution in 1848, he wrote, "No word spoke to the hearts, to the noble instincts, or to the higher feelings of the nation. Nothing but silence and stagnation." Actually, the fact that Andrian-Werburg and Kuranda and others wrote as they did gives evidence that Austria was not without men with independent and creative minds who wanted their country to join the modern world. They labored under painful restraints, confronted always by censorship and police surveillance. They had to resort to subterfuges, such as publication abroad, or to voluntary exile. Nonetheless they had their say and they were heard.

The undercurrent of intellectual life seemed well concealed from Paul Annenkov, a liberal Russian nobleman who visited Vienna in the winter of 1840–1841. Annenkov, who knew at first hand the lively life of the mind in Saint Petersburg and Moscow, called Vienna "a magnificently appointed wasteland" where one never encountered a single word or thought or piece of news or an opinion that did not come from the government.[28]

Vienna may have seemed an intellectual wasteland to Annenkov, who was a very serious young man, but the city enraptured most other visitors, who quickly succumbed to the spell of a city where everything seemed designed to please the senses and lift the spirits. Even the plan of the city had a special charm. Massive walls, fifty to seventy feet high and three miles around, built in the sixteenth century to defend the city against the invading Turks, surrounded the old city. The cannons were long since gone, and a promenade with trees and benches and coffee houses sat atop the walls. The Hofburg, the imperial palace, no less than 122 palaces of the nobility, government offices, museums, the best hotels, the houses of wealthy bourgeoisie, and fine shops all crowded the streets of the old city. The shops and inns had brightly painted signs, some of them worthy of hanging in a museum, in the opinion of the then Prussian captain and later field marshall Helmut von Moltke.[29]

A deep moat encircled the walls, planted with trees and crossed by bridges from each of the wall's twelve gates. Beyond the moat lay a broad open space, the glacis, fifty-five to a hundred yards wide, originally intended to compel an attacking enemy to advance without cover. Now it had a parade ground and paths and gardens and lawns that beckoned to the visitor. Then came a great circle of suburbs where most of the Viennese lived, with streets unpaved, muddy and dirty in wet weather, and dusty in dry. Factories and workshops were here, and military barracks, and also the summer palaces of the elite. Interspersed among the suburbs were gardens, theaters, inns, and dance halls. The public gardens, the walks with their charming bowers and graceful fountains, and the restaurants attracted happy throngs. And everywhere there was music, played by all manner of bands. Above all others were the orchestras led by Johann Strauss and his son Johann, and their chief—and some said their only—rival, Josef Lanner.

The Viennese themselves seemed a special breed. Baron von Hübner described the vast majority of them as good-natured and phlegmatic, adjusting easily to governmental repression. To a disapproving Czech the Viennese seemed interested only in having a good time. "It's always Sunday with them," he wrote in 1842, "always Carnival time, music everywhere, the countless inns full day and night with boozers." The English travel writer William Howitt, a dedicated conservative who approved of the repressive policies of the imperial regime, believed that the government deliberately promoted the pursuit of pleasure to divert the Viennese from thinking about political matters.[30]

The parks, the promenades, the bands, the inns, and all the other delights of Vienna were meant for the enjoyment of ordinary folk. Nobles, even members of the imperial family, sometimes ventured into the pleasure domes of the plebeians, perhaps to see how ordinary people entertained themselves. But the nobility lived in a world of its own. Indeed, to their peers in other lands, Austria seemed the Eldorado of the nobility, a society seemingly untouched by change, where ceremony and precedence were punctiliously observed, and where homage to high birth and rank was expected and given. In no other land did the nobles seem so proud and so tenacious of their position and their relative status vis-à-vis one another. Sometimes the pride reached ludicrous proportions. In the Viennese salons of the highest nobility, a sofa was reserved for princesses. If no princess attended, the sofa remained empty, or if only one princess came, she sat alone. Pride reached what was surely a hitherto unscaled pinnacle with the Esterhazys, the greatest of the Hungarian nobility. Painted on the wall of one of their castles was their version of the family tree, and what a tree it was. Adam lay gracefully reclining at the tree's base, and as it passed upward it contained every great name, biblical and heathen, from Moses to Attila the Hun. Beginning with Attila, each successive generation of the Esterhazys had their portraits painted with their wives and children.[31]

Not surprisingly, great wealth accompanied the highest social rank. In this overwhelmingly agricultural economy, wealth was measured in land and in the number of peasants who lived on the land. The ten wealthiest Bohemian families together had over one million peasants on their properties. The combined holdings of the five greatest Hungarian magnates covered over twelve thousand square miles.[32]

A handful of families of great wealth and old lineage stood at the peak of noble society. Called *la crème,* they scorned the rest of the nobility as inferior beings and barely recognized commoners as humans. Indeed, Prince Alfred Windisch-Grätz is supposed to have said, "Mankind begins with the barons." A closed coterie, related by generations of intermarriages, they associated almost exclusively with one another. They lived so extravagantly that despite their great wealth they often were deeply in debt. They spent great sums in building and remodeling their palaces, gambled for high stakes, and entertained with a lavish hand. In an earlier generation great nobles had patronized the arts. The compositions of Mozart, Haydn, and Beethoven often had their first performances in the palaces of the elite; Haydn had for twenty-nine years served as the musical director of the Esterhazys. By the 1840s the intellectual and artistic interests of *la crème* had all but disappeared. Great music was rarely heard in their palaces, and artists and intellectuals were seldom invited to their salons.[33]

Like the nobility of other European lands, *la crème* admired and imitated the English elite. They formed exclusive men's clubs, organized Jockey Clubs to race thoroughbreds and "improve the breed," and copied English fashions. Prince Trauttmansdorff introduced the English stovepipe hat with its narrow brim, which quickly became the favored headgear of the elite. An amused English visitor noticed that at the racetrack fashionable men tilted their tall hats to the back of their heads in proper English fashion. Trauttmansdorff also introduced fly-fishing from England, with its skillfully made lures. Hans Kudlich, once a peasant of Prince Liechtenstein, recalled that the prince, instead of supporting worthy causes such as art and scholarship, spent his money imitating what was called "English high life," which included wasting large sums on slow horses and fast women.

Lesser nobles owned proportionately less land and wealth, and so downward on a scale that ended with nobles who were landless or nearly landless. In Hungary the overwhelming majority of the nobility lived on the edge of economic ruin. Called the "sandal nobility" because its members could not afford boots, these people were said to own only "a house and four plum trees." The entirely landless among them often entered military service as hussars, the light cavalrymen famed as much—or more—for their dashing uniforms as for their military prowess. Other nobles in Hungary and other lands of the empire earned their livings in more mundane and often humble pursuits.[34]

All nobles, great and small, titled and untitled, enjoyed the same privileges guaranteed them by law. By far the most important of these privileges concerned taxation and the ownership of land. In Hungary nobles paid no taxes, tolls, tariffs, or tithes. In the rest of the empire, noblemen enjoyed preferential tax status. In Hungary only nobles could own land. In the rest of the empire, the law allowed commoners to own land, but in effect it remained a monopoly of the nobility. With ownership of the land went extensive political, economic, and judicial powers over the peasants who lived on the land and worked it.

The nobility, like the imperial family, the bureaucracy, the army, and the Church, all depended for most of their incomes upon the least in their society, the peasants. The peasant was "the stepchild of the age, the broad, patient back who bore the weight of the entire social pyramid ... the clumsy lout who was derided and mocked by court, noble and city. ... "[35] Nearly all of the peasants were the "hereditary subjects," as the law called them, of their landlords, to whom they paid dues in labor, kind, and cash. They made up three quarters of the 37.5 million people in the empire. Their payments to their lords, their taxes, and their tithes accounted for by far the largest share of the revenues of the landowners, the state, and the church.

The labor services demanded by the landowners were the most onerous of the obligations. Usually called *robot,* from the Slavic word for work, it varied with the size of the peasant's holding and with the custom of the crownland. All told, in the German-Slav crownlands alone the peasants performed over 68 million days of *robot* each year for their lords. In addition they had to make all manner of payments in kind to the landowner. Some were trifling, such as four hens and forty eggs each year; others were burdensome, above all the obligation to give the lord a set percentage, sometimes as much as one tenth, of the crops produced on the peasant's own holding. Peasants also paid a sizable fee to their lord when their holdings changed hands through inheritance or other kinds of transfer. In addition to their obligations to their lords, the peasants paid taxes to the state and tithes to the church. The state also required them to build and maintain roads and bridges in their neighborhoods, and house soldiers quartered on them. Finally, conscripted peasant youths filled the ranks of the army. Until 1845 they served for ten to fourteen years, depending upon the branch of the service. In 1845 the term became ten years for Hungarian conscripts and eight for those from the rest of the empire.[36]

Reforms ordered by Empress Maria Theresa and especially by her son Joseph II had set limits on the powers of the lord over his peasants and on the obligation he could demand. Concern for abstract principle had not motivated Maria Theresa or her son in their introduction of these reforms. They recognized the peasant as the paramount source of taxes and recruits. They feared that excessive exploitation by their lords would so impoverish the peasants that they could not pay more taxes, and would so weaken them physically that their numbers would decline and thereby reduce the flow of recruits into the army.

Opposition by the nobles and their near revolt, and then the outbreak of the French Revolution in 1789, brought the reform movement to its end. For the next sixty years, the peasant lived under a regime that resisted all change. Nonetheless, the peasants had far more rights and freedom than their forebears, though they still bore the yokes of their earlier serfdom. An outspoken criticism and even a defiant glance, and the lord could order confinement in the village jail. Within the village the peasants divided themselves into strata determined by the size of each household. They knew one another from the cradle, played and prayed and tilled their fields together. But the daughter of a prosperous peasant did not marry the son of a poor or landless peasant. The villagers censured such a marriage as a mésalliance. In the small mountainous lands of Tyrol and Vorarlberg, all of the peasants were free. They had won their release from the bonds of serfdom in the fifteenth and sixteenth centuries. A small number of free peasants were scattered through the rest of the empire. Most had gained freedom through individual acts of emancipation, usually in return for a cash payment by the peasant to his lord.[37]

Until the 1840s the middle class played an inconspicuous role in Austrian life. Concentrated in a few cities and towns, its numbers were relatively small. Most of its members earned their livings in small trade and handicrafts. Large-scale commerce and industry had barely gotten under way. A consciousness of sharing common middle-class interests had not yet appeared. The middle class accepted without caveat the established order in state, church, and social structure. The few dissident intellectuals and journalists, almost without exception from the middle class, had their number and influence limited by censorship and police surveillance.

The development of a bourgeois culture, with Vienna as its center in the 1840s, provided evidence of the growth of class consciousness. No matter what their ethnic origin, people of the middle class, especially of its upper and middle strata, became Germanized, adopting the language, values, tastes, and styles that radiated out from Vienna. The wealthiest of the bourgeoisie were the great Viennese bankers who did most of their lending to the government and to great nobles. The bankers dealt on equal terms with those who borrowed from them, but they were excluded from the social life of their clients. Apparently, this segregation did not trouble them since they lived on a grand scale and in a social world of their own. Their salons, presided over by their intelligent wives, attracted intellectuals and artists and important officials of the government who had risen from the ranks to their high posts. The interest in intellectual matters and the arts did not limit itself to the *haute bourgeoisie* but became an integral part of the life of prosperous middle-class families.[38]

Agriculture, which dominated the economy, and traditional modes of production of manufactured wares accounted for most of the empire's labor, capital, and goods. Capital for business expansion was hard to come by, and borrowers had to pay high rates of interest. Geographical barriers made communications difficult and heightened costs of transport. Import prohibitions and high tariffs insulated Austria from the economic and technological advances made in western Europe. A tariff barrier that separated Hungary from the rest of the empire, and the persistence of inefficient agriculture and poverty out on the land, restricted the size of the market.

Despite these obstacles, innovations in transportation and industry, introduced by men of the middle class, had taken root by the 1840s. The extension of the empire's road network and the introduction of railroads and river- and ocean-going steamships provided the stimulus for economic expansion. As with other lands in the first stages of industrialization, the greatest advances came in the manufacture of textiles, especially of cottons. Other branches of production lagged behind. It was very much a time of beginnings when new techniques and new organization of production took firm root, began to grow, and initiated the creation of an urban, industrial working class that included women and children.[39]

Men of the middle class, well aware of their increasing importance in the economic life of the empire, gained a new self-confidence. A growing number wanted liberal reforms that would end the absolutism and give them a voice, and even the controlling voice, in the running of the empire. They longed for judicial reforms with equality for everyone before the law, the end of special privilege, freedom of the press, and religious and academic freedom. The Catholic Church, and in particular the Jesuit and Redemptorist orders, became targets of liberal attacks as symbols of repression and as bastions of all that liberals found abhorrent in the regime. They resented the selfishness, snobbery, and irresponsibility of the nobility and the preference given them in appointments and promotions in the bureaucracy and the army. They realized, however, that the support of the nobility would greatly increase the chances for reform and so welcomed liberally inclined noblemen to their cause.

Leading members of the bourgeoisie formed clubs and organizations in Vienna and elsewhere in the 1840s to study and discuss matters of concern to them and to propose specific reforms. The discussions of political and economic matters at their meetings, and the liberal publications in their libraries, worried the censors and the police. The Legal-Political Reading Society that began to meet in Vienna in 1842 was a particular thorn in the side of the authorities. By 1847 it had 211 members and a number of associate members who could use the Society's library and participate in its activities. Count Sedlinitsky considered the Society a cradle of revolution, and it had frequent brushes with the law. Only the importance and influence of some of its members kept the police from shutting it down.

On December 23, 1844, the Society held a banquet to honor Friedrich List. As the first open political meeting in Austria, it created a sensation. The most important men of the business and professional world, high officials, and writers crowded the room. Count Colloredo-Mannsfeld, as president of the *Gewerbeverein*, the Trade Association, greeted the guests; Eduard Bauernfeld read a poem that ended with the lines, "If only ideas were tariff free, then we could talk of many things." With great applause, many raised their glasses, and List ended the toast with the words "Long live German union." A Viennese newspaper, in its report of the meeting, included List's toast. Prior to publication the censors passed the report up to Metternich, who changed "union" to "concord." Even so, many readers considered its publication a concession to the new times.[40]

Most of the nobility disdained men engaged in business. Prince Windisch-Grätz reflected that attitude when with an almost audible sniff he remarked, "No Windisch-Grätz engages in trade." Actually, nobles (including the haughty Windisch-Grätz) and other members of *la crème*, were not all that contemptuous of business and the making of profit. Time and envy of the wealth of successful bourgeois men of business had eroded the old prejudices, at least among some of the nobility. These men, most of them great landowners, awakened to the opportunity to profit from the improvements in transportation that enlarged old markets and created new ones for the products of their fields and forests. They built factories for the processing of agricultural products, especially beets to make sugar and potatoes to make whiskey. The beets and potatoes grew in their fields, the bricks to build the factories were made in their kilns, and the fuel for the factories came from their forests. Their peasants provided them with unpaid labor services that counted as part of their annual labor obligation, and furnished obligatory and unpaid transport services to carry the nobles' products to market—using the peasants' own carts and animals. To increase the productivity of their properties, the landowners introduced improved agricultural techniques, reclaimed land, and improved the bloodlines of their herds and flocks by selective breeding.

The most striking phenomenon of this new interest of nobles in profit-making was that the nobles, ostensibly the beneficiaries of the system that held the peasantry in hereditary subjection to them, pressed the government to end that system. A half-century earlier, the nobility had bitterly opposed the reforms in the lord-peasant relationship introduced by Joseph II. Now, in the 1840s, they wanted to abolish that system because they found it to be the chief obstacle to the most profitable exploitation of their estates. The *robot*, the unpaid labor services of their peasants, was their principal target. They pointed out that *robot* workers doing compulsory labor had no reason to work efficiently. Knowing that they could not be discharged, they scamped their work and used inferior draft animals. To document the inefficiency of *robot*

labor, nobles compared the work done in the same time span by hired laborers and unpaid *robot* workers. They found that hired labor did two to three
times as much.

Other motives also persuaded nobles to become advocates of agrarian
reform. The hobgoblin of peasant revolt and the desire to win the support of
the peasants for political or nationalistic programs played a part. The government for its part was not enamored of the system of hereditary subjection and
realized that benefits would accrue to the state from a more efficient agriculture. In addition, the agitations and unrest that the government dreaded
would inevitably accompany any major reform in the lord-peasant relationship. So it turned a deaf ear to the demands and petitions of the politically
powerless nobility of the German-Slav crownlands. In Hungary, where the
nobility had an effective voice in the government, the throne had to agree to
some change, although complete abolition of the system of hereditary subjection had to wait, as in the rest of the empire, until the revolutions of 1848.[41]

The growing disenchantment with the status quo among leading elements
of the bourgeoisie, and among some of the nobility, was a new phenomenon
that emerged in the 1840s. Until that decade only a bold few had dared publicly to criticize existing social and political arrangements. The failure of the
regime to introduce reforms after the death of Emperor Francis in 1835, and
the gradual perception by the educated public of the internal conflicts and
ineptitude of the State Conferences, persuaded increasing numbers to question and to criticize. "The Austrian has become serious," wrote the journalist
Franz Schuselka in 1843. "His belief in the infallibility of the regime has
ended: now he thinks, counts, compares." When Freiherr Franz von Andlaw,
Baden's ambassador to Austria, returned to Vienna in 1846 after earlier service there from 1832 to 1835, he was struck by the change. Under the surface
of traditional Viennese gaiety and unconcern he detected a deep-seated dis-
cordance that reached from the lowest to the highest circles. The censorship
seemed to lose some of its effectiveness, or perhaps to check the flood of criticism was beyond its powers. Political poems that attacked the regime
appeared. Theaters presented thinly veiled satires of the political system, and
liberal passages inserted in plays met with applause from sympathetic audiences. In 1847 a young doctor from Baden in Vienna for postgraduate study
was startled when medical men there spoke openly and sarcastically about the
inadequacies of the government.[42]

Early in the 1840s the demand for change surfaced in what seemed an
unlikely source—the provincial assemblies of German and Slav crownlands.
These groups, called estates, had little more than a shadow existence, rubber-
stamping whatever the government presented to them. After long decades of

acceptance of their emasculated role, nobles in six of these estates became restive. A new generation of leaders had taken over. The estates asked for the right to debate the proposals submitted to them by the central government and to suggest new legislation. When the government refused these moderate requests, the so-called "estates movement" took on the character of a loyal opposition. The assemblies, and especially the estates in Lower Austria, where Vienna was, and in Bohemia, proclaimed their dissatisfaction by the adoption of proposals for reform and by a general attitude of recalcitrance. The government rejected all of their proposals, so that the estates movement had no effect upon state policy. But this newly expressed defiance showed that men of the highest stratum in the empire no longer supported the paternalism and bureaucratic absolutism of the regime.[43]

The new phenomenon of nationalism provided another and, as time would prove, the most threatening element in the unprecedented wave of opposition that appeared in the 1840s. The peaceful coexistence of the many nationalities of the empire began to break down. The yearning for national self-expression, till now a dream among a few intellectuals, left the ivory tower and worked its way into the consciousness of an ever larger number of bourgeois liberals and of nobles who opposed the power of the German-directed central government.

In Hungary a movement inspired in large part by one of the country's greatest landowners, Count Stephen Széchenyi, aroused a birth of national pride among the nobility. Széchenyi himself identified the interests of the nation with those of his fellow magnates, whom he considered the only people able to carry out the reforms that he proposed. The new nationalism, however, aggravated the growing discontent, after 1840, among the lesser nobility who resented the domination of the magnates. In other lands middle-class liberals were the usual standard-bearers of nationalism. In Hungary, where the bourgeoisie were small in number and powerless, conservative nobles became the leaders of nationalism to preserve their traditional preeminence in their society. Unrest in Hungary grew so that already, in November 1841, a British observer wrote that "Austria has a running sore in the shape of Hungary."

To establish their national identity, the Hungarian nationalists revived their national language. Latin had been the official language of the government, of the laws, and of the debates in the Diet and the county assemblies, and German the language of general use. Only the lower strata of society spoke Magyar. In their enthusiasm the nationalists persuaded the Diet to pass a decree in 1843 that made Magyar the sole language of legislation and of debate in the Kingdom of Hungary.

In Bohemia the memories of when it had been an independent kingdom and a center of learning were all but forgotten. Most of the nobility were of foreign origin, implanted there by the victorious Habsburgs after the Battle of White Mountain in 1620, when Bohemia lost its independence. The nobility had little interest in Czech culture. The urban middle class had been Germanized, while the Czech language lived on as the language of the peasantry and the urban underclass. In the face of these formidable obstacles and despite the repressions of the government, a handful of middle-class intellectuals undertook studies and histories of the Czech language and literature. In other parts of the empire, too, scholars, writers, and political leaders devoted themselves to awakening their people to a consciousness of their nationality and to instilling a pride in their accomplishments, in their history—often much of it speculative and even imagined—and in their language and literature.[44]

Though they expressed their unhappiness with the status quo, the dissidents, with a few rare exceptions, did not advocate the overthrow of the dynasty and the dismemberment of the empire. They carped and complained, but they remained loyal to the throne. The writers who fled abroad for freedom to publish attacks on the government were patriots who passionately supported the honor and the integrity of the empire. Deeply concerned for the fate of Austria, they brooded over the repression and the inefficiency of the government and they berated the men who ruled the state and the bureaucrats who carried out their policies. They wanted reforms that would restore the empire to its past greatness.

A different story emerged in Galicia, which had been Austria's share of the booty in successive partitions of independent Poland by Russia, Prussia, and Austria. The Polish nobles of Galicia, like their fellows in Russian and Prussian Poland, never abandoned the dream of a reunited Polish state. As in Hungary, and for many of the same reasons, Polish noblemen became the leaders of Polish nationalism. Their propaganda met with considerable success among the Galician nobility. Only the peasants, who were Ruthenians, and who formed the great mass of Galicia's population, remained unaffected despite shining promises of land and freedom held out by the nationalists. The peasants had no reason to support a restoration of the Polish state. They hated their Polish lords, who had been their oppressors for centuries and who had always held them in contempt. Their only protection against their lords had come after Austria had annexed Galicia in 1772 and had introduced the eighteenth-century reforms that set limits to the powers of the seigniors.

The leaders of the independence movement realized that the peasantry was not with them. That did not deter them. In collusion with their fellows in

Russian and Prussian Poland, they planned for revolt to break out simultaneously on February 21, 1846, in all of what had once been independent Poland. On that date the rebels would assemble their peasants, give them freedom and land, and in return demand that they join in the uprising.

The secret of the planned revolt leaked out. The Russian and Prussian governments rounded up its leaders and aborted the rising. Arrests in Austria by the authorities almost prevented it there. Their hand forced, the Galician rebels moved up the date of the rising to February 18. Meanwhile, all manner of wild rumors spread among the peasantry. Not knowing whom or what to believe, but having always in their hearts a burning hatred of their Polish masters, the peasants decided to prepare themselves for any eventuality. Armed with sickles and scythes, with axes and pitchforks and flails, they took up posts at the crossroads and waited to see what was going to happen. Soon mounted noble insurgents began to appear on their way to their designated rallying points. The peasants would not let them pass; the nobles tried to fight their way through and fell before the numerically superior peasants. By daybreak of February 19, the revolt had been put down.

In the flush of their victory, the exultant peasants seized the opportunity to settle old scores. Organizing themselves into bands, they went from manor to manor, plundering, burning, and murdering. They despoiled over four hundred manors and slaughtered between 1,100 and 1,200 seigniors and their stewards. The Austrian government encouraged this violence by calling on the peasants to apprehend the rebels and by offering a reward for every captured insurgent. The jacquerie continued until the first days of March, when Austrian troops moved in and ordered the rampaging peasants to return to their villages. The peasants obeyed, convinced that their loyalty to the throne had won them release from their bonds. The rebels had promised them freedom and land, and they believed that the emperor for whom they had fought could do no less. Instead, army units marched from village to village to compel the peasants to resume their servile obligations. The rulers of Austria preened themselves on the loyalty of the peasants to the House of Habsburg. They realized, however, that they had to act quickly to hold that loyalty. The moment called for bold measures. Instead, with typical indecision and fear of change, the government issued decrees in April and December of 1846 that scarcely did more than repeat already existing legislation.

The failure of the government to institute meaningful reform stirred up waves of rural discontent not only in Galicia but in other parts of the empire, too. The peasants had long resented their subjection to the noble landowners. Yet despite their restiveness they had rarely resorted to open resistance, and these outbreaks had always been local in scale. Nonetheless, they made noble landowners aware of the always present threat of a peasant rebellion, made real by the example of Galicia. They feared not only the violence of a jacquerie but also the danger that the peasants would throw off their yoke without any indemnification to their erstwhile masters. Now their fears were realized. Peasants in many parts of the empire stopped rendering their obligations, whether in labor, cash, or kind, and made no offer of indemnification to the landowners. The government proved unable to compel the peasants to resume their obligations, nor did it come forward with plans for indemnification of the lords. Moreover, the failure of the government to protect the seigniors of Galicia from the vengeance of their peasants made nobles everywhere fear that they could not depend upon the regime to defend their lives, much less their privileges and their properties. So they became ever more eager for reforms that would appease the peasantry and at the same time provide them with indemnification for the land and privileges and services that they realized they would have to surrender.[45]

With the Galician revolt and its aftermath, the eleventh hour had struck for Austria. Till then the government had somehow managed to drift along, carried as it were by its own momentum. Now its bankruptcy became clear for all to see. To introduce changes that would have satisfied the discontented would have been relatively easy. These people were not incendiaries who wanted heads to roll, nor were they zealots who thought they knew how to create an earthly paradise. They were reasonable men who recognized the urgent need for reforms to save the empire and who were and remained loyal subjects of the throne. Austria's fate was that no one in the ruling elite had the strength, imagination, and vision to take over leadership and carry out reforms, and so avert the revolution that came in March 1848. In an autobiographical sketch that he wrote in retirement in the 1850s, Metternich acknowledged the responsibility of the government for the catastrophe of 1848. The seeds of revolution, he wrote, are always and everywhere present. They ripen only when the ruling power fails to carry out its obligations. "Revolts," he wrote, "rise up from below. Revolutions come from above."[46]

Despite Metternich's admission, all of the blame did not belong to the rulers of the empire. Happenings beyond their control made a bad situation much worse. Beginning in the mid-forties, a series of bad harvests, outbreaks of animal plagues, and the devastation of the potato crop—by a blight that spread throughout Europe—exacerbated the privation and misery of the peasantry. Simultaneously, a Europe-wide downturn in economic activity, aggravated by the rising prices for foodstuffs and raw materials, resulted in distress and widespread unemployment. The progress of factory industry had already displaced many craftsmen and the journeymen who worked for them.

Now the economic depression brought them, and the small shopkeepers who depended upon their custom, to the edge of ruin. Food riots broke out: food stores and warehouses were plundered, and long lines formed at emergency soup kitchens set up by private initiative. The crisis was deepened by the disarray of the government's finances. For years income had fallen behind expenditures. The government's indebtedness rose from 398 million gulden in 1815 to 748 million in 1848.[47]

Nobles, bourgeoisie, intellectuals, nationalists, peasants, artisans, proletarians, each for their own reasons, were disillusioned with their do-nothing government. Austria was ripe for revolution when word reached Vienna, on February 29, of the revolution in Paris five days earlier. That news had an electrifying effect. The ease with which the French revolutionaries had dethroned Louis Philippe made all things seem possible and exhilarated the opponents of the regime and frightened and confounded the ruling elite. Metternich had long expected revolution yet was as confused and unprepared as everyone else. "Everyone tells me that something must be done," he said to a friend a day after word came of the revolution in Paris. "Entirely true, but what? Our monarchy is an ancient house. One cannot except at great risk break through walls, open new doors and windows, and undertake greater internal changes. Yet something has to be done."[48] Nothing was done, and revolution engulfed the empire. Actually, there were a number of revolutions, each with its own goal. There was no central direction, no unity of purpose. There was a liberal revolution in Vienna and then a proletarian one; an agrarian revolution out in the countryside; and national revolutions in Hungary, Bohemia, Croatia, Galicia, and Lombardy-Venetia.

The news from Paris had set off an uproar in Vienna. Petitions to the government poured in, demanding liberal reforms and the dismissal of Metternich, the arch symbol in the popular mind of all that was wrong with the regime. On March 13 violence erupted in the streets and suburbs of Vienna. Troops were called out and, meeting resistance, fired into the unarmed mob, killing some and wounding many others. By late afternoon the soldiers had restored order. It was too late. Revolution had started and spread like wildfire throughout the empire.

The rising of the thirteenth forced the authorities to realize that they had to make immediate concessions: their first was to dismiss Metternich. At a hastily convened meeting, Metternich was told that his continuance in office would cause increased disorder. In defense, Metternich spoke for an hour and a half, until Archduke John pulled out his watch and told the chancellor that thus far he had really said nothing. At that Count Kolowrat, Metternich's old foe, could not resist saying, "It has always been his habit to talk without coming to the point." Metternich realized he had no choice, and after bitter words about the ingratitude of princes, he resigned. It became clear that Metternich was not safe in Vienna, and on the night of March 14, the seventy-five-year-old prince stole away from Vienna and headed for exile in England. Continued and often violent unrest in the streets persuaded the government to make further concessions on March 15, including the end of censorship, freedom of the press, and a convention to draw up a constitution as soon as possible.

News of the March Days in Vienna loosed a tidal wave of revolution that spread across the land. Nationalists and liberals everywhere held innumerable meetings to voice their grievances and to demand concessions. Their demands, programs, and manifestos, however, meant nothing to those who made up by far the largest part of the population of the empire—the peasants. They had only one demand: freedom from their servile status and from their dues and services. The revolutionaries and the government alike realized that victory would attend the side that won the support of the peasantry. The revolutionaries made freedom for the peasant part of their agenda. The government decreed the abolition of servile obligations but ordered that the peasant must indemnify his seignior for the obligations. Nor did the government order the end of the hereditary subjection of the peasantry. So the peasants almost everywhere threw in with the revolutionaries and remained with them until full freedom was theirs.

In Lombardy-Venetia, under Habsburg rule only since 1815, revolution broke out when word came of the insurrection in Vienna. For a time fortune favored the rebels, but the Austrian forces, led by the remarkably vigorous eighty-three-year-old Marshal Radetsky, won back Lombardy by August. The Venetians, who had proclaimed a republic, held out until May 1849 when, besieged by Radetsky's army, ravaged by cholera, and facing starvation, they finally surrendered. In Prague, too, the news from Vienna stirred up great excitement, and law and order began to break down. On April 8 an imperial rescript acceded to liberal demands for reform, but unrest continued, primed by radical students. Finally, on June 12 barricades went up in the streets. The rising lasted six days before troops, led by Prince Alfred Windisch-Grätz, crushed it. About 1,200 to 1,500 rebels had manned the barricades, 600 to 800 of them students and 300 to 400 workers. Under fifty were killed, and sixty or so were wounded.

The collapse of the rebellion forced the closing of a Slav Congress that had convened only days earlier. At the invitation of Czech leaders, 340 delegates had come to Prague to discuss the role of Slavs in the Austrian empire and the relations of Slavs everywhere with the other peoples of Europe. The

Congress issued only one statement, a Manifesto to the Nations of Europe. The pious hopes expressed in the Manifesto went unfulfilled, but the meeting itself took on historic significance. For the first time Slavs had joined together to express their awareness of their common ethnicity and to awaken the non-Slavic world to their existence and their importance.[49]

Meanwhile, in Vienna agitation by radical democrats, most of them students who had formed their own organization, the Academic Legion, led in mid-May to serious disturbances. The frightened government, on May 15, made new concessions, including consent for a unicameral national assembly, elected by universal male suffrage, to draw up a constitution. Two days later the emperor and his family fled for safety to Innsbruck. Unemployment, a poorly run public works program, and heightened radical agitation brought on riots of workers and increasing discontent. In early October violence burst forth again. This time it was a revolution of the proletariat of Vienna. The emperor, who had returned with his court to Vienna in August, once again fled, this time to Olmütz, a small town in Moravia. Once there he signed an order, drafted by Field Marshall Windisch-Grätz, ordering the army to march on Vienna. After a brief siege and bombardment, the city fell on October 30 at the cost of an estimated two thousand lives, most of them workers, and Vienna was placed under martial law.

During these troubled months, delegates had been elected to the national assembly convened in Vienna on July 11. Of its 383 members, 190 were Slavs and the rest Romanians, Italians, and German Austrians. Ninety-two of the delegates were peasants. Hungary, in revolt against the Habsburgs, sent no representatives. Many of the delegates neither spoke nor understood German, the official language of the assembly. Only after some time had passed were interpreters provided. On July 26 the youngest delegate, Hans Kudlich, university graduate and son of a Silesian peasant, moved that the assembly declare the immediate end of hereditary subjection. His motion carried unanimously. A month-long debate followed on whether the seigniors would receive indemnification for the land and for peasant dues and services they would relinquish. The assembly opted for indemnification of some of the obligations. On September 7, 1848, the emperor signed the bill and peasant emancipation became the law of the land.

The decree of September 7 proved to be the only lasting achievement of the revolution. It also sealed the fate of the revolution in the German and Slav lands of the empire. The peasants, having gained their freedom, lost all sympathy with the revolution and withdrew from it. Constitutions, democratic principles, popular sovereignty meant nothing to them. They resumed their innate conservatism, interested only in the protection of their gains from the demands for land from the rural proletariat—the cotters and the landless laborers. With their withdrawal the revolution in the German and Slav crownlands soon collapsed.[50]

With that collapse the time had come for the consummation of a long-held plan—the abdication of Emperor Ferdinand. The empress, who knew what a strain his duties placed on her husband, had for years wanted him to abdicate. In November 1847 she and Prince Metternich agreed that Ferdinand would renounce the throne, not in favor of his next eldest brother Francis Carl, but of Francis Carl's eldest son, Francis, when that young man reached the age of eighteen, in August 1848. That would make a regency unnecessary. Neither the empress nor Metternich nor anyone else felt that Francis Carl had the capacity to rule. A complete dullard, he possessed not a shred of personality, charm, or leadership. Revolution delayed the carrying out of the plan until the court fled to the security of Olmütz. Then it was agreed that Francis would succeed to the throne on December 2.

The plan proceeded in deepest secrecy known only to those directly involved. Ferdinand had wanted to remain on the throne, and it took much pressure and persuasion by his wife before he agreed to the plan. Then, at the very last moment, he suddenly became stubborn and had to be cajoled and then pushed into the room. Once inside, he renounced his throne in favor of his nephew, who now added Joseph to his name in honor of the reformer Emperor Joseph II. An eyewitness reported that everyone in the room wept, with one exception. The empress beamed. The next day Ferdinand and his devoted wife left to live in the imperial palace in Prague. There Ferdinand remained for the rest of his life, free at least of his cares, spending his time on his hobbies, enjoying the flowers that he loved, and listening to music.[51]

For all practical purposes, the revolution in the western half of the empire had ended in October. It raged on in Hungary for another ten months. The Hungarian Diet had been in session when word came of the February Revolution in Paris. The news tripped off great excitement. On March 3 Louis Kossuth, renowned as a journalist and orator, made a fiery speech in the Diet demanding wide-reaching reforms, including a constitution for Hungary. On March 15 the Diet adopted Kossuth's proposals. Among other provisions, the legislation freed the peasants with land, ordered equality before the law, and made Magyar the official language of the nation.

The reforms said nothing about the demands of the Slovaks, Serbians, Croats, Slovenes, and Romanians who lived in Hungary. This lack of recognition of their political existence, repressive actions against some of their representatives, and the official status accorded the Magyar tongue intensified nationalistic unrest among these peoples. The government in Vienna decided to take advantage of these dissensions. In Croatia the crown appointed Colonel Joseph Jellachich, a fanatical Croat nationalist, to the office of *ban*, or governor, of Croatia, promoted him to field marshall, and gave him command of the Croatian regiments. Jellachich declared Croatia independent of Hungary and prepared for war. In early September Jellachich invaded Hungary and after initial successes met Hungarian forces who in short order drove back his troops to within sight of Vienna.

After the accession of Francis Joseph, and the subsiding of revolution in the German and Slav lands, the government concentrated its forces against the Hungarian rebels. The beleaguered Hungarian Diet named Kossuth chairman of a committee of national defense. Then on April 14, 1849, the Diet, after listening to Kossuth's dramatic reading of a declaration of independence, proclaimed Hungary a republic and elected Kossuth "Responsible Governor-President" with dictatorial powers.

For a time fortune favored the Hungarians. Then Tsar Nicholas, enemy of all revolutions, offered to send aid in the suppression of the Hungarian rising. In mid-June, a Russian army marched into Hungary, while the Austrian General Haynau led an invasion from the west. Hungary's fate was sealed. On August 12 Kossuth fled to Turkey, and the next day Hungary surrendered.

Now at last all of the lands of the House of Habsburg again paid homage to their sovereign, the king-emperor in Vienna. The revolutions, save that of the peasants, had failed. In retrospect they were doomed to failure from their outset. Nationalist rivalries made a concerted revolutionary movement impossible. The bourgeois liberals who had taken the lead in the early days of revolution soon realized they had unleashed a radical-led proletariat that threatened them and their property. As the months wore on, the liberals, frightened by the demands and the antibourgeois propaganda of the radicals and the vandalism and violence of the workers, abandoned the revolution and welcomed the victories of the troops of the government. The peasants of the German and Slav crownlands withdrew from the revolution after the decree of September 7 freed them from their servitude. Finally, with the single exception of Louis Kossuth, no leader emerged who could move men by his words and by his vision of what the future might hold.

One might assume that the government, persuaded by the revolution of the need for reforms, would have followed conciliatory policies once it had reestablished its sovereignty. Instead, it embarked upon a program of repression, deception, and centralized despotism. The program began with the accession of Francis Joseph on December 2, 1848. The slim and energetic young emperor had a dignified manner, patience, and a sense of duty that belied his years. He impressed foreign rulers and statesmen who met him for the first time with his detailed knowledge and by the "rectitude," as one of them put it, of his ideas. Prince Feliz zu Schwarzenberg, the new chief minister, listing the young man's virtues in a letter to the exiled Metternich, wrote that courage was his outstanding quality. "Physically and morally he is fearless," Schwarzenberg wrote, "and I believe that the main reason why he can face the truth, however bitter, is that it does not frighten him."[52]

When he ascended the throne, Francis Joseph, aware of Schwarzenberg's experience, leaned heavily on his counsels and, indeed, became his pupil. The older man, a sophisticated, elegant, and highly intelligent man of the world, captivated the eighteen-year-old monarch. Schwarzenberg's life reads as if he stepped out of the pages of a romantic novel by Anthony Hope. Born in 1800, scion of one of Europe's oldest and wealthiest families, he began his career as a cavalry officer. He was the very image of an aristocrat, with a lean, sculptured face, a slim and erect carriage, an inborn elegance and an imperious manner. And always there were affairs with women of the great world. On April 5, 1852, he died suddenly of cardiac thrombosis while dressing for an assignation at a ball with the wife of a fellow officer.

Schwarzenberg's arrogance and supreme self-confidence were reflected in his contempt for nearly all of his fellow mortals. He sneered at highborn and lowborn alike. When Prince Windisch-Grätz suggested a House of Lords in an Austrian parliament, Schwarzenberg replied that there were not twelve men of their class in the entire empire who were fit to sit in an upper house. He believed that men could be ruled only by force and deception. He summed up his technique of governing when he once remarked, "You can do anything with bayonets except sit on them." In his reliance upon force and repression, and his disregard and even disdain for moral considerations, he was the prototype of the kind of statesmen, the *Realpolitiker,* who dominated European political life in the second half of the nineteenth century.[53]

Schwarzenberg wanted to transform Austria into a modern, centralized, unitary state ruled autocratically by the House of Habsburg. The proclamation that he prepared announcing the accession to the throne of Francis Joseph contained the promise that the new emperor would reign as a constitutional monarch. Schwarzenberg—and his willing pupil, the new emperor—had no intention of fulfilling that pledge, which he made only to win popular support for the throne at a time when Hungarian rebels were driving back government troops.

During the October rising in Vienna, the national assembly, called the *Reichstag,* which had convened in July 1848 to draw up a constitution, had moved to Kremsier, a small town in Moravia. There, out of the public eye, the deputies fell to work seriously on drafting a constitution. To Schwarzenberg the Reichstag was an assemblage of second-raters who lacked knowledge, understanding, political courage, and who had been elected by an "immature population." He had decided that a constitution drafted by representatives of the people was unacceptable. Instead, he and his ministers had drafted a constitution of their own that would come as a gift of the emperor to his people. The members of the Reichstag, unaware of this, had, on March 1, unanimously approved the final version of a constitution that provided for a genuine parliamentary government with ministerial responsibility and equal rights for all national groups. On March 4, three days after the Reichstag had approved its constitution, the emperor ordered the dissolution of the Reichstag. Orders went out to arrest certain of its members, and others fled, unable to return to Austria until years later. Then on that same March 4, the emperor promulgated the constitution drafted by Schwarzenberg and company.[54]

To the considerable surprise of conservative and liberal foreign observers alike, the new constitution was in many respects no less liberal than the Reichstag's constitution. The explanation of this seeming graciousness on the part of the emperor was a simple one. The constitution was a deliberate fraud perpetrated by Francis Joseph and Schwarzenberg. They had no intention of ever putting it into effect. They thought that they still needed to buy time to make sure that the last flicker of revolution had died out. By the end of 1851, this absolutism felt secure enough to throw off its mask. On December 31, the feast day of Saint Sylvester, the emperor issued the so-called Sylvester Patent. That patent formally abolished the constitution of March 4 and laid down the principles and guidelines of a new absolutism. Among its many provisions, it abolished the bill of rights that had been part of the Reichstag and March 4 constitutions, ended trial by jury, revived press censorship, and provided for the intervention of the central government in local government down to the smallest administrative unit, the rural commune. All branches of the government became directly responsible to the emperor. He closely supervised both civil and military affairs, presided over cabinet meetings, and on Schwarzenberg's death in 1854 assumed the office of prime minister.[55]

The revolutions had failed. The crown had emerged stronger than it had ever been. Yet the revolutions had not been in vain. On the one hand, they awakened and gave great impetus to nationalist movements everywhere in the empire. On the other hand, they forced the government to realize that it had to create a modern unitary state with uniform laws, equal rights for all of its subjects, and the end of the rights and privileges enjoyed by individual crownlands. The government chose to accomplish this by way of absolutism—or neoabsolutism, as historians have named it. The years of neoabsolutism lasted until 1859. Continued fiscal difficulties, swelling nationalist unrest, and defeat in war with France and Piedmont in 1859, and with Prussia in 1866, made it evident that drastic measures had to be taken. In desperation the emperor agreed to the Compromise of 1867. That famed agreement transformed the unitary empire into a Dual Monarchy of two equal states, Austria and Hungary, with one ruler. All the other nationalities became subservient to the Germans in the Austrian monarchy and to the Magyars in the Hungarian monarchy. Each monarchy had its own parliament, with ministers responsible to the parliament, and with its own civil service. Each parliament chose delegations who met with each other to discuss matters of common interest, and joint ministers handled foreign affairs, finances, and defense.

Dualism managed to hold the empire together for another fifty years, but throughout that half century the danger of collapse was never distant. The unsatisfied ambitions of the subject nationalities and their hostility to domination by Germans and Magyars gravely weakened the authority of the government. By the end of the century, nationalist passions had become so heated and so raucous that it became impossible for the legislature to carry on its business. Constitutional government had broken down, and the emperor and his ministers used their emergency powers to rule by decree, and made concessions to particular groups to gain support for particular measures.

Perhaps in time the new phenomenon of nationalism would have torn apart the empire. But history would not wait. The trauma of defeat in a war of hitherto unimaginable proportions, precipitated by nationalist unrest and terrorism, brought about the end, in 1918, of the centuries-old realm of the Habsburgs.

CHAPTER EIGHT

Germany on the
Threshold of Greatness

In one respect Germany seemed a mirror image of Austria. The Austrian empire contained an agglomeration of nationalities, languages, and cultures, all ruled by the same sovereign. The people of Germany shared the same nationality, the same language (albeit with many dialects), and the same culture, but were divided into thirty-nine independent polities, each with its own sovereign, its own soldiers, laws, and taxes. This arrangement represented a dramatic reduction in the number of independent states. Until the beginning of the nineteenth century, Germany had been divided into 314 sovereign entities, plus 1,475 imperial knights who held their small properties directly from the Holy Roman Emperor in Vienna. Napoleon, after conquering most of Germany, announced the dissolution of the Holy Roman Empire in 1806, and by amalgamation and redistribution reduced the number of states to thirty-seven (later increased to thirty-nine). The multitude of displaced sovereigns were "mediatized," which meant allowing them and their descendants to keep their titles and estates, and to become the principal nobles of the state into which their erstwhile princedom had been merged.

The size of the individual states ranged from Prussia, with over 71,000 square miles and around 11 million people, to tiny principalities of scarcely more than a hundred square miles and fewer than 50,000 inhabitants. The vagaries of marriage and inheritance had often splintered these lands into pieces divided from one another by a slice of territory that belonged to another sovereign. Thuringia, in central Germany, was the classic land of petty princedoms—of *Kleinstaaterei,* as the Germans called it. It once had twenty-eight sovereigns who ruled over a total of scarcely half a million people. Napoleon had reduced the number to nine states, but none of them had a consolidated territory. It was hardly possible to take a long walk in one of these princedoms without crossing a frontier, often marked only by a shield hanging from a tree. There were constant disputes among sovereigns over scraps of land; pieces passed back and forth between states; and towns were split between sovereigns.

Time seemed to stand still in these petty states. They resembled some fictional Graustark rather than parts of the real world. Their world was one of ceremonies, of narrowness, princely whims, courtiers with long and sonorous titles, and obedient townsmen and docile peasants.[1]

Anachronisms, eccentricities, and oddities abounded among these princes. Their behavior was not subject to the checks imposed by convention and law on the conduct of ordinary mortals. They loved to play at soldiering, with splendid uniforms and many generals for their minuscule armies. Some rulers majored, as it were, in profligacy. Three successive generations of the rulers of Electoral Hesse had spawned a profusion of illegitimate children, whom their fathers endowed from state revenues. Religious zeal inspired others. Prince Maximilian of Saxony had vowed to make a pilgrimage to Jerusalem, but family obligations made it impossible for him to go. Tormented by his failure to keep his vow, he turned to his confessor for advice. That sage cleric told him he could fulfill his vow and have the additional merit of going by foot, which few had done since the Crusades, and yet never leave Dresden. Simply measure the length of the long gallery in his castle, explained the priest, calculate the proportion that it bore to the distance to Jerusalem, and walk back and forth in the gallery the requisite number of times. The delighted Maximilian determined that meant pacing the gallery three hours daily for four years. He followed this routine faithfully for two years, after which a troubling problem occurred to him. There were mountains between Dresden and Jerusalem. Would God accept walking on a flat surface as the equivalent of the real thing? Again the trusted confessor provided the solution. Place chairs in the gallery, pray that God would accept them as mountains, and climb over them. A French diplomat who knew Maximilian intimately told a friend that he had often seen him on his "pilgrimage" climbing over the chairs.[2]

Some princes distinguished themselves by their dedication. King William of Württemberg, who ruled from 1816 to 1864, worked constantly for the welfare of his people. He lived frugally within his income, opposed mindless luxury, and neither gambled nor drank nor hunted. This paragon was not without a flaw. He engaged constantly in sexual liaisons, continuing them up to his death at eighty-three.[3]

Unusual and sometimes outrageous behavior was common currency among these princelings, but a few managed to exceed even these elastic limits. Among them was the king of Hannover. From 1714, when Hannover's king became King George I of Great Britain, until 1837, the two countries had the same sovereign, with Hannover very much the junior partner. The accession of Victoria to the British throne ended the connection because a woman could not inherit the throne of Hannover. That crown went to Victoria's uncle, Ernest Augustus, Duke of Cumberland, oldest surviving son of George III. The people of Hannover rejoiced at their independence from Britain and looked forward to having their own ruler who would bring to Hannover the blessings of freedom that had made Britain so great.

Rarely have popular hopes been so rudely shattered. Of all of George III's children, Ernest Augustus was by universal agreement the most vicious and the most detested of that unsavory brood. His own siblings spoke of him with horror. He was treacherous, profligate, cruel, and took delight in humiliating those around him. An English radical newspaper claimed that suicide was the only crime that he had not committed. In his obituary in 1851, the *Times* of London wrote that "little or no good could be said of him" and that "rumour persisted in attaching to his excesses a certain criminal blackness below the standard dye of aristocratic debauchery."[4]

His fierce face, deeply scarred and with only one piercing eye and a huge moustache, fitted his character. The scar and the eyeless socket were mementos of his service in war against the French. Not surprisingly, he was enormously unpopular in Britain, and when he left for Hannover, many expressed their heartfelt wish that he would never again set foot on British soil. He did make occasional visits, and as one wit observed, "goes about in an unwonted state of popularity—that is, generally unhissed." In 1815 he married a twice-widowed princess of Mecklenburg-Schwerin, who was said to have murdered her two previous husbands, both of them German princes. These two, who obviously deserved one another, were deeply in love and had a successful marriage, though marred by the blindness from early youth of their son and heir to the throne. With characteristic cruelty, Ernest Augustus could not forgive his son's handicap. Reputedly the young man suffered more from the raillery of his father than he did from his sightlessness.

Soon after his accession in 1837, Ernest Augustus abrogated the relatively liberal constitution granted in 1833 by his brother William IV, his predecessor as ruler of Hannover. He ordered all state officials, or "royal servants" as he called them, to renounce their oath to support the constitution and take a new oath of service to him. A few refused. Among them were seven professors at the University of Göttingen. The king dismissed them in what became a famous chapter in the history of academic freedom. In 1840, when he felt that he had firmly established his power, he granted a new constitution that, among its repressive features, imposed a rigid censorship, ended equality before the law, placed new restrictions upon Jews, and gave the king virtually absolute power.[5]

Louis I of Bavaria, king of Germany's second largest state, was another who stood out in the princely gallery of bizarre types. He distinguished himself on at least two counts. He led all other rulers in his devotion to the arts. He transformed Munich, his capital, from a sleepy provincial town into a major cultural center, with impressive buildings, museums, art galleries, and public gardens. He also distinguished himself as a man of many amours and, above all, by his last and greatest love. His devoutly Catholic subjects had tolerated his romances as conduct expected of a king. In late 1846, however, their tolerance began to wear thin when a twenty-six-year-old "Spanish" dancer who called herself Doña Maria de Delores de los Montes, known to history as Lola Montez, arrived in Munich to perform at the court's theater. Born the illegitimate daughter of a Scottish captain named Gilbert and a Creole mother, she had gone through an extraordinary succession of lovers from one end of Europe to the other. She was a dancer without noticeable talent, but she was outrageously beautiful, with glorious dark blue eyes, raven black hair, an olive complexion, and a marvelous and graceful figure which she displayed in tight-fitting black velvet gowns. As icing on this perfection she was an intelligent, witty, and spirited woman with great personal charm. She also possessed a fiery temper and no principles.

On arriving in Munich, Lola had a quarrel with the manager of the royal theater and went to the palace to complain. She created a scene when she was refused entrance, whereupon Louis, who heard the commotion, ordered her admitted so that he could reprimand her. That turned out to be the beginning of his end. Louis fell head over heels in love. In short order, he gave her a munificent pension, built her a palace, made her Countess Landsfeld, and wrote love poems to her. A bishop felt that the scandal required that he give Louis spiritual counsel, whereupon the king swore that his love for Lola was purely platonic. When the Prussian minister of foreign affairs learned of this, he said, "That makes his folly all the greater." Actually, Louis seems to have been telling the truth. The likelihood was that the sixty-one-year-old monarch was compelled to make a virtue of necessity. Lola proudly wrote "Maitresse de la Roi" beneath her signature, but with Louis's permission a young Lieutenant Nussbaumer served as her lover.

Louis might have survived his infatuation had not Lola decided to interfere in politics. Students at the University of Munich demonstrated against
Lola's domination of the king, and Louis ordered the university closed until
the following winter. Some foreign observers were amused by the goings-on.
The *Times* of London wrote that "our report states that Bavaria has been in
no such ferment since the ominous convulsion which succeeded a rise in the
price of beer." In early 1848 public outrage led to disturbances in the Army.
Louis had to yield, and on February 14 he banished his beloved from
Bavaria. In early March news of the February revolution in Paris reached
Munich, crowds filled the streets, and Louis, at heart a convinced absolutist
who had ridden roughshod over Bavaria's constitution, had to grant liberal
concessions. That, combined with the exile of Lola, proved too much for
Louis to take. In blind rage and disgust, he abdicated on March 20, turning
over his throne to his son Maximilian. After leaving Munich, Lola continued
her adventures and travel. She finally came to rest in New York where, after a
few years, she suffered a stroke and died. She was buried in Greenwood
Cemetery in Brooklyn under a simple marker that read, "Mrs. Elizabeth
Gilbert, died January 17, 1861, aged 41 years."[6]

Of all the *opéra bouffe* settings offered by the petty states of Germany,
none was more farcical than the principality of Reuss. That tiny state of 591
square miles with, in 1838, 101,800 people, was divided into four princedoms, each with its own ruler, all of them princes of the House of Reuss.
The Reuss family had ruled there since the twelfth century, and most of the
land was its private property. All of the men of the family bore the name of
Henry, supposedly in memory of their reputed ancestor, the tenth-century
Holy Roman Emperor Henry, called the Fowler because of his fondness for
falconry. At first the Henrys had been distinguished from one another by
such appellations as the Tall, the Short, the Fat, the Brave, the Pious, and
the like. As the centuries rolled by, the family, a remarkably fecund one, had
produced a host of Henrys. By the end of the seventeenth century, persuaded by the surfeit of Henrys, and doubtless by the exhaustion of suitable
adjectival appellations, a family council decided that starting with the new
century, the Henrys would have numbers to distinguish them. The elder line
decided to start with Henry the First, go up to Henry the Hundredth, then
start all over again. The younger line, who ruled over three of the four
princedoms, chose to call the first male born in each century Henry the
First, continue with successive numbers up to the century's end, and then in
each new century start afresh with Henry the First. The Henry who succeeded to the throne in each division retained his number in the birth order of
Henrys. That was why Prince Henry the Fourteenth of Reuss-Schleiz, the

younger line, was the son and successor of Henry the Sixty-Seventh, born in 1789.[7]

As could be expected, there was much intermarriage among the ruling families of these minuscule princedoms. Usually the progeny of these unions lived on in the same historical anonymity that shadowed their progenitors. There was one remarkable exception to that generalization. On June 13, 1777, Princess Augustine Caroline Sophia, daughter of Henry the Twenty-Fourth of Reuss-Lobenstein-Ebersdorff, married Franz Ferdinand Anton, duke of Saxe-Coburg-Saalsfeld. Their three daughters and four sons made excellent marriages, so far as rank and title were concerned, and thereby began a practice in the Coburg family of marrying upward. As a consequence, during the next two hundred years, direct descendants of that obscure marriage of 1777 sat on the thrones of Great Britain, Germany, Bulgaria, Belgium, Yugoslavia, Spain, Greece, Russia, Sweden, Portugal, and Norway.[8]

In 1815, after the fall of Napoleon, the German states had joined together with Austria into a loose and largely powerless league called the Germanic Confederation, or *Bund*. The act that created the Confederation had been largely dictated by Metternich at the Congress of Vienna. Metternich wanted to keep Germany disunited and so ensure Austrian domination of Central Europe. The founding act provided for a diet that met in Frankfurt, with delegates from each of the member states, and with Austria's representative as the permanent chairman. The act also called for each of the member states to grant a constitution that would establish civil and political equality for all of its citizens.

These and other good intentions, inspired by the principles loosed in Europe by the French Revolution, faded away in the wave of reaction that lasted until the 1840s. The rulers of Austria and Prussia, the two most important states of the *Bund*, refused to grant constitutions. The sovereigns of most other states provided constitutions as the gift of the ruler rather than the work of constitutional conventions. Not surprisingly, these documents left most of the governing power in the hands of the ruler.[9] Princely absolutism reestablished itself with its extravagance, its pomp, and its willfulness in both public and private behavior. The era of revolution with its message of freedom and equality seemed to have vanished almost without a trace. The great mass of the German people passively accepted the reaction, indifferent to such issues as natural rights and popular sovereignty that had once stirred them.

Not everyone, however, acquiesced in the reaction. The earliest organized opposition centered in the universities where, in 1815, students began to form fraternities called *Burschenschaften*. These organizations, inspired by a dawning nationalism, had as their aim the creation of a united Germany. They opposed absolute monarchy, rejected all foreign cultural influences, denounced the hierarchical social structure, and opposed capitalism and industrialization. Their program, their public demonstrations, indeed, their very existence, troubled the leaders of the reaction. Then on March 23, 1819, Karl Sand, a student of theology and a fanatical *Burschenschaft* member, assassinated August von Kotzebue, reactionary writer and formerly in the pay of the Russian tsar. The crime, along with an attempt upon the life of the ruler of the duchy of Nassau, sent shock waves throughout Germany. Metternich saw his opportunity to strike a punishing blow to nascent nationalism. In July he called a conference at Carlsbad of the ministers of several German states who happened to be vacationing at this famous Bohemian spa. At his urging, they drew up resolutions that were ratified in September by the Diet of the Confederation. Called the Carlsbad Decrees, the legislation bound the rulers of all the member states to impose a uniform strict censorship, to monitor schools and universities, and to discharge teachers deemed subversive. The Diet decided to set up a central bureau at Mainz to ferret out secret societies and other organizations and conspiracies directed against the status quo. The Diet ordered the dissolution of the student associations, which somehow managed to survive despite these and later attempts at their suppression.

The Carlsbad Decrees and other reactionary legislations introduced an era of severe repression in which scores of students, academics, professional men, and journalists were sentenced to long prison terms for their proscribed activities. The excessive punishments and miscarriages of justice aroused widespread horror and protests. The protests failed to persuade governments to mitigate their repression and persecution. Instead, they chose to combat dissent by increased oppression.[10] Actually, the degree of repression varied among the members of the *Bund*. That seemed especially true of censorship. The Carlsbad Decrees had ordered that each state must censor all publications of less than twenty pages. Some states obeyed this injunction, while others subjected all publications regardless of size to censorship. Approval by censors of one state did not protect the author from prosecution in another state. Publications banned in one state were freely published in another and then smuggled across the border. Brief experiments in the relaxation of censorship ended with the reintroduction of even more stringent controls.

The Germans had a special fascination with orders of honor and merit.

Their land seemed awash with a profusion of crosses, medals, stars, clusters, and ribbons awarded by sovereigns of states large and small. Their recipients delighted in them and wore them on every possible occasion. The Germans had a special passion, too, for uniforms. Rulers customarily appeared in them, with a dazzling display of decorations. They were appalled when Victoria's consort, Prince Albert, appeared at their courts on state occasions wearing an unadorned cutaway. Another trait that seemed especially German to foreigners was the prevalence of smoking. "Everyone, or nine out of ten," wrote one British writer, "has in his mouth a long pipe with a large earthen ware bowl."[11] In the principal cities, ordinances forbade smoking in the streets because of the danger of fires started by smokers, but apparently the prohibition was more honored in the breach than in the observance.

The German nobility, like their peers in other lands, delighted in the chase. Sometimes they hunted on foot, and on occasion, in imitation of the English, they rode to hounds. Often they organized "battues," in which beaters drove the game in front of a line of "sportsmen" who not only did not have to move but had their guns reloaded by servants who stood behind them. These battues were social events. In August 1845, when Queen Victoria visited Saxe-Coburg-Gotha, Prince Albert's homeland, a battue was arranged in honor of the guests. The slaughter lasted two hours, after which the ladies departed, walking through a carefully arranged avenue of the dead beasts, mostly stags. Queen Victoria, shocked at this butchery, wept. The right to hunt belonged exclusively to the elite (as it did in nearly every other European land). Poaching brought severe punishments, again as in other lands. Ernst Siemens, the famed engineer and inventor, who grew up in rural Hannover, remembered that the penalty for killing a deer was more severe than killing a human.[12]

Ordinary Germans found their pleasure in the public gardens and promenades that abounded in their towns. In good weather they flocked to these pleasant retreats to walk, to drink coffee and beer, to listen to the bands, and to waltz. They never seemed to tire of listening to music. Amateur singing societies and amateur musicians were everywhere. An American at the University of Göttingen wrote home that "it is almost impossible to meet a student who cannot sing a thousand songs and play at least one instrument." Sunday was the favored day for these recreations. Stores, cafés, and theaters were open and crowded, to the surprise of British visitors who knew only the British Sabbath with its puritanical blue laws that required the closing of all shops and places of amusement.[13]

From the end of May to early September, the elite migrated to the spas of

Germany and neighboring Bohemia to take the waters, to relax, and above all, to see and be seen. Central Europe had scores of spas—177 in Bohemia alone—but only a few attracted the so-called world of high fashion. Baden-Baden, in Germany's southwest corner, was especially popular, not only among Germany's princes and nobles, but among the social elite of all Europe. They brought servants and their finest carriages with them, so that in a summer's evening, the town's chief boulevard was said to offer a spectacle equaled only by the Champs Élysées or Hyde Park.

Vacationers filled their days and nights with concerts, balls, theater, gambling, endless writing of letters, gossiping, and of course, baths in the waters. If asked, they would have agreed with the enthusiastic young Russian nobleman who, in September 1840, wrote to his father that "Baden-Baden is a veritable terrestrial paradise, as much for the beauty of its location as for the delicious life one leads here." However, another and more serious Russian, who passed through Baden-Baden en route to a scientific expedition, called the vacationers "a fashionable and frivolous company of bored invalids" and wondered how people who lived in palaces and great mansions could spend entire months in "little boxes of rooms leading a barracks and corridor life."[14] Gambling casinos, housed in handsome salons, were prominent features of the German spas. Men and women of the highest rank crowded around the tables, shoulder to shoulder with professional gamblers, lowborn rogues, and adventurers. They played roulette and *rouge et noir* for high stakes.[15]

People of the middle class, too, visited the spas. Some came to seek relief from the illnesses that plagued them, but most came for rest and recreation. The costs were moderate and they drank the same sulphurous water, bathed in the same curative springs, enjoyed the same promenades and scenery, and listened to the same concerts as did the princes and barons. The enjoyment of these pleasures was one of the few occasions on which the elite and their social inferiors met on common ground. Supported by the conservatism of the era, the nobility continued to insist upon its traditional social supremacy. At theaters and concerts the best seats were reserved for nobles; at dances and garden parties a rope separated them from other guests. The wives of bourgeois cabinet ministers, or the middle-class wives or mothers of nobles, were not received in the court of the sovereign. At the universities the nobles sat separately, and in the few secondary schools in which nobles and commoners were fellow students, the nobles ate, slept, and bathed apart from their schoolmates. Nobles usually snubbed the bourgeoisie, often making no effort to conceal their disdain. Alexander von Humboldt told of a dinner at the palace of a duke at which someone remarked that there were thirteen at table—supposedly an ill omen. The host replied that two of his guests were not noblemen and so did not count. He said this in French, explaining that the two commoners would certainly not know that language.

The nobles had far less success in preserving their traditional preeminence in matters other than social status. The growing economic and political importance of the middle class was eroding the hierarchical structure of society. The nobility still enjoyed an elevated position, in part because nobles still owned most of the land, in part because of their dedication, especially in Prussia, to military service, and in largest part because of the persistence of traditional values that demanded respect for the nobility. They had lost most of their privileges, and those that remained were matters of form rather than special advantages. They no longer had the right of exclusive ownership of manors (*Ritterguter*). This especially chagrined the old nobility, who shuddered at the thought of men of common birth serving as judges and patrons of the peasants who lived on their manors, and naming the pastor of the village church. Nobles were embittered, too, by the loss of the monopoly on high office that had been theirs in times past. They resented, snubbed, and schemed against men of obscure pedigree who rose to importance in the councils of their sovereigns.[16]

A large increase in their number accelerated the declining importance of the nobility. An "inflation of honors" began in the last decades of the eighteenth century and continued on in the next century as each monarch continued to create new nobles. Most of these men and their progeny owned no land and depended for their livelihoods on service in the army or in the bureaucracy, in the lesser ranks and at low pay. Older families, too, including descendants of mediatized princes, fell on hard times.

These "noble proletarians," as a contemporary labeled them, brought discredit to the caste of the nobility. More important, the growing economic power and resulting self-confidence of the middle class had bred heightened resentment of the privileges and pretensions of the nobility. To many of these people, the nobility seemed an absurd anachronism. That was the way the popular writer Karl Immermann portrayed the nobility in his novel *Münchhausen,* which appeared in 1838-1839. He told of the bizarre household of Baron von Schnuck and his aging daughter Emerentia, who lived in the crumbling castle of Schnick-Schnack-Schnurr, and of their guest, the legendary master of lies, Baron von Münchhausen. Other novelists, too, lampooned the nobility, comparing them unfavorably with the capable and intelligent people of the middle class.[17]

As in other lands, the middle class stretched from small shopkeepers and craftsmen to the members of the professional and commercial elite, and from those who lived in provincial backwaters to the residents of important urban centers. Each stratum of the middle class had its own distinctive character and interests, but all were lumped together in what the Germans called the *Bürgertum*, the synonym for the humdrum, unpretentious, provincial, and complacent existence supposedly led by the middle class. In the early twentieth century critics and art historians gave the name Biedermeier (after a collection of parodies written between 1855 and 1859 by two writers who used the pseudonym of Gottlieb Biedermeier) to the bourgeois culture of the early decades of the nineteenth century.

There was much truth in that picture of German middle-class life, but new currents were at work that would alter it dramatically. The universities—there were nineteen of them scattered across Germany—drew ever larger numbers of youths of the bourgeoisie. Higher education became a vehicle for upward mobility, and a new university-trained elite emerged. University graduates entered into the higher ranks of the bureaucracy, and German professors and scientists began to make their universities and laboratories centers of learning that were to become famed throughout the world. Simultaneously, slow but steady economic advances, under the leadership of middle-class entrepreneurs, produced a new bourgeois patriciate of bankers and businessmen whose wealth won them the grudging respect of the old elite.

The successes of the middle-class bureaucrats, businessmen, academics, and scientists brought about a new kind of Germany that stressed the bourgeois virtues of work, of discipline, of attention to detail, and of precision. It was a Germany where men believed that the individual, by his diligence, served Germany and all humanity by the creation of wealth. The economist Friedrich List summed up that conviction when he wrote that "the power to create wealth is far more important than the wealth itself."[18]

Initially, the bourgeoisie did not dispute the domination of political and social life by the old elite; the tradition of hierarchy was too deeply imbedded in German life. Then, in the 1830s, some leading figures of the middle class, inspired by the success of the July revolution in France, started to question their exclusion from political life and to resent the preferment given to the nobility. They began to identify themselves as liberals. By the 1840s the doctrines of liberalism had won the allegiance of much of the upper and educated strata of the bourgeoisie. That the mass of the middle class remained indifferent to the movement did not trouble the liberals. Idealistic dreams of freedom, justice, and social welfare inspired the intellectuals among them, largely professors, lawyers, and journalists, while liberal businessmen wanted the way opened to the growth of capitalistic enterprises. Both the intellectual elite and the business elite, plus some nobles who were convinced by the arguments of the liberals, joined in the demand for a united Germany with a constitution and a parliament, free speech and free press, freedom to enter any occupation, the abolition of monopolies, and the end of social and legal barriers that impeded the rise of the individual. Like their fellow bourgeois liberals in other lands, they opposed universal suffrage. They believed that government belonged in the hands of the propertied and the educated. They feared that the masses were dependent, irrational, rootless, without a stake in society, and susceptible to the blandishments and promises of radicals and demagogues.[19]

The new assertiveness of middle-class liberals took place against a change in economic life. Germany's population grew steadily, from 23 million in 1800 to 35 million in 1850, an increase of over 50 percent. Two thirds of that increase occurred after 1820. The Germany of the 1840s stood on the threshold of a metamorphosis that transformed an overwhelmingly rural and backward economy in a politically fragmented country into a unified nation that by century's end contested with Great Britain for world economic leadership. Iron and steam and machines and factories began to replace the wood and the water and the wind power of the preindustrial stage of production. Improvements in agriculture that included rotation of crops instead of the three-field system with its wasteful fallows, and the spread of forage crops with consequent improvements in animal husbandry, began to provide increased amounts of food for the expanding population. It was very much a time of beginnings. The pace of economic change in these first years was slow. Most manufactured wares were made by artisans. In 1846 well over one quarter of all adult males (over fourteen) were craftsmen. Only 4.2 percent worked in factories. Merchants and peddlers bought and sold their wares at weekly markets and annual fairs. All-year-around marketing was only beginning to take hold. In 1849 the heavy industries of Prussia and Saxony, the two leading industrial states, employed an average of only twenty-five workers. Seventy percent of Germany's population still lived out on the land. But the breakthrough had been made. Germany had begun its "take-off" into self-sustained economic growth.

The internal tariffs and import and export duties that had retarded economic growth in each state all but disappeared with the famed *Zollverein*, the tariff union. In 1818 Prussia, with its eight provinces scattered across northern Germany from the French to the Polish borders, and with sixty different tariffs, adopted a single tariff for all of its possessions. As the years went by, other states joined, and by 1834 the *Zollverein* encompassed nearly all of Germany and provided a national market for the products of farm and factory. The removal of tariffs was only the first step. New roads were built, steam navigation began on the rivers, and most important of all, Germany entered the railroad age. The *Zollverein* made a unified national economy possible, while the railroad made it a reality. The first German railroad opened in 1835, and by 1850 Germany had over 3,600 miles of line, third in the world after the United States and Great Britain. The railroads not only promoted economic growth by their rapid and efficient carriage of goods and passengers. Their construction and operation created a demand for iron, coal, and labor, stimulating the growth of heavy industry and providing employment for thousands of workers. They served a significant political purpose, too, binding the German states together and helping to break down local loyalties in favor of pan-German nationalism.[20]

The upswing in economic life was only one facet in the transformation of Germany. Beginning in the late 1830s, a new restlessness, and a growing questioning and discontent with long-honored institutions and traditions, readied the way for the creation of a unified and mighty German empire. Prussia, largest and most important of the German states, provided the principal theater in which this historical process worked itself out. Prussia owed its dominant position to its ruling dynasty, the House of Hohenzollern. Beginning in the mid-seventeenth century, a remarkable succession of four of these dynasts forged their unimportant and scattered possessions into a kingdom that by the end of the eighteenth century had become one of Europe's five Great Powers. The state they created lacked natural frontiers and was split into two principal pieces, the largest lying on the east, next to Russian Poland, and the other on Germany's western border along the Rhine. In addition, the Swiss canton of Neuchâtel and several enclaves in Saxony belonged to the Hohenzollerns. The ruler was an absolute monarch, though the Englishman Richard Cobden, visiting in 1838 and impressed by the efficiency of the bureaucracy and the excellent educational system, pronounced it "the mildest phase in which absolutism has ever presented itself."

The bureaucrats who carried out the rules and regulations of the absolutism were as disciplined as an army. They formed a special kind of organization with its own code in which the supreme values were unswerving obedience to superiors, stern self-discipline, and hard work. Prussians bureaucrats were justly famed for their efficiency. Unfortunately, they were also famed for their arrogance, their tactlessness, and their attitude of superiority to the people they governed.

The Hohenzollerns owed their success as state makers above all to the effectiveness of the army which they created, and on which they spent the lion's share of the revenues of the state. It is a historical truism that the Prussian army made the Prussian state. The officers of the army, nearly all of them of noble birth, formed a proud caste that looked down upon the rest of society. They commanded a large standing army of career enlisted men. In addition, the law called for the universal conscription of all males at the age of twenty. The conscripts served for one year, then entered the reserve, going on active duty for two months each year until the age of thirty-nine. Other members of the German Confederation, too, had universal conscription, but their state of preparedness sometimes bordered on the farcical.[21]

Berlin, capital of Prussia, was Germany's largest city, with around three hundred thousand people in 1840. Despite having a distinguished university and other cultural institutions, visitors, and at least one of its most famous residents, found it singularly unattractive and dull. The famed scientist Alexander von Humboldt, who had reluctantly returned to his native Berlin in 1827, wrote bitterly about the city. In letters to friends, he wrote of its "monstrous dullness" and called it "a moral wasteland," "a small, illiterate, and malicious town," and said that "there was in Europe no other place where society was so dull, rude, and ignorant and proud of it." Henry Adams, who lived in Berlin in the 1860s, still found it "a provincial town, simple, dirty, uncivilized, and in most respects disgusting."[22]

The city sat on a flat plain so that water did not drain from its streets, and with no sewage system save that provided by the River Spree that meandered through the city, the stench from the river and from the festering messes in the undrained streets was so strong that, as one visitor put it, the city stank like a great sink. Another visitor, noting the many military monuments, remarked that if the statues could smell, they would be holding their noses instead of grasping their swords. The streets were broad but many were paved with small sharp stones that made walking unpleasant and even painful. Sidewalks were only beginning to be built. The city had one fine boulevard, Unter den Linden, but once away from there visitors were struck by the absence of people in the streets and by the lack of attractive shops. The slums of the city rivaled those of Manchester. A contemporary estimated that a quarter of the city's population lived in direst poverty.[23]

In November 1839 word spread through Berlin that the spectral "White Lady" had been seen at the royal palace. Legend had it that her appearance had always heralded the approaching death of the king of Prussia. Seven months later, Frederick William III, king for forty-two years, died after a long illness. An inarticulate and not very bright man, he had never courted public favor and in his later years made limited public appearances so that he seemed a distant figure to his subjects. Five times between 1810 and 1820 he had promised a written constitution to his people and a representative assembly but had never carried out his pledge. His subjects had not forgotten those promises, but in the years of reaction and repression that followed the end of the Napoleonic wars, they had not pressed him to keep his word but instead accepted his arbitrary rule. It was as if the people of his generation had reached an unspoken understanding not to disturb the calm of the old man's life by political unrest. With his death a new generation took over and a new era began in Prussia.

The hopes of the people entered on the person of the new king, Frederick William IV. A middle-aged man of forty-five, he was short, stout, full-faced with a weak mouth, near-sighted, balding, with a high-pitched voice and a loud laugh, awkward in his movements, and unhappy and clumsy astride a horse. In short, he did not cut a kingly figure; one observer thought that he looked more like a professor than a king.[24]

He was a knowledgeable and even intellectually gifted man who, according to someone who knew him well, thought that he was brighter than anyone else. Nonetheless, he recognized his limitations. In a conversation in 1849 with a nobleman, he said that to carry through a certain policy being discussed he would need "the spirit of a warrior, a hero, an unyielding statesman. You know, dear Saucken, I am none of these things. . . . " He had a deep interest in intellectual and cultural matters and delighted in talking and exchanging ideas with men of learning. Unlike other sovereigns of his line before and after him, army life held no fascination for him. He joked about the mistakes that he made at military reviews. He was the only Hohenzollern ruler who did not assume the office of commander-in-chief of his army. He turned that post over to his brother William, who delighted in it. He did leave his mark on the army by ordering its members to wear a new uniform that included the spiked helmet, a medieval fancy of the king. At first, people made fun of the *Pickelhaube*, as the Prussians named it, but in later years it became the honored symbol of German military might—and to Germany's enemies the symbol of German ruthlessness and brutality. The king was happily married to Elizabeth, second eldest daughter of the king of Bavaria. He depended heavily upon her for moral and emotional support. She never failed him, save that the marriage was childless. She shared his religious and charitable interests and gave generously from her own private fortune.[25]

When Frederick William was on his best behavior, as when he visited Queen Victoria in 1842, people found him amiable, well-meaning, and kind. It was a different story when he was among his own people. He had a violent and uncontrollable temper. When anger overwhelmed him, his wife would calm him by looking earnestly around the room and saying, "I am looking for the king." In his earlier years his mood would suddenly change from anger to amiability, and he would joke about his ill humor. As he grew older, physical weakness followed the tantrums, his brow became wet with perspiration, and he became despondent. As a young man he would engage in serious conversation and then suddenly would roar with laughter, jump up, shout and snort, and speaking loudly in the other person's ear would ask, "Have I scared you good and proper?"[26]

The fact was that the king of Prussia was a psychopath. His condition worsened as the years went by, and his problems mounted. Finally, he became so incapacitated that in 1858 he was adjudged insane, and his brother William took over the throne as regent. Four years later Frederick William died. It was a tragedy of historic dimensions that the absolute rulers of the two dominant powers of Central Europe were mentally ill. In Austria, where the weak-minded Ferdinand was incapable of ruling, no one was in charge, and the state drifted until his nephew replaced him in December 1848. In Prussia Frederick William was very much in charge, so that the destiny of Prussia, and of Germany during the crucial years of the forties and early fifties, was in the hands of a man who teetered on the brink of madness.

He was a dreamer, smitten with romantic and quixotic ideas, and affected by a deep religiosity. He had an idealized version of a Christian medieval past that never existed but for which he longed. He seemed uninterested and even repelled by practical, everyday concerns. He loved his people and he wanted them to love him, but he had no feeling for their problems so they became alienated from him. His intelligence enabled him to grasp and analyze a political situation, but he lacked the clear vision and the steadiness of character necessary for a systematic approach to a problem. Instead, he acted by fits and starts. Metternich, in 1847, observed that Frederick William was "impressed with the spirit of order, and creates disorder, he wants good and leads to evil." Less harsh critics thought it Frederick William's misfortune, and Germany's, too, that fate had made him a king. Someone said that he should have been a poet who had the right of poetic license and so, unlike a king, did not have to be taken at his word.[27]

As could be expected, the men closest to him shared his conservative convictions and his belief in enlightened absolutism. None of his advisors had any real power. Frederick William did as he pleased, following his own impulses. All that his confidants could do was to anticipate the wishes and fancies of the king and carry them out.[28] One of the most interesting of his advisors, and one of the unlikeliest figures of the era, was General Josef Maria von Radowitz. He was born in 1797 in central Germany into a newly ennobled Catholic family of Hungarian origin. He became a military cadet at fourteen and after service in other German armies, he joined the Prussian army as a captain in 1823. His outstanding intelligence won him rapid promotion and the friendship of important people, above all of them the Crown Prince Frederick William. His rapid rise in rank, his friendship with the powerful, and his marriage into the high Prussian nobility gained him the dislike and the envy of Prussian nobles. They resented, too, his Catholicism, his foreign origin, and his unimportant family background. It did not help that he made no effort to conceal his intellectual superiority, and that, supremely self-confident, he monopolized conversations, holding forth in the tones of a lecturer.[29]

Frederick William's first acts as monarch met and even exceeded the great expectations that had greeted his accession. He appointed liberal ministers, granted amnesty to political prisoners, and eased the censorship and thought control. These and other measures persuaded liberal and radical Prussians that their new king would grant the constitution and the parliament that his father had promised. The press, able now to write about political matters, excitedly discussed the question of a constitution.

Rarely was a new monarch greeted with such enthusiasm and rarely was the enthusiasm so quickly dashed. The reaction of his subjects to his first actions surprised and angered Frederick William. He had initiated these measures as the father of his people who knew what was best for them, and not as part of a liberal agenda. He cherished freedom so long as it did not diminish his royal prerogative. He did not hesitate to withdraw a freedom if he felt that his subjects misused it. That happened with the comparative freedom of the press that he had permitted. He thought that he could be indifferent to published criticisms of himself and his policies, but he quickly discovered that his skin was not as thick as he thought it was. By early 1843 the old oppressive censorship had been restored. The demands for a constitution and a representative assembly particularly offended him. He early made it clear that he intended to continue the absolute rule of his forebears. In his mind constitutions and representative governments were legacies of the hated French Revolution and had no place on German soil.

Religion was of great importance to Frederick William. He felt that he must use his God-given power to combat the philosophical and humanistic currents that seemed to him to be undermining traditional religion and values. He dreamed of a Christian monarchy in which monarch and people lived according to the teachings of the Christian faith. Baron von Meyendorff, Russia's ambassador to Berlin, an unusually perceptive man, reported in September 1841 that to Frederick William the goal of the state was not to ensure the material and cultural well-being of its subjects. Rather, it was to provide them with the spiritual means to live on earth according to the will of God, as a preparation for afterlife.[30]

Royal reveries such as these could not still growing discontent, aggravated by the economic downturn of the mid-forties. So Frederick William decided to implement an idea that had occupied his mind for some time. In February 1847 he summoned the representatives of Prussia's eight provincial diets to a general assembly that he called the United Diet. He planned that the Diet would meet periodically at his pleasure, discuss such matters as he assigned to it but without making decisions, and give its approval to state loans and taxes that he might propose. He honestly believed that he had made a master stroke that would end all talk of constitutions and representative assemblies.

The Diet had 613 delegates, divided into four estates: 70 princes, 237 nobles, 182 burghers, and 124 peasants. The delegates recognized the limitations imposed upon the Diet, but many saw it as a preliminary step toward representative government. Whatever hopes they had for reform were quickly dispelled by the king's address that opened the first session of the Diet on April 11. He reminded the delegates that they represented the estates of the realm and not the people as a whole. He warned them that liberal doctrines would undermine state and church, that he would never allow "a piece of paper with writing on it to rule us by its paragraphs," and that he neither could nor should rule in accordance with the will of the majority. Exasperated by the king's declaration of unregenerate absolutism, many conservative delegates joined with liberal ones to demand some small reforms. The king refused to make any concessions. The delegates responded by refusing to approve state loans. The deadlock made it clear that the Diet could accomplish nothing, and on June 26 Frederick William ordered its adjournment.

The king was not without his defenders among the delegates. One of them was the thirty-two-year-old Otto von Bismarck, who began his spectacular career as a substitute for an elected delegate who had become ill. He quickly made a reputation as a fearless debater. An overage *enfant terrible,* he said whatever came to his mind, delighted in making his opponents uncomfortable, and spared no one. Older conservatives said that he went too far and would come to no good end.[31]

The summoning of the Diet had turned out to be a great mistake and not the great triumph that the king had hoped it would be. The Diet had made it clear for all to see that Frederick William stood in the path of progress. Even more important, for the first time it had provided an official and public platform for a discussion of the constitutional question, and had given national exposure to the able and self-confident middle-class delegates who led in the debate. The impact of their arguments and the obduracy of the king gave new strength to the reform movement. Had Frederick William been wise enough to bend a little and make some concessions, Prussia might have been spared the turmoil of revolution.[32]

In other German states, too, rulers disregarded a rising tide of discontent. At the outset of the 1840s, as if at some agreed-upon signal, political and nationalistic agitation swept through the land, dispelling the apathy that had prevailed for so long. Nationalism became a burning issue, stirred up by the threat of war with France in 1840 and then controversy with Denmark about sovereignty over the duchies of Schleswig and Holstein. Liberal businessmen, encouraged by the success of the *Zollverein,* looked forward to a united Germany that could withstand the competition of more advanced nations. At scholarly meetings academics discussed the need for national unification, and writers of all stripes, conservative and radical, dreamed of a united Germany that stretched from the Alps to the sea. Poets wrote patriotic effusions, among them Hoffman von Fallersleben's *Deutschland über Alles,* which later became the national anthem of the unified German state.

There was as yet no open enmity between sovereigns and their subjects, no threatening confrontations, no desire to overthrow governments. Instead, a malaise compounded of political discontent and social and economic dislocations spread through the land and enlisted people of all classes in the ranks of the disaffected. Liberals formed the most prominent element. Led by men of the upper bourgeoisie, the demand for political equality gained increasing support among the middle class. The liberal press openly defied the censorship with articles critical of the status quo, liberal leaders met and approved reform programs, and criticism mounted of the ineffectiveness of the German Confederation. People talked more and more of the need for a much closer link among the German states and the strengthening of a national consciousness. Critics called these liberals *Kammerliberalen,* "parlor pinks."

A more threatening attack on the establishment came from what W. H. Riehl called in his 1851 book the "intellectual proletariat." Composed of alienated educated members of the middle class, this group counted among its members minor bureaucrats, schoolmasters, underpaid university lecturers, perennially unemployed clergymen, journalists, and artists. As Riehl put it, they were "the yeast who first set the working class into action." Germany produced more educated men than its predominantly rural society needed or could reward adequately. German universities, supported by the state, were inexpensive, so that boys from poor families could afford to attend with the hope of becoming bureaucrats or professional men. The result was an oversupply of university graduates, unable to achieve the status and income that they felt appropriate to their education and intellectual abilities. Frustrated in their ambitions for a successful career, they turned to political action in the hope of reforming the society that had failed them. Unlike their peers in later generations, only a few of them were attracted to the socialistic doctrines that made their debut in the 1840s. Most of them rejected the idea of the class struggle and the socialization of the means of production. Their program included universal manhood suffrage, welfare legislation, and a republican form of government.[33]

New social pressures and economic distress underlay and aggravated the political discontent. The growth of population had outstripped the growth of the economy. Germany's economy could not provide enough jobs for all its people, nor could its traditional agriculture produce enough to feed them adequately. Destitution became the lot of millions in town and country alike. The European-wide downturn in economic life of the mid-1840s and crop failures that pushed up food prices worsened the distress. By mid-1847 the price of wheat in the Rhineland was 250 percent higher than in 1845, of rye 300 percent, and of potatoes 425 percent. In Berlin the so-called Potato Riots erupted on April 21, 1847. For four days the city was in turmoil, with mobs plundering food stores, wine shops, and warehouses. Troops had to be used to suppress the rioters. Other cities experienced similar outbreaks. Those able to scrape together passage money fled overseas in ever increasing numbers. In the decade of the thirties, 124,726 Germans migrated to the United States. Between 1840 and 1849, that number had more than tripled to 385,434. A few thousand left their homeland for political or religious reasons, but most migrated to escape the hard times and to start life anew.[34]

Artisans, Germany's principal producers of manufactured wares, were especially discontented. They bitterly opposed legislation that began to undermine the centuries-old monopolistic privileges of their guilds. The advances of factory industry, the *Zollverein*, the new railroads that brought in competing goods, and the economic downturn of the mid-forties aggravated their frustration. Their protests, and especially those of the journeymen, became more frequent and sometimes violent. The best known of these outbursts occurred in June 1844 when the spinners and weavers of linen in Silesia rose in fury against their employers. The rising was immortalized by Heinrich Heine's poem "The Weavers" and a half century later by Gerhart Hauptmann's play *The Weavers*, one of the classics of German literature.[35]

Out in the countryside, where 70 percent of Germany's people lived, life seemed unchanged. Peasants, men and women, young and old, worked endlessly as they always had to make ends meet, letting nothing that they could possibly use go to waste. They held on to their old customs and to their communal life. But they could not withstand the forces that were bearing down on all of German society. The pressure of population growth brought about the subdivision of their holdings and a great increase in the landless. These landless people earned their meager livings by working as farm laborers for other peasants or for the landowner, and by cottage industries, especially spinning and weaving. Still others gave up the struggle to survive on the land and fled to the cities in search of employment. Some became vagabonds, wandering from place to place, begging and stealing to keep body and soul together. The serfdom that had bound many of Germany's peasants to their lords had ended in much of Germany, but most peasants remained in some degree of servile dependency upon their seigniors. To add to their burdens, the peasants had to meet the state's demand for taxes and for military service. The upper classes, for their part, regarded peasants as scarcely human and derogated them. The powerless peasants had to accept this treatment, but it bred deep resentment among many countrymen. The resentment sometimes led to violence, but far more usually it produced passive resistance, such as the refusal to perform services for the lord or the threat of a strike at harvest time. None of these incidents reached serious proportions, but there was evidence of growing rural discontent, exacerbated by the crop failure of the mid-forties that left many peasants near starvation.[36]

As the years of the forties went by, a sense of crisis spread through all levels of society. Predictions of revolution, and more specifically of social revolution, became commonplace. In June 1844 Prince Hohenlohe-Schillingsfürst, who had just accepted an appointment in the Prussian bureaucracy, wrote in his journal that unless the supreme authority made a complete change, revolution could break out on the slightest provocation. In December 1845 Varnhagen von Ense wrote that people had accepted the inevitability of a revolution. The American consul in Amsterdam reported in late 1847 that the German immigrants who passed through that port expressed the belief that "the present crisis . . . is but the commencement of that Great Revolution, which they consider sooner or later is to dissolve the present constitution of things." In an article on Prussia in the *Edinburgh Review* in 1846, Richard Monkton Milnes foresaw revolution, "when sullenness will burst into rage, and political rights be forcibly wrung from the hand that withheld them."[37]

By 1847 Germany seemed teetering on the edge of anarchy. Food riots, strikes, and increased pauperism and crime threatened the fabric of society. Liberal and radical critics grew bolder in their speeches and writings, societies formed with demands for reform, and religious agitation stirred up old animosities between Catholics and Protestants. News of risings in Italy and of civil war in neighboring Switzerland added to the general unrest. At the end of 1847, Hohenlohe-Schillingsfürst wrote in his journal, "The real peril lies not in the parties of the Communists, Socialists, and Radicals . . . not in the secret machinations of the Jesuit Fathers and their friends . . . but in the fact that the discontent of which each party makes such skillful use, is so universal and so well-founded."[38]

The storm broke when word came of the February Revolution in Paris. Popular demonstrations, demands for reform, and then risings followed the news from Paris as it spread eastward. Every corner of Germany had its fiery orators and its tumult. Demands for change bombarded the princes and made them tremble on their thrones. Despite the many warnings the monarchs seemed surprised and unprepared when revolution came. Overwhelmed and frightened by the threatening oratory, mass demonstrations, and outbreaks of violence, they hastened to make concessions, to dismiss old ministers, and to name new ones who they hoped would placate the rebels. Particularism was too strong to allow the forging of a united revolutionary movement, and no great leader emerged who could speak for such a movement. So there were many 1848 revolutions in Germany, each within a specific state, and each with its own leaders and objectives. There was much high-flown verbiage that served to obfuscate rather than to illuminate. Nonetheless, four main demands emerged everywhere: freedom of the press, trial by jury, the right of the people to bear arms, and the summoning of a German national assembly. The first three demands reflected the concern of the middle-class liberal revolutionaries for effective guarantees of political freedom. The fourth demand reflected the desire of Germans from every class for a united Germany. The nationalism born in the struggle against Napoleon had matured simultaneously with the desire for political liberties.

The liberals, who made up by far the largest number of the bourgeois supporters of the revolution, wanted constitutional monarchies with representative assemblies, ministers responsible to the assemblies, and with greater or lesser limits on the powers of the sovereign. The republicans, small in number but vociferous in volume, wanted to establish republics with universal manhood suffrage, led by propertied men of the middle class, favorable to the growth of industrial capitalism but sensitive to the need for welfare legislation. The radicals, or the "red republicans" as contemporaries called them, wanted socialist republics. Though their preachments ignited a "Red Scare," they had a negligible influence, serving only as bogeymen. None of the many risings were inspired by their teachings, and none of their followers sat in any of the revolutionary assemblies.[39]

The middle-class leaders of the revolution excluded workers and peasants from their councils but depended upon them as shock troops of the revolution. The workers, like their fellows in the cities of France and Austria, provided the bodies for the demonstrations, for the riots that precipitated the revolutions, and for the fighting in the streets. Factory workers, still relatively few in number, were minor participants in the revolutions. Artisans accepted middle-class leadership, but most of them were not concerned about the ideologies of bourgeois revolutionaries. They were driven not by ideologies but by their fears of a future in which factories and machines would take away their livelihoods, by the misery and the hopelessness of their lives, and by a hatred of their exploiters.

Ideologies meant even less to peasants. Their traditional mistrust of educated city people aroused their suspicions of such concepts as constitutions and parliaments and freedom of the press. Their enemies were not the monarchs against whom the burghers rebelled, nor the threat of industrialization that frightened the artisans. Their enemies were the lords who still held power over them, and the village usurers and the shopkeepers who exploited them. When, with the help of their middle-class allies, they achieved their goal of freedom from their servile bonds, they withdrew from the revolution. They made no significant political demands and remained monarchists and conservatives. When they withdrew, the revolutionary movement foundered, just as it had in Austria.[40]

When word of the revolution in Paris reached Berlin, excited crowds filled the streets, eagerly discussing rumors and exaggerated reports about events in France and in other parts of Germany. Then came the news of the revolution in Vienna on March 13 and the fall of Metternich. Excitement and rejoicing peaked, except at the royal court. King Frederick William, in his palace in Potsdam, made the mistake of going to Berlin. The deluded man thought his presence there would prevent the outbreak of revolution. Had he remained in Potsdam, he would have been spared much grief and humiliation. Demonstrations and demands for reform mounted. On March 16 the efforts of soldiers to clear the streets of some barricades led to bloodshed. The king, beginning to panic, decided to put himself at the head of a revolution he could not suppress. On March 18 he abolished the censorship, ordered the reconvening of the United Diet, and declared his readiness to help transform Germany into a federal union with a constitution. The overjoyed Berliners poured into the great square before the palace to show their gratitude to their sovereign and to ask for the withdrawal of troops from the city. A cavalry squadron advanced to clear the square when suddenly two shots rang out, fired probably by a nervous trooper. No one was hurt, but the crowd assumed that the soldiers had been ordered to attack. Cries of "treachery" and "to arms" echoed through the city, barricades went up, and soldiers and civilians battled in the streets. Fighting continued throughout the night, burning houses providing eerie illumination for the combatants. By the next morning, the soldiers had the insurgents surrounded. Then, to the great surprise of the soldiers, the king ordered the army to withdraw from Berlin. Though they had lost the battle, the insurgents won.[41]

The fighting cost the lives of about 230 civilians, though some reports set the casualties as high as 1,500. Of the civilian dead who were identified, 88 percent were workers, nearly half of them journeymen. On the afternoon of the nineteenth, long processions marched into the palace square, bearing the bloodstained bodies of the civilian dead, and heaped them at the foot of the palace stairs. The crowd called for the king to come out. He came down the stairs and, bareheaded, bowed before the corpses. His weeping queen fainted. Then a deep voice in the hushed crowd began singing, "Jesus My Refuge" and the people joined in. It was an unforgettable scene. When still more corpses were borne in, the king, who had returned to his palace, no longer responded to cries for his appearance. The crowd became excited and seemed ready to break into the palace. Young Prince Felix Lichnowsky, a noble of liberal sympathies, leaped upon a table in the middle of the square and in a loud voice announced, without any authority, that the king would grant all demands, and the crowd dispersed peacefully.[42]

The king's brother and heir, William, was known to be an enemy of the revolution. When a false rumor spread that he had given the order to fire on the crowd on March 18, popular fury turned against him. Other rumors told of William's strong disagreement with his brother's withdrawal of the army from Berlin. To placate the insurgents, the king on March 19 ordered William to leave the country. That night in disguise, William fled to England. On the twentieth the king ordered amnesty for all political prisoners. On the twenty-first he issued a proclamation announcing that he placed himself at the head of a "united Fatherland." That same day he ordered the army to wear a cockade of the revolutionary colors: black, red, and gold. Only a few days earlier, certain punishment had awaited those who had dared to wear these colors. Then, in a supreme act of humiliation, he rode through the streets of Berlin with members of his family and his ministers all wearing armbands of black, red, and gold. He told his cheering subjects who lined the streets that he sided with the revolution. His actions and his words were deliberate lies by a frightened and demoralized man who hated the revolution but lacked the honesty and the courage to acknowledge his true feelings openly. He remained an absolutist to the core of his being who believed, as he wrote in a letter to a friend, that liberalism, "a sinful, God-cursed frenzy," led to certain ruin and Godlessness, where "black is called white and darkness light."[43]

Others shared Frederick William's dismay and despair over the events of the March Days. Army officers felt dishonored by the king's order for them to withdraw from Berlin. The youthful Frederick, son of Prince William and destined to be his successor in 1888, who fled to Britain with his father, told the Duke of Argyll that he could hardly speak of the disgrace. He told Argyll that he felt inclined to break his sword, the ultimate symbol of an officer's humiliation. Helmut von Moltke, who five years later became chief of the Prussian General Staff, wrote that the March Days had shattered authority in Berlin and in all Germany. "It's no longer about Monarch and Republic," he wrote, "but about Law or Anarchy. Our enemies do not come from without, we have them within. . . . What a responsibility for those who allowed these conditions." Moltke did not name those whom he felt responsible. Others put the blame squarely on Frederick William. King Frederick William himself told the historian Leopold von Ranke that the March Days "was when we all crawled on our bellies." Ranke, who opposed the revolution, said that when he saw Frederick William that summer the king impressed him as "a young man full of intelligence and knowledge who, excuse the professor in me, had by some mischance failed in his examinations."[44]

Like Louis Philippe of France, Frederick William's resolve had failed him at the time of crisis. Unlike Louis Philippe, he did not run away. He thought of doing that on the night of March 19, and he continued to think of abdication in succeeding months. But he stuck it out, determined to resist as well as he could the diminution of his royal prerogatives. The course of events after the victory of the revolution enabled him to do just that. Instead of inaugurating an era of domestic reform, months of near anarchy followed the March Days. The machinery of government broke down. A National Assembly, elected by universal male suffrage, endlessly wrangled over the draft of a constitution. Economic life was at a standstill. Increasing numbers of the unemployed thronged the streets and, stirred up by demagogues, demonstrated, rioted, and often stole. A public-works program proved a failure. The breakdown of order, the unbridled license, and the insecurity of daily life depressed and frightened Berliners, especially the middle-class liberals who had welcomed the revolution. The army remained faithful to Frederick William, but even the most loyal of his officers thought that the sky was about to fall.[45]

The 1848 Revolution had not started in Berlin. In the first two weeks of March, unrest in Baden, Württemberg, Bavaria, Nassau, Saxe-Meiningen, and Hohenzollern-Sigmaringen had erupted into revolutions that forced their rulers to make concessions. But the March Days in Berlin, capital of Germany's leading state, seemed to all Germans the dawn of a new age, with its promises of a united Germany, of constitutions, of parliaments, and of the end of censorship. Revolutions spread through the land, though nearly every-where the insurgents triumphed without violence over their frightened rulers, who, unnerved by demonstrations of rebellious subjects, made concessions such as constitutional and responsible government, freedom of the press, trial by jury, and similar reforms. Sometimes, though, events did not proceed so peacefully. Peasants in various parts of Germany burned and sacked manor houses, paying special attention to the destruction of all records of the servile obligations they owed to their seigniors. In Heidelberg artisans took advantage of street turmoil to attack the shops and factories that they felt were depriving them of their livelihoods.[46]

The Grand Duchy of Baden, in Germany's southwest corner, became a fountainhead of revolutionary radicalism. On April 12, 1848, Friedrich Hecker, a lawyer, and Gustav Struve, a journalist, proclaimed the German Republic. Within eight days government troops had defeated the ragtag army of the newly proclaimed republic. Meanwhile, German political refugees in neighboring Switzerland had come over the border to fight for the republic. Among them were around seven hundred men of the so-called German Democratic Legion of Paris, led by George Herwegh, whose radical poetry had some years earlier won him acclaim. Herwegh, wrapped in a great black cloak, headed the column, accompanied by his wealthy wife, Emma, whose money supported the Legion. By the time the poorly armed Legion arrived in Baden, Hecker's *putsch* had collapsed. The Legion, after a brief skirmish with government troops, broke up. Herwegh and his wife escaped into Switzerland. An apocryphal but widely believed story recounted that Emma Herwegh had driven a cart over the border with Herwegh hiding ignominiously under the leather splashboards.

Gustav Struve, captured after the collapse of the rising, was exiled to Switzerland. A vegetarian and a devotee of phrenology, he believed that mankind could be saved by proper diet and ruled by phrenology. He told Alexander Herzen that he chose his wife because she lacked the cranial bump of passion (Herzen thought that this was grounds for divorce). The lady proved a shrewd and loyal wife, blessed with far more common sense than her spouse. In September of 1848 he and a dozen unarmed friends walked across the Swiss border to a small town in Baden, seized the city hall, and again proclaimed the German Republic. The conspirators took over a local print shop and ran off proclamations and appeals for volunteers. In thirty-six hours, Struve had an army of ten thousand men and began to lead them toward Freiburg. In a few days, government troops surrounded Struve's army and ended the rising. This time Struve was sentenced to five years, and his wife, too, was jailed. She was released in April 1849 and succeeded in rousing a mob to storm Struve's jail and free him. Struve and spouse fled to Switzerland, then England, and, in 1851, to the United States.[47]

Two of the largest German states, Württemberg and Hannover, were barely touched by unrest. King William of Württemberg, on March 8, in reply to popular demand, replaced his ministers with a new cabinet headed by Friedrich Römer, who till then had led the opposition, and dissolved the diet and announced elections for a new one. Revolutionary fervor, placated by these concessions, faded away. Before revolutions swept over Germany, the king of Hannover had been the most hated of German princes. The seventy-seven-year-old Ernest Augustus was an arrogant, cruel, intolerant, and insufferable man, but he was not a fool. Unlike the king of Prussia, he kept his self-possession. On March 17, of his own volition, he restored freedoms that he had suppressed years before, released political prisoners, and appointed Johann Stuve, a leading liberal, as his principal minister. Contrary to all expectations, the king quickly entered into a warm personal relationship with Stuve. The king himself said that he had always looked upon Stuve as a republican, a demagogue, and a public menace. When he came to know him, he continued, he found him to be the monarchy's most loyal supporter.[48]

Meanwhile, from the very outset of the revolutionary movement, liberals began to plan for a united Germany that would include Austria. A self-appointed committee of fifty-one men met in Heidelberg on March 5 to call for elections to a national assembly. They invited "trustworthy men" to meet in Frankfurt on March 31 to lay plans for such an assembly. Five-hundred-and-seventy-four delegates appeared, nearly all of them self-appointed and most of them from the small states of southern Germany. Known as the Pre-Parliament, they met for four days. They decided that a National Assembly would convene in Frankfurt on May 18, its delegates elected by universal male suffrage, with one delegate for every fifty thousand people, and with the mission of drawing up a constitution for a united Germany. Actually, the universal male suffrage ordered by the Pre-Parliament was honored more in the breach than in the observance. Many states denied the vote to men of the working class, and everywhere people receiving relief were automatically disenfranchised. In any event, a general lack of interest held down the turnout. In some places, less than 10 percent of the eligible males voted. Average participation is estimated to have been well below 50 percent of the adult male population.

Of the 831 deputies elected, only 339 appeared in the opening session of the assembly. Thereafter, attendance averaged between 400 and 500. Over four fifths of the deputies had attended universities. Two thirds were judges, lawyers, professors, school masters, and bureaucrats. Only seventy-five came from the business community and sixty-eight were landowners, many of them noblemen. A scattering of clergymen, writers, journalists, medical men, and army officers made up the rest of the assembly. Not a single deputy came from the proletarist, a scant four were artisans, and only one was a peasant. The intellectual eminence of the academicians and of many other members won the Parliament the reputation of "the most distinguished constitutional body in history, unequalled in the quality and depth of the debates on the basic problems of political life." Others of a more critical attitude called it the "Professors Parliament" where learned doctrinaires, without practical experience and without an understanding of politics and of ordinary mankind, held forth endlessly on their favorite themes of governance.

Most of the deputies were moderate liberals who supported constitutional monarchy. They wanted freedom for the individual but wanted the suffrage limited to exclude the uneducated and the propertyless. Only a minority of radicals wanted universal male suffrage and sweeping social and economic reforms. The Parliament met in Saint Paul's Church, a large, circular, and architecturally unattractive building that proved an ill-chosen meeting place. The galleries that encircled the auditorium seated a thousand or more spectators whose raucous behavior, applause, and catcalls affected the debates. The building had no side rooms. When deputies wanted to confer privately with one another or with constituents, they had to meet elsewhere or during a session had to go out in the streets.[49]

In his opening remarks at the first session, the elected president of the Parliament, Heinrich von Gagern, a noble landowner and longtime liberal leader, declared, "We shall draw up a constitution for Germany, for the entire realm." Tumultuous applause greeted his words. Actually von Gagern had greatly simplified the task that confronted the assembly. To begin with, the deputies had to decide on the organization of the Parliament and to agree on its rules and regulations. Once organized, the assembly had to create a provisional government with its own executive and ministers. It had to decide whether to include non-German provinces such as Prussia's Posen and Austria's Bohemia in a united Germany. It had to establish and organize a federal government for the nonexistent German state and decide whether Austria or Prussia should lead the new state. The assembly set itself an enormous task, and with the wisdom gained by hindsight, an insuperable one. Its members overestimated the power of ideas and underestimated the strength of tradition and the importance of power in the making of political decisions.

The establishment of a provisional government with a regent as chief executive and a cabinet took six weeks of heated debate. Finally, the assembly chose Archduke John of Austria as regent. Some years earlier at a celebration in the Prussian city of Cologne, John had incautiously proposed a toast, "No Austria! No Prussia! One united Germany!" That toast, word of which spread through Germany, his marriage to the daughter of a peasant, his contribution to the economy and culture of the Austrian province of Styria, and his alienation from the imperial court in Vienna made him a popular figure among the liberals. Actually, as head of the provisional government, his powers were mostly meaningless. He named the ministers but had no authority over them. He was authorized to supervise the nonexistent armed forces of the government and name its commanders, to make appointments to nonexistent embassies and consulates, and with the assent of Parliament, to make war, peace, and treaties with other governments. Yet, despite the shadow existence of this provisional government, the diet of the Germanic Confederation, the *Bund,* transferred its own nebulous powers to the new government and went out of existence.[50]

At the outset the deputies divided themselves into monarchists and republicans. Six parties quickly formed, ranging from the extreme left, who wanted a unitary republic, to the extreme right, who wanted a unified German monarchy but with the preservation of the individual sovereign states. These groups became the forerunners of German political parties. Each party had its acknowledged leader who, by virtue of his position, became a leading figure in the Parliament. Whether radical or conservative, all of the deputies agreed on the unification of Germany, but the form of the union proved a thorny problem. Some form of a federal empire seemed to recommend itself, in which the component parts retained local autonomy. But which states should be included and who should be emperor? How could Austria, already an empire, be included in another empire? Or should Austria be excluded from the new empire?[51]

While these and other great questions remained unresolved, the Parliament involved itself in an even more pressing matter—war with Denmark over the duchies of Schleswig and Holstein. These two duchies lay in a peninsula stretching north from the German mainland between Germany and Denmark. Each had as its hereditary duke the king of Denmark, although Schleswig's population was more than half German and Holstein's almost entirely German. The duchies, which regarded themselves as indivisible because of arcane dynastic and genealogical entanglements, refused to recognize the hereditary claim of the Danish king, who wanted to integrate Schleswig into the Danish state. When he sent in his troops, the duchies revolted and declared themselves for the Frankfurt Parliament. The Parliament decided to come to the aid of the rebels in the name of German nationalism. It had no army and so asked the German states, and particularly Prussia, to provide the needed military forces. The mostly Prussian troops entered the war in April and pushed back the Danes. Then pressure from Russia, Britain, and France, who did not want Prussia in control of the peninsula, persuaded the king of Prussia to agree to an armistice in late August. The terms of the armistice strongly favored Denmark.

Germans, intoxicated with the new nationalist spirit, saw the armistice as a cowardly retreat before the great powers. Parliament at first refused to ratify the treaty, but reason quickly prevailed. Without their own troops to continue the war, the deputies had to acknowledge reality. On September 16 the Parliament, by a small majority of twenty-one, voted to accept the armistice. Outraged by the Parliament's about-face, mobs vandalized Saint Paul's Church and chased out the deputies. Armed rioters, joined by peasants who poured in from the surrounding countryside, filled the streets. Radical demagogues denounced the Parliament's majority as traitors to the German people. The badly frightened Parliament called for troops from the neighboring Grand Duchy of Hesse. When the soldiers arrived in Frankfurt, they quickly restored order, but not the prestige of the Parliament. Having knuckled under on the armistice, the Parliament had to call on the old princely order to protect itself from the people whom it claimed to represent. That move cost the assembly the support of many on the left. Meanwhile, the Parliament's involvement in the rebellion in Schleswig-Holstein had caused the powers to adopt a hostile stance toward German unification. The excesses of the rioters persuaded many middle-class liberals to reconsider their support of the revolution. Popular sovereignty began to lose its appeal, in favor of the peace and order of the days before the revolutions.[52]

The threat of radicalism and its program of social reform and republicanism had alarmed bourgeois liberals almost from the outset of the revolutions. A radical physician in Cologne, in a letter of March 26, 1848, to Moses Hess wrote, "You have no idea of the fear of our bourgeoisie of the word republican. To them it's identical with robbery, murder, Russian invasion. . . . " New waves of unrest stirred up by radicals aroused the growing numbers of the unemployed. Many of the middle class sensed that a new revolution threatening the sanctity of private property was in preparation. For their part, artisans and proletarians alike became increasingly disenchanted with middle-class leadership.[53]

In contrast to the swelling unrest in the cities, the revolutionary tide had ebbed out in the countryside. The peasant risings in early spring and the threat of a nationwide jacquerie frightened princes and revolutionary assemblies alike. No longer was there any question about emancipation. Everyone supported freedom. The debate concerned the details, especially whether to pay indemnification of the seigniors and how much. Beginning in late March, in state after state, decrees were issued that gave the peasants land and freedom. With their aims achieved, the peasants lost interest in the revolutions and withdrew from them.

The alienation of the workers, the withdrawal of the peasants, and the growing disillusionment of the middle classes opened the way for counter-revolution. The Junkers, the conservative landowners of eastern Prussia, organized a parliament of their own, and started what became an influential newspaper, the *Neue Preussische Zeitung*, whose motto was "Forward with God, for King and Fatherland," better known as the *Kreuzzeitung*, from the large cross on its front page. Emboldened by the turn of events, Frederick William began to consider a *coup d'état*. In late October the king decided the time had come. His newly appointed chief minister, Count Friedrich Wilhelm von Brandenburg, suspended the Prussian Assembly. On November 10 General von Wrangel, at the king's command, marched into Berlin with thirteen thousand soldiers and sixty cannons. Without firing a shot, he occupied the capital. Martial law was declared; police and soldiers shut down the clubs; newspapers or posters could not appear without official permission; the citizens' militia, formed in March, meekly surrendered its arms; and politically suspect persons were made to leave town.[54]

On December 5 the king dissolved the Prussian Assembly, which had spent months bickering over the draft of a constitution. On the same day the king promulgated a constitution as a free gift from the throne. Frederick William still believed that a constitution represented an illegal incursion into his sovereign power, and only after strong pressure from Count Brandenburg did he give in. Prussia had at last become a constitutional monarchy, but with a constitution that, in fact, established a barely disguised absolutism. The constitution affirmed the principle of divine right monarchy, allowed the monarch to suspend civil liberties, to issue decrees when the parliament was not in session, and to have control over the armed forces. It provided for a bicameral diet in which the upper house was to be a hereditary house of lords. The lower house was to be elected by a three-tier system of universal male suffrage based upon the amount of taxes paid. The king had the right of absolute veto over the diet's actions, and the cabinet ministers, appointed by the king, were responsible only to him. That constitution, which became even more restrictive with time, served as the model for Germany's constitution after unification in 1871 and remained the basic law of Prussia until 1918.[55]

The triumph of the counterrevolution in Berlin and Vienna inevitably reverberated in the lesser states that took their cues from Prussia and Austria.

The fires of revolution burned lower but were not yet extinguished. The Frankfurt Parliament continued to meet. On March 28, 1849, it adopted the long-debated constitution for a united Germany. The new state would have a hereditary emperor who would share authority with a ministry whom he would name but who would be responsible to a bicameral parliament. The governments and legislatures of the member states of the empire would name the members of the upper house, and the lower house would be elected by universal male suffrage.

The assembly, by a unanimous 290 votes, but with 248 abstentions, offered the crown to Frederick William. On April 3, in a carefully worded statement, the Prussian king thanked the assembly, but said that he could not accept its offer without the free consent of the rulers of the other German states. His explanation was a reasonable one, but that was not why he refused the offer. In letters to a confidant, he called the crown "a fictitious coronet baked out of mire and clay," that it "stank of the Revolution of 1848," and said that the Frankfurt Parliament "wanted to buckle a dog's collar on that fool, the Prussian king, that would shackle him indissolubly to the sovereignty of the people, and make him a bondsman of the Revolution of 1848."

Meanwhile, twenty-eight states had indicated their approval of the Parliament's proposed constitution, but the most important states—Prussia, Bavaria, Saxony, and Hannover—rejected it. Their rejection and Frederick Williams' refusal of the imperial crown gave the finishing blows to the Frankfurt Parliament. Some states recalled their deputies, and others left of their own volition. Only a rump of assorted radicals remained and continued to meet in Frankfurt until the end of May. Finding the official atmosphere there unfriendly, the rump moved to Stuttgart. Its radical proposals quickly alienated the government there, and on June 18 troops occupied the meeting hall and locked out the deputies. Such was the inglorious end of the Frankfurt Parliament.[56]

The cost in human lives in the revolutionary movements was relatively small. Germany suffered a greater human loss in the political refugees who fled after the defeat of the revolutions. These "Forty-Eighters," as they came to be called, included men of outstanding abilities who, like the refugees from Hitler's Germany, contributed significantly to the life and culture of the countries to which they migrated. Others who fled, abandoning or repressing their revolutionary ardor, returned to Germany, and had important careers there, among them Richard Wagner and the famed historian Theodor Mommsen.[57]

The revolution had failed. The counterrevolution had triumphed. The hopes of the bourgeois liberals that they could establish a united, constitutional German empire faded before the unrest and anarchy that were spawned by the deprivations and frustrations of artisans and workers and by the agitation of radicals. Disillusioned and dreading further disorders that might endanger the right of private property, the bourgeoisie did not oppose the counterrevolution, and, indeed, often actually supported it. Most, still seeking unification, abandoned the liberalism that had proven ineffective and chose the *Realpolitik* of Bismarck. In return for the support of the bourgeoisie, the state guaranteed social order and provided a favorable climate for business enterprise. By abandoning their liberalism, the bourgeoisie created a tradition of abdication of political responsibility and acquiescence in authoritarianism that has haunted German history since that time. That was the heavy and ultimately tragic price that Germany paid for the failure of the revolutions of 1848.[58]

Berliners joked that the only thing that the revolution accomplished was to allow smoking in the streets, hitherto prohibited. Actually, the revolutions were not without their lasting achievements. In state after state, they had completed the process of the emancipation of the peasantry. Aspects of seigniorial authority persisted in some places, especially in the eastern provinces of Prussia. Nonetheless, the emancipation of the peasantry spelled the end of the old order—with its hierarchical arrangement of society into separate estates, each with its own privileges and responsibilities. Now all were citizens of the state in which they lived, equal before its laws and, theoretically at least, possessed of the same rights and privileges as all other citizens.

Above all, the revolutionary movement had prepared the way for the ultimate unification of Germany. Despite their failures, the revolutions had welded the German people into a single political community. The dream of unification had once been restricted to bourgeois liberals and to intellectuals. The revolutions had converted that dream into a national movement supported by most Germans, and insuring that the effort would continue until unification became a reality.

Frederick William had his own plan for unification, which called for a voluntary association of German states with Prussia's king as its head and with a bicameral legislature representing the member states. The Union, as it was called, would join with Austria in an indissoluble federation headed by Austria. By October 1849 twenty-five of the thirty-seven German states had accepted the Prussian proposal. In March 1850 a parliament met at Erfurt, in Prussia, where the 195 delegates—138 of them from Prussia—approved the constitution of the new Union. Unification at last seemed on the verge of becoming a reality when the dream was shattered by Austria's Prince Felix zu Schwarzenberg. Until the late summer of 1848, the revolution in Hungary had occupied Austria's attention. With the Hungarians crushed, Schwarzenberg could concentrate on beating down the Prussian Union. With an amalgam of promises and threats, he lured away some of the German states. Then, at his invitation, representatives of smaller states met at Frankfurt in May 1850 and resurrected the Germanic Confederation that everyone thought had died quietly in the revolutionary spring of 1848. Now Germany had two unions. Confrontation was inevitable and came when the ruler of Hesse-Cassel asked for help to quell a revolt. Austria dispatched troops of the revived Confederation, and so did Prussia, since Hesse-Cassel had joined the Prussian Union. War seemed inevitable and both powers mobilized. Frederick William, dismayed by the turn of events and counseled by close advisers and army commanders that the war would result in revolution, abandoned his plans for union. Instead, he asked for a conference at Olmütz, in Moravia.[59]

On November 29, 1850, Otto von Manteufel, Prussia's chief minister, signed the document officially called the Punctuation of Olmütz, but that Germans called the Humiliation of Olmütz. Prussia yielded at every point. It gave up the Prussian Union, recognized and joined the reestablished Germanic Confederation, and accepted the supremacy of Austria in German affairs. The Prussian surrender had a devastating effect on the morale of many Germans. Rudolf von Delbruck, then in his early thirties and later a leading German statesman, remembered it as the saddest time of his life and in the lives of friends and acquaintances. Many feared the growth of Russia's power and influence. They believed that Napoleon's reputed prophecy at St. Helena—that in fifty years Europe would be either a republic or dominated by Russia—was about to come true.

The disappointment and the fears passed with time. Instead, Germans came to see Olmütz as a great turning point in the history of the relations between Austria and Prussia. Germans had long accepted the supremacy of Austria in Central Europe as a matter of course. Now things had changed with the rise of a pan-German national consciousness. Olmütz had taught those Germans who had their hearts and minds set on unification that Austria had to be excluded from German affairs.

With the rebirth of the Germanic Confederation, it seemed as if the clock had been turned back. The Confederation once again became the central agency of reaction and resolved to erase what it called "the democratic filth of the years of shame." It established a central committee to administer the policies of reaction and to make certain that no organization or institution would develop in any of the member states that would threaten internal order. The Confederation restored censorship and instituted controls on education to ensure a docile citizenry. Everywhere governments crushed or crippled dissident movements. The Prussian government, in its zeal to smash all opposition, confused Friedrich Fröbel, founder of the kindergarten movement, with his nephew Julius, a leader of the far left during the revolution, and so banned kindergartens on the grounds that they spread socialism and atheism.[60]

The reaction and the repressions notwithstanding, there was much that augured well for Germany's future in the postrevolutionary years. Above all else, the Germany economy that had "taken off" in the 1840s entered upon years of growth that would in a few decades carry Germany to the front rank of the economic powers of the world. Banking, industry, and commerce took on new life. Agriculture, till now preeminent in the economy, retreated before the emergence of a new kind of society increasingly dominated by industry. Conservative governments, recognizing the need to win and hold the support of the working class, introduced factory legislation. A number of states, at the demand of artisan guilds, had reintroduced restrictions on the freedom to enter certain trades, but within a few years repealed the legislation as industry grew and the importance and number of artisans dwindled.[61]

Finally, in a few short years, the seeming burial at Olmütz of the hope for unification was forgotten. The star of a great new leader began its ascent when Otto von Bismarck went to Frankfurt as Prussia's representative at the diet of the Germanic Confederation. An uncompromising conservative, he was determined to preserve traditional authority against the forces of change. He believed that it was Germany's destiny to become a unified and great power under the leadership of Prussia and its king. He chose guile and force as the way to achieve that goal. After three wars, with Denmark in 1864, with Austria in 1866, and with France in 1870–1871, success was his when on January 18, 1871, a new German empire was officially proclaimed with the king of Prussia as its emperor. His success was destined to have only a brief life. The empire, an anachronism in its own time, lasted only until 1918. German unification died in the rubble of Berlin in 1945, and proud Prussia itself disappeared, wiped out as a political entity by the victorious Allied Powers. Now, after 1989, the world watches and wonders and worries while a newly reunified Germany begins to shape its own future.

CHAPTER NINE

Russia:
Autocracy and
Intelligentsia

Baron Sigismund von Herberstein, in Muscovy in 1517 and again in 1526 as ambassador of the Holy Roman Emperor, reported that the tsar, "in the sway which he holds over his people, surpasses all the monarchs of the whole world. . . . He holds unlimited control over the lives and property of all his subjects; not one of his counsellors has sufficient authority to dare to oppose him, or even differ from him on any subject. They openly confess that the will of the prince is the will of God, and that whatever the prince does, he does by the will of God. . . . " Three hundred years later, visitors discovered that nothing had changed. "No one man in the world has as much power as the tsar," wrote one visitor. "The will of the tsar is the supreme law: he orders and all obey." The first article of the *Svod Zakonov*, the code of laws of the Russian empire, first published in 1832 in forty-five huge volumes, declared, "The Tsar of All the Russias is an autocratic and absolute monarch. God himself commands us to obey the Tsar's supreme authority, not from fear alone, but as a matter of conscience."

Europe knew other absolute monarchs, but none possessed the plenitude of power held by the ruler of Russia, Tsar Nicholas I. Even crowned heads held him in awe. Queen Victoria, whom Nicholas visited in 1844, wrote to her uncle Leopold that "it really seems like a dream when I think that we breakfast and walk out with the greatest of earthly Potentates as quietly as we walked . . . with anyone."[1]

A vast empire owed its allegiance to this one man. His realm marched more than halfway around the world, from the borders of Central Europe through Siberia and across the Bering Sea to Alaska, and from the shores of the Arctic Ocean to the Caspian and Black Seas. Nearly all of this immense realm was a vast tableland, interrupted only by occasional hills and by the long low ridge of the Urals that separated European Russia from Siberia. Without visible boundaries and with few geographical features to lend it variety, the landscape seemed to stretch on into infinity. Even the climate had a sameness. With no neighboring great sea to temper the extremes of its weather, winters were long and hard and summers short and hot.

Between 60 and 70 million people lived scattered across these millions of square miles. Nearly all of them lived in the European part of the empire. The monotony of the landscape seemed to mirror itself in the lack of variety in the villages and towns and in the people themselves. Visitors from the West found a startling homogeneity that seemed to them unnatural. Most of the towns seemed indistinguishable from one another. They had wide, unpaved streets, low buildings, a military barrack, and nearly everything made of wood, including the sidewalks. The oldest cities always had a kremlin—a fortified walled citadel on a commanding rise.[2]

The two capitals, Moscow with 365,000 people in the center of European Russia, and Saint Petersburg, in the far northwest corner with about 485,000, were the greatest cities of the empire. Travelers described as breathtaking their first view of Moscow with its myriad of towers and golden church domes, and its great kremlin rising out of a sea of red roofs. Saint Petersburg, built at great cost in human lives by Peter I early in the eighteenth century, was a European and not a Russian city in architecture and appearance. It was a handsome city and much admired by visitors when first they arrived. Accustomed to the noise and bustle of the great cities of the West, they quickly became disconcerted by the almost eerie silence that ruled over the city. Even at times of public celebration, when people thronged the streets, such as at the end of Lent, there seemed almost no noise save the sound of carriages and occasional bursts of music from open theater doors.[3]

To the foreign visitor, and to many Russians, life in Nicholas's empire, whether in town or village, was clouded by dark ignorance, by despotic misgovernment, by pervasive corruption, by hateful prejudices, by brutality, and above all, by the servitude of its millions of peasants. Marquis de Custine, after visiting Russia in 1839, wrote that anyone who lived there would be happy to live anywhere else. Visitors noticed that when Russian nobles, fortunate enough to get the required permission to travel abroad, left Russia they seemed as happy as schoolboys on a holiday. When they came back, they were subdued and unsmiling and talked little and then in low tones, and seemed saddened by the prospect of returning to their homeland. Wealthy nobles and intellectuals fleeing from tsarist oppression made Paris their Mecca. The nobles, spending with a free hand, astounded Parisians by their opulence and scandalized them by the behavior of some of their women. To the intellectuals, as Alexander Herzen explained, Paris was synonymous with freedom. They immersed themselves in the literary, political, and philosophical movements that flourished in the French capital.[4]

Visitors to Russia were dismayed by the dirt that gathered everywhere, in streets, in public buildings, and in homes. They discovered, to their disgust, that vermin of all varieties infested hotels, inns, and private homes. They found even more offensive and shocking the seemingly universal Russian habit of striking with fists, sticks, or whips persons lower on the social scale, for no perceptible reason and with no fear of reprisal. Ivan Golovin, a Russian exile living in Paris, explained that his countrymen imbibed the mania of beating with their mother's milk. The pecking order began at the throne and continued on down to the peasant who was beaten by everyone. The peasant, for his part, cruelly beat his wife and his horse. As Golovin put it, every Russian was both hammer and anvil.[5]

As elsewhere in Europe the people who lived in this vast land were divided into three great categories—nobles, middle class, and lower class. In Russia, however, the nature and characteristics of each of these categories differed sharply from its analogue in the rest of Europe. In these other lands the nobles formed an independent privileged caste whose origins reached back to feudal times before the emergence of national states. They had contended for power with their sovereigns, and had successfully limited the authority of the throne. In Russia the nobility was the creation of the absolutism and its creature. The princes of Muscovy in their savage ascent to power over all of Russia had all but wiped out the old aristocracy of the princedoms they had conquered. They chose new men to serve them. These new nobles, whose status depended upon service to the tsar, proved willing instruments of his absolutism, subservient to his every wish. Peter I (who gave himself the appellation of Great) regularized the principle that social rank and privilege rose from service to the tsar when, in 1722, he established a Table of Ranks that contained fourteen grades. Men of nonnoble birth acquired hereditary nobility when they entered the fourteenth grade in the military service, or when they reached the eighth grade in the bureaucracy. This automatic elevation to nobility made the Russian nobility an open-ended caste. New men constantly flowed into it as the army and the civil service grew. Between 1825 and 1845, some twenty thousand men of nonnoble birth gained hereditary nobility through promotion in the Table of Ranks. All of the children of the new hereditary nobles acquired noble status along with their fathers, so that the total number of nobles rose sharply to about 550,000 to 600,000 people, or about 1 percent of the empire's population. Upper ranks of the nobility feared that their class was becoming too common. In response to their wishes, Tsar Nicholas I, in 1845, decreed that henceforth hereditary nobility would come only with the eighth rank in the military and the fifth in the civil service.[6]

As the reward for service to the state, the tsars gave the nobility special and valuable privileges. These included a monopoly on the ownership of serfs, nearly unlimited powers over the persons and belongings of these serfs, the exclusive right to own populated land, broad local police and judicial authority, exemption from military conscription, freedom from taxation, and freedom from corporal punishment. Until 1762 every adult male noble had to serve in the military or civil service in order to retain his status as a nobleman. Then Peter III ended the compulsory service. Despite this relaxation most nobles chose to serve if only because refusal to serve diminished them in the eyes of their peers. In the usual pattern the young nobleman entered the tsar's service at twenty, continued in it for five to ten years, and then, reaching a respectable rank, retired and returned to his estate.[7]

The Russian nobility differed from other European nobilities even in the matter of titles. Prince (*kniaz*) had been the sole native title. Until the eighteenth century, only descendants of the rulers of the medieval Russian princedoms could claim it. Then the tsars awarded the title to favorites, albeit sparingly. They also awarded the titles of count or baron to others whom they wished to honor. These titles did not possess the luster attached to them in the rest of Europe. Some of the greatest families had no titles and apparently felt no need for them. The relative unimportance of titles did not mean that the Russian nobility was indifferent to the symbols of status and rank. For instance, every grade in the Table of Ranks had an honorific term of address attached to it, ranging from "Well-born" to "Excellency." The appropriate title had always to be used when addressing these men. Decorations, too, had great symbolic and social significance. Peter I, on his return home from a famed trip to Western Europe in 1697–1698, had created the first Russian order. His successors created other orders—in the 1840s there were eight of them—each with its own medal and ribbon, and most with a stipend attached to them. In addition, the throne awarded a large number of decorations in recognition of outstanding services in the army or in civilian life. Foreigners were struck by the large number of people that they saw wearing decorations.[8]

In law and in theory, all nobles were equally noble and equally privileged. In actuality they ranged from men of fantastic wealth and great influence to petty nobles who could scarcely be distinguished from their serfs. Still others owned neither land nor serfs and depended for their livelihoods upon their inadequate salaries as army officers or bureaucrats and whatever they could make by corruption. Russians measured real property—by far the empire's most important form of wealth—not by acreage but by the number of adult male serfs, called "souls," owned by a nobleman. That way of measuring wealth ended only in 1861 with the emancipation of the serfs. Official data from the 1850s showed that of the 103,880 nobles who owned "souls," 43 percent owned only 3 percent of the 10.5 million serf souls. At the other end of the scale, 1 percent of the serf owners owned 29 percent of all serf souls. These greatest proprietors lived in unbelievable luxury, waited upon by hundreds of servants chosen from among the serfs. They had serf orchestras and actors and dwarfs and jesters and teachers and singers and artists, all existing for the pleasure and convenience of their masters. Lesser proprietors had smaller staffs, but still kept more servants than seemed reasonable by any other than Russian standards.

Despite their enormous wealth, these greatest proprietors could not meet the costs of their lavish way of life. They piled up debts of spectacular proportions. In 1838 Count D. N. Sheremetyev, who owned 300,000 people, spent 3,442,500 rubles, exceeding his income for that year by 1,200,000 rubles. So he borrowed and kept on borrowing, and by 1858 he owed six million rubles. Grandees like Sheremetyev and men of lesser wealth borrowed money by mortgaging their serfs with government lending agencies that the state had established for their convenience. By the mid-forties, nobles had mortgaged off 50 percent of their adult male serfs with these agencies, and by 1859 that number had risen to 66 percent. The lenient policy of the government's lending agencies encouraged excessive borrowing and fostered improvidence and profligacy. These institutions granted extensions freely and rarely foreclosed, since they had as their purpose to preserve the land of the nobility. They allowed delinquents to remain in possession of gifts from the state. Whether a man owned thousands of serfs or was a landless, serfless bureaucrat, the nobleman held his noble status at the sufferance of the tsar. At any time and for any reason, the autocrat could strip him of his noble rank and reduce him to whatever status the tsar wished.[9]

In Western Europe the nobility had not been alone in contending with royal authority. Men of the urban middle class had struggled for the rule of law, for the rights of the individual, and for freedom from arbitrary interference by the government. In Russia the middle class was so small and inconsequential that it seemed all but nonexistent. It lacked the wealth, the status, and the inclination to challenge the autocracy. Like the nobility, it acquiesced in the tradition of compulsion and servility. The unimportance of the middle class served as both cause and effect of Russia's economic backwardness. In earlier centuries the economic policies of the emergent absolutism had favored the nobility and the monasteries with extensive commercial privileges at the expense of urban merchants. Unlike the nobility of most of continental Europe, Russian nobles engaged in trade without losing caste; indeed, the tsar himself had, through his agents, been the chief trader of the realm. As a consequence an important bourgeois class failed to develop in the formative years of the Russian empire. The competition of peasants had further inhibited the growth of a middle class. These peasants, many of them serfs, produced goods and services in their villages for the consumption of their masters, opened up shops in town, became peddlers and even interregional traders. A few of them started factories, nominally owned by their masters, and employed other peasants as their workers.

The absence of a sizable, aggressive middle class meant that Russia lacked the pools of capital, the private banking system, the commercial technique and skills, and the political and social ambitions that the bourgeoisie of other lands had developed over the centuries. The typical Russian merchant, bearded and clad in a caftan, resembled the haggling merchant of the Orient rather than the educated and sophisticated Western man of business. Every sizable town had its bazaar where the merchants displayed their wares in their small shops or stalls. Many cities and towns had annual fairs; by the mid-nineteenth century, there were over five thousand of these fairs. Most were small operations that served as markets for local products, or, at most, as regional markets. A few had interregional and even international connections. The greatest fair of them all was held each summer at Nizhni Novgorod at the confluence of the Oka and Volga rivers, not far from the borders of Asia. Beginning in early June and lasting for six weeks, the fair attracted thousands of merchants from Europe and from Asia to buy and sell a myriad of products from and to one another.

In Western Europe the expansion of trade and industry had produced an ever increasing class of the proletariat. Poor, exploited, and miserably housed, the proletarians depended for their livelihoods upon the sale of their labor to their employers. In Russia, where agriculture was far and away the chief industry, that class barely existed. Over 90 percent of the empire's 60 million inhabitants belonged to the peasantry. Save for a relative handful, they were not free. Over half of them belonged to the state and the imperial court. The rest were serfs owned by noble landowners. Serfdom took root in Russia during the same centuries in which it largely disappeared in the West. By the middle of the seventeenth century, peasants who lived on land owned by nobles or monasteries lost their freedom and became the serfs of their land-lords. The rationale for their enserfment lay primarily in the thrust of the tsars to achieve absolute rule. To reach that goal they needed the services of the new nobility that they had created. As time went on, the tsars intensified the bonds of serfdom and transformed millions of peasants who lived on state-owned land into the less onerous but still unfree status of state peasant.[10]

Serfdom in Europe had a thousand-year history so that, not unexpectedly, it took many forms with differing degrees of dependence. The tragic fate of the Russian peasant was that his serfdom was of the deepest and most com-plete kind. His owner could remove him from his holding and convert him into a domestic servant or a landless field hand. He could sell him without land, give him to someone else, or gamble him away. He could demand what-ever obligations he wanted in cash, kind, or labor. Generally, these obligations were fixed by custom, but the serfowner could always change them. He could have his serfs whipped or jailed. Laws of the 1830s and 1840s set limits to the punitive powers of the serfowners, but lords freely exceeded these limits and openly bragged about it.

In short, the Russian serf was indistinguishable from a slave save in one respect. The law recognized the serf as a legal person, while the slave was the chattel of his owner. In practice this meant that the serf had the dubious priv-ilege of paying taxes to the state and of being drafted into the army. The serf lived at the mercy of the whims, appetites, and temper of his owner. Many, and probably most, serf owners did not abuse their people. Nonetheless, the nearly unlimited authority they had over their serfs, the fact that the serfs had no legal recourse, and perhaps most important, the absence of social disap-proval by the serfowner's peers of mistreatment of his peasants, opened the door to callousness and brutality.

In addition to the obligations they owed to their owner, whether a noble-man or the state, the peasants had to meet the demands of the government. Of these, the most important were the soul tax and military service, both of them introduced by Peter I. The soul tax, levied annually upon each adult male was the same amount for all, with only noblemen, clergy, and a few numerically unimportant groups exempted from it. The tax seemed small, but with large acreages it accumulated. The obligation to provide recruits for the army came every other year. Usually the call was for less than seven recruits per thousand male souls. Each village, or its lord, chose the recruits from among men between twenty and thirty-five. Each village had to outfit its recruits and pay for their transportation to their military posts. Army service was a cruel and heavy burden that tore away the recruit from family and village and forced him to live under harsh and even barbarous discipline. Until 1793 the recruit served for life. In that year the term of service was reduced to twenty-five years, and in 1834 to twenty years on active duty and five years in the reserve.

Nearly all peasants lived in village communes that periodically redistributed the land of the village to equalize the holdings of each household. The frequency of the redistribution fluctuated from every year to every ten years or more. The heads of each household met together at set intervals to supervise the redistribution of the land, to elect communal officials, to levy and collect from each household the taxes levied upon the village as a unit, and to conduct any other communal business. Despite the leveling effected by the redistribution of the land, some peasants were more prosperous than others. They had more fertile land, or supplemented their incomes by trade or handicraft production. A handful managed to gain much wealth through trade or manufacturing. Their achievement paid tribute to their outstanding entrepreneurial skills. Most peasants lived out their lives on the margin of subsistence. When famines or other calamities struck, they rarely had the resources to carry them through the bad times. Starvation, death, brigandage, and mass flights marked those evil days. As in other lands, observers were overwhelmed by the filth, stench, vermin, and general wretchedness of most peasant housing.[11]

The subservience of the peasant, the appalling squalor in which he lived, and his ragged and filthy clothing made him an object of contempt to the rest of society. His social superiors thought of him as different from and inferior to mankind. In turn, the centuries of servility and the contempt and disdain that was their lot left their mark upon the peasants. They were ignorant, superstitious, and uncooperative, instinctively resisting any innovations in their traditional way of doing things. Most of the time peasants accepted their oppression without protest. They tried, as men have ever since organized society began, to evade their obligations, and they paid up peacefully enough when they were caught. But every once in a while, they would suddenly decide that they had enough and would fight back. Often only a single village would rebel, but sometimes mass discontent and disturbances convulsed an entire region. Most often the protests were nonviolent, such as the refusal to render certain dues or services, or flight to the open land of the frontiers in search of freedom. But sometimes they seized up their scythes and sickles and pitchforks and axes and, driven by some blind fury, poured out of their villages to beat and murder the lords and estate officials who ruled over them, and to pillage the homes and burn the records of their oppressors. They protested against specific injustices of their masters, such as an increase in obligations, rather than against the servile system that held them in bondage. They did not direct their discontents and their risings against the tsar. On the contrary, they cherished the tsar as their "Little Father," and thought of him as their protector. Their enemies were their masters who, they believed, gave the tsar evil counsels, kept the knowledge of the true state of affairs from him, and circumvented orders that they believed he gave to raise the peasantry from their lowly condition.[12]

Nearly always the disturbances quickly burned themselves out. Then during the reign of Nicholas, peasant unrest took on a new dimension and a new significance. Soviet scholars counted 1,904 rural disturbances between 1826 and 1849, some so threatening that troops had to be called out to restore order 381 times. Contemporary reports of the Ministry of the Interior revealed that between 1835 and 1854 rioting peasants killed 144 estate owners and twenty-nine of their stewards and made unsuccessful attempts on the lives of seventy-five other lords and stewards. Meanwhile, an always increasing number of peasants fled to still open frontiers.[13]

The rise in peasant unrest was both cause and effect of a new and steadily growing conviction among people of the upper orders that Russia must rid itself of serfdom. Tsar Nicholas, fearfully concerned with the increase of rural risings, became convinced that the continued existence of serfdom menaced the power and the well-being of the state itself. Reports from trusted officials, such as Count Beckendorff, his chief of police, deepened his concern. Beckendorff, in 1839, told the tsar that "The entire soul of the people turns to one goal, to liberation. . . . Serfdom is a powder keg under the state." Nicholas appointed special committees and spent long hours with them discussing reforms. But he could not bring himself to take decisive measures. He not only had a built-in repugnance toward any change. He also feared that ending or even limiting the powers of the serf owners might work against the absolutism. A discontented nobility might seek new powers for itself at the expense of the throne as compensation for the privileges it had lost. And clearly most serf owners looked upon any move to reform serfdom as a direct threat to their property rights over land and peasants.

In an autocratic society the views of the autocrat obviously have enormous influence in shaping the opinions of his subjects. But Nicholas was not alone in shaping the opinion that serfdom must end. Already in the late eighteenth and early nineteenth centuries, economists had attacked serfdom as unprofitable, intellectuals had charged it as being immoral, and writers had condemned it as inhuman. By 1836 the French ambassador at Saint Petersburg reported that "everyone agrees that the welfare of Russia depends upon the freeing of the serfs."[14] The heaviest attack on the institution came in the

1840s, in what is justly called the Golden Age of Russian Culture. Nicholas's empire became the scene of a spectacular intellectual outburst by a new generation of writers, philosophers, and critics. The educated Russian public, small in number but influential, listened intently to what these young men, most of them from the nobility, had to say. Nearly every one of them had a burning hatred of serfdom and wanted to rid Russia of it. The conviction in the highest circles that serfdom must go, stimulated by the intensification of peasant unrest, served in turn to encourage more unrest. Somehow word of the high-level concerns and debates filtered down to the villages, carried there probably by servants in the great houses who overheard their masters discussing these matters. Misinformation and false rumors of impending emancipation spread through the land.

Nicholas did allow certain limited reforms in serfdom but they had a barely perceptible effect. He had more success with the state peasantry where, under the inspired leadership of Count P. D. Kiselev, material improvements were introduced in the condition of the peasants. Finally, his unending preoccupation with the peasant problem readied the empire for ultimate emancipation. His concern created and encouraged an awareness of the problem in the highest circles of government. By the time he died in 1855, it was clear that reform was inevitable. For that realization Nicholas, more than anyone else, was responsible. That was his greatest legacy to Russia and to his son and heir, Alexander II, who won fame as the Tsar-Liberator when, in 1861, he decreed the emancipation of the serfs.[15]

Nicholas, the man who ruled as autocrat and absolute monarch over noble, burgher, and peasant alike, had not expected to wield this mighty power. He was the third son of Tsar Paul. In 1801 a band of Guards officers burst into Paul's bedroom and brutally murdered him. Paul's eldest son and successor, Alexander, knew of the plot to depose his father, but may not have known that the plan included his father's assassination. In any event, as Alexander I, he did not punish the murderers. An indecisive man, he was given to sudden enthusiasms that he then abandoned. The uncertainties that clouded his reign pursued him even after his death in 1825. For years a fanciful story persisted that he had feigned death and had gone to Siberia where he lived as a saintly monk until his death in 1864.

Alexander had no children and normally Paul's second son, Constantine, would have succeeded him. Constantine had a remarkably unattractive personality and manner. Princess Lieven, who knew him well and had for a time been his mistress, described him as dissolute, cruel, and generally hated and feared by his countrymen, who allowed him one quality, that of being a coward. Princess Lieven, in light of her ended liaison with Constantine, might not have been impartial in her opinion, but other contemporaries held closely parallel views.[16] Russia escaped his rule because in 1822, Constantine renounced his right of succession in favor of his younger brother Nicholas. Constantine wanted to divorce his wife, from whom he had been separated for twenty years (finding him unbearable, she had returned home to Germany and refused to return), and marry a commoner. Tsar Alexander granted his permission on the condition that Constantine would give up his right of succession. Constantine, who had long indicated that he did not look forward to ascending the throne, readily agreed.

No public announcement was made of Constantine's stepping aside in favor of Nicholas. When Alexander died unexpectedly in 1825, confusion ruled for nearly three weeks. Constantine, obnoxious as always, refused to make a public announcement of his renunciation of the throne, even though he had no intention of claiming it. A secret society of young noble army officers, taking advantage of the turmoil, attempted a *coup d'état* on December 14 in Saint Petersburg. They wanted to transform the autocracy into a constitutional monarchy, along with other reforms that included the emancipation of the serfs. On that same day, Nicholas took the oath as Tsar Nicholas I and proceeded to put down the ill-planned attempted *coup*. His speedy and ruthless repression of the rising, the opening act of his reign, set the tone for his rule that endured for thirty years. For their part the Decembrists, as they came to be called, became the symbols of the struggle against the autocracy, and they won lasting fame as the founders of Russia's revolutionary tradition. Actually, most of the defeated rebels nearly fell over one another in their haste to beg the tsar's forgiveness and to tell all that they knew about the conspiracy.

The new tsar, twenty-nine when he ascended the throne, was an extraordinarily handsome man. Over six feet tall, with an erect carriage, a perfect profile, and a deep and sonorous voice, he was a striking and truly majestic figure. In his forties he put on weight and began to lose his hair, but people still thought him a grand-looking personage. John Lothrop Motley, in 1841 the newly appointed secretary of the American legation at Saint Petersburg, thought him one of the most handsome men he had ever seen: "every inch a king," wrote Motley, and deserving of all the praise of his appearance. His eyes were his most striking feature. Large and bright, they had pale lashes so that they appeared unshaded. They were wintery eyes, the color of pewter, that to Alexander Herzen seemed without a trace of mercy. He smiled rarely and when he did, his eyes did not smile, nor was his smile a happy one. On his visit to Britain in 1844, he gave Queen Victoria and Prince Albert the impression of an unhappy man whose immense power and position weighed heavily and painfully on him. In fact, he was by nature a pessimist and a worrier who, as his foreign minister, Count Nesselrode, said, was inclined "always to see black."[17]

In his youth distinguished scholars had served as his tutors, but their efforts seemed only to create a contempt in their erstwhile student for intellectual matters—he called them "abstractions." He enjoyed and showed aptitude for military science, especially military engineering. He was a hard and cruel man, a ruthless disciplinarian with a passion for precision and orderliness in small matters. He had an unforgiving and vindictive nature, and ordered harsh and sometimes barbarous punishments and tortures for those who ran afoul of his laws or his whims. Like many such people, he was also very emotional and sentimental, easily moved to tears, whether of sympathy, of sorrow, or of rage. He had an inordinate, indeed, almost a pathological sense of duty, devoting nearly every waking hour to governing his empire. He carefully read reports and made extensive marginal comments, involved himself in all manner of decision, no matter how trivial, and sometimes personally directed investigations of persons accused of being subversive. He went on endless tours of inspection of military installations and schools, often without warning, and he frequently traveled abroad. He was deeply religious, attended church services faithfully, and felt certain that God directed him in whatever he did.[18]

Life at court was formal and stiff, punctuated by brilliant balls attended by the elite of society. Twice a year, on New Year's Day and on the emperor's birthday, Nicholas held public receptions. A throng of several thousands, which included carefully selected burghers and peasants, poured in to pay their respects to their sovereign and his empress. Despite precautions, nimble-fingered guests in 1839 relieved the Sardinian ambassador of his watch; others lost silk handkerchiefs, and a French visitor had his purse lifted. Easter, the most important holy day of the Orthodox Church calendar, was celebrated by a great gala at the court. Only the elite of the empire attended the court's receptions and balls, but Nicholas did not shut himself off from his lesser subjects. He often rode in an old open barouche or on a sleigh in the streets of Saint Petersburg, or walked along Nevsky Prospekt, the great avenue of the capital. On his constant travels, too, through his empire, many of his subjects saw him.[19]

As a younger son, Nicholas had been destined for a military career. He gained a life-long infatuation with army life, specifically of the spit-and-polish parade ground variety. The discipline and the unquestioning obedience of soldiers to the commands of their superiors appealed to his passion for precision and orderliness. He believed that man's most noble calling was that of a soldier, ready to give his life in defense of tsar and country. He considered a strong and loyal army his first concern. With about one million men in uniform, Russia had by far the largest army in Europe. The government spent much of its revenues on the army, but it proved not enough, and economies at the expense of other governmental functions became the order of the day. The soldiers themselves spent most of their time in preparing for parades and reviews and too little time in training for combat, and the officers lacked knowledge of military techniques. The fact was that the army, in which Nicholas took so much pride, was in lamentable shape as a fighting machine.[20]

A despot to his innermost being, Nicholas seemed haunted by a fear of freedom. He could not abide even the expression of the slightest objection to absolute rule. He harbored a particular hatred of constitutional monarchy, calling it a government of lies, fraud, and corruption. In what an English contemporary called "the insolence of unbridled power," Nicholas had an unshakable faith in his own infallibility. One of his favorite expressions was "God is with Us! Understand it, you people, and submit, for God is with Us!" In his mind that justified his despotism. He insisted that all decision-making powers must rest with him. One of his ministers wrote in 1849, "I have neither my own thoughts nor my own will. I am a blind tool of the tsar."[21]

An obsessive insecurity underlay Nicholas's insistence that he alone must run his empire. The Decembrist revolt at the outset of his reign and his own paranoia had convinced him that he must be always on guard against ideas and innovation that would dispute his autocratic rule. "The time, the talents, the activity and ambition of Nicholas," wrote the secretary of the American legation at Saint Petersburg who succeeded Motley, "are devoted almost wholly to suppress the whispers that speak of revolution or of liberty. Haunted with real or fancied dangers, troubled with dreams or imaginings of conspiracy, he strives with his forebodings as with an enemy at his palace gates, and would obliterate the very shadows proclaiming events which are to come."[22]

In seeking to run his vast empire single-handedly, Nicholas set an impossible task for himself, made even more impossible by the corruption and inefficiency of the bureaucrats and army officers upon whom the tsar depended. Bribery of officials was universal, from the steps of the throne down to the petty clerk in a distant provincial town. For a suitable cash payment, a person could gain exemption from the decrees of the tsar. Thieves caught red-handed escaped punishment by splitting their booty with the police. Bureaucrats stole government supplies with impunity. Most of the corruption was petty, if only because of limited opportunity. The higher the bureaucrat, the greater the peculation. The chief of police in Saint Petersburg stole over 100,000 rubles from money provided to send 17,000 recruits to the Caucasus. The men set out with inadequate food and supplies, and over half of them perished before they arrived at their destination. Army officers of high rank concealed casualties and continued to draw money for rations and equipment for dead soldiers.

Corruption flourished because the throne allowed it and the public accepted it as a normal pattern of behavior. In his famed play, *The Inspector-General*, which he wrote in 1836, N. V. Gogol portrayed the entire bureaucracy of a provincial city as knaves who preyed on the people whom they were supposed to serve. Gogol intended his play as a critical satire, but instead his audiences regarded it as a delightful comedy. Reportedly, Nicholas himself told the author, "I've never laughed so much, dear Gogol, as I did at your play," to which Gogol replied, "I did not write it for your laughter, Your Majesty."[23]

The curse of corruption was aggravated by the inefficiency of the bureaucracy. The men recruited for the lower positions were often barely literate. They spent their days copying, often in nearly illegible handwriting and with many misspellings, the enormous number of documents spawned by the bureaucracy. Pushing papers from one desk to another became the chief occupation of many bureaucrats. Agencies, flooded with official documents, burned older ones to make room in their files for the new ones. Every official action produced an enormous amount of paper. Understandably, enormous backlogs piled up, so that it could take years for a government agency or a court of law to carry through a routine procedure.[24]

Miraculously, in this swamp of corruption and inefficiency, there appeared in the 1840s a group of young second-level bureaucrats devoted to the public service and its reform. Most of them came from impoverished and often landless noble families or from the middle class, so that they had no special stake in the existing state of affairs. Ambitious to advance, they made it their concern to learn as much as they could about the inner workings of the government and about local conditions throughout the empire. Themselves men of education and intellect, they associated with and were influenced by men of the intelligentsia, some of whom had themselves joined the bureaucracy. This new generation of bureaucrats, men like N. A. Miliutin, Y. Solovyev, Y. F. Samarin, and others, were destined to be the principal architects of the great movements of reform that began with the emancipation of the serfs in 1861.[25]

Tsar Nicholas was not alone in the insecurity that haunted him. The upper ranks of Russian society suffered an insecurity of their own that revealed itself in their feeling of inferiority to Western Europeans. The Russians felt, with reason, that they lagged behind the West in just about every aspect of life. To narrow the gap, they imitated Western ways and apologized for Russian mannerisms. Friedrich von Gagern, in Russia in 1839 as a member of a visiting Dutch prince's entourage, asked General Kavelin, tutor of the heir apparent to the throne, in what branches of science and industry Russia had made the greatest progress. The General, in all seriousness, replied "in every branch" because, said he, "Russians possess the genius of imitation." Gagern, amused by the answer, called that "an entirely new kind of genius." The Russians had a special regard for the Germans, whom they both admired and disliked for their diligence, their perseverance, and their superior education. Germans handled much of Russia's foreign trade and had a major role in the early stages of Russia's industrialization. Germans from the Baltic provinces of Courland, Livonia, and Estonia, which Russia had annexed in the eighteenth century, held a disproportionately large number of high offices at court, in the army, and in the bureaucracy, particularly in the Foreign Ministry. The importance of these Balts stirred resentment among Russian nationalists, who regarded them as a foreign element who refused to become Russified. Russians especially resented the air of superiority affected by the Germans. Prince P. Dolgorukov undoubtedly spoke for many Russians when he said of Count Nesselrode, the foreign minister and a native German (albeit not a Balt), that "he is one of those who believe that God, after resting on the seventh day of creation, on the eighth day created the first German."[26]

The travel accounts of Westerners who visited Russia added fuel to the Russian feeling of insecurity. Almost to a man the visitors were critical and often contemptuous of most of what they saw and heard. The account of Marquis de Custine, published in Paris in 1843, described the Russians as a half-savage, almost barbaric, and lackluster people. Custine's account contained many shortcomings. His tour lasted less than three months, and he himself wrote that he did not see much and guessed a great amount. He dealt in sweeping generalizations, repeated unfounded gossip with not even the pretense of objectivity, and was often factually in error. Despite these flaws the book, quickly translated into other languages, enjoyed great popular success, doubtless because it confirmed long-held Western prejudices about the Russians. Russian readers publicly expressed their outrage, but in private conversations they admitted that the book held much that was true.[27]

The sense of inferiority and the imitation of Western ways proved strongest at the pinnacle of Russian society. Clustered in Saint Petersburg and

Moscow, the manners, dress, and entertainments of these people differed not at all from the elite of the great capitals of the West. They all spoke French, the common language of Europe's high society, some of them speaking and writing it more fluently and correctly than Russian. The tsar himself habitually spoke in French, and wrote his letters to his wife in that language. The Europeanization of the elite received its greatest impetus in the late eighteenth century. Émigrés fleeing the French Revolution sought sanctuary in Russia. To earn their livings they became tutors of the children of the great families and indoctrinated their pupils with the social graces and aristocratic values of the West. Those noblemen who by choice or by economic necessity did not abandon the traditional ways were derided and made the butt of jokes. Their embrace of Western European culture isolated the upper strata of the nobility from the culture and traditions of the mass of the Russian people. About the only things that the elite had in common with their countrymen were the Orthodox religion and subservience to the will of the tsar.[28]

Nicholas feared that Western political ideologies would filter into his empire along with Western manners and culture. His dread of new political ideas impelled him to take extraordinary measures to combat them. He attacked at two levels: he advanced an ideology of his own, and he intensified the government's repression of men and ideas. The ideology, called Official Nationalism, justified and defended his autocratic rule and the established order. The triad "Orthodoxy, Autocracy, Nationality" epitomized its principles. Orthodoxy meant the control of the spiritual lives of the people by the official state religion, the Russian Orthodox Church. Autocracy meant the absolute rule of the tsar, because man was weak and needed a strong hand to govern him. The meaning of Nationality was obscure but included the idealization of the Russian people as superior to the people of other nations and as supporters of the tsarist regime.

The tsar attacked at the second level by the creation of a new police force, called the Third Section of His Majesty's Private Imperial Chancery. The Third Section, headed by Count A. N. Beckendorff, became the most powerful arm of the government. Nicholas assigned it the mission to discover and keep him informed about the dangers, real, potential, and imagined, that threatened the regime. The Third Section had no limits on its power to investigate any organization or any individual. Surveillance did not end at the frontiers. Beginning in the 1840s special efforts were made to report on the activities of Russians abroad. Russians who wanted to visit other lands had to ask for the tsar's personal permission. That could not be without its risks. Nicholas considered such requests as evidence of ingratitude for his rule and an implied criticism of the regime. To discourage foreign travel, he ordered that no one could go abroad before the age of twenty-five and imposed a tax of 800 rubles a year on passports. The Russians who succeeded in gaining the emperor's permission could not stay abroad for more than five years and could be summoned back to the homeland at any time.[29]

As part of the defense against the importation of Western ideas, the bureaucracy placed many obstacles against the entry of foreign visitors. The inconveniences encountered by visitors before they disembarked at Saint Petersburg were intensified by a decree in 1844 that ordered visitors to report to the Third Section immediately upon arrival at the city for another examination of their passports and for interrogation. Annoying as the procedures were at Saint Petersburg, they seemed almost trivial compared to the delays, red tape, and deliberate inefficiencies that beset those who sought to enter Nicholas's empire at other places.

Censorship, already severe by any standard, became more rigorous, especially after the outbreak of revolutions in Central and Western Europe in the spring of 1848. Despite its severity, the censorship allowed a certain amount of toleration, possibly because of the inefficiency of the censors. Journals printed articles about conditions in other lands, but sophisticated readers read criticism of Nicholas's regime between the lines. Bookstores openly displayed Western books forbidden to enter the country, and Muscovites could easily procure radical Western writings. In 1847 alone, 862,000 volumes of foreign literature came into Russia legally, and undoubtedly many thousands more were brought in illegally.[30]

Nicholas took a special interest in and a deep suspicion of education from the outset of his reign. Once, when riding past the University of Moscow, he pointed to the building and said, "There is the wolf's den." Count Uvarov, then Vice-Minister of Education, in a report to the tsar wrote that education had for its proper aim to produce "useful and zealous instruments of government" and devoted supporters of conservative principles. To reach that goal he proposed that the government closely supervise all schools and that each class of society be provided with an education that corresponded to its social status. New legislation reduced the autonomy of the six universities in the empire, revised the curriculum, ordered students to wear a distinctive uniform, and appointed inspectors to check on the behavior of students outside the classroom. Admission was open to all who passed the entrance examinations. Tuition was free. Those who could not afford the costs of maintenance received scholarships that paid for room and board. In return the students had the obligation to serve in the government for six years. In 1847 enrollments ranged from 1,198 students at the University of Moscow to 368 at the University of Kazan. The majority of the students came from nonnoble families, but in the classrooms and in university intellectual life, nobles and commoners were on the same footing, with intellectual ability and not birth the sole criterion. There were no sharp social distinctions as there were at Oxford and Cambridge, and no fraternities, such as existed in German universities, to mirror the snobberies of the great world. Instead, as Alexander Herzen, one of the students of that day put it, young men of all sorts and conditions "were quickly fused into a compact mass of comrades." Despite the controls and the careful conservatism of the professors, students with inquiring minds immersed themselves in the supposedly banned writings of German philosophers and French socialists. That was especially true of the University of Moscow, but at provincial universities, too, radical philosophical and political ideas had wide currency.[31]

The regimentation, the suppression of dissent, the swift and harsh punishment visited on those who failed to conform, the omnipresent secret police, the censorship—all should have resulted in a stagnant and barren society. Instead, in one of the great paradoxes of history, Nicholas's empire became the setting in the 1840s for a spectacular intellectual outburst that justly deserves the name of the Golden Age of Russian culture. Nicholas's unending campaign of intellectual repression turned out to be his greatest failure. Men of superior talent, and some graced with the transcendent ability and vastly original creative power of genius, seemed to spring up on all sides. Literature was the greatest glory of the Golden Age, but the era also saw the beginnings of modern Russian music, drama, and art. Above all, the decade of the forties witnessed the emergence of an intense social conscience among a small group of young men repelled by the repression, injustice, and corruption of Nicholas's regime.

Around a hundred or so young men, nearly all of them of noble birth and many of them students or former students at the University of Moscow, made up this intellectual elite. In their twenties and early thirties, and some still in their late teens, in later times they were hailed as "the men of the forties." They began the organized struggle for political freedom and civil equality in Russia. They hated the repression, spurned service in the corrupt and oppressive bureaucracy, and disdained material success. As a consequence, they became increasingly alienated from their society and lived in a sort of internal exile. The government's suspicion of their activities served to increase their isolation. The police and the censorship made it difficult if not impossible to discuss and write about political matters, so, perforce, they immersed themselves in philosophical discussions, debates about the future of Russia, and literary criticism. As Alexander Herzen, one of their leaders, explained, they threw themselves into the world of books and there voiced "muffled and in undertones, the protest against the oppression of Nicholas."

These young men were the first generation of a new class that transcended old class lines and that the Russians came to call the *intelligentsia*. This new class was destined to have enormous importance for Russian history and ultimately for world history. A self-conscious and self-appointed intellectual elite, they devoted themselves with a barely credible intensity to the life of the mind and the pursuit of truth—truth that took many guises as their philosophies shifted. They spent their days and their nights, sometimes to the small hours of the morning, in their quest, writing and, above all, talking and arguing with one another. Some of them, from landowning families, had private incomes. Others lived precariously on what they could earn from translating Western writings and from contributions to the intellectual (and often suppressed) journals published during the forties. They all shared in a vital moral sense that was outraged by the injustices of their society. They suffered because of their compassion for the plight of the oppressed. Being young and romantic, they also suffered because they believed that suffering ennobled the sufferer. They also shared in a youthful and sometimes impassioned intolerance of ideas that conflicted with their own views. They constantly fell out with one another and then became reconciled. Sometimes their intellectual disagreements brought them to the point of challenge to a duel. Others announced a break in friendship in a gentler manner. K. S. Aksakov came to Timofey Granovsky's home late one night, awakened him, embraced him, and with tears flowing declared that he was breaking off relations with Granovsky because of the difference in their views about Russia vis-à-vis the rest of Europe.[32]

In their search for truth, the men of the forties looked to the West for philosophical guidance. They turned first to the German philosophers, above all others to Hegel. His teachings seemed to them to offer the answer to their search and the justification for their own existence as intellectuals. They read everything by Hegel or about his philosophy that they could find, and they argued endlessly about the meaning of the abstruse and the nebulous all-embracing concepts. To these enthusiasts the only thing that mattered was the life of the spirit. Then some became disenchanted with the obscurities of German idealism. They decided that they must confront the problems of the real world. So they fastened on to the no less abstruse but seemingly practical solutions proposed by French utopian socialists such as Cabet, Fourier, and others.

Whatever their differences and whatever their philosophies, these young men all had an intense love of their homeland and a deep concern for its welfare. They were preoccupied with Russia, its history, its virtues and its vices, and the character of its people. They exalted nationality and were convinced that man was nothing without it. Ivan Turgenev, in his first novel, *Rudin* (1855), voices that conviction when he has Lezhev—like Turgenev a man of the forties—say, "Russia can get on without any of us, but not one of us can get on without Russia. . . . Cosmopolitanism is rubbish, and the cosmopolitan is a nonentity, worse than a nonentity. Outside nationality there is no art, no truth, no life, nothing."[33]

Above all else, they saw it as their duty to erase the injustices and the corruption that defiled their beloved homeland. This challenge split the men of the forties into two antagonistic camps, the Westernizers and the Slavophiles. Their disagreement centered on Russia's relation to Western Europe. Peter Chaadayev had focused the debate when, in 1836, he published his "First Philosophical Letter" in *Teleskop*, a Moscow journal. Chaadayev wrote that Russia had contributed nothing to civilization. He blamed this on Russia's alienation from the main currents of European history that began in the ninth century, when the Eastern and Western churches had split from each other. Since then, Russian history explained nothing and proved nothing. Russia's salvation lay in absorbing Western culture and thereby making up for all Russia had missed. That included, wrote Chaadayev, reunion with the Roman Catholic Church.[34]

The letter created a great furor. Herzen said that it had "the effect of a pistol shot in the dead of night; it forced everyone to awaken." "Everyone" included an outraged Tsar Nicholas, who considered the letter as an insult to Russia and its Orthodox Church. He officially declared Chaadayev insane, confined him to his home under the care of a physician, suppressed the *Teleskop*, exiled its editor to Siberia, and dismissed the censor who had approved the publication of the article. Despite the suppression the article aroused heated arguments between those who substantially agreed with Chaadayev, who were given the name of Westernizers, and those who vehemently disagreed, called the Slavophiles. The Westernizers insisted that although Russia was an integral part of Europe, it had been bypassed by the mainstream of European history and civilization. Russia had never experienced the Renaissance and the Reformation, the genesis and growth of parliamentary institutions, the spread of industrialization, and all the other great developments that had shaped Western society. The Westernizers urged that the state must use its power to bridge the great gap by adopting changes and reforms modeled after Western societies. That did not mean slavish imitation of the Western way of life or the thoughtless adaptation of Russian institutions to those of the West. Rather, Russia should study and gain an understanding of the Western experience that would allow Russia to draw the lessons of that experience and so avoid the traumas and crises that punctuated and that still plagued Western history. The Westernizers were largely drawn from men of the liberal professions, notably academicians and journalists. Most of the Westernizers advocated a gradual and moderately liberal program of reform. A small but influential radical wing turned to socialist solutions.

The Slavophiles, made up largely from men of the landed nobility, were inflamed by the Westernizers' derogation of Russian life and institutions. To their way of thinking, Russia was a civilization separate from and superior to the West. The West, polluted by materialism and rationalism, convulsed by unrest and threats of revolution, was nearing collapse. The Orthodox Church, unsullied by the plague of rationalism that had corrupted Western Christianity, remained the only true faith. Indeed, far from needing to adopt the Western model, Russia was destined to be the bearer of a great religious and social rebirth that would bring rejuvenation and salvation to the decadent West.

The Slavophiles, idealizers of everything uniquely Russian, took a particular interest in the Russian peasant, whom they saw as the truest of Russians, innocent of all knowledge of the West, and preserver of the values of old Russia and of its church. They took a special interest in the peasant commune. Ironically, it was a book on Russia by a Western European, August von Haxthausen, published in 1847, that drew their attention to the commune. Haxthausen, a proud nobleman and defender of traditional values, deplored the inroads made in Western Europe by individualism and industrialization. He saw the land-equalizing commune as the bulwark that would save Russia from the fate of the West. The commune would save Russia from the creation of a rootless proletariat and the pauperism that bedeviled the West, and from the anti-Christian panaceas offered by the radicals and communists of the West. The Slavophiles quickly seized upon Haxthausen's exaltation of the peasant commune. In their enthusiasm they immersed themselves in the study of the customs and values of the peasantry and in the roots of Russian culture.[35]

The Slavophiles stoutly defended the autocracy as a uniquely Russian institution. It had successfully defended Russia from the corrupting influence of the West. A natural harmony united people and tsar in a divinely inspired synthesis. The Slavophiles' support of the autocracy was, however, tempered by their conviction that the state existed for the people rather than the people existing for the state. They also accorded preeminence over the autocracy to the Orthodox Church, so that state power must yield before Christian faith and Christian principles. These and similar attitudes raised doubts and suspicions in official circles. A police report in 1846 said of the Slavophiles that "expressing themselves pompously and ambiguously, they have often led one to consider whether perhaps their patriotic outcries concealed purposes against our government."[36]

Whether Slavophiles or Westernizers, these intellectuals formed "circles," as they were called, informal organizations of like-minded men who met to discuss ideas with a freedom and openness not possible anywhere else. The circles coalesced around individuals of outstanding intellect whose interests set the tone of the group. For example, the circle led by N. V. Stankevich (who was only twenty-seven when he died), concentrated on philosophy, art, and literature, while the circle that gathered around Herzen dealt mainly with political and social issues. The circle led by M. V. Butashevich-Petrashevsky attracted left-leaning intellectuals of Saint Petersburg.

Ivan Turgenev, who attended one of the circles, remembered the intellectual exhilaration of the meetings. In his novel *Rudin* he has one of his characters recall those times. "Imagine a gathering of half a dozen boys, our only light a tallow candle, tea like slops and biscuits as old as Adam—but if you'd only heard our speeches and looked at our faces! Excitement in everyone's eyes, cheeks on fire, our hearts beating fast, and we'd talk about God, about truth, abut the future of humanity, about poetry, sometimes talking nonsense, carried away by empty words, but what did that matter! . . . And the night would fly away calmly and smoothly as if on wings. And then gray dawn would break and we'd go our different ways, brimful of feeling, happy, honorable, sober (we never even thought of having strong drink), and with a kind of pleasant drowsiness in our souls."[37]

The forties, too, saw the flourishing of salons in the homes of ladies of high social rank. The salons met regularly on a set evening of the week. Here the intelligentsia met and talked with officials of the government. The most famous of these salons was that of the Grand Duchess Elena Pavlovna, wife of the tsar's brother Michael. Elena, born a princess of Württemberg, was a woman of intelligence, spirit, and considerable beauty. She did not get along well with her husband, reportedly in no small part because she let him know that he was her intellectual inferior. Because of her exalted rank and her own reformist views, those who came to her Thursday evenings in her Saint Petersburg palace felt that they could speak without fear of reprisal.[38]

The intellectual journals that began to appear offered a more lasting medium for the opinions of the intelligentsia and provided a meager source of income for their often needy contributors. They had small circulations but they were closely read and discussed by their readers. The censorship made it impossible for those "thick journals," as they were called, to publish articles about politics or about proposals for reforms. Instead, they dealt with literature, literary criticism, and philosophical ideas. Under the guise of these seemingly apolitical subjects, the authors of the articles managed to convey their discontents and to strike a blow, however muffled, for freedom.

The men of the forties counted many striking personalities among their number. But three who stand out could each personify a type among the intelligentsia of that time: Alexander Herzen, the dissident nobleman; Timofey Granovsky, the academic; and Vissarion Belinsky, the critic. Herzen, born in 1812, the illegitimate son of a moody, eccentric, and wealthy landowner and the German woman with whom he lived but never married, told the story of his life in one of the world's great masterpieces of autobiography. A leader of the Westernizers, he became a convert to the socialistic ideas that came into Russia from France. He was a man of remarkable intellectual powers, articulate almost to a painful degree, spoiled, wealthy so that he could indulge his whims, yet sensitive and warmhearted, and destined to a life filled with disappointments. In 1846 his father died and left Herzen a large fortune. The next year he left Russia, never to return. He spent the rest of his life in Western Europe (he died in 1870), actively engaged in international socialist activities, moving from place to place, always the exile. He never ceased in his struggle for freedom in his homeland, writing books and articles, and above all, founding a journal, *The Bell*, that was smuggled into Russia and widely read, and where it served to fuel the continuing agitation against the autocracy.

Timofey Granovsky's greatest strength lay in what Herzen called "his positive moral influence, in the absolute confidence which he inspired . . . the calm serenity of his spirit, the purity of his character, and in his constant profound protest against the existing order in Russia." He inspired the love and admiration of his friends. Turgenev, who knew him well, wrote that "He was an idealist in the best sense of that word, in the sense that he was not an idealist in isolation. He had a perfect right to say *Humani nil a me alienum puto*, and therefore nothing human felt alien to him."

Born in 1813, the son of a lesser provincial landowner, Granovsky studied at the University of Moscow and then in Germany. In 1839, at only twenty-six, he became Professor of History at the University of Moscow. His lectures there had a deep and lasting influence on his students. Like Herzen, he was a Westernizer, but unlike Herzen he had no talent or interest in the abstruse philosophical speculations in which his friends delighted. Instead, he studied the European past and found in it meaning and guidance for the Russian present. Once close to Herzen and his intimates, Granovsky broke away from them because of their atheism and their materialistic philosophy and their advocacy of revolutionary socialism. Repelled by their determinism, he emphasized the importance of the individual. He believed that history had for its purpose the attainment, to use his own words, "of a moral and enlightened individual personality, independent of fatalistic categories; and of a society which is appropriate to the demands of such a personality." In the dark years of brutal repression that marked the last eight years of Nicholas's reign, Granovsky managed to keep his chair at the University and to retain his intellectual independence until his early death at forty-two in 1855.[39]

Herzen and Granovsky, like most of the men of the forties, belonged to the privileged class of the nobility. The intelligentsia of the years and decades that followed came mainly from petty bourgeois or clerical families. They had broken away from the patriarchal domination, the superstitions, and the submissiveness of their origins. They belonged to no class, a new phenomenon in the rigid class structure of Russian society. Vissarion Belinsky was the progenitor of this new breed of classless men. He has been called the Everyman of the Russian intelligentsia, the personification of its strengths and its weaknesses, of its way of life, of its love of words written or spoken, of its singular dedication to an ideal and a cause, of its seeking for what it believed to be the final truth.[40]

Born in 1811, the son of a drunken small-town doctor, Belinsky grew up in poverty. A bright, serious, and hardworking schoolboy, he gained the attention of his teachers and won a scholarship to the University of Moscow. After three years there, he was expelled because of his poor grades and because of a play he had written that denounced serfdom. He enriched his formal education by omnivorous reading and by long discussions with his fellow students. He persisted in this way of self-education throughout the remaining years of his brief life. In 1834, soon after his dismissal from the University, he found employment with a Moscow journal and quickly gained a reputation for his literary criticism. From then on, first in Moscow and, from 1839, in Saint Petersburg, he earned his living by writing scores of essays and reviews of literature, poetry, and history. His irreverence toward long-accepted literary standards and his enchantment with the foreign philosophical and social ideas appealed to the men of the new generation.

His unprepossessing appearance and his seeming shyness belied the fiery personality that made his intimates call him "Vissariono furioso." He was a small, stoop-shouldered man with a sunken chest, painfully thin, pale, with a sad and pensive expression and a grating voice. Tuberculosis racked him from his early years and finally killed him. He lacked the social graces of his well-born friends and became flustered on meeting strangers. He possessed neither the skill nor the taste for the amenities of ordinary polite social inter-course. His awareness of these shortcomings doubtless explained his scorn for what he called "tea table affability." In this, as in so much else, he set the style for the calculated rudeness of the intelligentsia in the years that followed.[41]

The shyness and the self-consciousness vanished when he was in his own element, with men like himself, concerned above all with the search for some kind of truth that would give meaning to man's fate. Then he was full of life, seeking always to provoke, disposed to find fault and to cavil, and never con-ceding victory to an opponent. He gloried in argument, waving his arms, walking endlessly back and forth, the words tumbling out, his cheeks glowing with excitement. Sadly, as Herzen wrote, "the dispute would end with blood flowing from the sick man's throat, pale, gasping, with his eyes fixed on the man with whom he was speaking, he would lift his handkerchief to his mouth with shaking hand and stop, deeply mortified, crushed by his physical weak-ness. How I loved and how I pitied him at those moments."[42]

The harsh climate of Saint Petersburg worsened his consumption, and he grew ever weaker. In 1847 friends paid for a trip to the waters at Salzbrunn, reported to have curative powers for tuberculosis. The disease had progressed too far for the baths to have any effect. He returned home, where he died in late May of 1848. He was only thirty-seven and at the height of his intellectu-al powers.

In his unending quest for the answers to his questions about the nature of man and of society, he moved through a spectrum of philosophical enthusi-asms. Like so many of his contemporaries, he began as a devotee of the meta-physical abstractions of German philosophers. In 1837 he came under the influence of Mikhail Bakunin, the future revolutionary anarchist, who at that point in his career was a leading proselytizer of Hegel. Belinsky became a convinced Hegelian, given to extremes that made even Bakunin protest. Accepting without question Hegel's famous proposition, "All that is real is rational, all that is rational is real," he urged the acceptance of the autocracy and its institutions. They existed, and therefore they must be rational and a necessary stage in the inevitable evolution of history. Opposition to the autoc-racy was irrational and immoral.

As could be expected, these extremist positions aroused controversy and opposition from his contemporaries. It was not long before the controversy and the opposition had their effects, and Belinsky turned his back on Hegelianism. He now despised the very institutions that he had called upon men to accept. He began to read translations of French utopian socialists (he did not know enough French to read them in the original). With the impetuosity that was part of his being, he quickly became a perfervid socialist. By the fall of 1841, he wrote to his friend, V. P. Botkin, "You know my nature: it is always at extremes and never strikes the center of an idea. I part with the old idea with difficulty, renounce it down to the ground, and take up the new idea with all the fanaticism of a proselyte. And so I am now at a new extreme, which is the idea of socialism that has become for me the idea of ideas, the being of beings, the question of questions, the alpha and the omega of being and knowledge. It is the all and end. It is the question and the solution. It has (for me) engulfed history and religion and philosophy."

Together with Herzen he became the leader of the radical Westernizers. He now believed that human progress was possible only with the adoption of revolutionary change in the structure of society. "Evil is latent in society, and not in man," he wrote in 1844, "since society, namely the forms of human development, have by no means yet reached perfection." The influence of his writings served to persuade others to abandon the abstract thought of German thinkers for a philosophy that at least had the appearance of basing itself upon the real world. P. V. Annenkov went abroad in 1840, when Belinsky was in his Hegelian mode. When he returned in the fall of 1843, he found "whole phalanxes" reading the French utopians.[43]

Whatever his ideological position of the moment, Belinsky was always the moralist and the preacher. His reviews and essays were sermons in which he conveyed his benedictions or his condemnation to his readers. He drew his texts from literature, his great love. He believed that the writer must concern himself with life as it really was, and not with some imagined world. Literature could and must serve as the conscience of society, describing its evils, providing camouflage under which lay concealed propaganda for reform.

Belinsky reached the pinnacle of his influence in a famed open letter to Gogol that he wrote in July 1847, on the trip abroad for his health. He once told a friend that the censorship obliged him to act against his natural character. "Nature has condemned me," he wrote, "to bark like a dog and howl like a jackal, but circumstances compel me to mew like a cat and wave my tail like a fox." Free of these restraints outside of Russia, and in the last stages of consumption, he let himself go in the letter to Gogol.[44]

The letter was inspired by the publication of Gogol's *Selected Passages from Correspondence with Friends*. In that book Gogol eulogized the autocracy, the Church, serfdom, and the other institutions that he had mercilessly satirized in his earlier writings. Now he proclaimed that complete submission to the will of the tsar and to the teachings of the Orthodox Church would cure all of the ills that afflicted Russia. This strange *volte face* outraged Gogol's friends, and no one more than Belinsky. He had once hailed Gogol as Russia's premier literary artist, indeed, as one of its greatest geniuses. Now, in his letter, he denounced Gogol as an apostle of obscurantism and bitterly attacked the institutions that Gogol had praised. Russia, he wrote, needed laws and rights that protected the individual from the arbitrary acts of the autocracy, and from the church, the handmaiden of the autocracy. Russians must awaken to a realization of their human dignity, which had been trampled upon for centuries by their rulers. They must have guarantees for their persons, their honor, and their property, now at the mercy of a corrupt officialdom. Serfdom, corporal punishment, and all the other anachronistic trappings of the despotism must be abolished, along with the oppression and censorship that prevented the free exchange of ideas.

The letter so outraged officialdom that the head of the Third Section said that he regretted Belinsky's death because he would have jailed Belinsky in the Fortress of Saint Peter and Saint Paul and "let him rot there." The censorship not only attempted to ban the publication of the letter, but for several years even forbade the mention of Belinsky's name in any publication. The attempts at suppression proved failures. Soon thousands of copies of the letter circulated throughout Russia.[45]

Belinsky once told a friend that all his best articles were "unpremeditated, just improvisations; in sitting down to them I never knew what I was going to write." His writing style, ponderous with overlong and involved sentences, reflected the lack of plan. So, too, did his leaping in the course of a review from one subject to another entirely extraneous one. He lacked objectivity, a failing to which he readily admitted without apology. "I know that I take a one-sided position," he wrote, "but I do not wish to change it and I feel sorrow and pity for those who do not share my opinion." He more than shaded the truth when he said that he felt sorrow and pity for those who disagreed with him. As a friend put it, "he expended his energies on enmity and indignation"—not only for contemporaries but people who were long dead. Most important, he defined the mission of Russian literature in his own time and for long years to come. As he explained in the last months of his life, the chief task of literature "is that it should call forth questions. If it achieves that goal, even without poetry and artistry, for me it is *nonetheless* interesting, and I do not read it, I devour it."[46]

So impassioned were his convictions, so honest and sincere were his reviews, so apparent was his love of literature, and so candidly did he express what was in the minds of his peers that he became the voice of the men of the forties and the most important cultural force of his time. Nor did his influence vanish with the forties. His social idealism, his lack of objectivity, his intolerance for those who disagreed with him, his irritability, the vehemence of his attacks, his disdain for religion, his scorn of aesthetes, and even his clumsy style and humble origins set the pattern for the radical intelligentsia of later years. They elevated him into the pantheon of Russia's heroes as their patron saint. He received the final accolade when Lenin hailed him, Herzen, and Chernyshevsky as the precursors of Russian social democracy and thereby automatically guaranteed him reverent admiration in Soviet society.[47]

The intellectual outburst of the forties came to an abrupt halt in 1848. The outbreak of revolution in the West made Nicholas fear catastrophic consequences in Russia and everywhere else in Europe. When he learned that revolution had broken out in Berlin in mid-March, he drafted a manifesto declaring that revolution threatened all of Europe, and called on God's help to destroy Russia's enemies. His fear that the revolutionary infection would spread to Russia was aggravated by a succession of domestic calamities that included a cholera epidemic that carried away thousands of his subjects; a widespread crop failure and resulting famine; a rash of fires, many of them the work of arsonists, that destroyed thousands of homes and businesses; an alarming increase in violent peasant risings; a sharp drop in foreign demand for grain, Russia's chief export; and rumors of discontent in the officers corps of the army.[48]

Cooler heads than Nicholas were less fearful of the danger of revolution in Russia. Baron M. A. Korff, a longtime advisor to the tsar, confided to his diary that Russia had neither the elements nor the instruments for revolution because "freedom of the press, popular representation, national guards, and things of that nature . . . are complete nonsense to nine-tenths of the Russian population." But Nicholas believed in taking no chances, and he ordered an intensification of the bonds of repression. He leveled an especial attack on intellectual life. He ordered a drastic tightening of the censorship and a suppression of all forms of political and social criticism. The censors went to ridiculous extremes to carry out the orders of their emperor. They purged all references to "republic" and "republicanism" from studies on ancient Greece and Rome. Nicholas exiled the secretary of the Society of Russian History and Antiquities because the Society had published a Russian translation of Giles Fletcher's *Of the Russe Commonwealth,* an account of Fletcher's visit to Russia in 1588–1589. The book contained an adverse description of conditions in Russia at that far-off time, but that did not matter to Nicholas.[49]

Nicholas's police and informers had, of course, kept him informed of the intellectual ferment of the forties, and repressive actions had been taken against publications and individuals. Now the tsar decided to move against the universities as the breeding ground of the intellectuals. He banned the teaching of philosophy and the constitutional law of European states and ordered that theologians should give the lectures in logic and psychology to ensure that their content conformed to the teaching of the Orthodox Church. Another decree ordered that enrollment at each university could not exceed three hundred, and that universities could not accept applicants until their enrollment had fallen to that number. Sons of noble families had to be given preference for admission. The universities could accept applicants of non-noble origin only if the list of noble applicants had been exhausted and vacancies still existed.[50]

Nearly any intellectual of any importance experienced difficulties—some of them were jailed or exiled, and many were placed under police surveillance. Official oppression—and sadism—culminated in the arrest, in April 1849, of the members of the Saint Petersburg circle led by Butashevich-Petrashevsky. They stood accused of plotting the overthrow of the regime. Among the accused was the twenty-eight-year-old Fyodor Dostoyevsky, former army officer and already successful novelist, charged initially with reading Belinsky's letter to Gogol to a meeting of the circle. After eight months in jail, the prisoners were led to the huge Semevsky Square, whose four sides were lined with soldiers, and behind them a crowd of onlookers. A general read the indictment that listed their offenses and then announced their sentence. Only at that moment did the accused men learn that they had been tried and sentenced to death by a firing squad. A priest called upon them to repent and held a small cross to their lips. Then soldiers handed them white shrouds and hoods and helped them put them on. The first three were tied to posts, the drum roll began, the firing squad took aim, only awaiting the command "Fire!" At that moment an imperial aide-de-camp galloped into the square holding a sealed dispatch. It contained a reprieve of the death sentence, and instead exiled the accused to hard labor in Siberia. This sentence had been agreed upon by the court days before. Nicholas himself had ordered this incredibly cruel travesty, supposedly to teach these men a lesson they would never forget.[51]

During the years of heightened repression that lasted until Nicholas's death in 1855, autocracy reached its zenith in Russia and began its decline. Nicholas's reign ended in failure. His drive to suppress independent thought had a numbing effect on intellectual life but did not destroy it. When death removed his heavy hand, that life flourished more mightily than ever before. His efforts at thought control served only to intensify an intellectual activity critical of the absolutism and demanding reform. In foreign policy, too, Nicholas's dreams turned to ashes. His aggressive diplomacy, his huge army, and his intervention and success in crushing revolution in Hungary in 1849 brought Russia and Nicholas to the peak of international power. Prince Albert of Britain called him "the master of Europe."[52] Then, in 1853, Nicholas made the mistake of getting into a war with the crumbling Ottoman Empire. That conflict, called the Crimean War, was an episode in what the diplomats of the nineteenth century called the Eastern Question: would the Ottoman Empire survive, and if it did not, how was it to be divided among the Great Powers? Nicholas found himself at war not only with the Ottomans, but also with Britain and France. They knew that a Russian victory would severely weaken their influence in the Near East and lessen or even cancel their share of the spoils of a carved-up Ottoman Empire. Almost from the outset the war went badly for the Russians. Inefficiency, ineptitude, inferior matériel, corruption, and lack of adequate means of supply led inevitably to defeat. Troubles piled up on the home front, too. The state's finances buckled under the strain of the war effort, and deficits soared. Even more serious, a great new wave of peasant unrest and violence swept across and shook much of the empire. The failure of his diplomatic schemes, the collapse of the army of which he had been so proud, and the domestic disorders were more than Nicholas could bear. Both his spirit and his health gave way, and on March 2, 1855, he died. There was even talk that he had committed suicide by taking poison.

Nicholas's death cleared the way for the emergence of a new era in Russian history that had its origins in the 1840s. That was when the most important man in Russia, Tsar Nicholas himself, became convinced that the continued existence of serfdom threatened the power and well-being of his empire. He could not bring himself to order its abolition, but he prepared the way for the emancipation that came only six years after his death. The ending of serfdom made possible the introduction of other sweeping reforms; it took the cork out of the bottle.

The new tsar, Nicholas's son Alexander II, convinced by the defeat in the Crimean War and by the growing threat of rural unrest that his state teetered on the edge of political collapse, had the will to introduce reforms and the determination to carry them out. The autocracy remained, but not with the plenitude of power that it possessed in Nicholas's time. The serfs and the state peasants were emancipated, although restrictions still remained on the freedom of the individual peasant. Elected district and provincial assemblies, the *zemstvos*, represented a first step toward representative government and whetted the appetite of many Russians for a greater voice in running the country. Municipal government was reformed by arrangements much like those of the *zemstvo* system. The corrupt and unfair judicial system was reconstructed on the Western model to provide equality before the law, uniform judicial procedures, public trials, juries, defense lawyers, and judges who could not be dismissed except for misconduct in office. As one of Nicholas's biographers observed,[53] Nicholas was the last ruler of Russia to hold undivided power, and so, in a real sense, he was Russia's last truly absolute ruler.

EPILOGUE

In 1842 Alfred Tennyson, himself a member of the new generation, wrote,

> For I dipt into the future, far as human eye could see,
> Saw the Vision of the world, and all the wonder that would be

Tennyson's poetic imagination, of course, could not conceive of all the wonders that would be. No one could. The most striking feature of the modern age has been the astonishing acceleration in the pace of change. Once the beginning was made, advances came with ever increasing swiftness, ultimately transforming the tempo and the condition of human life throughout the world. The first steps in the 1840s in the creation of a railway network and the introduction of the electric telegraph, of photography, and of cheap mail marked the onset of a flood of innovations that opened a new age of communication. The world is now linked by a global network created by such triumphs of science and technology as radio, television, airplanes, satellites, and computers. They transmit information and word of happenings great and small throughout the world, seemingly at lightning speed.

In science, too, the advances have come with dizzying swiftness. The insistence upon research and experiment and the use of mathematics that began in the forties has led to a new era in the interpretation of nature. No science has experienced more rapid and sweeping changes than has physics. The gradual understanding of the complex structure of the atom opened great theoretical possibilities and a tremendous new source of energy. Enormous progress, too, has been made in medical science. The emphasis upon research and experiment, and the employment of physics, chemistry, and biology, first stressed in the 1840s, have lessened human suffering and prolonged life. So, too, have the giant strides that have been made in sanitary engineering and the concern with public health since the first steps that were taken in the forties. The application of science to industrial processes, barely beginning and still suspect in the 1840s, has become a commonplace. Indeed, scientific advance has become the prerequisite and associate of technological advance. The social sciences, too, have experienced a remarkable growth, with their emphasis upon precise measurement, the testing of hypotheses, and mathematics. Once principally employed as university professors, social scientists now serve also in the worlds of commerce and banking and in governmental and international agencies.

By 1840 Britain alone among the nations of the world had experienced the changes in industrial production that go by the name of the Industrial Revolution. Yet not until 1851 did workers in British industry outnumber those in agriculture. In the rest of Europe, agriculture and the employments associated with it remained by far the dominant sector of the economy. In the 1840s, however, tentative beginnings had been made in some lands in the process of industrialization. In France, Germany, and Austria the new techniques of production had barely taken root. In the succeeding decades, the diffusion of the new technology led these and other nations to industrialize—first in Europe and the United States, and then, in the twentieth century, in other parts of the globe.

The advance of industrialization and its accompanying phenomenon of urbanization spelled the end of the society of orders whose origins reached back a thousand years. The disintegration of the traditional society with its hierarchical structure based upon birth was greatly accelerated in the 1840s by the growing numbers, importance, and impatience of the middle and working classes, and by the emancipation of the peasantry in central Europe. A class society has replaced the traditional society, with membership in each class determined not by birth but by the role the individual plays in the production of goods and services and by his income. With the breakdown of the traditional society, governments became increasingly responsive to the demands of the middle and then of the working class. These demands were expressed through political pressure groups and militant labor organizations, both innovations of the forties. The response of governments manifested itself in the extension of the suffrage to ever widening circles, the growth and proliferation of political parties, and the increasing participation of the middle and working class in the affairs of government. These developments, and a growing social consciousness of the plight of the poor, were reflected in the gradual acceptance by governments of their responsibility for the welfare of their citizens. That concern for public welfare, first evidenced in Britain in the 1840s, spread gradually to other lands. The wealth created by modern developed society allows such societies to assure everyone of an income sufficient to provide the basic necessities of life. In the modern welfare state, such guarantees are viewed not as charity but as a right of all of its people.

The "scientific" socialism heralded by Karl Marx and Friedrich Engels in the 1840s provided the foundation for effective socialist movements and of powerful political parties, first in Germany in the 1870s and then in country after country around the world. Some of these parties advocate revolutionary action, but most have adopted a more gradual approach, believing that socialism can be established by political action rather than by revolution. The writings of Pierre-Joseph Proudhon helped shape the modern anarchist and syndicalist movements that have their greatest appeal in Latin countries.

Another ideology, that of chauvinistic nationalism and the racism that often accompanies it, also emerged in the 1840s. This creed has had an even greater impact upon the world than has socialism. Absorbed by people of nations everywhere, it continues to inflame national and ethnic rivalries and hatreds; has left a heritage of insecurity and suspicion; and often brings war, devastation, and death in its train.

Tennyson's "Vision of the world, and all the wonder that would be" foresaw war and "a ghastly dew" raining from "airy navies grappling in the central blue." Then, true Romantic that he was, Tennyson allowed his poetic imagination to soar when he wrote,

> Till the war-drum throbbed no longer and the battle flags were furled
> In the Parliament of man, the Federation of the world.

NOTES

INTRODUCTION

1. Kübeck (1909), suppl. 135–136; Martin (1875–80), I, 312–313; Stahl and Yuill (1970), III, 156; Riehl (1861), 342.

2. Boigne (1907–8), IV, 273; Tocqueville (1958), 67–69; Kübeck (1909), I, ii, 716; Varnhagen von Ense (1972), II, 324, 378, III, 268; O'Boyle (1970), 489, 490; Meyendorff (1923), I, 276.

3. Musset (1977), 46.

4. Mitchell (1981), 87ff.

5. Lewis (1955), 55.

6. Greville (1958), I, xiii; Hodder (1887), II, 243; Riehl (1861), 6–7.

7. Johnson (1963), 49; Wigand (1846–52), IX, 156–157; Sheehan (1978), 47; Wallis (1853), 187–188.

8. cf. Cohen (1935), 23; Varnhagen von Ense (1972), II, 139, 227–228; Apponyi (1913–26), III, 362; Macauley (1974–81), III, 304; Bismarck (1966), I, 215–216; Rotteck and Welcker (1845–48), III, 699; Greville (1938), IV, 40–41.

9. Croker (1885), II, 114; Thureau-Danzin (1884–92), III, 194; Apponyi (1913–26), III, 225–227; Castellane (1895–97), III, 208–209; Senior (1978), I, 46–47.

10. Friedrich (1921), 114–115.

11. Senior (1978), I, 92; cf. Gerlach (1903), 483.

12. Robertson (1952), vii.

CHAPTER ONE

1. Blum (1943), 26; Bodenstedt (1888), 77; Riedel (1961), 122.
2. Kussmaul (1900), 101; Schnabel (1929–37), III, 435; Treitschke (1915–19), VI, 108, 117; Corti (1929), 91, 112; Ratcliffe (1972), 199; Christie (1928) 247.
3. Heine (1893), VI, 382; Broughton (1909–11), V, 3; Cockburn (1874), II, 129; Bone (1862), IX, 150; Anderson (1967), 18; London *Times*, ec. 16, 1871.
4. Clapham (1930), I, 92–93; Macaulay (1974–81), III, 270; Schnabel (1929–37), III, 387.
5. Custine (1843), IV, 5–6; Blum (1961), 282–283; Haywood (1969), 34–36; Wallace (1877), 13–14; Senior (1973), I, 91; Tenison (1853), 291–297; Durrieu (1845), 625.
6. Kirby (1956), 201–202.
7. Dyos and Aldcroft (1969), 222; Clapham (1930), I, 93–94; Perkin (1971), 19–20, 67–68, 113; Barker and Savage (1974), 55, 120–121.
8. Milward and Saul (1973), 335; Herrmann (1981), 32–33; Varnhagen von Ense (1972), III, 376; Blum (1943), 27–28; Czoernig (1858), 313–316; Heywood (1969), 24–26; Maxwell (1848), 182.
9. Pollock (1887), I, 89, 169; Fish (1838), 86; Mohl (1902), II, 265–266; Motley (1889), I, 103; Schnabel (1929–37), III, 386; Thackeray (1840), 16; Durbin (1844), I, 187–188.
10. Pinkney (1986), 14; Beyle (1838), I, 78; Vizitelly (1893), I, 116; Gottschall (1898), 119, 188; Falloux (1888), I, 138; Robinson (1948), 233.
11. Maxwell (1848), 307–308; Demidoff (1855), I, 337–338; Blum (1961), 282–283, 500–501; Custine (1843), IV, 5–6; Heywood (1969), 34–36.
12. Pinkney (1986), 14; Granville (1837), I, 183.
13. Pinkney (1986), 51; Clapham (1930), I, 80–84; Blum (1961), 283–284.
14. Dyos and Aldcroft (1969), 211; Perkin (1971), 112; Acworth (1889), 21–25, 29; Clapham (1930), I, 401; Barker and Savage (1974), 14–15; Musgrave (1848), I, 5.
15. Mitchell (1980), 609–610; Blum (1961), 284.
16. Baker and Savage (1974), 57–64, 72–74; Evans (1936), 3.
17. Evans (1936), 9–10, 13–14, 24–25; Henry (1979), III, 197n.; Dyos and Aldcroft (1969), 195–196.
18. Baxter (1962), 32, 35–36; Spencer (1926), I, 140; Evans (1859), 8.
19. Peacock and Joy (1971), 9–14, 19; *Dictionary of National Biography*, X, 145.
20. Lewin (1968), 261–262; Perkin (1971), 186; Lambert (1934), 55, 5; Smiles (1859), 420–423.
21. Evans (1859), 70–72; Lambert (1934), 90, 127, 172–176.
22. Lambert (1934), 186, 192, 254, 265, 268–273; Lewin (1968), 352–353, 359–363; Evans (1936), 102.

23. Cockburn (1874), II, 129; Greville (1938), V, 234–235; Evans (1848), 9–19; Morgan (1963), 96–97; Jenks (1938), 374n.

24. Pollins (1954), 233; Boot (1984), 7; Killick and Thomas (1970), 103–104; Reid (1890), I, 356.

25. Spencer (1926), 283–284, 288–289; Vizetelly (1893), I, 298–299; Evans (1848), 2–8, 39–40, 45–46; Jackman (1966), 570–571, 593–598; Evans (1958), 6–7; Lambert (1934), 11–19.

26. Guest (1950), 167; Evans (1936), 100–102; Ward-Perkins (1966), III, 265; Lambert (1934), 164; Dyos and Aldcroft (1969), 127–128, 135; Clapham (1930), I, 387.

27. *Dictionary of National Biography*, X, 146; Evans (1859), 2; Lambert (1943), 20–27, 158–159, 218; Peacock and Joy (1971), 32; Bancroft (1904), 113–114.

28. Gregory (1894), 132; Greville (1938), IV, 162; Campbell (1881), II, 216, 217n.; Lennox (1877), I, 185–191.

29. Guest (1950), 132; Evans (1848), 31–33; Evans (1958), 45; Boot (1984), 8–12, 51, 63, 67; Malmesbury (1884), I, 199.

30. London *Times*, Dec. 16, 22, 1871; Schumpeter (1939), I, 344n.; Gourvish (1980), 9; Evans (1859), 3; Dyos and Aldcroft (1969), 130.

31. List (1927–36), III, pt. i, 346, VII, 510.

32. Ibid., VIII, 355; Henderson (1983), 2–67; Mohl (1902), I, 93–94.

33. List (1927–36), III, pt. i, 155–195, pt. ii, 820–826, VIII, 81; Henderson (1983), 133–136; Gehrig (1966), 78.

34. List (1927–36), III, pt. ii, 1009ff., IX, 190ff.; Schnabel (1929–37), III, 337, 369; Treitschke (1915–19), V, 116; Mohl (1902), II, 8–9.

35. Delbruck (1905), I, 134–135; Friedrich (1921), 52; Schnabel (1929–37), 372–384.

36. *Cambridge Economic History*, IX, i. 415; Milward and Saul (1973), 382–383; Henderson (1983), 244.

37. Gille (1965), I, 263; Ratcliffe (1972), 207–209.

38. Blum (1943), 31–32; Corti (1928), 84–112; Mitchell (1981), 609.

39. Ratcliffe (1972), 197–198; Dunham (1955), 49–53.

40. Kemp (1972), 127; Jardin and Tudesq (1983), 195; Baxter (1962), 44–47, 53.

41. Gourvish (1980), 20–21; Mitchell (1964), 322–324.

42. Chandler (1965), 16–19; Gourvish (1973), 280–290; Tilly (1978), 555.

43. Jenks (1938), 130–132; Killich and Thomas (1970), 96; Mitchell (1964), 330–333.

44. Aldcroft (1972), 240–242; Fremdling (1977), 584–585; Tilly (1978), 414.

45.   Pollock (1887), I, 194; *Edinburgh Review* (1840), LXXII, 12; Treitschke (1915–19), VI, 126–127.
46.   Silliman (1980), II, 311–312; Spencer (1926), 130; Musgrave (1848), I, 101; Adams (1968), 49–50; Vignoles (1889), 104.
47.   Silliman (1980), II, 390; Neumann (1928), II, 311; Barker and Savage (1974), 83–84.
48.   Goudsmit (1980), 83; Maunder (1900), 152–153; Dyos and Aldcroft (1969), 199.
49.   Dyos and Aldcroft (1969), 181; Cockburn (1874), II, 130–132.
50.   Churlton (1951), I, 20–21; Musgrave (1848), I, 130–131, 169.
51.   Blum (1943), 29–30; Kirby (1956), 246, 252–263; Barker and Savage (1974), 70–72; *Dictionary of National Biography*, V, 300.
52.   Motley (1889), I, II, 63; Gardner (1848), 1–3; Silliman (1980), I, 14; Mitchell and Deane (1962), 218; Kirby (1956), 263–265.
53.   Singer (1958), IV, 646; Kirby (1956), 336–337; Raikes (1856–57), III, 44; Macaulay (1974–81), III, 341; Bamberger (1899), 241.
54.   Singer (1958), IV, 657–660; Kirby (1956), 339–340.
55.   Siemens (1922), 50–51, 55–58, 62, 67; Mather (1953), 48–49; Flaubert (1980–82), I, 134n.
56.   Shee (1893), 83; Hill (1880), II, 419.
57.   Falloux (1888), I, 203; Vizetelly (1893), I, 179–180; Robinson (1948), 192, 194, 220.
58.   Hill (1880), I, 241; Robinson (1948), 257.
59.   Robinson (1848), 260–269; Hemmeon (1912), 66; *Dictionary of National Biography*, IX, 867–869.
60.   Robinson (1948), 272–281, 319–320.
61.   Ibid., 324–330, 335–336.
62.   Hill (1880), I, 29; Trollope (1950), 133, 283; Trollope (1951), 148.
63.   Robinson (1948), 371ff.
64.   Gernsheim (1955), 1–151.

CHAPTER TWO

1.   Mill (1849), 34; Greville (1938), IV, 94; Hodder (1887), I, 322–323; Andlaw (1862), II, 119; Biedermann (1886–87), I, 160.
2.   Biedermann (1886–87), I, 160.
3.   Haencken (1930), 29; Jagow (1938), 163; Martin (1875–80), II, 69; Campbell (1881), II, 247; Kübeck von Kubau (1909), II, 50; Varnhagen von Ense (1972), VII, 1.
4.   Croker (1884), II, 205; Macaulay (1935), 189, 195; Edmonds (1964), 102; Raikes (1856–57), IV, 133; Lyell quoted in Dickens (1965–) III, 156n.; Humboldt (1860), 305; Colman (1849), I, 224.

5.   Cockburn (1874), II, 3; Hodder (1887), I, 323; Villermé (1840), *passim;* Pinkney (1986), 102; Carlyle (1840), 1–3; *Working Class* (1973), II, 659.

6.   Blum (1978), 178–193, 271–276; Carlyle (1882), 64, 69, 128–129; Hohenlohe-Ingelfingen (1897–1907), I, 5–7; Argyll (1906), I, 282–286.

7.   Engels (1968), 10–11; Adams (1804), 96–97; *Edinburgh Review* quoted in Saville (1973),151.

8.   Saville (1973), 151; Cooper (1971), 140–141; Levasseur (1969), II, 262; Hamerow (1958), 30–35; Langer (1969), 182; Rath (1969), 15.

9.   *Historical Statistics* (1949), 34.

10.   Kitson-Clark (1967), 127; Villermé (1840), I, 36; Blum (1978), 48.

11.   Corson (1848), 321, 323–324; Levasseur (1969), II, 291; Chevalier (1973), 116, 455; Villermé (1840), II, 34–38, 49–54.

12.   Taylor (1842), *passim;* Cockburn (1874), II, 2, 5; Villermé (1840), II, 203–209; Fourastie (1962), 27–28; Clapham (1930), I, 175; Deane and Coale (1962), 142; Pinkney (1958), 9.

13.   Hodder (1887), I, 215.

14.   Edmonds (1964), 56.

15.   Ibid., 56, 68–69.

16.   Walling (1931), 76.

17.   Cazamian (1973), 46–47; Hodder (1887), 60–66, 108–112; Best (1964), 43–44.

18.   Birnie (1930), 204–205, 207–208; Slade (1840), 82; Levasseur (1969), II, 130–131; Rigaudias-Weiss (1975), 112.

19.   Taylor (1842), 37, 75, 212; Villermé (1840), I, 82–83; Faucher (1845), I, II; Buret (1839), I, 310–349; Chadwick (1965), 5; Walker (1839), 146ff.; Engels (1968), 53–63; Pinkney (1958), 19–21, 145–146.

20.   Villermé (1840), II, 245; Levasseur (1969), II, 267; Pinkney (1958), 24; Gottstein (1901–2), I, 241–242; Owen (1965), 135.

21.   Ackerknecht (1948), 117–145; Finer (1952), 2–6; Lewis (1952), 107.

22.   Chadwick (1965), 51–53, 58–61.

23.   *Ibid.*, 66–71; Finer (1952), 209–212; Best (1964), 133–136.

24.   Gottstein (1901–2), 244–245; Chadwick (1965), 71–73; Best (1964), 133–136.

25.   Gottstein (1901–2), 245; Pettenkofer (1941), 478ff.; Pinkney (1958), 122ff.

26.   Guest (1950), 211; Roberts (1960), 178–179; Owen (1965), 95.

27.   Owen (1965), 123–124, 163; Dickens (1965–), IV, 556n.

28.   Owen (1965), 93, 164–165; Feingold (1987), 164–165; Greville (1938), V, 169; *Edinburgh Review* quoted in Saville (1973), 130; *Economist* quoted in Clapman (1930), I, 545.

29.   Talmon (1961), 357; Treitschke (1915–19), VI, 596, 600, VII, 299, 310; Biedermann (1886–87), I, 155–156; Varnhagen von Ense (1972), II, 395; Noyes (1966), 47.

30.   *Times* quoted in Owen (1965), 166; Best (1964), 42, 50, 126, 138–139; Hodder (1887), II, 295–296.

31.   Hodder (1887), I, 106; Battiscombe (1975), 3.

32.   Hodder (1887), I, 36–40, 50–52, 117, 228; Argyll (1906), I, 223.

33.   Hodder (1887), I, 55, 101, 105.

34.   Ibid., I, 101, 229, 231, 406; II, 359.

35.   Ibid., II, 121–122; Greville (1938), IV, 162.

36.   Hodder (1887), I, 111, 112, 502, 519; II, 127, 143, 274, 314.

37.   Hodder (1887), I, 67, 441, 359–395; Battiscombe (1975); 99–101, 129, 136–137.

38.   Hodder (1887), II, 304–307, 331, III, 30–32; Battiscombe (1975), 158; Robinson (1948), 330.

39.   Hodder (1887), II, 377; *Dictionary of National Biography*, IV, 1061.

40.   Greville (1883–1905), 375; Edmonds (1964), 76; Ernest August (1925), 229; Price (1957), 61.

41.   Deane and Coale (1962), 26–27; Hartwell (1970), 170–173, 177–179; Chadwick (1965), 3–4.

42.   Villermé (1840), II, 5–7, 25; Fourastie (1962), 73, 89; Levasseur (1969), II, 268; Chevalier (1973), 20.

43.   Edmonds (1964), 37–38; Lovett (1920), I, 100.

44.   Thompson (1964), 711ff.; Lovett (1920), I, v, vii, xi–xiii, 94, 103, II, 93, 155.

45.   Rath (1957), 14–15; Engels (1967), 193; Rietra (1980), 22.

46.   Clapham (1951), 76–81; Dunham (1955), 203; Talmon (1961), 367; Johnson (1974), 65.

47.   Herwegh (1898), 13; Herzen (1968), II, 673; O'Boyle (1970), 477, 493–495.

48.   Herzen quoted in Carr (1933), 29; Nesselrode (1908–12), VII, 322–323; Senior (1878), I, 113.

49.   Herzen (1968), II, 684–686; Bamberger (1899), 198–201, 208–218; Billington (1980), 259–260.

50.   Heine (1893), VI, 427–428.

51.   Bestor (1948), 259–261, 277–282; Lacassagne (1973), 127; Noyes (1966), 41–42.

52.   Valentin (1930), I, 279–280; Stein (1964), 33; Frank (1983), 122–123.

53.   Clapham (1930), I, 314–315, 599.

54.   Bornstein (1884), 347–348, 350–354; Frobel (1890–91), I, 96–97.

55.   Walter (1963), 209; Johnson (1971), 647–657; *idem* (1974), 61.

56.   Cabet (1973), introd. *passim*.

57.   Johnson (1974), 59–60, 80, 83–85; Cabet (1973), xiv–xx; Zeldin (1979), 85–88.

58.   Hayek (1952), 375; Popper (1950), 30.

59. Born (1898), 68–69.
60. Hess (1959), 79–80, 256; Annenkov (1968), 167–168; Kamenka (1980), 29.
61. Ritter (1969), 104–106.
62. Proudhon (1970), 88–89, 221; Ritter (1969), 104–106.
63. Dorpalen (1970), 344–350; Herwegh (1898), 225.
64. Heine (1893), VI, 215–216; Herzen (1968), I, xxi.

CHAPTER THREE

1. Hugo (1957), 73.
2. Van Tieghem (1948), 7; Lovejoy (1941), 258; Manuel (1987), 135.
3. Hugo (1957), 65; Arendt (1944), 50.
4. Grimm quoted in Kohn (1950), 454.
5. Evans (1931), 98, 100; Van Tieghem (1948), 519.
6. Thackeray (1903), 191; Carr (1933), 63.
7. Halsted (1969), 253; Hayes (1968), 138–160; *idem* (1966), 52–54.
8. Shafer (1955), 4; Kedourie (1961), 9.
9. Goethe quoted in Kedourie (1961), 12.
10. Fichte quoted in Kedourie (1961), 50; Hayes (1968), 160; Shafer (1955), 189–190.
11. Herder quoted in Jaszi (1966), 258; Hayes (1927), 726.
12. Hayes (1968), 294.
13. Broch and Skilling (1970), 33–52.
14. Slomka (1941), 167–173.
15. Mazzini (1894), vii.
16. Gregory (1894), 88–89.
17. Michelet (1973), 183.
18. Normanby (1857), II, 14, 14n.
19. Cobban (1978), 146–148; Trevelyan (1876), II, 228; Emerson (1968), 150.
20. Billington (1980), 165–166.
21. Herzen (1968), II, 1014; Mazzini (1894), ix; Fichte (1968), 73; Stambrook (1969), 33.
22. Noyes (1944), 13–29.
23. Herzen (1968), II, 1014.
24. Noyes (1944), 13–29, 371–415.
25. UNESCO (1955), 106; Kohn (1960), 43.
26. Noyes (1944), 17, 42; UNESCO (1955), 92; Mills (1952), 37; Herzen (1968), II, 666–667.
27. UNESCO (1955), 31–32; Noyes (1944), 40; Walicki (1982), 253.
28. Noyes (1944), 53–56; Gardner (1911), 206–207, 211–218, 245–266.
29. Noyes (1944), 53–56; UNESCO (1955), 2–7.
30. Linton (1894), 152; Langer (1969), 113; Herzen (1968), II, 697.

31. Mazzini (1979), 123.
32. Bamberger (1899), 219.
33. Mazzini (1929), 41–50.
34. *Idem* (1974), 139–140, 147, 156.
35. *Idem* (1929), 58–59, 176–177; *idem* (1894), xxx; Salvemini (1957), 79–80.
36. Salvemini (1957), 70; Mazzini (1979), 4.
37. Mazzini (1929), 148.
38. Eyck (1958), 360–362, 369–373; Barr (1975), 34–40.
39. Linton (1892), 152; Dickens (1965–), IV, 485n.
40. Barr (1975), 40–41, 132; Herzen (1968), II, 694.
41. Nasson (1908), 206; Herzen (1968), II, 694.
42. Mazzini (1979), 41, 43–44, 101–102; Barr (1975), 232.
43. Barr (1975), 179–223.
44. Salvemini (1957), 44.
45. Meinecke (1970), viii–ix; Pflanze (1966), 136.
46. Kohn (1965), 76–77, 116–117; Liptzin (1944), 102–103; Varnhagen von Ense (1972), I, 13.
47. Klein (1914), 294–296; Dahlmann quoted in Hock (1957), 102–103.
48. Marx and Engels (1972), 114–116.
49. Kohn (1955), 51; *idem* (1957), 14–15.
50. King (1899), II, 153.
51. Mill (1849), 30–31; Senior (1973), I, 263.
52. Schuselka (1845), 1–13; Blum (1982), 622–623, 629.
53. Poliakov (1947), 24–25; Arendt (1944), 54–57; Barzun (1937), 50–57.
54. Pflanze (1966), 131.
55. Sand (1964), 23–24, 30; Monas (1961), 191; Ray (1945–46), II, 316.
56. Balzac (1968–71), I, 14; *idem* (1965), I, 51.
57. Magill (1948), 494n.; Thureau-Danzin (1884–92), VI, 66–67.
58. Beales (1969), 156; Balabine (1914), I, 48; Bamberger (1899), 13.
59. Evans (1931), 105–106; Rohr (1963), 52–53; Liptzin (1926), 47ff.
60. Masson (1908), 253; Riehl (1861), 26.
61. Parker (1899), III, 441; Martineau (1969), II, 377–378; Michelet (1973), 6–7; Andlaw (1862), II, 79; Marx and Engels (1975–88), IV, ch. V, vi; Balzac (1968–71), xviii, i.
62. Balzac (1968–71), I, 12, 14–15.
63. Masson (1975); 254; Ray (1945–46), II, 353–354.
64. Minogue (1967), 7.

CHAPTER FOUR

1. Crossland (1967), 75–76, 433; Silliman (1980), II, 322.
2. Martineau (1869), 149; Bitterling (1959), foreword; *Dictionary of Scientific Biography* (hereafter referred to as DSB), VI, 549ff.

3. Treitschke (1915–19), VI, 323–326; Eilers (1856), V, 155–156; Reumont (1885), 145.

4. Reumont (1885), 144–147; Müller (1928), *passim*; Humboldt (1860), *passim*.

5. Klein (1926), I, 17–18; Du Bois-Reymond (1982), 44; Agassiz (1869), 44.

6. Humboldt (1860), 35–38; Du Bois-Reymond (1982), 44; Treitschke (1915–19), VII, 194–196.

7. Carrière (1967), 15; Henry (1979), III, 393; Du Bois-Reymond (1982), 58; Ben-David (1984), 95, 100.

8. Merz (1903–14), I, 174–176; Caneva (1978), 132–136, 138–139; Liebig (1891), 33–34.

9. Kuhn (1959), 338; Haines (1957), 31; Merz (1903–14), I, 178n., 204; Liebig (1891), 38; Turner (1971), 147.

10. Langer (1969), 535; Du Bois-Reymond (1982), 39; Liebig (1891), 33; Caneva (1978), 131.

11. Coleman (1971), 4, 7; Ben-David (1984), 123–124; Du Bois-Reymond (1982), 54; Merz (1903–14), I, 212–216; Caneva (1978), 137.

12. Merz (1903–14), I, 183; Hayek (1952), 33; Gillispie (1960), 352–353; Caneva (1978), 68–69, 95, 136; Helmholtz (1971), 233.

13. Coleman (1971), 122; DSB, II, 531; Du Bois-Reymond (1848), xxxviii–xix; Goodfield (1981), 135–139; Temkin (1946), 324–325.

14. Ackerknecht (1932), 78–80; Du Bois-Reymond (1982), 8–13, 18; DSB, XIV, 40–41.

15. Du Bois-Reymond (1982), 39, 41, 79.

16. Ackerknecht (1932), 90; Du Bois-Reymond (1982), viii; DSB, VIII, 541.

17. Rossiter (1975), 26; Liebig (1891), 31–33, 35–36, 38; Pottenkofer (1874), 3–8.

18. Liebig (1891), 36–38; Pottenkofer (1874), 18; Crossland (1967), 435.

19. Rossiter (1975), 10, app. 1, 2, 5; Schnabel (1929 37), III, 213.

20. F. L. Holmes, introd. to Liebig (1924), cxiv–cxvi.

21. Coleman (1971), 138; Bernal (1953), 78–79.

22. Carrière (1967), 112, 165, 185, 199, 233; Liebig (1924), lxi–lxii; Koenigsberger (1906), 82.

23. Du Bois-Reymond (1918), 143; Gillispie (1960), 382; Klein (1926), I, 224; Helmholtz (1966), 20.

24. Helmholtz (1966), 20–37; Klein (1926), I, 223–224; DSB, VI, 241ff.; Du Bois-Reymond (1912), II, 518, 520.

25. Du Bois-Reymond (1918), 122–123, 128–132.

26. Koenigsberger (1906), 31, 44–45; Helmholtz (1966), 21–22; Elkana (1970), 163–264, 274–275.

27. Helmholtz (1966), 23.

28. Gillispie (1960), 382; Koenigsberger (1906), 44; Helmholtz (1966), 42.
29. Kuhn (1959), 321; Coleman (1971), 122; Du Bois-Reymond (1912), II, 520, 570.
30. Helmholtz (1966), 25–26; Shryock (1936), 202; Du Bois-Reymond (1912), II, 520, 570.
31. Carrière (1967), 134.
32. Hyman (1982), 90–98; Carrière (1967); 134; Haines (1957), 18–19.
33. Fisk (1838), 571; Mohl (1902), II, 410–411; Silliman (1980); Lyell (1856), 237–238; Bristed (1852), I, 176–177.
34. Quoted in Merz (1903–14), I, 239n.
35. DSB, IV, 527–529; Henry (1979), III, 318–319; Helmholtz (1884), II, 277.
36. DSB, IV, 527–540; Cohen (1985), 301–305; Holton and Roller (1958), 495–497.
37. Ringer (1979), 212; Mendelsohn (1964), 39.
38. Haines (1957), 294; Gillispie (1951), 192–201; Greville (1938), IV, 42.
39. Langer (1969), 543–544; Gillispie (1951), x–xi, 126–133, 187.
40. Gillispie (1951), 149–183, 217; Coleman (1971), 70–71.
41. DSB, III, 563 ff.; Haines (1957), 39–41.
42. Jacobi quoted in *Deutsche Akademie* (1959), 89; Helmholtz quoted in Merz (1903–14), I, 175n.; Liebig quoted in Lyell (1856), I, 244–246.
43. Schnabel (1929–37), III, 209; Landes (1969), 276–277.
44. Dance (1976), 62–64; Varnhagen von Ense (1972), IV, 59.
45. Spencer (1926), 200–201, 297; Morley (1881), 27, 377; Hayek (1952), 331; *North American Review* (1838), 461.
46. Garrison (1929), 409–410, 428–429, 437–438; Dodds (1952), 118.
47. Schieferdecker (1844), vi–xii; Granville (1837), *passim*; Sealsfield (1828), 43–44.
48. Dallas (1892), 77; Kerner (1897), II, 350–351; Kaplan (1975), 25–26; Martineau (1969), I, 474, 513–514; Varnhagen von Ense (1972), III, 325; Lorenz (1896), 150–151.
49. Helmholtz (1971), 232–243; *idem* (1884), I, 361.
50. Engelmann quoted in Kamen (1986), 232.
51. Virchow quoted in Major (1954), II, 790; Helmholtz (1971), 234–235; *idem* (1966), 21, 36–37.
52. Major (1954), II, 793–795; Kussmaul (1900), 390.
53. DSB, XIV, 40–41; Garrison (1929), 457; Shryock (1936), 120; Major (1954), II, 806.
54. DSB, II, 24–34; Shryock (1936), 197, 203–204; Olmstead (1938), 7–19.
55. Greville (1938), V, 472; Varnhagen von Ense (1972), IV, 4.
56. Garrison (1929), 472, 505–506; Dodds (1952), 287.

57.   Simon (1973), 4, 9; Hayek (1952), 385, 388; Zeldin (1979), II, 595–596.

58.   Simon (1973), 6; Manuel (1962), 261–268, 272–273.

59.   Hayek (1952), 353, 361–362; Zeldin (1969), II, 595; Billington (1960), 808–814.

60.   DSB, XI, 236–239; Porter (1986), 18; Hayek (1952), 74.

61.   Carlyle (1885), 80; Trevelyan quoted in Stern (1956), 241; Gooch (1959), 163–164.

62.   Greville (1938), V, 474; Cockburn (1874), II, 232–235; Croker (1885), III, 12; Langer (1969), 550.

63.   Droysen (1929), I, 278.

64.   Gooch (1959), 274; Macaulay (1968), I, 1–2; Strachey (1931), 174–175.

65.   Neville (1963–64), I, 273.

66.   Gershoy (1951), 140–142.

67.   Fueter (1914), 667; Neff (1947), 107.

68.   Gooch (1959), 101–102; Ranke (1867–90), LIII–LIV, 61; Von Laue (1950), 25.

69.   Gooch (1959), 83; Krieger (1977), 361.

70.   Krieger (1977), 162; Von Laue (1950), 122; White (1973), 169.

71.   Delbruck (1905), I, 71–72; Von Laue (1950), 145.

72.   Dodds (1952), 201; Jagow (1938), 132; Martin (1875–80), II, 170.

73.   List (1927–36), V, 514–515.

74.   Schnabel (1929–37), III, 338–339; Schmoller quoted in Gehrig (1966), 10.

75.   Schnabel (1929–37), III, 125–127; James (1989), 69–71.

CHAPTER FIVE

1.   Gerlach (1903), I, 239.

2.   Greville (1938), III, 222; Foord (1952), 401, 404–410; *Annual Register* (1839), 2–3.

3.   Creevy (1904), I, 27, 277; Greville (1938), I, 337; Plumb (1956), 148–152.

4.   Bagehot (1889), 46, 322; Blakiston (1972), 409; Plumb (1956), 150; Greville (1938), IV, 244; Apponyi (1913–26), IV, 22.

5.   Treitschke (1915–19), VI, 449; St. Aulaire (1925), 262.

6.   Martin (1875–80), I, 241.

7.   Neville (1963–64), I, 20, 24, 31; Dino (1909–10), II, 174–176.

8.   Croker (1884), II, 318–319; Benson and Esher (1907), I, 199; Greville (1938), IV, 110; Argyll (1906), I, 151; Strachey (1969), 50–52, 75.

9.   Victoria quoted in Petrie (1961), 34; Croker (1884), II, 341; Parker (1899), II, 396–397.

10.   Eyck (1959), 28; Campbell (1881), II, 101; Pollock (1887), I, 82–83; Benson and Esher (1907), I, 268; Greville (1938), 174–175.

11.   Bagehot (1829), 83; Hanham (1969), 41.

12.   St. Aulaire (1925), 268; Mill (1849), 13–14; Senior (1968), I, 34.

13.   Bagehot (1929), 103.

14.   Parker (1899), II, 414.

15.   Greville (1938), IV, 241.

16.   Jagow (1938), 67; Benson and Esher (1907), I, 251; Parker (1899), II, 408–409; Anson quoted in Ames (1968), 26–27.

17.   Martin (1875–80), II, 547; Broughton (1909–11), VI, 235–236.

18.   Jagow (1938), 97–98, 108; Martin (1875–80), II, 366–367; Hodder (1887), II, 245–246.

19.   Greville (1938), VII, 304; Parker (1899), II, 414.

20.   Jagow (1938), 108; Ernst (1888), I, 94; Senior (1878), I, 101.

21.   Greville (1938), IV, 413–414; Eyck (1959), 30.

22.   Scott quoted in Bagehot (1858), 51.

23.   Ponsonby (1942), 350.

24.   Hanham (1969), 33–36.

25.   Lipscomb (1903), XII, 376.

26.   Gregory (1894), 58–59; Guttsman (1963), 53–54; Kitson-Clark (1967), 210; Morley (1881), 272–273.

27.   Emerson (1968), 364; Kitson-Clark (1967), 300; Morley (1923), I, 88, 287; Parker (1907), II, 34; Gladstone quoted in Le May (1979), 183.

28.   Tocqueville (1958), 42; Broughton (1909–11), VI, 263–264.

29.   Ward (1970), 13; Arnstein (1973), 216; Christie (1928), 165; Russell quoted in Le May (1979), 10; Guizot (1858–67), V, 132–133.

30.   Parker (1907), I, 336; Gash (1979), 18; Spring (1977), 37–38.

31.   Spring (1977), 2–3; Spring (1971), 39–42.

32.   Colman (1849), I, 27–29; Hertford quoted in Guttsman (1968), 71; Gash (1979), 17–18.

33.   Spring (1977), Tocqueville (1958), 76–77; Trevelyan quoted in O'Boyle (1970), 482.

34.   Ticknor (1876), 446–447; Greville (1938), I, 227n, XII, 212n.

35.   Blum (1978), 11, 24n.; Gash (1979), 18.

36.   Stone (1984), 412–413; Arnstein (1973), 245, 248; Morley (1881), 346.

37.   Christie (1928), 143; Greville (1938), VI, 360–361; Greville (1883–1905), 433; Argyll (1906), I, 315–316; Raikes (1956–57), IV, 203; Guedella (1931), 479; Trevelyan (1876), II, 118.

38.   Raikes (1856–57), IV, 188; Neumann (1928), II, 169; Senior (1878), II, 391.

39.   Cooper (1971), 330; Masson (1908), 230; Greville (1938), V, 25; Mohl (1902), I, 418.

40.   Tocqueville (1958), 42–43; Surtees (1827), 201.x.

Notes

41. Greville (1838), vi, 369–372; Guedella (1931), 477–481.
42. Faucher (1845), xvi–xvii.
43. Aydelotte (1866), 102; Gash (1953), 94–97.
44. Benson and Esher (1907), I, 491; Kitson-Clark (1967), 104; Gash (1979), 160–163; Le May (1979), 37, 59.
45. O'Connell quoted in Trevelyan (1946), 221; Hodder (1887), I, 244.
46. Kitson-Clark (1936), 7; Broglie (1938–41), I, 112; Greville (1938), II, 163; Hodder (1887), I, 244.
47. Parker (1899), III, 430–432, 551; Martin (1875–80), 221; Broughton (1909–11), VI, 262; Broglie (1938–41), 113; Woodward (1938), 110.
48. Bright quoted in Morley (1881), 127; Trevelyan (1913), 1–2, 171.
49. Chaloner (1970), 135–151; Trevelyan (1913), 1–2; Briggs (1967), 59–60.
50. Cockburn (1874), 276–277; Croker (1884), III, 65–69; Macaulay (1974–81), IV, 188.
51. Crocker (1884), II, 247; Peel (1920), 265; Bentinck quoted in Gregory (1894), 107.
52. Morley (1881), 260–261; McCord (1967), 94; Gash (1972), 703–705; *Annual Register* (1950), 174–180; Guest (1950), 245.
53. Greville (1938), VI, 242; Peel (1920), 280–282.
54. Croker (1884), II, 239, 261; Parker (1907), II, 99–100.
55. Faucher (1845), II, 331; Pumphrey (1959), 4–5.
56. *Edinburgh Review* (1840), LXXII, 13, 41; Emerson (1968), 199; Croker (1884), III, 220.
57. Morley (1881), 346, 348–349; Duffy (1892), 26; Vaughan (1843), 1–5; Howitt (1846), 135; Ticknor (1876), II, 150; Emerson (1968), 198.
58. Calvert (1852), 12; *cf.* Greville (1938), V, 51.
59. Faucher (1845), II, 328; Guest (1950), 133, 164; Morley (1881), 373, 375–376; Trevelyan (1913), 177.
60. Guest (1950), 131–133; Greville (1938), II, 75, 222; Bagehot (1889), 43–44.
61. Kitson-Clark (1967), 290ff.; Morley (1881), 457; Bagehot (1929), 24–25.
62. Cannadine (1980), 46–47; Abramowitz and Eliasberg (1957), 9–11.
63. Edmonds (1964), 77.
64. Benson and Esher (1907), I, 533; Greville (1938), V, 29; Carlyle (1843), Book I, ch. 3; Senior (1968), 22–23; Victoria quoted in Gaskell (1972), lviii.
65. Heine (1893), VI, 363–364, 366; Marx and Engels (1975–88), IV, 581–583.
66. Kitson-Clark (1967), 61; Dodds (1952), 140–142; Linton (1894), 89.
67. Linton (1894), 42; McCarthy (1879), I, 79; Randell (1972), 25–33; Wilson (1970), 118–132; Cooper (1971), 175, 177; Trevelyan (1913), 79.

68. Cooper (1971), 179; Adams (1968), 209; Read and Glasgow (1961), 60–61.
69. Mather (1953), 49–53; Taylor (1885), II, 35; Malmesbury (1884), 225; Greville (1938), VI, 5.
70. Greville (1938), VI, 52–53; Postgate (1975), 122–125; Smith (1979), 111–113.
71. *Morning Chronicle* quoted in Smith (1979), 115; Shee (1893), 157; Marx and Engels (1959), VI, 77–78.
72. Read and Glasgow (1961), 140.
73. Colman (1849), 244, 253–254; Mokyr (1983), 7–8, 218; Carlyle (1882), 30; Parker (1899), III, 177; Parker (1907), II, 78–79.
74. McCarthy (1879), I, 189, 192; Gwynn (1949), 12.
75. Parker (1899), III, 18.
76. Treble (1970), 165; Parker (1907), I, 367; Parker (1899), III, 116.
77. Campbell (1881), II, 184–187.
78. Mokyr (1983), 31, 263–264; Macaulay (1974–81), V, 310n.; Slicher van Bath (1963), 270.
79. Gwynn (1949), 239ff.
80. Cockburn (1874), II, 211–212.
81. Greville (1938), VI, 47, 75; Dickens (1965), V, 254; *Annual Register* (1848), 36–37.
82. *Annual Register* (1848), 128–147; Colman (1849), II, 370–371.
83. Peel quoted in Morley (1881), 320; Rude (1969), 242–243.
84. *Annual Register* (1848), 124.
85. Dodds (1952), 474–475; Benson and Esher (1907), II, 383–384; Shee (1893), 187–188, 190.

CHAPTER SIX

1. Metternich (1880–84) VI, 166; Brougham quoted in Monin (1887), 295.
2. Lucas-Dubreton (1929), 170; Guizot quoted in Woodward (1929) 144–145; Jardin and Tudesq (1983), 94, 97–101; Pinkney (1964), 37.
3. Joinville (1970), 45n.
4. Blanc (1848), I, 269.
5. Apponyi (1913–26), IV, 48.
6. Boigne (1907–8), IV, 396; Tocqueville (1942), 28–29; Senior (1878), II, 390; Howarth (1961), 272–275.
7. Boigne (1907–8), IV, 370.
8. Normanby (1857), I, 30–31; Remusat (1958–67), II, 581, III, 501.
9. Meyendorff (1923), II, 104; Martin (1875–80), II, 134.
10. Kemp (1972), 113; Mitchell (1981), 609, 610; Pinkney (1986), 30, 44, 45; Crouzet (1974), 170; Cameron (1967), 105–107.

11. Guizot (1858–67), IV, 240.

12. Ibid., V, 32; cf. Blanc (1848), I, 269–271.

13. Guizot (1858–67), IV, 272; Michelet (1973), 83n.; Daumard (1970), 5.

14. Ponteil (1968), 68–69; Daumard (1970), 338.

15. Guizot (1858–67), IV, 274–275; Rémond (1968), I, 87–88; Chaussinard-Nogaret (1975), 290.

16. Nesselrode (1908–12), VIII, 95–96; Rémond (1968), I, 84–85; Remusat (1958–67), III, 88–90.

17. Alton-Shee (1869), I, 122–123; Pinkney (1986), 151; Newman and Simpson (1986), II, 741–742.

18. Flaubert (1980–82), I, xvii; Tocqueville (1970), 5; Senior (1968), I, 134; Mill (1849), 7.

19. Zeldin (1979), I, 416.

20. Tocqueville (1970), 5; Higonnet (1967), 207.

21. Gutman (1978), 145–146; Lhomme (1960), 36–42; Thackeray (1883), 118; Newman and Simpson (1987), I, 488.

22. Beyle (1838), I, 30–31; Normanby (1857), I, 18; Alton-Shee (1869), I, 136–143, 146.

23. Senior (1968), I, 32, 68–69, 122–123, 157, 161; Castellane (1895–97), III, 373.

24. Toutain (1963), 50; Blanqui (1851), 9–10; Fish (1838), 89; Weber (1976), 131–133; 144; Blum (1978), 185.

25. Fish (1838), 89–90; Durbin (1844), I, 183; Weber (1976), 170–174.

26. Weber (1976), 3–8, 23–29, 67–69; Pinkney (1986), 6–8, 49; Ross (1893), 315; Margedant (1979), 338–339; Zeldin (1979), I, 179–180, 478.

27. Metternich (1880–84), VI, 452; Senior (1878), I, 135; Newman and Simpson (1987), I, 771; Jardin and Tudesq (1973), I, 385; Pouthas (1952), 143–148; Durbin (1844), II, 42–43.

28. M'Culloch (1844), II, 546–556; Gardner (1848), 45; Musgrave (1848), I, 201; Jardin and Tudesq (1983), 374; Newman and Simpson (1987), 773.

29. Blanc (1843–51), III, 26; Hoetzsch (1923), II, 32.

30. Veron (1853–55), IV, 124; Hugo (1926), II, 157, 159; Boigne (1907–8), IV, 362–365; Castellane (1895–97), IV, 362–365; Senior (1878), I, 131–133; Cass (1840), 26–29.

31. Ponteil (1968), 101; Pinkney (1986), 65–66; Price (1972), 33.

32. Senior (1878), I, 127; Normanby (1857), I, 17.

33. Heine (1893), VI, 302; La Hodde (1850), *passim*; Alton-Shee (1869), I, 270; Cass (1840), 32–34.

34. Vincent (1968), 59–61; Cass (1840), 23–24, 93–94; Villermé (1840), II, 325–326; Heine (1893), VI, 238–239.

35. Falloux (1925–26), I, 220–221; Broglie (1938–41), I, 70–71; Perrier quoted in Lucas-Dubreton (1929), 179; Nesselrode (1908–12), VIII, 128.

36. Thackeray (1903), 151–152; Thureau-Danzin (1884–92), I, 427–429; Morse (1896), 106, 127; Newman and Simpson (1987), I, 291, II, 1067–1068.

37. September laws in Collins (1970), 99–100; Annenkov (1968), 72; Rush (1860), 338; Greville (1938), III, 340; Durbin (1844) I, 120, 141, 150; Sherburne (1847), 179.

38. Thureau-Danzin (1884–92), II, 296ff., III, 34, 146, IV, 343, III, 116; Howarth (1961), 230–231.

39. Apponyi (1913–26), III, 281–282; Cass (1840), 8–9; Raikes (1856–57), III, 133; Croker (1884), II, 163–164; Ross (1893), 215.

40. Martin (1875–80), I, 156; Humboldt (1860), 246.

41. Heine (1893), VI, 233; Börnstein (1884), I, 319–321, 326; Guizot (1858–67), VII, 38–39; Joinville (1895), 236–238; Dino (1909–10), 153; Normanby (1857), I, 210–211; Remusat (1958–67), IV, 36.

42. Andlaw (1857), II, 56–57; Heine (1893), VI, 351; Remusat (1958–67), IV, 36; Boigne (1907–8), IV, 330–332, 394–395; Broglie (1981), 306.

43. Heine (1893), VI, 344–345; Guizot (1858–67), I, 216; Woodward (1929), 140–141, 144–145; Priouret (1959), 71–72; Remusat (1958–67), II, 404–405.

44. Balabine (1914), I, 23–24; Broughton (1909–11), V, 354; Hohenlohe-Schillingsfürst (1906), I, 67; Priouret (1959), 72–73; Woodward (1929), 116.

45. Naville (1963–64), I, xlv, 199–205, II, 272; Broglie (1938–41), I, 83; Remusat (1958–67), IV, 41–43; Quennell (1980), 97–98; St. Aulaire (1925), 249–250.

46. Guizot (1858–67), VI, 4; Johnson (1963), 11–13, 432.

47. Remusat (1958–67), III, 53–58; Castellane (1895–97), III, 213.

48. Ernst (1888), I, 214; Greville (1938), V, 392.

49. Motley (1889), I, 106; Apponyi (1913–26), III, 253; Priouret (1959), 72.

50. Castellane (1895–97), III, 273, 331, 392; Normanby (1857), I, 37–40; Johnson (1963), 253–254; Raikes (1856–57), IV, 128–129; Higonnet (1967), 212–213; Tocqueville quoted in Howarth (1961), 310n.

51. Loomis (1967), 15, 124ff.; *Economist* quoted in Hirsch (1976), 3; Vitzthum von Eckstädt (1886), 55.

52. Jardin and Tudesq (1983), 201–203; Baughman (1959), 1ff.

53. Mill (1849), 2; Falloux (1925), I, 235; Hoeztsch (1923), II, 35–36.

54. Falloux (1925–26), I, 236; Ernst (1888), I, 214; Remusat (1958–67), IV, 241–246; Greville (1938), VI, 22, 24.

55. Newman and Simpson (1987), I, 20, 169–170, 545–546, II, 836–840, 897–900; Tilly (1970), 158; *idem* (1972), 228–232; Langer (1969), 348–350; Clark (1973), 13.

56. Normanby (1857), II, 280, 281.
57. Newman and Simpson (1987), II, 898–900.
58. Fröbel (1890–91), I, 74; Guedella (1922), 141; Senior (1968), I, 256–257; Guizot (1858–67), V, 258–259.
59. Castellane (1895–97), III, 278; Apponyi (1913–26), III, 422; Echard (1985), 346–347.
60. Normanby (1857), I, xii.
61. Senior (1968), 56, 101, 104–105; Newman and Simpson (1987), I, 257; Echard (1985), 523–524.
62. Bagehot (1879), I, 310ff.; Senior (1887), I, 219–223; Echard (1985), 146–147; Margedant (1984), 672, 677–678; Tilly (1970), 159–160.
63. Bagehot (1879), 310ff.; Echard (1985), 171, 613–614.

CHAPTER SEVEN

1. Andrian-Werburg (1843–47), I, 48–49; Friedrich (1921), 81–82; Beidtel (1896–98), II, 47, 235.
2. Palacky quoted in Thomson (1943), 165–166; Rietra (1980), 31; Ross (1893), 194.
3. Thompson (1849), 339–340.
4. Hübner (1891), 11–12; Hartig (1853), 25; Blum (1943), 24–25; Metternich (1880–84), VII, 620.
5. Hartig (1850), 12; Srbik (1925), I, pt. 1, 453–454.
6. Hübner (1891), 79–80; Trollope (1838), I, 382.
7. Mohl (1902) II, 110; Kudlich (1873), I, 139; Grillparzer (1924); Metternich (1880–84), VI, 220–221.
8. Kübeck (1909), I, ii, 679; Radvany (1971), 68–69.
9. Kübeck (1909), I, ii, 679; Raikes (1856–57), III, 326; St. Aulaire (1925), 113; Ross (1893), 194.
10. Friedrich (1921), 68; Frankl (1910), 166; Treitschke (1915–19), VI, 31.
11. St. Aulaire (1925), 337–338; Knappich (1969), 279–280; Slade (1840), 108–109; Friedrich (1921), 68–69; Raikes (1856–57), III, 326.
12. Radvany (1971), 74; Hübner (1891), 8; Kübeck (1909), I, i, 846–847, I, ii, 768; Metternich (1880–84), VI, 218–219, 224, 226–227.
13. Kübeck (1909), I, i, 787, suppl. 91; Radvany (1971), 128; Metternich (1880–84), VIII, 212.
14. St. Aulaire (1925), 110–111, 185–186; Posch (1954), 364–368, 377; Sutter (1963), 165ff.
15. Broglie (1938–41), I, 89; Hoeztsch (1923), I, 7; Metternich (1880–84), III, 224–225; Prokesch (1881), II, 196; Ticknor (1909), II, 13; Guizot (1858–67), V, 21; Naville (1963–64), I, 70; Greville (1883–1905), I, 243; Senior (1878), 391.

16. Ticknor (1909), II, 13; St. Aulaire (1925), 110; Radvany (1971), 138, 140; Vitzthum (1886), 72.

17. Kissinger (1964), 321; Walker (1968), 328; Kübeck (1909), suppl. 39.

18. Metternich (1880–84), VII, 220–221; Hartig (1853), 50.

19. Ticknor (1909), II, 13; Metternich (1880–84), VI, 443, VII, 211, VIII, 427.

20. Woodward (1929), 29–30; Metternich (1880–84), VII, 336; Meyer (1924), 25.

21. Kübeck (1909), I, ii, 439, 681; Metternich (1880–84), VII, 48–49, 595; Veuillot (1924–38), 359.

22. Grillparzer (1924), VI, 428; St. Aulaire (1925), 24–28; Srbik (1925), I, 244–246; Grunwald (1953), I, 234, 236–237; Castle (1921–23), I, 497–498.

23. Kissinger (1964), 8. For historiographical discussion see Milne (1975), 1ff.; Schroeder (1961), 237ff.

24. Frankl (1910), 248–249; Stiles (1852), I, 86–78, 90; Emerson (1968), 33–34, 36ff.; Srbik (1925), I, 493–494; Castle (1921–23), 496; Bertier de Sauvigny (1962), 438.

25. Seton-Watson (1939), XVII, 524–525; Redlich (1920–26), I, 63n; Rietra (1980), 6–7.

26. Bauernfeld (1923), 247; Hartig (1853), 38–30; Frankl (1910), 260–261; Stern (1894–1929), VI, 354; Rietra (1980), 7–9.

27. Kudlich (1873), I, 59, 77; Springer (1892), 25, 48, 74; Bauernfeld (1923), 244; Thompson (1849), 96–99; Stekl (1973), 104–114.

28. Andrian-Werburg (1843–47), I, 45–46; Hübner (1891), 82–83; Annenkov (1968), 67.

29. Moltke (1891), I, 125–126. In 1857 destruction of the wall began, to be replaced in 1867 by the grand boulevard, the *Ringstrasse.* May (1966), 33.

30. Hübner (1891), 79–80; Bauernfeld (1923), 258; Schuselka (1843), 24; Howitt (1842), 383; Grillparzer quoted in Redlich (1929), 3.

31. St. Aulaire (1925), 39–40; Andrian-Werburg (1843–47), I, 25; Paget (1971), I, 49, 237.

32. Polisensky (1980), 79; Sealsfield (1828), 163; Blum (1947), 36, 101n.

33. St. Aulaire (1925), 38, 41–43, 83, 378; Kübeck (1909), I, 237; Raikes (1856–57), IV, 263; Friedjung (1908–12), II, 273; Stekl (1973), 27; Uhl (1888), 490; Friedrich (1921), 85; Kudlich (1873), I, 118.

34. Kudlich (1873), 45; Neumann (1928), II, 61–62; Brunner (1949), 333; Uhl (1888), 487–488; Blum (1947), 37; Janos (1982), 64.

35. Hinrichs quoted in Abel (1967), 256.

36. Blum (1947), 70–80; *idem* (1978), 69; Polisensky (1980), 47.

37. Blum (1947), 45–46; Kudlich (1873), I, 46, 65; Prinz (1962), 3.

38. Friedjung (1908–12), I, 335, II, 293; Redlich (1920–26), I, 47–53; Springer (1892), 50–53; Kimmel (1970), 119; St. Aulaire (1925), 43–44; Stekl (1973), 132–133.

39. Blum (1943), 26ff.
40. Rietra (1980), 26–27; Rath (1969), 8, 9, 16, 26, 30–32; Bibl (1911), 52–53; Bauernfeld (1923), 247; Frankl (1910), 176–179; Falk (1948), 139–143.
41. Blum (1947), 91–132, 171–192.
42. Schuselka quoted in Bibl (1911), 28; Andrian-Werburg (1843–47), I, 48; Andlaw (1862), II, 98; Kussmaul (1900), 360.
43. Blum (1947), 204–205; Redlich (1920–26), I, 74–76.
44. Shee (1893), 113; Ernst (1888), I, 174; Janos (1982), 50–54; Sugar (1967), 112–115; Pesek (1970), 131–132; Jaszi (1966), 132; Zacek (1970), 95–96.
45. Blum (1947), 207–208, 225–231; *idem* (1978), 340; Reid (1891), 422; Namier (1944), 15–16.
46. John quoted in Posch (1954), 382–383; Redlich (1920–26), I, 71; Metternich (1880–84), VII, 623.
47. Marx (1965), 141ff.; Rath (1969), 15–16; Falk (1948), 143–144, 147; Vitzthum (1886), 72–73, 75.
48. Hübner (1891), 11. Except where otherwise indicated the following account of the 1848 revolution is from Rath (1969) and Robertson (1952).
49. Pech (1969), 123ff; Carr (1937), 156–157.
50. Falk (1948), 154n.; Blum (1947), 232–236; Friedjung (1908–12), I, 362.
51. Hubner (1891), 317, 320–321; Schwarzenberg (1946), 34, and n.; Knappich (1969), 283.
52. Schiemann (1904–19), IV, 195 and n.; Redlich (1929), 49; Hoeztsch (1923), II, 359; Friedjung (1908–12), II, 245.
53. Schwarzenberg (1946), 206–207; Redlich (1929), 34–37; Joinville (1895), 232, 331; Bibl (1922–24), II, 186; Langer (1969), 483.
54. Schwarzenberg (1946), 26; Redlich (1929), 30–31; Falk (1848), 156.
55. Schwarzenberg (1946), 109–110, 109n.; Janos (1982), 88.

CHAPTER EIGHT

1. Ernest (1888), 136–138; Ernest August (1925), 250–54.
2. Ticknor (1909), I, 407; Senior (1871), II, 275–276; D'Auvergne (1911), 13–14; Valentin (1930), I, 141–142, 148–149, 191, 209–210, 229, 231.
3. Mohl (1902), II, 17–19.
4. Bodenstedt (1888), 118; Plumb (1956), 150–151; Longford (1964), 17; *Times* quoted in Willis (1954), 413.
5. Reid (1890), I, 301; Willis (1954), 413; Treitschke (1915–19), VI, 186–191; Valentin (1930), I, 197–207.
6. Leland (1893), 160; Nesselrode (1908–12), IX, 15; *Times*, Mar. 2,

1847, 5; Varnhagen von Ense (1972), IV, 246–247; Kussmaul (1900), 323–325; Treitschke (1915–19), VII, 64–65, 475–491; Pottendorff (1955), 427.

7.   M'Culloch (1844), II, 679; Adam (1897), 259; Legge (1910), 168.

8.   Lorenz (1896), 293–294, 302.

9.   Bauernfeld (1923), 207–209.

10.   Treitschke (1915–19), VI, 142–151, VII, 494–495; Valentin (1930), I, 43–50; Laing (1850), 430–431; Varnhagen von Ense (1972), I, 341, II, 132, 232, 234–235; Sheehan (1989), 405–408.

11.   Motley (1889), I, 151; Edmunds (1964), 91; Fish (1838), 455; Howitt (1842), 10, 223.

12.   Howitt (1842), 70; Moltke (1960), 174–175; Dodds (1952), 198–199; Martin (1875–80) I, 247–248; Friedrich (1921), 14; Siemens (1922), 6.

13.   Howitt (1842), 31–32, 58–59, 64, 77–78, 197, 238–239; Motley (1889), I, 23; Laing (1850), 456–460; Trollope (1834), 125.

14.   Nesselrode (1908–12), VIII, 45; Demidoff (1855), I, 21–22; Friedrich (1921), 21–22; Varnhagen von Ense (1972), I, 324–327, III, 388–389; Granville (1837), I, 301, II, 27–33, 81, 94–95, 119, 260, 350.

15.   Trollope (1834), 179–180, 192; Granville (1837), II, 209; Varnhagen von Ense (1972), II, 271–272, 279; Treitschke (1915–19), VII, 520.

16.   Motley (1889), I, 32; Delbruck (1905), I, 194; Varnhagen von Ense (1972), I, 28, II, 283, III, 216; Humboldt (1860), 392; Bülow-Cummerow (1842), I, 93–96; Riehl (1861), 307.

17.   Riehl (1861), 152–153, 155–156, 367–368, 373–377, 380; Bismarck (1899), I, 16; Stahl and Yuell (1970), III, 159–160; Bramsted (1964), 47–48.

18.   Riehl (1861), 246, 248, 256–257; Stahl and Yuell (1970), III, 144–145; Schnabel (1929–37), III, 437.

19.   Dronke (1953), 273–274; Sheehan (1978), 32; Rohr (1963), 10, 131–162; Bramsted (1964), 71–73, 129, 174–175.

20.   Noyes (1966), 17, 20–21; Rostow (1964), 109–111; Rohr (1963), 35–39; Schnabel (1929–37), III, 439; Delbruck (1905), I, 142–143.

21.   Motley (1889), I, 70; Morley (1881), 88; Treitschke (1915–19), VI, 172, 407, 412; M'Culloch (1844), I, 303; Faulkner (1932), I, 286.

22.   Deutsche Akademie (1959), 90n.; Humboldt (1860), 29, 50, 121; Ross (1893), 187; Henry Adams quoted in Von Laue (1950), 140.

23.   Gleig (1839), I, 61–62, 67; M'Culloch (1844), I, 357; Laing (1850), 239–240; Gottstein (1901–2), 244; Ackerknecht (1932), 67.

24.   Greville (1938), V. 10; Broglie (1938–41), I, 88; Born (1898), 10.

25.   Varnhagen von Ense (1972), VI, 112; Taylor (1946), 66; Valentin (1930), I, 36; Lorenz (1896), 140; Reumont (1885), 143; Humboldt (1860), 150; Treitschke (1915–19), VI, 310–311.

26.   Benson and Esher (1907), I, 475–476; Greville (1938), V, 7; Ernest (1888), II, 325; Reumont (1855), 310; Varnhagen von Ense (1972), 166, 284.

Notes

27. Benson and Esher (1907), I, 476n.; Metternich (1880–84), 333–334; Gottschall (1898), 97; Born (1898), 16.

28. Humboldt (1860), 136–137; Varnhagen von Ense (1972), I, 253, III, 95; Treitschke (1915–19), VI, 322.

29. Ernest August (1925), 181; Hohenlohe-Ingelfingen (1897–1907), I, 192–194; Morris (1976), 168; Hamerow (1958), 72–73.

30. Treitschke (1915–19), VI, 525–554; Hoetzsch (1923), I, 184–185; Gerlach (1891–92), I, 96; Eilers (1856), III, 211; Sheehan (1989), 621–624.

31. Schiemann (1904–19), IV, 101; Metternich (1881–84), VII, 379–382; Craig (1955), 88–89; Klein (1914), 91; Hohenlohe-Ingelfingen (1897–1907), I, 201–202; Gottschall (1898), 263.

32. Vitzthum (1886), 47; Ernest (1888), I, 149–150.

33. Riehl (1861), 313, 367, 384–385; Laing (1850), 176n.; O'Boyle (1970), 478; Hawkins (1838), 187–188; Hamerow (1958), 64–67.

34. Noyes (1966), 32–33; *Historical Statistics* (1949), 34; Walker (1971), 770–780; Hamerow (1958), 75–86; Sheehan (1989), 639–642.

35. Valentin (1930), I, 52–54; Klein (1914), 79–83; Varnhagen von Ense (1972), II, 307–314; Sheehan (1989), 643–645.

36. Riehl (1861), 55–60; Howitt (1842), 42–44; Silliman (1980), II, 341–342; Faulkner (1832), 44, 80–81; Bülow-Cummerow (1847), n.; Kussmaul (1900), 39–40; Blum (1978), 105–106, 387.

37. Hohenlohe-Schillingsfürst (1906), I, 25–26; U.S. consul quoted in Hansen (1945), 252; Apponyi (1913–26), IV, 72; Milnes quoted in Fischer (1922), 31–32; Biedermann (1886–87), I, 215–216.

38. Andlaw (1862), 116–117; Treitschke (1915–19), VII, 440, 502–518; Hohenlohe-Schillingsfürst (1906), I, 40.

39. Duckwitz (1877), 72, 215; Valentin (1930), I, 246; Johann (1958), 194; Hamerow (1958), 64–69; Ticknor (1876), II, 237.

40. Noyes (1966), 9, 11, 60–61; Hamerow (1958), 67, 102–106, 260–261; Blum (1978), 370–371; Franz (1959), 179–186; Riehl (1861), 124–126.

41. Siemens (1922), 35; Martin (1875–80), II, 25–26.

42. Noyes (1966), 68–72; Schurz (1907–08), I, 12; Valentin (1930), I, 444–445; Siemens (1922), 36–37.

43. Varnhagen von Ense (1972), IV, 311, 325, 334, 350; Hoetzsch (1923), II, 51; Eyck (1972), 68–69; Valentin (1930), 445–451; Legge (1919), 354.

44. Argyll (1906), I, 305; Moltke (1960), 234; Greville (1938), VI, 146; Ernest August (1925), 148; Lorenz (1896), 133; Legge (1919), 142–143.

45. Hoetzsch (1923), II, 104; Delbruck (1905), I, 212; Moltke (1891), I, 181; Marwitz (1908), 469; Legge (1919), 434.

46. Martin (1875–80), II, 23, 25; Bamberger (1899), 35.

[359]

47. Born (1898), 106–107; Robertson (1952), 168–173; Pinson (1954), 83–85; Herzen (1968), III, 690–691; Fröbel (1890–91), I, 169; Zucker (1950), 301–302.

48. Droz (1957), 161; Mohl (1902), II, 16; Ernest August (1925), 146–147, 151; Hoetzsch (1923), II, 101; Valentin (1930), I, 362–365, II, 400–402; Hess (1959), I, 197.

49. Hamerow (1961), 15–33; Mohl (1902), II, 34–35; 36–38; Mommsen (1949), 218; Sheehan (1978), 57; King-Hall and Ullman (1954) 49–50; Martin (1875–80), II, 71; Franz (1959), 190; Fröbel (1890–91), I, 172.

50. Klein (1914), 261–262; Beseler (1884), 58–59; Morris (1976), 71–72; Blum (1898), 271–272, 279–281; Andlaw (1862), II, 129; King-Hall and Ullman (1954), 50.

51. Eyck (1968), 396; Bamberger (1899), 52; Mohl (1902), 58–59; Valentin (1930), I, 220–224; Schmidt (1970), 367.

52. Klein (1914), 301, 305–309; Duckwitz (1877), 81–82, 88–89; Senior (1878), I, 93; Laube (1849), II, 295–307.

53. Hess (1959), 176; Droysen (1929), I, 416; Moltke (1960), 237; Marquardt (1966), 204; Noyes (1966), 378–379; Hamerow (1968), 156–158.

54. Sagarra (1971), 181; Martin (1875–80), II, 128–129; Craig (1955), 107–114; Gottschall (1898), 322–323.

55. Craig (1955), 122–123; Varnhagen von Ense (1972), V, 338; Reumont (1885), 361.

56. Klein (1914), 415–417; Pinson (1954), 101–104; Legge (1919), 513; Gottschall (1898), 83–84; Fröbel (1890–91), I, 265–266; Duckwitz (1877), 286, 320.

57. Valentin (1930), II, 1; Bamberger (1899), 174–176, 244; Hess (1959), 220–221.

58. Riehl (1861), 314; Duckwitz (1877), 282; Droz (1957), 627n., 632–637; Bismarck quoted in Sturmer (1974), 228.

59. Langer (1969), 505–506; Morris (1976), 96–124; Redlich (1929), 72.

60. Reumont (1885), 362; Delbruck (1905), I, 272; Siemens (1922), 72; Sagarra (1971), 188.

61. Laing (1850), 169–170; Hamerow (1958), 238–252; Walker (1971), 409–414.

CHAPTER NINE

1. Herberstein (1852), I, 30, 32; Custine (1843), II, 114; Lacroix (1845) 10–11; *Russkaia Starina* (1901), CIX, 122; Benson and Esher (1907), II, 14; *Svod Zakonov* (1832), I, 1.

2. Morley (1881), 307; Haxthausen (1847–52), I, 306, 308–309, 466–467; Custine (1843), IV, 31, 310–311, 316; Nifontov (1931), 25–26.

3. Dallas (1892), 85; Maxwell (1854), 134; Cadot (1967), 285–287; Haxthausen (1847–52), I, 48; Custine (1843), II, 105.

4. Maxwell (1854), 90; Custine (1843), I, 97–98, IV, 310–311, 374–376; Gerlach (1903), I, 480; Hommaire de Hell (1934), 29n.; Cadot (1967), 51–67, 325; Annenkov (1968), 165.

5. Custine (1843), 15–16, 52, 125; Bodenstedt (1888), 186; Maxwell (1854), 95–96, 315; Golovin (1846), I, 88–89, 92, 104; Rozanov (1894), 79; Frank (1976), 70–71.

6. Korelin (1971), 65; Romanovich-Slavatinskii (1870), 508–509; Tsentral'yi statisticheskii komitet (1863), 174, 267; Blum (1978), 24n.

7. Brower (1975), 54; Haxthausen (1847–52), III, 56–57, n.

8. Romanovich-Slavatinskii (1870), 38–41; Lacroix (1845), 42; Golovin (1846), 81–112; Pelchinsky (1845), 67; Bismarck (1966), I, 243.

9. *Russkaia Starina* (1881), XXX, 746–747; Blum (1961), 368–370, 379–384, 456–457; Custine (1843), I, 5 6; Slade (1840), 365.

10. Blum (1961), 289–291; Bodenstedt (1888), 51, 125; Haxthausen (1847–52), I, 10, 54–55, 62; Golovin (1846), I, 124.

11. Blum (1961), 414ff.; Matossian (1968), 4–8; Rozanov (1894), 106; Maxwell (1854), 241–243.

12. Blum (1961), 551–557.

13. Ibid. 557–558.

14. Barante (1890–91), V, 521.

15. Blum (1961), 546–551.

16. Temperley (1925), 23.

17. Andlaw (1862), II, 25; Motley (1889), I, 86; Benson and Esher (1907), II, 14, 17; Martin (1875–80), I, 185n.; Herzen (1968), I, 50; Custine (1843), II, 9; Stupperich (1939), 81.

18. Henningsen (1844), 106; Martin (1875–80), 181, 189; Riasanovsky (1959), 7–8, 12, 194; Lincoln (1978), 85–86, 244, 350; Curtiss (1965), 52.

19. Metternich (1880–84), VI, 295; Nesselrode (1908–12), VIII, 199; Schiemann (1904–19), IV, 17–18; Custine (1843), II, 109–110; Mandt (1923), 165–171; Maxwell (1854), 135.

20. Barante (1890–91), V, 469; Curtiss (1965), 46–48, 52–53; Starr (1972), 15–16.

21. Guizot (1974), VI, 269; Greville (1938), III, 262; Schiemann (1904–19), IV, 143–144, 233, 421–422.

22. Maxwell (1854), 223–224.

23. Bodenstedt (1888), 130–131; Golovin (1846), I, 164–166; Schiemann (1904–19), IV, 119, 258–259; Lagny (1854), 116; Cottrell (1842), 24–27; Gagern (1856), III 13.

24. Starr (1972), 19–20; Lincoln (1972), 321–322; Lincoln (1975), 82–100.

25. Lincoln (1972), 325–330.

26. Gagern (1856), III, 376, 380; Dolgorukov quoted in Grunwald (1945), 178n.; Haxthausen (1847–52), III, 19–22; Riasanovsky (1959), 144–145; Bodenstedt (1888), 50–51.

27.   Custine (1843), I, 196; Cadot (1967), 173, 229–230.
28.   Bodenstedt (1888), 135; Haxthausen (1847–52), I, 117–118, III, 5–6; Rozanov (1894), 50; Cadot (1967), 324.
29.   Lincoln (1978), 89; Bernhardi (1894–1900), II, 75; Golovin (1846), I, 5–7, 27–28; Monas (1961), 92–93, 95.
30.   Elliott (1838), I, 217–235; Brower (1975), 173; Berlin (1948), 327–349; Bodenstedt (1888), 135.
31.   Masaryk (1961–67), I, 111; Monas (1961), 158, 246n.; Balmuth (1960), 497–498; Hans (1964), 61–67; Herzen (1968), I, 96; Haxthausen (1847–52), II, 129–130; Bodenstedt (1888), 135.
32.   Herzen (1968), II, 530–531; Panaev (1950), 147; Annenkov (1968), 24–25, 94.
33.   Turgenev (1975), 158.
34.   Raeff (1966), 160ff.
35.   Haxthausen (1847–52), I, 138–157; Blum (1982), 628.
36.   Riasanovsky (1952), 127–130; Monas (1961), 263.
37.   Frank (1983), 8; Walicki (1979), 153; Turgenev (1975), 98.
38.   Metternich (1880–84), VII, 82; Gagern (1856), 355; Herzen (1968), II, 534–535; Annenkov (1968), 92, 266; Lincoln (1970), 374ff.
39.   Annenkov (1968), 86; Herzen (1968), II, 499–500; Turgenev (1975), intro. 14; Granovsky quoted in Schapiro (1967), 78.
40.   For a superlative appreciation of Belinsky see Berlin (1978), 150–185.
41.   Herzen (1968), II, 409–410; Annenkov (1968), 92; Berlin (1978), 176.
42.   Herzen (1968), II, 411; Annenkov (1968), 102, 226.
43.   Belinsky (1948), 159, 235; Annenkov (1968), 77.
44.   Belinsky (1948), 503–512, 527–529.
45.   Ibid., 529–530.
46.   Ibid., 528; Frank (1976), 180; Annenkov (1968), 103–104.
47.   Belinsky (1948), vi.
48.   Schiemann (1904–19), IV, 139, 143–144, 156–157; Nifontov (1931), 19–34; Lincoln (1978), 288–290.
49.   Masaryk (1961–67), I, 113; Schiemann (1904–19), 149–150; Lincoln (1978), 319.
50.   Hans (1964), 77–80; Schiemann (1904–19), IV, 187, 234; Florinsky (1953), 804–806.
51.   Frank (1983), 51–59.
52.   Lincoln (1978), 329.
53.   Ibid., 352.

LIST OF WORKS CITED

Abel, W. (1967), *Geschichte der deutschen Landwirtschaft von frühen Mittelalter bis zum 19. Jahrhundert*. 2nd ed. Stuttgart.

Abramovitz, M., and V. E. Eliasberg (1957), *The Growth of Public Employment in Great Britain*. Princeton.

Ackerknecht, E. H. (1932), "Beiträge zur Geschichte der Medizinalreform von 1848," *Sudhoffs Archiv für Geschichte der Medizin*, XXV.

Ackerknecht, E. H. (1948), "Hygiene in France, 1815–1848," *Bulletin of the History of Medicine*, XXIII.

Acworth, W. M. (1889), *The Railways of England*. London.

Adam, K. (1896–97), "Kulturgeschichtliche Streifzuge durch das Jahr 1848–49," *Zeitschrift für Kulturgeschichte*, III, IV.

Adams, J. Q. (1804), *Letters on Silesia, Written during a Tour through that Country in the Years 1800, 1801*. London.

Adams, W. E. (1968), *Memoirs of a Social Atom*. 2 vols. in 1, 1st ed. 1903.

Agassiz, L. (1869), *Address delivered on the Centennial Anniversary of the Birth of Alexander von Humboldt*. Boston.

Aldcroft, D. H. (1972), "Railways and Economic Growth," *Journal of Transport History*, n.s. I.

Alton-Shee, E. de L, Comte de (1869), *Mes mémoires (1826–1848)*. 2 vols. Paris.

Anderson, E. N., and P. R. (1967), *Political Institutions and Social Change in Continental Europe in the Nineteenth Century*. Berkeley and Los Angeles.

List of Works Cited

Andlaw, F. (1862), *Mein Tagebuch. Auszüge aus Aufschreibungen der Jahre 1811 bis 1861*. 2 vols. Frankfurt am Main.

Andrian-Werburg, V. von (1843–47), *Oesterreich und dessen Zukunft*. 2 vols. in 1. 2nd ed. Hamburg.

Annenkov, P. V. (1968), *The Extraordinary Decade*, Tr. from Russian by I. R. Titunik. Ann Arbor, Mich.

Annual Register.

Apponyi, R. (1913–26), *Vingt-cinq ans à Paris (1826–1852). Journal du Comte Rodolph Apponyi. Attaché de l'ambassade d'Autriche à Paris*. Ed. by E. Daudet. 4 vols. Paris.

Arendt, H. (1944), "Race-Thinking before Racism," *Review of Politics*, VI.

Argyll, G. D., duke of (1906), *Autobiography and Memoirs*. 2 vols. London.

Arnstein, W. L. (1973), "The Survival of the Victorian Aristocracy." In F. C. Jaher, ed., *The Rich, the Well Born, and the Powerful*. Urbana, Ill.

Aydelotte, W. O. (1966), "Parties and Issues in Early Victorian England," *Journal of British Studies*, V, no. 2.

Bagehot, W. (1889), *Biographical Studies*. 2nd ed. London.

Bagehot, W. (1929), *The English Constitution*. 1st publ. 1867. London.

Bagehot, W. (1858), *Estimates of Some Englishmen and Scotsmen*. London.

Bagehot, W. (1879), *Literary Studies*. 2 vols. London.

Balabine, V. de (1914), *Paris de 1842 à 1852. Journal de Victor de Balabine*. Ed. by D. Daudet. Paris.

Balmuth, D. (1960), "The Origins of the Tsarist Epoch of Censorship Terror," *American Slavic and East European Review*, XIX.

Balzac, H. de (1965), *La comédie humaine*. Paris.

Balzac, H. de (1968–71), *Oeuvres complètes*. Paris.

Bamberger, L. (1899), *Erinnerungen*. Berlin.

Bancroft, E. D. (1904), *Letters from England, 1846–49*. New York.

Barante, A. G. P. C. (1890–99). *Souvenirs 1782–1866*. Ed. by C. de Barante. 8 vols. Paris.

Barker, T. C., and C. I. Savage (1974), *An Economic History of Transport in Britain*. 3rd ed. London.

Barr, S. (1975), *Mazzini. Portrait of an Exile*. New York.

Barzun, J. (1937), *Race: A Study in Modern Superstition*. New York.

Battiscombe, G. (1975), *Shaftesbury: The Great Reformer 1801–1885*. Boston.

Bauernfeld, E. (1923), *Erinnerungen aus Alt Wien*. Linz.

Baughman, J. (1959), "The French Banquet Campaign of 1847–48," *Journal of Modern History*, XXXI.

Baxter, R. D. (1962), "Railway Expansion and its Results." In E. M. Carus-Wilson, ed., *Essays in Economic History*, III.

Beales, D. E. D. (1969), *From Castlereagh to Gladstone, 1815–1885*. London.

Beidtel, I. (1896–98), *Geschichte der österreichischen Staats-verwaltung 1740–1848*. Ed. by A. Huber. 2 vols. Innsbruck.

List of Works Cited

Belinsky, V. G. (1948), *Selected Philosophical Works*. Moscow.

Ben-David, J. (1984), *The Scientist's Role in Society: A Comparative Study*. Englewood Cliffs, N.J.

Benson, A. C., and R. B. Esher (1907), *The Letters of Queen Victoria*. 3 vols. New York.

Berlin, I. (1948), "Russia and 1848," *Slavonic Review*, XXVI.

Berlin, I. (1978), *Russian Thinkers*. New York.

Bernard, J. D. (1953), *Science and Industry in the Nineteenth Century*. London.

Bernhardi, T. von (1894–1900), *Aus dem Leben Theodor von Bernhardis*. 9 pts. Leipzig.

Bertier de Sauvigny, G. de (1962), *Metternich and his Times*. Tr. from the French. London.

Beseler, G. (1884), *Erlebtes und Erstrebtes, 1809–1859*. Berlin.

Best, G. (1964), *Shaftesbury*. New York.

Bestor, A. E., Jr. (1948), "The Evolution of the Socialist Vocabulary," *Journal of the History of Ideas*, IX.

Beutin, L. (1953), *Bremen und Amerika*. Bremen.

Beyle, M. H. (1838), *Mémoires d'un tourist*. 2 vols. Brussels.

Beyle, M. H. (1971), *Travels in the South of France*. Tr. from the French. London.

Bibl, V. (1922–24), *Der Zerfall Österreichs*. 2 vols. Vienna.

Bibl, V. (1911), *Die niederösterreichischen Stände im Vormärz*. Vienna.

Biedermann, K. (1886–87), *Mein Leben und ein Stück Zeitgeschichte*. 2 vols. Breslau.

Billington, J. H. (1980), *Fire in the Minds of Men*. New York.

Billington, J. H. (1960), "The Intelligentsia and the Religion of Humanity," *American Historical Review*, LXV.

Birnie, A. (1930), *An Economic History of Europe*. London.

Bismarck, O. von (1966), *Bismarck. The Memoirs*. 2 vols. New York.

Bismarck, O. von (1898), *Gedanken und Erinnerungen*. 2 vols. Stuttgart.

Bitterling, R. (1959), *Alexander von Humboldt*. Berlin.

Blakiston, G., ed. (1972), *Lord William Russell and his Wife 1815–1846*. London.

Blanc, L. (1843–51), *Histoire de dix ans 1830–1840*. 7 vols. in 4. Brussels.

Blanc, L. (1948), *The History of Ten Years, 1830–1840*. Tr. by W. K. Kelly. 2 vols. Philadelphia.

Blanqui, A. (1851), "Tableau des populations rurales en France en 1850," *Journal des économistes*, XXVIII, XXX.

Blum, H. (1898), *Die deutsche Revolution 1848–49*. Florence, Leipzig.

Blum, J. (1982), "Agricultural History and Nineteenth-Century European Ideologies," *Agricultural History*, LVI.

Blum, J. (1978), *The End of the Old Order in Rural Europe*. Princeton.

Blum, J. (1961), *Lord and Peasant in Russia from the Ninth to the Nineteenth Century*. Princeton.

Blum, J. (1948), *Noble Landowners and Agriculture in Austria 1815–1848*. Baltimore.

Blum, J. (1943), "Transportation and Industry in Austria 1815–1848," *Journal of Modern History*, XV.

Bodenstedt, F. (1888), *Erinnerungen aus meinem Leben*. Berlin.

Boigne, C. L. E. A., comtesse de (1907–8), *Mémoires de la comtesse de Boigne née d'Osmond*. 4 vols. Paris.

Boot, H. M. (1984), *The Commercial Crisis of 1847*. Hull.

Born, S. (1898), *Erinnerungen eines Achtundvierzigers*. Leipzig.

Borne, L. (1862), *Gesammelte Schriften*. Vol. IX.

Börnstein, H. (1884), *Fünfundsiebzig Jahre in der alten und neuen Welt. Memoiren einer Unbedeutenden*, 2nd ed. 2 vols. Leipzig.

Bramsted, E. K. (1964), *Aristocracy and the Middle-Classes in Germany*. Chicago.

Briggs, A. (1967), "The Language of 'Class' in Early Nineteenth Century England." In A. Briggs and J. Saville, *Essays in Labor History*. London.

Bristed, C. A. (1852), *Five Years in an English University*. 2 vols. New York.

Broch, P., and H. G. Skilling, eds. (1970), *The Czech Renascence of the Nineteenth Century*. Toronto.

Broglie, A., duc de (1938–41), *Mémoires du duc de Broglie*. 2 vols. Paris.

Broglie, G. de (1981), *L'Orléanisme*. Paris.

Broughton. See Hobhouse, J. C.

Brower, D. R. (1975), *Training the Nihilists. Education and Radicalism in Tsarist Russia*. Ithaca, N.Y.

Brunner, O. (1949), *Adeliges Landleben und Europäischer Geist*. Salzburg.

Bülow-Cummerow, E. G. G. (1842–43), *Preussen, seine Verwaltung, seine Verfassung, sein Verhältniss zu Deutschland*. 2 vols. Berlin.

Buret, E. (1839), *De la misère des classes laborieuses en Angleterre et en France*. Paris.

Cabet, E. (1973), *Voyage en Icarie*. Clifton, N.J.

Cadot, M. (1967), *La Russie dans la vie intellectuelle française, 1839–1856*. Paris.

Calvert, G. H. (1852), *Scenes and Thoughts in Europe*. New York.

Cambridge Economic History (1966–89), 9 vols. Cambridge.

Cameron, R. et al. (1967), *Banking in the Early Stages of Industrialization*. New York.

Campbell, J. C. (1881), *Life of John, Lord Campbell*. 2 vols. London.

Caneva, K. L. (1978), "From Galvanism to Electrodynamics. The Transformation of German Physics and its Social Context," *Historical Studies in the Physical Sciences*, IX.

Cannadine, D. (1980), *Lords and Landlords: The Aristocracy and the Town, 1774–1967*. Leicester.

Carlyle, T. (1840), *Chartism*. London.

Carlyle, T. (1898), "Hudson's Statue," *Latter Day Pamphlets*. New York.

Carlyle, T. (1885), "Memoirs of the Life of Scott," *Critical and Miscellaneous Essays*. New York.

Carlyle, T. (1843), *Past and Present*. Boston.

Carlyle, T. (1882), *Reminiscences of my Irish Journey in 1849*. New York.

Carr, E. H. (1937), *Michael Bakunin*, New York.

Carr, E. H. (1975), *The Romantic Exiles*. New York.

Carrière, J., ed. (1967), *Berzelius und Liebig. Ihre Briefe von 1831–1845*. Wiesbaden.

Cass, L. (1840), *France, its King, Court, and Government*. New York.

Castellane, E. V. E. B. (1895–97), *Journal de Maréchal de Castellane 1804–1862*. 5 vols. Paris.

Castle, E. (1921–23), "Aus dem Tagebuch des Freiherrn Max von Löwenthal," *Historische Blätter*, I.

Cazamian, L. F. (1973), *The Social Novel in England 1830–1850*. Tr. from the French. London and Boston.

Chadwick, E. (1965), *The Sanitary Condition of the Labouring Population of Great Britain*. New ed. with introd. by M. W. Flinn. Edinburgh.

Chaloner, W. H. (1970), "The Agitation Against the Corn Laws." In J. T. Ward, ed., *Popular Movements c. 1830–1850*. London.

Chandler, A. D., Jr. (1965), "The Railroads: Pioneers in Modern Corporate Management," *Business History Review*, XXXI.

Chaussinand-Nogaret, G., ed. (1975), *Une histoire des élites 1700–1848*. Paris.

Chevalier, L. (1973), *Laboring Classes and Dangerous Classes in Paris during the First Half of the Nineteenth Century*. Tr. from the French. London.

Christie, O. F. (1928), *The Transition from Aristocracy 1832–1867*. New York.

Churton, E. (1973), *The Railroad Book of England*. London.

Clapham, J. H. (1951), *The Economic Development of France and Germany 1815–1914*. Cambridge.

Clapham, J. H. (1930), *An Economic History of Modern Britain*, vol. 1. Cambridge.

Clark, T. J. (1973), *The Absolute Bourgeois: Artists and Politics in France 1848–1851*. London.

Cobban, A. (1978), *Edmund Burke and the Revolt Against the Eighteenth Century*. London.

Cockburn, H. T. (1874), *Journal of Henry Cockburn, being a Continuation of the Memorials of his Time 1831–1854*. 2 vols. Edinburgh.

Cohen, I. B. (1985), *Revolution in Science*. Cambridge.

Cohen, L. (1935), *Lady de Rothschild and her Daughters 1821–1931*. London.

Coleman, W. (1971), *Biology in the Nineteenth Century*. Cambridge.

Collins, I., ed. (1970), *Government and Society in France 1814–1848*. New York.

Colman, H. (1849), *European Life and Manners, in Familiar Letters to Friends*. Boston and London.

Cooper, T. (1971). *The Life of Thomas Cooper*. New York.

Corson, J. W. (1848), *Loiterings in Europe*. New York.

Corti, E. (1928), *The Reign of the House of Rothschild*. London.

Cottrell, C. H. (1842), *Recollections of Siberia in the Years 1840 and 1841*. London.

Craig, G. A. (1955), *The Politics of the Prussian Army 1640–1945*. Oxford.

Creevy, T. (1904), *The Creevy Papers*. 2 vols. London.

Croker, J. W. (1884), *The Croker Papers*. Ed. by L. J. Jennings. 2 vols. New York.

Crosland, M. (1967), *The Society of Arcueil*. Cambridge.

Crouzet, F. (1974), "French Economic Growth in the Nineteenth Century Reconsidered," *History*, LIX.

Curtiss, J. S. (1965), *The Russian Army under Nicholas I, 1825–1855*. Durham.

Custine, A. L. L. (1842), *La Russie en 1839*. 4 vols. Paris.

Czoernig, C. von (1858), *Oesterreichs Neugestaltung 1848–1858*. Stuttgart and Augsburg.

Dallas, G. M. (1892), *Diary while United States Minister to Russia 1837 to 1839, and to England 1856 to 1861*. Philadelphia.

Dance, P. (1976), *Animal Fakes and Frauds*. Maidenhead.

Daumard, A. (1970), *La bourgeoisie parisienne de 1815 à 1848*. Paris.

D'Auvergne, E. B. (1911), *The Coburgs*. New York.

Deane, P., and W. A. Coale (1962), *British Economic Growth 1688–1959*. Cambridge.

Delbrück, R. von (1905), *Lebenserinnerungen 1817–1867*. 2 vols. Leipzig.

Demidoff, A. de (1855), *Travels in Southern Russia and the Crimea . . . during the Year 1837*. 2 vols. London.

Deutsche Akademie der Wissenschaften (1959), *Alexander von Humboldt. Gedenkschrift zur 100. Wiederkehr seines Todestages*. Berlin.

Dickens, C. (1965–). *The Letters of Charles Dickens*. M. House and G. Storey, eds. 6 vols. Oxford.

Dictionary of National Biography, (1885–1901), 60 vols. London.

Dictionary of Scientific Biography (1970–80). C. C. Gillispie, ed. 16 vols. New York.

Dodds, J. W. (1952), *The Age of Paradox*. New York.

Dorpalen, A. (1970). "Die Revolution von 1848 in der Geschichts-schreibung der DDR," *Historische Zeitschrift*, CCX.

Dronke, E. (1953), *Berlin*. 1st publ. 1846. Berlin.

Droysen, J. G. (1929), *Briefwechsel*. Ed. by R. Hübner. 2 vols. Stuttgart.

Droz, J. (1957), *Les révolutions allemandes de 1848*. Paris.

Du Bois-Reymond, E. H. (1918), *Jugendbriefe*. Berlin.

Du Bois-Reymond, E. H. (1912), *Reden*. 2 vols. Leipzig.

Du Bois-Reymond, E. H. (1982), *Two Great Scientists of the Nineteenth Century. Correspondence of Emil Du Bois-Reymond (1818–1896) and Carl Ludwig (1816–1895)*. Tr. from the German. Baltimore.

Duckwitz, A. (1877), *Denkwürdigkeiten aus meinem öffentlichen Leben von 1841–1866*. Bremen.

Duffy, C. G. (1892), *Conversations with Carlyle*. New York.

Dunham, A. L. (1955), *The Industrial Revolution in France 1815–1848*. New York.

Durbin, J. P. (1844), *Observations in Europe*. 2 vols. New York.

Durrieu, X. (1845), "Le Portugal en 1845," *Revue des deux mondes*, Feb. 1845.

Dyos, H. J., and D. H. Aldcroft (1969), *British Transport. An Economic Survey from the Seventeenth Century to the Twentieth*. Leicester.

Echard, W. E., ed. (1985), *Historical Dictionary of the French Second Empire, 1852–1870*. Westport, Conn.

Edinburgh Review (1840–41), "Democracy in America," LXII.

Edmonds, E. L., and P. O., eds. (1964), *I Was There. The Memoirs of H. S. Tremenheere*. Eton.

Eilers, G. (1856), *Meine Wanderung durch Leben. Beitrag zurinneren Geschichte der ersten Hälfte der 19. Jahrhundert*. 6 pts. in 3 vols. Leipzig.

Elkana, Y. (1970), "'Kraft': An Illustration of Concepts in Flux," *Historical Studies in the Physical Sciences*. II.

Elliott, C. B. (1838), *Travels in the Three Great Empires of Austria, Russia and Turkey*. London.

Emerson, D. E. (1968), *Metternich and the Political Police. Security and Subversion in the Habsburg Monarchy*. The Hague.

Emerson, R. W. (1968), *English Traits*. New York.

Engels, F. (1968), *The Condition of the Working Class in England*. Tr. and ed. by W. O. Henderson and W. H. Chaloner. Stanford.

Engels, F. (1967), *Germany: Revolution and Counter Revolution*. In *The German Revolutions*, L. Krieger, ed., Chicago.

Ernest II (1888), *Memoirs*. 4 vols. Tr. from the German.

Ernest August (1925), *Letters of the King of Hannover to Viscount Strangford*. London.

Eyck, F. (1968), *The Frankfurt Parliament 1848–1849*. New York.

Eyck, F. (1959), *The Prince Consort*. London.

Eyck, F., ed. (1972), *The Revolutions of 1848–49*. New York.

Falk, M. R. (1948), "Alexander Bach and the *Leseverein* in the Viennese Revolution of 1848," *Journal of Central European Affairs*, VIII.

Falloux, A. P. F. de (1888), *Memoirs of the Count de Falloux*. Tr. from the French. 2 vols. London.

Faucher, L. (1845), *Études sur l'Angleterre*. 2 vols. Paris.

Faulkner, A. B. (1832), *Visit to Germany and the Low Countries in the Years 1829, 30 and 31*. 2 vols. London.

Feingold, M. (1987), "Philanthropy, Pomp, and Patronage," *Daedulus*, Winter 1987.

Fejtö, F., ed. (1948), *The Opening of an Era: 1848*. London.

Fichte, J. G. (1968), *Addresses to the German Nation*. New York.

Finer, S. E. (1952), *The Life and Times of Sir Edwin Chadwick*. London.

Fischer, W. (1922), *Die Briefe Richard Monkton Milnes . . . an Varnhagen von Ense (1844–1854)*. [*Anglistische Forschungen*, vol. 57]. Heidelberg.

Fisk, W. (1938), *Travels in Europe*. New York.

Flaubert, G. (1980–82), *The Letters of Gustave Flaubert*. 2 vols. Cambridge.

Florinsky, M. (1953), *Russia: A History and an Interpretation*. 2 vols. New York.

Foord, A. S. (1952), "The Waning of the 'Influence of the Crown.'" In R. L. Schuyler and H. Ausubel, eds., *The Making of English History*. New York.

Fourastié, J. (1962), *Machinisme et bien être*. Paris.

Frank, J. (1976), *Dostoevskii. The Seeds of Revolt*. Princeton.

Frank, J. (1983), *Dostoevskii. The Years of Ordeal 1850–1859*. Princeton.

Frankl, L. A. (1910), *Erinnerungen*. Prague.

Franz, G. (1959), "Die agrarische Bewegung in Jahre 1848," *Zeitschrift für Agrargeschichte und Agrarsoziologie*, VII.

Fremdling, R. (1977), "Railroads and German Economic Growth," *Journal of Economic History*, XXXVII.

Freville, J. (1936), *Sur la littérature et l'art. Karl Marx, Friedrich Engels*. 2 vols. Paris.

Friedjung, H. (1908–12), *Österreich von 1848 bis 1860*. 2 vols. Stuttgart and Berlin.

Friedrich I of Baden (1921), "Jugenderinnerungen 1826–1847," *Sitzungsberichte der Heidelberger Akademie der Wissenschaften*, phil.-hist. Klasse, XII.

Fröbel, J. (1890–91), *Ein Lebenslauf. Aufzeichnungen, Erinnerungen und Bekenntnisse*. 2 vols. Stuttgart.

Fuctcr, E. (1914), *Histoire de l'historiographie*. Tr. from the German, Paris.

Gagern, F. von (1856), "Journal meiner Reise nach Russland im Jahre 1839." In H. von Gagern, *Das Leben des Generals Friedrich von Gagern*, 3 vols. in 4. Leipzig and Heidelberg.

Gardner, A. K. (1848), *Old Wine in New Bottles*. New York.

Gardner, M. (1911), *Adam Mickiewicz*. London.

Garrison, F. H. (1929), *An Introduction to the History of Medicine*. 4th ed. Philadelphia.

Gash, N. (1979), *Aristocracy and People. Britain 1815–1865*. Cambridge.

Gash, N. (1953), *Politics in the Age of Peel*. London.

Gash, N. (1972), *Sir Robert Peel. The Life of Sir Robert Peel after 1830*. London.

Gaskell, E. (1972), *Mary Barton*. New York.

Gehrig, H. (1966), *Friedrich List. Wegbereiter einer neuen Wirtschaft. Hauptgedanken aus seinen Schriften*. Berlin.

Gerlach, E. L. von (1903), *Aufzeichnungen aus seinem Leben und Wirkung, 1795–1877*. Ed. by J. von Gerlach. 2 vols. Schwerin.

Gerlach, E. L. von (1891–92), *Denkwürdigkeiten*. 2 vols. Berlin.

Gernsheim, H. (1955), *The History of Photography*. London.

Gershoy, L. (1951), "Three French Historians and the Revolution of 1848," *Journal of the History of Ideas*, XII.

Gille, B. (1965), *Histoire de la Maison Rothschild*. Paris.

Gillispie, C. C. (1960), *The Edge of Objectivity*. Princeton.

Gillispie, C. C. (1951), *Genesis and Geology*. Cambridge.

Gleig, G. R. (1839), *Germany, Bohemia and Hungary visited in 1837*. 3 vols. London.

Golovin, I. (1846), *Russia under the Autocrat, Nicholas the First*. 2 vols. London.

Gooch, G. P. (1959), *History and Historians in the Nineteenth Century*. Boston.

Goodfield, G. J. (1981), *An Imagined World: A Story of Scientific Discovery*. New York.

Gottschall, R. von (1898), *Aus meiner Jugend. Erinnerungen*, Berlin.

Gottstein, A. (1901–2), "Geschichte der Hygiene im neunzehnten Jahrhundert." In G. Stockhausen, ed., *Das deutsche Jahrhundert*. 2 vols. Berlin.

Goudsmit, S. A. et. al. (1980), *Time*. Alexandria, Va.

Gourvish, T. R. (1973), "A British Business Elite: The Chief Executive Managers of the Railway Industry, 1850–1922," *Business History Review*, XLVII.

Gourvish, T. R. (1980), *Railways and the British Economy, 1830–1914*. London.

Granville, A. B. (1841), *The Spas of England*. 3 vols. London.

Granville, A. B. (1837), *The Spas of Germany*. 2 vols. Paris.

Gregory, W. (1894), *An Autobiography*. Ed. by Lady Gregory. London.

Greville, C. C. F. (1938), *The Greville Memoirs 1814–1860*. Ed. by L. Strachey and R. Fulford. 8 vols. London.

Greville, H. W. (1883–1905), *Leaves from the Diary of Henry Greville*. Ed. by Countess Enfield. 4 vols. London.

Grillparzer, F. (1924), *Werke*. 6 vols. Vienna.

Grunwald, C. de (1953), *Metternich*. Tr. from the French. London.

Grunwald, C. de (1945), "Nesselrode et le 'gendarme de l'Europe,'" in *Trois siècles de diplomatie russe*. Paris.

Guedella, P. (1922), *The Second Empire*. London.

Guedella, P. (1931), *Wellington*. New York.

Guest, C. (1950), *Extracts from her Journal, 1833–1852*. Ed. by the Earl of Bessborough. London.

Guizot, F. P. G. (1858–67), *Mémoires pour servir à l'histoire de mon temps*. 8 vols. Paris.

Gutman, S. (1978), "Changing Conceptions of Elite," *The Consortium on Revolutionary Europe*. Proceedings, 1978. Athens, Ga.

Guttsman, W. L. (1963), *The British Political Elite*. London.

Guttsman, W. L., ed. (1969), *The English Ruling Class*. London.

Gwynn, D. (1949), *Young Ireland and 1848*. Cork.

Haenchen, K., ed. (1930), *Revolutionsbriefe 1848*. Leipzig.

Halsted, J. B., ed. (1969), *Romanticism*. New York.

Hamerow, T. S. (1968), "1848." In L. Krieger and F. Stern, eds., *The Responsibility of Power*. London.

Hamerow, T. S. (1961), "The Elections to the Frankfurt Parliament," *Journal of Modern History*, XXXIII.

Hamerow, T. S. (1958), *Restoration, Revolution, Reaction*. Princeton.

Hanham, H. J., ed. (1969), *The Nineteenth Century Constitution 1815–1914*. Cambridge.

Hans, N. A. (1964), *History of Russian Educational Policy* (1701–1917). New York.

Hansen, M. L. (1945), *The Atlantic Migration*. Cambridge.

Hartig, F. von (1853), *Genesis*. Tr. from the German in W. K. Kelly, *History of the House of Austria*. London.

Hartwell, R. M., ed. (1970), *The Industrial Revolution*. Oxford.

Hawkins, B. (1838), *Germany*. London.

Haxthausen, A. von (1847–52), *Studien über die inneren Zustände, das Volksleben und insbesondere die ländlichen Einrichtungen Russlands*. 3 vols. Hannover and Berlin.

Hayek, F. A. (1952), *The Counter-Revolution of Science*. Glencoe.

Hayes, C. J. H. (1927), "Contributions of Herder to the Doctrine of Nationalism," *American Historical Review*, XXXII.

Hayes, C. J. H. (1966), *Essays on Nationalism*. New York.

Hayes, C. J. H. (1968), *The Historical Evolution of Modern Nationalism*. New York.

Haywood, R. N. (1969), *The Beginnings of Railway Development in Russia in the Reign of Nicholas I, 1835–1842*. Durham.

Heine, H. (1893), *Lutetia* in *Gesammelte Werke*, VI. Berlin.

Helmholtz, H. von (1971), *Philosophische Vorträge und Aufsätze*. Berlin.

Helmholtz, H. von (1966), *Ueber sich selbst*. Leipzig.

Helmholtz, H. von (1884), *Vorträge und Reden*. 2 vols. in 1. Braunschweig.

Hemmings, F. W. J., ed. (1974), *The Age of Realism*. Baltimore.

Henderson, W. O. (1983), *Friedrich List. Economist and Visionary*. Totowa, N.J.

Henningsen, C. F. (1844), *Revelations of Russia*. 2 vols. London.

Henry, J. (1979), *The Papers of Joseph Henry*, III. Washington.

Herberstein, S. von (1852), *Notes upon Russia*. Tr. from the Latin. *Works Issued by the Haklyut Society*, X, XII.

Hermann, K. (1981), *Thurn und Taxis-Post und die Eisenbahnen*. Kallmünz.

Herwegh, M., ed. (1898), *Briefe von und an Georg Herwegh*. Munich.

Herzen, A. (1968). *My Past and Thoughts*. Tr. from the Russian, 4 vols. New York.

Hess, M. (1959), *Moses Hess Briefwechsel*. Ed. by E. Silberner. The Hague.

Higonnet, P. L., and T. Higonnet (1967), "Class, Corruption, and Politics in the French Chamber of Deputies, 1846–1858," *French Historical Studies*, V.

Hill, R., and G. B. Hill (1880), *The Life of Sir Rowland Hill*. 2 vols. London.

Hingley, R., tr. and ed. (1965), *The Oxford Chekhov*, 8 vols. London.

Hirsch, H. (1976), "Karl Ludwig Bernays und die Revolutions-erwartung von 1848, dargestellt am Mordfall Praslin," *Schriften aus dem Karl-Marx-Haus* XVII. Trier.

Historical Statistics of the United States (1949), Washington.

Hobhouse, J. C. (1909–11), *Recollections of a Long Life, with Additional Extracts from his Private Diaries*. 6 vols. New York.

Hock, W. (1957), *Liberales Denken im Zeitalter der Paulskirche. Droysen und die Frankfurter Mitte*. Münster.

Hodder, E. (1887), *The Life and Work of the Seventh Earl of Shaftesbury*. 3 vols. London.

Hoetzsch, O., ed. See Meyendorff.

Hohenlohe-Ingelfingen, K. zu (1897–1907), *Aus meinem Leben*. 4 vols. Berlin.

Hohenlohe-Schillingsfürst, C. von (1906), *Memoirs*. Tr. from the German. 2 vols. New York.

Holton, G., and D. H. D. Roller (1958), *Foundations of Physical Science*. Reading, Mass.

Hommaire de Hell, A. (1934), *Mémoires d'une aventuriére (1833–1852)*. Paris.

Howarth, T. E. B. (1961), *Citizen King. The Life of Louis Philippe*. London, New York.

Howitt, W. (1846), *The Aristocracy of England*. London.

Howitt, W. (1842), *The Rural and Domestic Life of Germany*. London.

List of Works Cited

Howitt, W. (1842), *The Student Life of Germany*. Philadelphia.

Hübner, J. A. (1891), *Ein Jahr meines Leben 1848–1849*. Leipzig.

Hugo, H. E., ed. (1957), *The Romantic Reader*. New York.

Humboldt, A. von (1860), *Letters of Alexander von Humboldt to Varnhagen von Ense*. Tr. from the German. New York.

Hyman, A. (1982), *Charles Babbage, Pioneer of the Computer*. Princeton.

Jackman, W. T. (1966), *The Development of Transportation in Modern England*. London.

Jagow, K. (1938), *Letters of the Prince Consort 1831–1861*. Tr. from the German. New York.

James, H. (1989), *A German Identity Crisis 1770–1990*. New York.

Janos, A. C. (1982), *The Politics of Backwardness in Hungary 1825–1945*. Princeton.

Jardin, A., and A. J. Tudesq (1973), *La France des notables*. 2 vols. Paris.

Jardin, A., and A. J. Tudesq (1983), *Restoration and Reaction. 1815–1848*. Tr. from the French. Cambridge.

Jaszi, O. (1966), *The Dissolution of the Habsburg Monarchy*. Chicago.

Jenks, L. H. (1938), *The Migration of British Capital to 1875*. New York.

Johann, King of Saxony (1958), *Lebenserinnerungen des Königs. Eigene Aufzeichnungen des Königs über die Jahre 1801 bis 1854*. (Historische Kommission bei der Bayerischen Akademie der Wissenschaften, *Deutsche Geschichtsquellendes 19. und 20 Jahrhunderts*, vol. 42). Göttingen.

Johnson, C. H. (1971), "Communism and the Working Class before Marx; the Icarian Experience," *American Historical Review*, LXXVI.

Johnson, C. H. (1974), *Utopian Communism in France. Cabet and the Icarians 1839–1851*. Ithaca, N.Y.

Johnson, D. (1963), *Guizot. Aspects of French History 1787–1874*. London.

Joinville, F., Prince de (1895), *Memoirs*. Tr. from the French. London.

Joinville, F., Prince de (1970), *Vieux souvenirs de Mgr. le prince de Joinville 1818–1848*. Paris.

Kamen, M. D. (1986), "On Creativity of Eye and Ear: A Commentary on the Career of T. W. Engelman," *Proceedings of the American Philosophical Society*, CXXX.

Kamenka, E., ed. (1980), *The Portable Karl Marx*. New York.

Kamenka, E., and F. B. Smith, eds. (1979), *Intellectuals and Evolution. Socialism and the Experience of 1848*. London.

Kaplan, F. (1975), *Dickens and Mesmerism*. Princeton.

Kedourie, E. (1961), *Nationalism*. New York.

Kemp, T. (1972), *Economic Forces in French History*. London.

Kerner, J. (1897), *Briefwechsel mit seinen Freunden*. 2 vols. Berlin.

Killick, J. R., and W. A. Thomas (1970), "The Provincial Stock Exchanges, 1830–1870," *Economic History Review*, XXIII.

Kimmel, B. H. (1970), "Karel Havlicek and the Czech Press before 1848." In Broch and Skilling, q.v.

[374]

List of Works Cited

King, B. (1899), *A History of Italian Unity*, 2 vols. New York.

King-Hall, S., and R. K. Ullman (1954), *German Parliaments*. New York.

Kirby, R. S. et al. (1950), *Engineering in History*. New York.

Kissinger, H. A. (1964), *A World Restored*. New York.

Kitson Clark, G. (1967), *The Making of Victorian England*. New York.

Kitson Clark, G. (1936), *Peel*. London.

Klein, F. (1926), *Vorlesungen über die Entwicklung der Mathematik im 19. Jahrhundert*. 2 vols. Berlin.

Klein, T., ed. (1914), *1848. Der Vorkampf deutscher Einheit und Freiheit*. Leipzig.

Knappich, W. (1969), *Die Habsburger-Chronik*. Salzburg, Stuttgart.

Koenigsberger, L. (1906), *Hermann von Helmholtz*.

Kohn, H. (1965), *The Mind of Germany*.

Kohn, H., ed. (1955), *Nationalism*.

Kohn, H. (1960), *Pan-Slavism: Its History and Ideology*. New York.

Kohn, H. (1950), "Romanticism and the Rise of German Nationalism," *Review of Politics*, XII.

Komlos, J., ed. (1983), *Economic Development in the Habsburg Monarchy in the Nineteenth Century*, New York.

Korelin, A. P. (1971), "Rossiiskoe dvorianstvo: ego soslovnaiaorganizatsiia (1861–1904 gg.)," *Istoriia SSSR*, 1971, no. 5.

Korff, M. A. (1899–1900), "Iz zapisok barona Korff," *Russkaia Starina*, XCVIII–CI.

Krieger, L. (1977), *Ranke: The Meaning of History*. Chicago.

Kübeck von Kübau, K. F. (1909), *Tagebücher*, 2 vols. in 3 parts.

Kudlich, H. (1873), *Rückblicke und Erinnerungen*. 3 vols. Vienna.

Kuhn, T. S. (1959), "Energy Conservation as an Example of Simultaneous Discovery." In M. Clagget, ed., *Critical Problems in the History of Science*.

Kussmaul, A. (1900), *Jugenderinnerungen eines alten Arztes*. Stuttgart.

Lacassagne, J. P., ed. (1973), *Pierre Leroux et George Sand. Histoire d'une amitié*. Paris.

Lacroix, F. (1845), *Les mystères de la Russie*. Paris.

Lagny, G. de (1854), *The Knout and the Russians*. Tr. from the French. New York.

LaHodde, L. de (1850), *Histoire des sociétés secrètes et du parti républicain de 1830 à 1848*. Paris.

Laing, S. (1850), *Observations on the Social and Political State of the European People in 1848 and 1849*. London.

"L'Allemagne du présent. Lettres au prince de Metternich" (1846), *Revue des deux mondes*, XIII–XIV.

Lambert, R. S. (1934), *The Railway King: A Study of George Hudson and the Business Morals of his Time*. London.

Landes, D. S. (1960), *The Unbound Prometheus*. Cambridge.

Langer, W. L. (1969), *Political and Social Upheaval, 1832–1852*. New York.

Laube, H. (1849), *Das erste deutsche Parliament*. 3 vols.

Legge, J. G. (1919), *Rhyme and Revolution in Germany: A Study in German History, Life, Literature, Character, 1813–1850*. London.

Leikina-Svirskaia, V. R. (1958), "Formirovanie raznochinskoi intelligentsii v Rossii v 40-kh godakh XIX veka," *Istoriia* SSSR, no. 1 (Jan., Feb. 1958).

Leland, C. G. (1893), *Memoirs*. New York.

Le May, G. H. L. (1979), *The Victorian Constitution*. New York.

Lennox, W. P. (1877), *Celebrities I Have Known*. 2nd ser. 2 vols. London.

Levasseur, E. (1969), *Histoire des classes ouvrières et de l'industrie en France de 1789 à 1870*. 2 vols. New York.

Lewin, H. G. (1968), *The Railway Mania and its Aftermath, 1845–1852*. Newton Abbot.

Lewis, R. A. (1952), *Edwin Chadwick and the Public Health Movement*. London.

Lewis, W. A. (1955), *The Theory of Economic Growth*. London.

Lhomme, J. (1960), *La grande bourgeoisie au pouvoir (1830–1880)*. Paris.

Liebig, J. (1924), *Animal Chemistry or Organic Chemistry in its Application to Physiology and Pathology*. New York (The Sources of Science, no. 4).

Liebig, J. (1891), "Eigenhändige biographische Aufzeichnungen," *Deutsche Rundschau*, LXVI.

Lincoln, W. B. (1970), "The Circle of the Grand Duchess Elena Pavlovna, 1847–1861," *Slavonic and East European Review*, XLVIII.

Lincoln, W. B. (1975), "The Daily Life of St. Petersburg Officials in the Mid-Nineteenth Century," *Oxford Slavonic Papers*, VIII.

Lincoln, W. B. (1972), "The Genesis of an 'Enlightened' Bureaucracy in Russia, 1825–1855," *Jahrbücher für Geschichte Osteuropas*, XX.

Lincoln, W. B. (1978), *Nicholas I: Emperor and Autocrat of All the Russias*. Bloomington.

Linton, W. J. (1892), *European Republicans*. London.

Linton, W. J. (1894), *Threescore and Ten Years, 1820 to 1890. Recollections*. New York.

Lipscomb, A. A., ed. (1903), *The Writings of Thomas Jefferson*, XII. Washington.

Liptzin, S. (1944), *Germany's Stepchildren*. Philadelphia.

Liptzin, S. (1926), *The Weavers in German Literature*. Baltimore.

List, F. (1927–36), *Schriften, Reden, Briefe*. 10 vol. in 12. Berlin.

Longford, E. (1964), *Queen Victoria*. New York.

Loomis, S. (1967), *A Crime of Passion*. Philadelphia and New York.

Lorenz, O. (1896), *Staatsmänner und Geschichtsschreiber des neunzehnten Jahrhunderts*. Berlin.

List of Works Cited

Lovejoy, A. (1941), "The Meaning of Romanticism," *Journal of the History of Ideas*, II.

Lovett, W. (1920), *Life and Struggles of William Lovett*. New York.

Lucas-Dubreton, J. (1929), *The Restoration and the July Monarchy*. Tr. from the French. New York.

Lyell, C. (1856), *Travels in North America 1841–2*. 2 vols. in 1. New York.

McCarthy, J. (1879), *A History of Our Own Times*. 4 vols. New York.

McCord, N. (1967), "Cobden and Bright in Politics, 1846–1857." In Robson, ed., q.v.

M'Culloch, J. R. (1844), *M'Culloch's Universal Gazeteer*. 2 vols. New York.

Macaulay, T. B. (1968), *The History of England from the Accession of James the Second*. 5 vols. New York.

Macaulay, T. B. (1974–81), *The Letters of Thomas Babington Macaulay*. 6 vols. Cambridge.

Magill, C. P. (1948), "The German Author and his Public in the Mid-Nineteenth Century," *Modern Language Review*, XLIII.

Major, R. H. (1954), *A History of Medicine*. 2 vols. Springfield.

Malmesbury, J. H. H., Earl of (1884), *Memoirs of an Ex-Minister*. 2 vols. London.

Mandt, M. W. (1923), *Ein deutsche Artz am Hofe Kaiser Nikolaus I von Russland*. Munich and Leipzig.

Manuel, F. E. (1987), "Lovejoy Revisited," *Daedulus*, Spring 1987.

Manuel, F. E. (1962), *The Prophets of Paris*. Cambridge.

Margadant, T. (1979), *French Peasants in Revolt: The Insurrection of 1851*. Princeton.

Margadant, T. (1984), "Tradition and Modernity in Rural France during the Nineteenth Century," *Journal of Modern History*, LVI.

Marquardt, F. D. (1969), "*Pauperismus* in Germany during the *Vormärz*," *Central European History*, II

Marquardt, F. D. (1966), "A Working Class in Berlin in the 1840's?" In H. U. Wehler, ed., q.v.

Martin, T. (1875–80), *The Life of His Royal Highness the Prince Consort*. 5 vols. New York.

Martineau, H. (1969), *Autobiography*. 2 vols. London.

Martineau, H. (1869), *Biographical Sketches*. New York.

Marwitz, L., ed. (1908), *Vom Leben am Preussischen Hofe 1815–1852*. Berlin.

Marx, J. (1965), *Die wirtschaftlichen Ursachen der Revolution von 1848 in Österreich*. Graz, Köln.

Marx, K., and F. Engels (1975–88), *Collected Works*. 43 vols. New York and Moscow.

Marx, K., and F. Engels (1972), *The Revolution of 1848–49*. Articles from the *Neue Rheinische Zeitung*. New York.

Masaryk, T. G. (1961–67), *The Spirit of Russia*. 3 vols. New York.

Masson, D. (1908), *Memories of London in the 'Forties*. Edinburgh.

Mather, F. C. (1953), "The Railways, the Electric Telegraph and Public Order during the Chartist Period, 1837–1848," *History*, n.s. XXXVIII.

Matossian, M. (1968), "The Peasant Way of Life." In W. S. Vucinich, ed., *The Peasant in Nineteenth Century Russia*. Stanford.

Maunder, E. W. (1900), *The Royal Observatory, Greenwich*. London.

Maxwell, J. S. (1854), *The Czar, his Court and People*. New York.

May, A. J. (1966), *Vienna in the Age of Franz Josef*. Norman, Okla.

Mazzini, J. (1929), *The Duty of Man and Other Essays*. London.

Mazzini, J. (1894), *Essays*. London.

Mazzini, J. (1979), *Mazzini's Letters*. Westport, Conn.

Meinecke, F. (1970), *Cosmopolitanism and the National State*. Tr. from the German. Princeton.

Mendelsohn, E. (1964), "The Emergence of Science as a Profession in Nineteenth Century Europe." In K. B. Hill, ed., *The Management of Scientists*. Boston.

Merz, J. T. (1903–1914), *A History of European Thought in the Nineteenth Century*. 4 vols. Edinburgh and London.

Meyendorff, P. von (1923), *Politischer und Privater Briefwechsel 1826–1862*. O. Hoetzsch, ed. 3 vols. Berlin.

Meyer, A. O. (1924), *Fürst Metternich*. Berlin.

Michelet, J. (1973), *The People*. Tr. from the French. Urbana, Ill.

Mill, J. S. (1849), "The French Revolution of 1848 and its Assailants," *Westminster Review*, LI.

Mills, C. (1952), *Adam Mickiewicz. Selected Poems*. New York.

Milne, A. (1975), *Metternich*. Totowa, N.J.

Milward, A. S., and S. B. Saul (1973), *The Economic Development of Continental Europe 1780–1870*. London.

Minogue, K. R. (1967), *Nationalism*.

Mitchell, B. R. (1969), "The Coming of the Railway and United Kingdom Economic Growth." In M. C. Reed, ed., *Railways in the British Economy*. Newton Abbot.

Mitchell, B. R. (1981), *European Historical Statistics 1750–1975*. New York.

Mitchell, B. R., and P. Deane (1962), *Abstract of British Historical Statistics*. Cambridge.

Mohl, R. von (1902), *Lebenserinnerungen 1799–1875*. 2 vols. Stuttgart and Leipzig.

Mokyr, J. (1983), *Why Ireland Starved. A Quantitative and Analytical History of the Irish Economy*. Manchester.

Moltke, H. von (1960), *Briefe 1825–1891. Eine Auswahl*. Stuttgart.

Moltke, H. von (1891), *Letters of Field-Marshal Count Helmuth von Moltke to His Mother and His Brothers*. Tr. from the German. 2 vols. London.

Mommsen, W. (1949), *Grösse und Versagen des deutschen Bürgertums*. Munich.

Monas, S. (1961), *The Third Section: Police and Society in Russia under Nicholas I*. Cambridge.

Monin, H. (1897), "Le pressentiment sociale, à propos de la Revolution de 1848 en France," *Revue Internationale de Sociologie*, V.

Morgan, B., ed. (1963), *The Railway-Lover's Companion*. London.

Morley, J. (1923), *Life of Gladstone*. 3 vols. London.

Morley, J. (1881), *The Life of Richard Cobden*. Boston.

Morris, W. B., Jr. (1876), *The Road to Olmütz. The Career of Joseph Maria von Radowitz*. New York.

Morse, J. T., Jr. (1896), *Life and Letters of Oliver Wendell Holmes*. 2 vols. Boston, New York.

Motley, J. L. (1889), *Correspondence*. 2 vols. New York.

Müller, C., ed. (1928), *Alexander von Humboldt und das Preussische Königshaus. Briefe aus den Jahren 1835–1857*. Leipzig.

Musgrave, G. M. (1848). *The Parson, Pen and Pencil*. 3 vols. London.

Musset, A. de (1977), *Confessions of a Child of the Century*. Tr. from the French. New York.

Namier, L. B. (1944), *1848: The Revolution of the Intellectuals*. London.

Naville, J., ed. (1963–64), *Lettres de François Guizot et de la princesse de Lieven*. 3 vols. Paris.

Neff, E. (1947), *The Poetry of History*. New York.

Nesselrode, C. de (1908–12), *Lettres et papiers du chancelier comte de Nesselrode 1760–1856*. 11 vols. Paris.

Neumann, P. von (1928), *The Diary of Philipp von Neumann 1819 to 1850*. Tr. from the German. 2 vols. Boston and New York.

Newman, E. L., and R. L. Simpson, eds. (1987), *Historical Dictionary of France from the 1815 Restoration to the Second Empire*. 2 vols. Westport, Conn.

Nifontov, A. S. (1931), *1848 god v Rossii*. Moscow and Leningrad.

Normanby, C. H. P. (1857), *A Year of Revolution*. 2 vols. London.

North American Review (1838).

Noyes, G. R., ed. (1944), *Poems by Adam Mickiewicz*. New York.

Noyes, P. K. (1966), *Organization and Revolution: Working Class Associations in the German Revolution of 1848–1849*. Princeton.

O'Boyle, L. (1970), "The Problem of an Excess of Educated Men in Western Europe 1800–1850," *Journal of Modern History*, vol. 42.

Olmsted, J. M. D. (1938), *Claude Bernard, Physiologist*. New York.

Owens, D. E. (1965), *English Philanthropy 1660–1960*. Cambridge.

Paget, J. (1971), *Hungary and Transylvania*. 1st publ. 1850. New York.

Panaev, I. I. (1950), *Literaturnye Vospominaniia*. Moscow.

Parker, C. S. (1907), *Life and Letters of Sir James Graham*. 2 vols. London.

Parker, C. S., ed. (1899), *Sir Robert Peel from his Private Papers*. 3 vols. London.

Peacock, A. J., and D. Joy (1971), *George Hudson of York*. Clapham.

Pech, S. (1969), *The Czech Revolution of 1848*. Chapel Hill, N.C.

Peel, G. (1920), ed. *The Private Letters of Sir Robert Peel*. London.

Pelchinsky, V. (1845), *La Russie en 1844*. Paris, Leipzig.

Perkin, H. *The Age of the Railway*. Newton Abbot.

Pesek, T. G. (1970), "The 'Czechoslovak' Question on the Eve of the 1848 Revolution." In Broch and Skilling, q.v.

Petrie, C. A. *The Modern British Monarchy*. London.

Pettenkofer, M. von (1874), *Dr. Justus Freiherrn von Liebigzum Gedächtnis*. Munich.

Pettenkofer, M. von (1941), "The Value of Health to a City," Tr. by H. E. Sigerist, *Bulletin of the History of Medicine*, X.

Pflanze, O. (1966), "Characteristics of Nationalism in Europe: 1848–1871," *Review of Politics*, XXVIII.

Pinkney, D. H. (1964), "The Crowd in the French Revolution of 1830," *American Historical Review*, LXX.

Pinkney, D. H. (1986), *Decisive Years in France, 1840–1847*. Princeton.

Pinkney, D. H. (1958), *Napoleon III and the Rebuilding of Paris*. Princeton.

Pinson, K. (1954), *Modern Germany, its History and Civilization*. New York.

Plumb, J. H. (1956), *The First Four Georges*. London.

Poliakov, L. (1947), *The Aryan Myth*. London.

Polisensky, J. (1980), *Aristocrats and the Crowd in the Revolutionary Year 1848*. Tr. from the Czech. Albany, N.Y.

Pollins, H. (1954), "The Marketing of Railway Shares in the First Half of the Nineteenth Century," *Economic History Review*, VII.

Pollock, F. (1887), *Personal Remembrances*. 2 vols. London.

Ponsonby, A. (1942), *Henry Ponsonby, Queen Victoria's Private Secretary*. London.

Ponteil, F. (1968), *Les classes bourgeoises et l'avénement de la démocratie, 1815–1914*. Paris.

Popper, K. R. (1950), *The Open Society and its Enemies*. Princeton.

Porter, T. M. (1986), *The Rise of Statistical Thinking, 1820–1900*. Princeton.

Posch, A. (1954), "Erzherzog Johann und Metternich." In B. Sutter, ed., *Festschrift Julius Franz Schütz*, Graz-Cologne.

Postgate, R. (1975), *Story of a Year, 1848*. Westport, Conn.

Pottendorf, E. (1955), *Lola Montez, die spanische Tänzerin*. Zurich.

Pouthas, H. (1952), *Le population française pendant le première moitié du XIXe siècle*. Paris.

Price, R. (1972), *The French Second Republic. A Social History*. London.

Price, R. G. G. (1957), *A History of Punch*. London.

Prinz, F. (1962), *Hans Kudlich (1823–1917)*. Prague.

Priouret, R. (1959), *La République des Députés*. Paris.

Prokesch von Osten, A. (1881), *Aus dem Nachlasse des Grafen Prokesch-Osten*. 2 vols. Vienna.

Proudhon, P. J. (1970), *Selected Writings*. Ed. by S. Edwards. London.

Pumphrey, R. E. (1959), "The Introduction of Industrialists into the British Peerage," *American Historical Review*, LXV.

Quennel, P., ed., (1980), *Affairs of the Mind*. Washington.

Radvany, E. (1971), *Metternich's Projects for Reform in Austria*.

Raeff, M., ed. (1966), *Russian Intellectual History: An Anthology*. New York.

Raikes, T. (1956–57), *A Portion of the Journal Kept by Thomas Raikes, Esq. from 1831 to 1847*. 4 vols. London.

Randell, K. H. (1972), *Politics and the People 1835–1850*. London.

Ranke, L. von (1867–90), *Sämtliche Werke*. 54 vols. Leipzig.

Ratcliffe, B. (1972), "The Origins of the Paris–St. Germain Railway," *Journal of Transport History*, n.s. I.

Rath, R. J. (1957), *The Viennese Revolution of 1848*. Austin, Tex.

Ray, G. N., ed (1945–46), *The Letters and Private Papers of William Makepeace Thackeray*. 4 vols. Cambridge.

Read, D., and E. Glasgow (1961), *Feargus O'Connor*. London.

Redlich, J. (1920–26), *Das österreichische Staats- und Reichsproblem*. 3 vols. Leipzig.

Redlich, J. (1929), *Emperor Francis Joseph of Austria*. New York.

Reid, T. W. (1891), *The Life, Letters and Friendships of R. M. Milnes*. 2 vols. London.

Rémond, R. (1968), *Les droits en France*. 2 vols. Paris.

Remusat, C. de (1958–67), *Mémoires de ma vie*. 5 vols. Paris.

Reumont, A. von (1885), *Aus Friedrich Wilhelm's IV gesunden und kranken Tagen*. Leipzig.

Riasanovsky, N. V. (1959), *Nicholas I and Official Nationality in Russia, 1825–1855*. Berkeley and Los Angeles.

Riasanovsky, N. V. (1952), *Russia and the West in the Teachings of the Slavophils*. Cambridge.

Riedel, M. (1961), "Vom Biedermeier zum Maschinenzeitalter: zur Kulturgeschichte der ersten Eisenbahnen in Deutschland," *Archiv für Kulturgeschichte*. VIII.

Riehl, W. H. (1861), *Die bürgerliche Gesellschaft*. Stuttgart.

Riehl, W. H. (1861), *Land und Leute*. Stuttgart.

Rietra, M., ed. (1980), *Jung Österreich*. Amsterdam.

Rigaudias-Weiss, H. (1936), *Les enquêtes ouvmères en France entre 1848*. Paris.

Ringer, F. K. (1979), *Education and Society in Modern Europe*. Bloomington.

Ritter, A. (1969), *The Political Thought of Pierre-Joseph Proudhon*. Princeton.

Roberts, D. (1960), *Victorian Origins of the British Welfare State*. New Haven.

Robertson, P. (1952), *Revolutions of 1848*. Princeton.

Robinson, H. (1948), *The British Post Office. A History*. Princeton.

Robson, R., ed. (1967), *Ideas and Institutions of Victorian Britain*. London.

Rohr, D. G. *The Origins of Social Liberalism in Germany*. Chicago.

Romanovich-Slavatinskii, A. (1870), *Dvorianstvo v Rossii otnachala XVIII veka do otmeny krepostnago prava*. St. Petersburg.

Rosdolsky, R. (1964), "Friedrich Engels und das Problem der 'geschichtlichen' Völker. Die Nationalitätenfrage in der Revolution 1848–1849 im Lichte der *Neuen rheinischen Zeitung*," *Archiv für Sozialgeschichte*, IV.

Ross, J. (1893), *Three Generations of English Women*. London.

Rossiter, M. (1975), *The Emergence of Agricultural Science: Justus Liebig and the Americans 1840–1880*. New Haven.

Rostow, W. W., ed. (1964), *The Economics of Take-Off into Sustained Growth*. London.

Rotteck, K. von, and K. Welscker, eds. (1845–48), *Das Staats-Lexikon*. 12 vols. Altona.

Rozanov, A. I. (1894), *Erinnerungen eines Dorfgeistlichen*. Tr. from the Russian. Stuttgart.

Rudé, G. (1969), "Why was there no Revolution in England in 1830 or 1848?" In M. Kossok, ed., *Studien über die Revolution*. Berlin.

Rush, R. (1860), "A Glance at the Court and Government of Louis Philippe in 1847–1848," in *Occasional Productions*. Philadelphia.

Russkaia Starina (1901), vol. CIX.

Sagarra, E. (1971), *Traditions and Revolution: German Literature and Society 1830–1890. New York*.

St. Aulaire, L. (1925), "Souvenirs de mon ambassade à Londres," *La Revue de Paris*, XXXII.

St. Aulaire, L. (1924), "Souvenirs de mon ambassade à Vienne," *La Revue de Paris*, XXXI.

Salvemini, G. (1957), *Mazzini*. Tr. from the Italian.

Sand, G. (1964), *Le mare au diable*. Paris.

Saville, J., ed. (1973), *Working Conditions in the Victorian Age*. Farnborough.

Schapiro, L. *(1967), Rationalism and Nationalism in Russian Nineteenth-Century Political Thought*. New Haven and London.

Schieferdecker, C. C. (1844), *Vincent Priessnitz or the Wonderful Power of Water in Healing the Diseases of the Human Body*. Philadelphia.

Schiemann, T. (1904–19), *Geschichte Russlands unter Kaiser Nikolaus I*. Berlin.

Schmidt, S. (1970), "Robert Blum." In K. Obernabb et al. *Männer der Revolution von 1848*. Berlin.

Schnabel, F. (1929–37), *Deutsche Geschichte im neunzehnten Jahrhundert*. 4 vols. Freiburg.

Schroeder, P. W. (1961), "Metternich Studies Since 1925," *Journal of Modern History*, XXXIII.

Schumpeter, J. (1939), *Business Cycles*. 2 vols. New York.

Schurz, C. (1907–08), *The Reminiscences of Carl Schurz*. 3 vols. New York.

Schuselka, F. (1843), *Deutsche Worte einer Oesterreichers*. Hamburg.

Schuselka, F. (1845), *Mittelmeer, Ost- und Nordsee*. Leipzig.

Schwarzenberg, A. (1946), *Prince Felix zu Schwarzenberg*. New York.

Sealsfield, C. (1828), *Austria as It Is*. London.

Senior, N. W. (1878), *Conversations with M. Thiers, M. Guizot, and other Eminent Persons*. 2 vols. London.

Senior, N. W. (1968), *Correspondence and Conversations of Alexis de Tocqueville with Nassau William Senior from 1834 to 1859*. New York.

Senior, N. W. (1973), *Journals kept in France and Italy 1848–1852 with a Sketch of the Revolution of 1848*. 2 vols. New York.

Seton-Watson, R. W. (1939), "Metternich and Internal Austrian Policy," *Slavonic Review*, XVII, XVIII.

Shafer, B. (1955), *Nationalism. Myth and Reality*. New York.

Shee, W. A. (1893), *My Contemporaries*. London.

Sheehan, J. J. (1989), *German History 1770–1866*. Oxford.

Sheehan, J. J. (1978), *German Liberalism in the Nineteenth Century*. Chicago and London.

Sherburne, J. H. (1847), *The Tourist's Guide*. Philadelphia.

Shryock, R. H. (1936), *The Development of Modern Medicine*. Philadelphia.

Siemens, W. von (1922), *Lebenserinnerungen*. Berlin.

Silliman, B. (1980), *A Visit to Europe in 1851*. 2 vols. New York.

Simon, W. (1973), *European Positivism in the Nineteenth Century*. Ithaca, N.Y.

Singer, C. et al. (1958), A History of Technology. Oxford.

Slade, A. (1840), *Travels in Germany and Russia . . . in 1838–39*. London.

Slicher van Bath, B. H. (1963), *The Agrarian History of Western Europe A.D. 500–1850*. Tr. from the Dutch. London.

Slomka, J. (1941), *From Serfdom to Self-Government. Memoirs of a Polish Village Peasant*. Tr. from the Polish. London.

Smiles, S. (1859), *The Life of George Stephenson*. London.

Smith, F. B. (1979), "The View from Britain." In Kamenka and Smith, q.v.

Solovyev, Y. A. (1881), "Zapiski Senatora Ia. A. Solov'eva o krest'ianskom dele," *Russkaia Starina*, XXX.

Spencer, H. (1926), *An Autobiography*. 2 vols. London.

Spring, D. (1971), "English Landowners and Nineteenth-Century Industrialism." In J. T. Ward and R. G. Wilson, eds., *Land and Industry*. Newton Abbot.

Spring, D., ed. (1977), *European Landed Elites in the Nineteenth Century*, Baltimore.

Springer, A. (1892), *Aus meinem Leben*. Berlin.

Springer, A. (1863–65), *Geschichte Oesterreichs seit dem Wiener Frieden, 1809*. 2 vols. Leipzig.

Srbik, H. von (1925–54), *Metternich: der Staatsmann und der Mensch.* 3 vols. Munich.

Stahl, E. L., and W. E. Yuill (1970), *German Literature of the Eighteenth and Nineteenth Centuries.* New York.

Stambrook, F. G. (1969), *European Nationalism in the Nineteenth Century.* London.

Starr, S. F. (1972), *Decentralization and Self-Government in Russia, 1830–1870.* Princeton.

Stein, L. von (1964), *The History of the Social Movement in France, 1789–1850.* Tr. from the German. Totowa, N.J.

Stekl, H. (1973), *Österreichs Aristokratie im Vormärz. Herrschaftstyl und Lebensformen der Fürstenhauser Liechtenstein und Schwarzenberg.* Munich.

Stern, A. (1894–1929), *Geschichte Europas von der Verträgenvon 1815 bis zum Frankfurter Frieden von 1871.* 10 vols. Stuttgart and Berlin.

Stern, F., ed. (1956), *The Varieties of History.* New York.

Stiles, W. H. (1852), *Austria in 1848–49.* 2 vols. New York.

Stone, L., and J. C. F. Stone (1984), *An Open Elite? England 1540–1880.* Oxford.

Strachey, L. (1931), *Portraits in Miniature.* London.

Stupperich, R. (1939), *Die Anfänge der Bauernbefreiung in Russland.* Berlin.

Stürmer, M. (1974), "1848 in deutscher Geschichte." In Wehler, q.v.

Sugar, P. (1967), "The Rise of Nationalism," *Austrian History Yearbook,* III, pt. 1.

Surtees, R. S. (1927), *The Hunting Tours of Surtees.* Edinburgh, London.

Sutter, B. (1963), "Erzherzog Johanns Kritik an Österreich," *Mitteilungen des österreichischen Staatsarchiv,* XVI.

Talleyrand-Perigord, D. (1909–10), *Memoirs of the duchess de Dino 1831–1862.* Tr. from the French. 3 vols. London.

Talmon, J. L. (1961), *Political Messianism. The Romantic Phase.* New York.

Taylor, A. J. P. (1946), *The Course of German History.* New York.

Taylor, A. J. P. (1948), *The Habsburg Monarchy 1809–1918.* London.

Taylor, H. (1885), *Autobiography 1800–1875.* 2 vols. London.

Taylor, W. C. (1842), *Notes on a Tour in the Manufacturing Districts of Lancashire.* London.

Temkin, O. (1946), "Materialism in French and German Physiology in the Early Nineteenth Century," *Bulletin of the History of Medicine,* XX.

Temperley, H., ed. (1925), *The Unpublished Diary and Political Sketches of Princess Lieven.* London.

Tenison, L. (1853), *Castile and Andalucia.* London.

Thackeray, W. M. (1883), *The Paris Sketch Book.* New York.

Thompson, E. P. (1849), *Austria.* London.

Thompson, E. P. (1964), *The Making of the English Working Class.* New York.

Thompson, R. L. (1947), *Wiring a Continent*. Princeton.

Thomson, S. H. (1943), *Czechoslovakia in European History*. Princeton.

Thureau-Danzin, P. (1884–92), *Histoire de la Monarchie de Juillet*. 7 vols. Paris.

Ticknor, G. (1876), *Life, Letters and Journals*. 2 vols. Boston.

Tilly, C. (1970), "The Changing Place of Collective Violence." In M. Richter, ed., *Essays in Social and Political History*. Cambridge.

Tilly, C. (1972), "How Protest Modernized France." In W. O. Aydelotte et al., *The Dimensions of Quantitative Research in History*. Princeton.

Tilly, R. H. (1978), "Capital Formation in Germany," *Cambridge Economic History of Europe*, VII, pt. 1.

Tocqueville, A. de (1958), *Journeys to England and Ireland*. Tr. from the French. New Haven.

Tocqueville, A. de (1958), *Recollections*. Tr. from the French. New Haven.

Toutain, J. C. (1963), *La population de la France de 1700 à 1959*. Cahiers de l'Institut de Science Economique Applique, suppl. no. 133.

Treble, J. H. (1970), "The Irish Agitation." In Ward, *Popular Movements*, q.v.

Treitschke, H. von (1915–19), *History of Germany in the Nineteenth Century*. Tr. from the German. New York.

Trevelyan, G. M. (1946), *British History in the Nineteenth Century and After*. London.

Trevelyan, G. M. (1913), *The Life and Letters of Lord Macaulay*. 2 vols. New York.

Trevelyan, G. M. (1913), *The Life of John Bright*. London.

Trollope, A. (1950), *An Autobiography*. Oxford.

Trollope, A. (1951), *Letters*. Oxford.

Trollope, F. (1834), *Belgium and Western Germany in 1833*. Philadelphia.

Trollope, F. (1838), *Vienna and the Austrians*. 2 vols. London.

Tsentral'yi statisticheskii komitet (1863), *Statisticheskiia tablitsy Rossiiskoi Imperii*. St. Petersburg.

Turgenev, I. S. (1975), *Rudin*. Tr. from the Russian. Baltimore.

Turner, R. S. (1971), "The Growth of Professional Research in Prussia, 1818–1848. Causes and Context," *Historical Studies in the Physical Sciences*, III.

Uhl, F. (1888), "Die Gesellschaft." In *Wien 1848–1888*. 2 vols. Vienna.

UNESCO (1955), *Adam Mickiewicz*. Zurich.

Valentin, V. (1930), *Geschichte der deutschen Revolution von 1848–49*. 2 vols. Berlin.

Van Tieghem, P. (1948), *Le romanticisme dans la littérature européenne*. Paris.

Varnhagen von Ense, K. A. (1972), *Tagebücher*. 15 vols. Bern.

Vaughan, R. (1843), *The Age of the Great Cities*. London.

Veron, L. (1853–55), *Mémoires d'un bourgeois de Paris*. 6 vols. Paris.

Veuillot, L. (1924–38), *Oeuvres complètes*. Paris.

List of Works Cited

Vignoles, O. J. (1889), *Life of C. B. Vignoles*. London.

Villermé, L. R. (1840), *Tableau de l'état physique et moral des ouvriers*. 2 vols. Paris.

Vincent, H. P. (1968), *Daumier and His World*. Evanston, Ill.

Virchow, R. (1906), *Briefe an seine Eltern 1839 bis 1864*. Leipzig.

Vitzthum von Eckstädt, K. F. (1886), *Berlin und Wien in den Jahren 1845–1852*. Stuttgart.

Vizetelly, H. (1893), *Glances Back through Seventy Years*. 2 vols. London.

Von Laue, T. H. (1950), *Leopold Ranke: The Formative Years*. Princeton.

Walicki, A. (1982), *Philosophy and Romantic Nationalism*.Oxford.

Walicki, A. (1975), *The Slavophile Controversy*. London.

Walker, G. A. (1839), *Gatherings from Graveyards*. London.

Walker, M. (1971), *German Home Towns: Community, State, and General Estate 1648–1871*. Ithaca, N.Y., and London.

Walker, M. (1968), *Metternich's Europe*. New York.

Wallace, D. M. (1877), *Russia*. New York.

Walling, R. A. J., ed. (1931), *The Diaries of John Bright*. New York.

Wallis, S. T. (1853), *Spain. Her Institutions, Politics, and Public Men*. Boston.

Walter, F. (1963), "Eine österreichische Denkschrift über den Stand der sozialistischen Bewegung zu Anfang des Jahres 1850." *Vierteljahrschrift für Sozial- und Wirtschaftsgeschichte, L.*

Ward, J. T., ed. (1970), *Popular Movements c. 1830–1850*. London.

Ward-Perkins, C. N. (1966), "The Commercial Crisis of 1847" In E. M. Carus-Wilson, ed., *Essays in Economic History*, III.

Weber, E. (1976), *Peasants into Frenchmen*. Stanford.

Wehler, H. U., ed. (1966), *Sozialgeschichte heute*. Göttingen.

White, H. (1973), *Metahistory: The Historical Imagination in Nineteenth Century Europe*. Baltimore.

Wigand, O., ed. (1846–52), *Conversations-Lexikon für alle Stände*. 15 vols. Leipzig.

Willis, G. M. (1954), *Ernest Augustus, Duke of Cumberland and King of Hannover*. London.

Wilson, A. (1970), "Chartism." In J. T. Ward, q.v.

Woodward, E. L. (1938), "Les caracères genéraux des relations franco-anglaises de 1815–1870," *Revue d'histoire moderne*, XIII.

Woodward, E. L. (1929), *Three Studies in European Conservatism*. London.

Working Classes in the Victorian Age (1973). 4 vols. Farnsborough.

Zacek, J. F. (1970), "Metternich's Censors: The Case of Palacky." In Broch and Skilling, q.v.

Zeldin, T. (1979), *France 1848–1945. Politics and Anger*. Oxford.

Zucker, A. E. (1850), *The Forty-Eighters*. New York.

INDEX

on socialism, 78
  Struve and, 294
Herzen, Natalie, 82
Hess, Moses, 73, 298
Hesse, Grand Duke of, 122
Highland Railway, 10
Hill, Frederic, 35, 37
Hill, Rowland, 34–37, 39
Historical School of Political Economy, 150
history, 143–48
  economics and, 150
Hitler, Adolf, 300
Hobhouse, John, 162
Hofmann, August Wilhelm, 133
Hohenlohe-Schillingsfürst, Prince, 289
Hohenzollern, House of, xv, 105, 144, 281, 283
Holy Alliance of the Peoples, 97
Holy Family, The (Marx and Engels), 110
Holy Roman Empire, 242, 269
Home Rule, 195
homeopathy, 135
homing pigeons, 32
Hood, Thomas, 110
Hope, Anthony, 266
Howard, Elizabeth, 230, 231
Howitt, William, 249
Hübner, Count J. A. von, 248, 249
Hudson, George, 12–14, 16–20, 24
Hugo, Victor, 81, 88, 107, 211–12
Humboldt, Alexander von, 42, 113–17, 121, 122, 126, 277, 282
Humbolt, Wilhelm von, 114
Hume, David, 247
Hungary
  monarchy in, 236, 268
  nationalism in, 84, 102, 257
  nobility of, 250, 251
  peasantry of, 252
  railroads in, 25
  revolution in, xvi, xviii, 261, 264–65, 302
Huss, John, 99

Hutton, James, 131
Huxley, T. H., 141
hydrotherapy, 135
hypnotism, 136

Icarians, 71
Immermann, Karl, 278
India, British, 170
individualism, 67, 96
industrialization, x, xii, 63, 336
  in Austria, 254, 255
  economics of, 149–50
  in Germany, 280
Industrial Revolution, 48, 336
infant mortality, 53
insane, treatment of, 50–51
Inspector General, The (Gogol), 317
intellectuals, Russian, 306, 313, 317, 321–33
Ireland, xvi, 191–96
  Chartism in, 189
  emigration from, 46
  nationalism in, 88
  poverty in, 44
Irish Confederation, 194–95
Isabella, Queen of Spain, xiv–xv
Italy
  nationalism in, xviii, 84, 87, 90, 94–100
  railroads in, 26
  revolution in, xvi–xviii, 94, 289
  unification of, 105–6

Jacobins, 201
Jeanne d'Arc, xiv
Jefferson, Thomas, 166
Jellachich, Colonel Joseph, 265
Jena, University of, 118
Jersey, Earl of, 176
Jesuits, 254, 290
Jews, 58, 73
  Austrian, 236, 247
  French, 223
  German, 272
Jockey Clubs, 251

ABOUT THE AUTHOR

Jerome Blum, whose previous books include *Our Forgotten Past* and *The End of the Old Order in Rural Europe,* was chairman of the history department at Princeton University. He was a Guggenheim Fellow, a National Endowment for the Humanities Fellow, a Shreve Fellow, and a Fellow of the American Academy of Arts and Sciences. Prizes for his writing include the Herbert Baxter Adams Prize and the Higby Prize, and he was on the editorial board of *The Journal of Modern History.* He died in 1993.